The Social Space of Language

SOUTH ASIA ACROSS THE DISCIPLINES

South Asia across the Disciplines is a series devoted to publishing first books across a wide range of South Asian studies, including art, history, philology or textual studies, philosophy, religion, and interpretive social sciences. Contributors all share the goal of opening up new archives, especially in South Asian languages, and suggesting new methods and approaches, while demonstrating that South Asian scholarship can be at once deep in expertise and broad in appeal.

Edited by Dipesh Chakrabarty, Sheldon Pollock, and Sanjay Subrahmanyam

Funded by a grant from the Andew W. Mellon Fondation and jointly published by the University of California Press, the University of Chicago Press, and Columbia University Press.

The Social Space of Language

Vernacular Culture in British Colonial Punjab

Farina Mir

UNIVERSITY OF CALIFORNIA PRESS

Berkeley   Los Angeles   London

University of California Press, one of the most distinguished university presses in the United States, enriches lives around the world by advancing scholarship in the humanities, social sciences, and natural sciences. Its activities are supported by the UC Press Foundation and by philanthropic contributions from individuals and institutions. For more information, visit www.ucpress.edu.

University of California Press
Berkeley and Los Angeles, California

University of California Press, Ltd.
London, England

An earlier version of Chapter 1 was published as "Imperial Policy, Provincial Practices: Colonial Language Policy in Nineteenth-Century India," *Indian Economic and Social History Review* 43, 4 (2006): 395–427. Chapter 5 is reprinted in revised and expanded form from "Genre and Devotion in Punjabi Popular Narratives: Rethinking Cultural and Religious Syncretism," *Comparative Studies in Society and History* 48, 3 (July 2006): 727–58; reprinted with permission from Cambridge University Press.

Library of Congress Cataloging-in-Publication Data

Mir, Farina.
    The social space of language : vernacular culture in British colonial Punjab / Farina Mir.
        p.   cm. — (South Asia across the disciplines ; 2)
    Includes bibliographical references and index.
    ISBN 978-0-520-26269-0 (cloth : alk. paper)
    1. Panjabi literature—19th century—History and criticism.   2. Panjabi literature—20th century—History and criticism.   3. Literature and society—India—Punjab—History—19th century.   4. Literature and society—India—Punjab—History—20th century.   5. Punjab (India)—Intellectual life—19th century.   6. Punjab (India)—Intellectual life—20th century.   I. Title.
    PK2650.5.M57   2010
    891.4'209355—dc22   2009049413

Manufactured in the United States of America

19   18   17   16   15   14   13   12   11
10   9   8   7   6   5   4   3   2   1

This book is printed on Cascades Enviro 100, a 100% post consumer waste, recycled, de-inked fiber. FSC recycled certified and processed chlorine free. It is acid free, Ecologo certified, and manufactured by BioGas energy.

CONTENTS

ILLUSTRATIONS

MAPS

FIGURES

TABLES

ACKNOWLEDGMENTS

This book would not have been possible without the support of a number of people and institutions. Research and writing were supported at various stages by: the Social Science Research Council, American Institute of Pakistan Studies, International Institute of Education (Fulbright), Columbia University, Mrs. Giles Whiting Foundation, and the University of Michigan. A faculty fellowship from the Eisenberg Institute for Historical Studies made the final preparation of the manuscript possible. Research in Pakistan, India, and Britain was facilitated by the superb staffs at the following institutions: in Lahore, the Dyal Singh Trust Library, the Punjab Public Library, and the Punjab University Library; in Delhi, the National Archives of India; in Chandigarh, the Panjab University Library and the Punjab Provincial Archives; in Patiala, the Bhai Kahan Singh Nabha Library, Bhasha Vibhag, Musafir Memorial Central Library, and the Patiala State Archives; in Amritsar, the Bhai Gurdas Library at Guru Nanak Dev University; and in Britain, the Oriental and India Office Collection at the British Library.

My deepest gratitude is to Ayesha Jalal, who supervised the Ph.D. dissertation that provided the foundation for this book. Ayesha is a model teacher, and her intellectual engagement at every stage from this project's inception has shaped it for the better. In addition to giving unfailingly in intellectual matters, Ayesha has been a caring friend whose thoughtfulness and generosity have helped me weather many storms. My years at Columbia were marked by the generosity of others as well. I feel extremely fortunate to have stumbled into Richard Bulliet's welcoming office, where I learned about Islamic history and so much more. My thanks to him for modeling creativity in the historian's endeavor, and my gratitude for his enduring support. Gurinder Singh Mann's interventions have been manifold and his influence is manifest in this work, as also in my life; without him both would have taken a different, and less fulfilling course. My thanks are also due to David Armitage and David Cannadine. I am fortunate to have had teachers beyond Columbia's gates, also. My thanks to Sugata Bose for his challenging questions and keen literary sensibility, and his mentoring. David Gilmartin has been similarly giving. A valued interlocutor, David's critical engagement helped me clarify key arguments in this book.

Lahore became a second home during my research there, largely due to the kindness of Nighat and Bashir Patel, and their daughter Halima, who made me part of their family. Thanks also to Anwar Mir, for his hospitality and care; to Nusrat, Shahid, and Sehr Jalal, for welcoming me in their home; and to Zakia Jalal for her unparalleled warmth. Najm Hossain Syed extended every kindness to me. His scholarship and the weekly *sangat* in his home have had a profound impact on how I understand Punjabi literature, and our many conversations helped me find my way in Lahore. Nadir Ali showed me that the Punjabi tradition continues to thrive. Delhi would not have been the same if not for Sanjay Muttoo. In Chandigarh, Savipal Singh Gyani and his family were exceedingly kind hosts and Professor Indu Banga introduced me to Panjab University. In London, Farhad Karim was a generous host, as always. My thanks to him for these many years of friendship and support.

Over the years it took to revise this manuscript, I was affiliated with Cornell University, the University of Virginia, and the University of Michigan. A Mellon Postdoctoral fellowship at the Society for the Humanities at Cornell allowed me to begin the revision process. My thanks to Dominick LaCapra and other members of the society, and to Chris Minkowski. In Charlottesville, my colleagues provided a most congenial atmosphere. I would like to thank Rich Barnett, Chuck McCurdy, Sophie Rosenfeld, and Elizabeth Thompson, in particular.

The University of Michigan has been an exceptionally supportive environment. I have had the enviable opportunity to work with fellow South Asian historians Juan Cole, Barbara Metcalf, Sumathi Ramaswamy, and Thomas Trautmann; my thanks to each of them for their support and encouragement. I am grateful to my three chairs—Sonya Rose, Mary Kelley, and Geoff Eley, in particular—for helping negotiate this manuscript and so much more. For their warmth, friendship, and intellectual engagement, my gratitude goes to Kathleen Canning, Christian de Pee, Nancy Hunt, and Helmut Puff. I must also thank John Carson, David Cohen, Kali Israel, Gina Morantz-Sanchez, and Penny Von Eschen for helping me find my feet in the department. The feedback provided by colleagues at my manuscript workshop had a profound impact on the final shape of this book. I am indebted to Miriam Angress, David Gilmartin, Barbara Metcalf, and Damon Salesa for serving as internal and external readers, and to all those who participated.

My experience of the field of South Asian studies suggests that critical engagement and generosity are guiding principles of interaction. Certainly, that is what I have learned from Antoinette Burton, Vasudha Dalmia, Ann Gold, Anshu Malhotra, Tom Metcalf, Gail Minault, Carla Petievich, Lee Schlesinger, Christopher Shackle, Tony Stewart, and Muhammad Qasim Zaman. It is what I experienced with audiences at conferences, and when I presented parts of this work at University of California, Santa Barbara; University of Texas, Austin; and Harvard University. This same generosity is manifest in the institution of the South Asia across the Disciplines series. I would like to express my gratitude to Dipesh Chakrabarty, Sheldon Pollock, and Sanjay Subrahmanyam for creating this opportunity. Thanks are also due to Reed Malcolm of the University of California Press for shepherding this book through publication, to David Akin and Terre Fisher for their editorial assistance and friendship, and to Paul Tierman for producing the maps. My sincerest thanks to Nilima Sheikh for permission to reproduce a detail of her extraordinary painting, *River–Carrying Across Leaving Behind*.

I would also like to thank Simone Almeida, Amita Baviskar, Anna Bigelow, Preeti Chopra, Iftikhar Dadi, Kavita Datla, Don Davis, Tom Guglielmo, Charles Hirschkind, Akbar Hyder, Webb Keane, Lisa Klopfer, Jayati Lal, Saba Mahmood, Karuna Mantena, Rama Mantena, Monika Mehta, Adela Pinch, Mary Rader, Mridu Rai, Mahesh Rangarajan, Parna Sengupta, Eric Tagliocozzo, and Clare Talwalker for their friendship and support through these years. Munis Faruqui has been a particularly stalwart friend, as has Kathryn Babayan; my thanks to them both for their ethic of friendship. My brother, Farhaan Mir, has been unfailingly supportive and loving. My parents, Akhtar and Naseem Mir, are remarkable people whose fortitude was my example at every turn of what was at times an arduous task.

No words are adequate to express my gratitude to Will Glover. His intellect inspires me, his love sustains me, and his laughter reminds me of all that is joyful in life.

A NOTE ON TRANSLATION, TRANSLITERATION, AND USE OF FOREIGN TERMS

This book uses many Hindi, Persian, Punjabi, and Urdu words. Except in the case of proper nouns or words that are familiar in English, all foreign terms are italicized in the text. Foreign terms are defined the first time they are used either through context, a parenthetical or bracketed remark, or in a note. For all of the foreign words used I have chosen a simple form of transliteration rather than using diacritical marks. The only exception is my use of an inverted apostrophe for the Arabic character *ayin,* as in *sama'.* I have chosen to transliterate terms in a way that I believe renders them phonetically correct for an American reader. Spellings of words in direct quotations have been left as they were in the original. Two different spellings of the word *Punjab* (the other being *Panjab*) are common in the secondary scholarship. I have kept the spelling used in the original wherever this word appears. Where publication dates of primary source texts were given in the Hijri or Bikrami calendars, I have retained these dates and provided their C.E. equivalents. All translations from Punjabi and Urdu are mine, unless otherwise noted.

Introduction

The following story has been circulating in northwest India for at least the past four hundred years: A young man named Dhido sets out from his village Takht Hazara on an epic journey in search of the renowned beauty named Hir. Through trials and tribulations, he makes his way to Hir's hometown of Jhang, where the two fall in love at first sight. Their love blossoms on the banks of the Chenab River, where Ranjha (as Dhido is always called) takes cattle to pasture each day, Hir's father having hired him—at her suggestion—as a cowherd. Hir and Ranjha's idyll is soon interrupted, however, when Hir's family learns of her liaison. Her parents reject Ranjha as a suitor for their daughter because of his low-status occupation and they betroth Hir to Seido Khera, a bridegroom Hir's father considers more appropriate to his family's landlord status. Hir is forcibly married to Khera but refuses to consummate her marriage, and Ranjha makes his way, disguised as a yogi, to her married home. In this disguise, Ranjha is able to contact Hir and the two elope. The Kheras pursue the lovers and in most renditions of this tale commonly known as *Hir-Ranjha*, or simply as *Hir*, the two die for their love.

Hir-Ranjha—part epic, part romance, and almost certainly fictional—has circulated orally and textually for centuries in north India, principally in the Punjab (map 1). Its longevity alone is not what makes this tale noteworthy, however, given that epics such as the *Mahabharata* have circulated in South Asia (and beyond) for millennia. What makes *Hir-Ranjha* particularly compelling is that this ostensibly simple love story surfaces repeatedly in Punjab's history in places one would least expect to find it or any other love story. For example, it is embedded in Ganesh Das's *Char Bagh-i Punjab*, a Persian-language history of the Punjab from earliest antiquity through the period of Sikh sovereignty (1799–1949).[1] Written in 1849 as

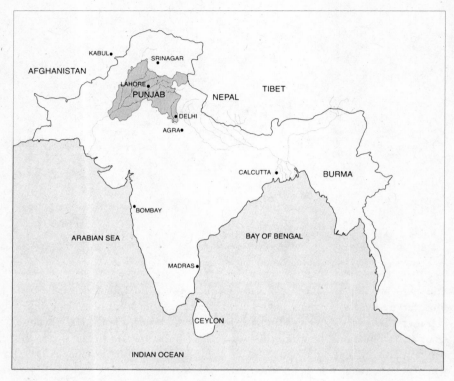

MAP 1. Punjab in the British Indian empire.

the English East India Company annexed the Sikh kingdom of Lahore and transformed its territories into the colonial Punjab province, the *Char Bagh-i Punjab* is primarily a political history of the establishment, decline, and fall of Sikh rule in the region, along with a detailed account of many of the area's towns, cities, and villages.[2] Nestled in the middle of Das's work is an account of *Hir-Ranjha* alongside other fictional love stories, including *Sohni-Mahival* and *Mirza-Sahiban.* Why did Ganesh Das find *Hir-Ranjha,* and the Punjabi-language *qissa* (epic-romance; pl. *qisse*) tradition, to which all three romances belong, relevant to writing the region's history?

Many years later, in a very different setting, an Indian revolutionary stood trial for the murder of Michael O'Dwyer, who had been lieutenant-governor of the Punjab in 1919 when the Jallianwala Bagh massacre took place.[3] Today this revolutionary is popularly known by his given name, Udham Singh, but while in custody he gave his name as Ram Mohammad Singh Azad, a name that invoked the three major religious communities of the Punjab—Hindu, Muslim, and Sikh—as well as his anticolonial sentiment (*azad* means "free"). At his trial in England in April 1940, Udham Singh asked to take the required oath on *Hir Waris*, an eighteenth-century rendition of *Hir-Ranjha* by the poet Waris Shah, which he had requested from a friend while in jail.[4] Why did Udham Singh–Ram Muhammad Singh Azad want to swear on this Punjabi epic–romance in place of religious scripture? What authority was vested in the romance of Hir and Ranjha for this political revolutionary?

In 1947, the British Indian province of Punjab was divided between the newly independent nation-states of India and Pakistan. Partitioned along ostensibly religious lines, the Punjab was mired in religious violence in which at least one million people were killed. The poet Amrita Pritam (b. 1919) fled Lahore for Delhi in 1947 and expressed through her poetry the anguish caused by partition and its attendant violence. Her "To Waris Shah" is perhaps the most famous Punjabi poem of the twentieth century. It is an exceptionally vivid and evocative tableau of the events of 1947:

> Today I call on Waris Shah—from beyond the grave—speak!
> And turn, today, a new page in the Book of Love!
> Once wept a daughter of the Punjab [Hir], your pen unleashed a million cries.
> Today millions of them weep, and to you, Waris Shah, they say:
> O sympathizer of sufferers! Rise, and look at your Punjab!
> Today corpses lie in the thickets and full of blood is the Chenab [River].
> Somebody mixed poison into the five rivers,
> And those waters watered the earth.
> . . . .
> Lost is the flute where once sounded the pipings of love.
> Ranjha and his kind have forgotten how to play.
> Blood upon the earth has even seeped into graves.
> Love's princesses cry today in their mausoleums.
> . . . .
> Today where can we find another Waris Shah?
> Today I call on Waris Shah—from out of your grave—speak!
> And turn today a new page of the Book of Love![5]

In evoking the violence and tragedy of Punjab's partition, Amrita Pritam turned to Waris Shah, the eighteenth-century *qissa* poet whose *Hir-Ranjha* continues to enthrall audiences to this day. Why did Pritam use *Hir-Ranjha* as a metaphor in her lament on the tragedy of Punjab's partition in 1947?

The narrative *Hir-Ranjha* and its principle genre, the *qissa*, are both deeply embedded in Punjab's history, as these examples suggest. The *qissa* was a leading genre of Punjabi literary production from the seventeenth through the early twentieth centuries, and *Hir-Ranjha* was among its most popular texts. Punjabi *qisse* served as both high literature and popular entertainment, and were widely accessible due to their being composed in a vernacular language and disseminated through oral performance and printed media. The examples above also indicate that *qisse* functioned as more than literary texts, and more than forms of popular entertainment. Ganesh Das's history, Udham Singh's actions, and Amrita Pritam's poem suggest that the *qissa*—and *Hir-Ranjha* in particular—was central to constructing and narrating historical imaginations in colonial Punjab.

This book is a study of Punjabi language literary traditions during the colonial period (1849–1947), with a particular focus on the *qissa*. Punjabi literary culture was particularly vibrant in the late nineteenth and early twentieth centuries, marked by an abundance of original literary compositions, a burgeoning print culture, and ubiquitous oral performances. Syad Muhammad Latif's 1892 history of Lahore provides an indication of this vitality, describing the soundscape of a Punjabi city street in which "young people . . . recite [Punjabi] epic and other poetry, or sing songs descriptive of love or intrigue."[6] Latif's remarks give little indication of how the colonial state attempted to marginalize Punjabi through policies that denied the language and its literature almost all forms of state patronage (something taken up in chapter 1). Despite those policies, however, Punjabi, both as a colloquial language and a literary tradition, thrived during the colonial period (map 2).[7]

Punjabi's survival and continuous vitality through the colonial period signals a discernible limit to colonial dominance in British India. Mapping the limits of the colonial state by tracing the resilience of a Punjabi cultural formation is one of my critical objectives, and the historical dynamic between the Punjabi language and the colonial state is centrally important to the arguments presented here. Although some scholars have chosen to read the Punjabi language's survival as a mode of Indian resistance to colonialism,[8] my approach in this book emphasizes resilience over resistance by showing that Punjabi literary culture operated at considerable remove from colonial institutions and venues. Indeed, I argue that Punjabi literary culture enjoyed relative independence from the colonial state, particularly vis-à-vis certain other Indian vernacular languages such as Hindi, Urdu, and Bengali.[9] This relative independence allowed greater scope for continuity with precolonial practices. Punjabi literary culture offers, therefore, a particular instance of stability through a period usually marked for its ruptures, as people and institutions traversed the divide between precolonial and colonial rule. In examining this continuity, the chapters that follow concentrate on how a regional literary tradition was kept vibrant and socially meaningful despite the profound transformations taking place in the institutional sites of its production and the social milieus of its reception.

These transformations occurred largely as a result of colonialism, and language was a key site of colonial intervention. It was also a site where colonial officials felt

MAP 2. The Punjabi language area, showing major dialects.

sure of their ability to effect change. When asked in 1863 about the language practices of the people in his Punjab division (a subprovincial administrative unit),
one British divisional commissioner proclaimed, "The Punjabee [language] itself
is dying out."[10] His conviction that colonial policies would precipitate this demise,
that they would bring about the death of a language, were misplaced, however, for
nothing of the sort happened. Throughout the colonial period, Punjabi language
and literature were robust and they remain so today. Reading evidence of the limits
of colonial rule in Punjabi's resilience is one aspect of a more complicated history,

however. Why did colonial policy not cause Punjabi to atrophy? What sustained the language and its literary traditions throughout the colonial period?

At the broadest level, the answer to these questions is that this cultural formation's pragmatic engagements with colonial institutions were far less important than the affective attachments its adherents had established with a place and with an old but dynamic corpus of stories. These attachments were produced, in part, through the pleasures of composing, performing, reading, and listening to Punjabi literature. But pleasure alone did not preserve this tradition. Punjabi literature's survival also hinged on a distinctive array of devotional practices, social relations, vocations, and commerce that accompanied its production and circulation from the seventeenth through the late nineteenth and early twentieth centuries. Equally important was a continued commitment on behalf of composers, performers, readers, and listeners to the moral sensibilities that suffused a key genre of this literature, the *qissa*. Punjabi *qisse* present a widespread, religiously plural, and place-centered poetics of belonging, strong enough and deeply embedded enough in society to withstand well-organized efforts to dismiss outright the language and its literature. Fundamental to a historical understanding of *qisse* is that this tradition was the focal point of what I will call a *Punjabi literary formation*: those individuals who shared the practices of producing, circulating, performing, and consuming Punjabi literary texts. For this formation, the *qissa* was a key site for the construction, contestation, and articulation of a particular historical imagination. By analyzing the *qissa* through the colonial period, with its precolonial history as an important reference, we can analyze the extent to which colonialism shaped and transformed the literary formation's historical imagination.

The history of the *qissa* and the Punjabi literary formation for which it was a focal point also allows for a reconsideration of two fundamental aspects of South Asian historiography. First, the vitality of the Punjabi *qissa* tradition in the colonial period, despite predictions of its imminent demise, forces a reevaluation of the nature and extent of colonial power in British India. Not only did the British deny patronage to the Punjabi language, they actively promoted another vernacular language in the Punjab: Urdu. Their efforts to change the linguistic and literary practices of the region's inhabitants were only partially successful. Though Urdu became an important language of literary production and the principal language of Punjab's incipient public sphere, Punjabi continued to be the main colloquial language in the province and Punjabi literary activity not only continued unabated, but may even have enjoyed a resurgence during the colonial period. Second, this history redirects inquiry into late nineteenth- and early twentieth-century cultural formations in north India away from a focus on religious communal identities and nationalist politics—the dominant emphases in the present historiography—to analyze a set of practices and ideas that Punjab's inhabitants shared, no matter what their religious persuasion, which were not easily assimilated to nationalist agendas. Before elaborating on these points, let me briefly situate the Punjabi *qissa* tradition historically and discuss some of the key terms used in this book.

THE PUNJABI *QISSA*

I begin with the earliest known Punjabi-language *qissa:* the poet Damodar's early seventeenth-century text *Hir-Ranjha* (completed c. 1605). Damodar's text was not without antecedents, in terms of both genre and narrative content. As a genre, Punjabi-language *qisse* are rooted in Arabic and Persian storytelling traditions of the same name.[11] They have particular affinity with the Persian romance *qissa*, a subgenre marked by its use of the *masnavi* poetic form, which dates from c. 1000 C.E.[12] This latter tradition, both its literary norms and its repertoire of stories, was transmitted to South Asia from Central Asia and Persia during the medieval period, likely crossing regional boundaries with court poets, merchants, traders, Sufis, and mendicants. Indian litterateurs took up the genre by composing *qisse* principally in Persian, the literary language of much of north India during the medieval and early modern periods. Amir Khusraw's poetry provides one of the earliest examples of this adoption. Khusraw (1254–1325) composed the romances *Laila-Majnun* (originally Arabic) and *Shirin-Khusraw* (originally Persian) in Persian and in *masnavi* (the standard form of the Persian romance *qissa*).[13]

The form and narratives of the *qissa* were gradually adopted into Indian vernacular literatures. Punjabi poets took up the genre in the early seventeenth century, some five hundred years into the development of Punjabi literature (discussed in chapter 1). The Punjabi *qissa* retained the *masnavi* form and rhyme scheme, but used indigenous rather than Persian meters. Another way in which the cosmopolitan Persian *qissa* tradition was localized in Punjab was through the inclusion of indigenous romance narratives. Punjabi poets used stories originally brought from the Arabian peninsula and Persia, such as *Laila-Majnun* and *Shirin-Khusraw*, but they also composed stories that were local in origin, situated in the local landscape and embedded in local social relations. Among these, some that continue to be popular beyond the geographic locale of the Punjab are *Puran-Bhagat*, *Sohni-Mahival*, *Sassi-Punnun*, *Mirza-Sahiban*, and, perhaps most popular of all, *Hir-Ranjha*. These latter tales did not originate in *qissa* compositions, however. They had been circulating in manuscripts and orally earlier, at least since the sixteenth century. *Hir-Ranjha* serves as a typical example.

The earliest textual reference to *Hir-Ranjha* comes not from Damodar's seventeenth-century *qissa* but in the poetry of four near contemporaries: Hari Das Haria (c. 1520s–50s), Shah Husain (c. 1530s–1600), Bhai Gurdas Bhalla (c. 1550s–1635), and Gang Bhatt (c. 1580s–90s).[14] Their poetry provides important insights into the *Hir-Ranjha* narrative tradition prior to its adaptation by *qissa* poets.[15] Dialect differences among these four poets show that by the sixteenth century the narrative was familiar in both central and southern Punjab.[16] The varied social backgrounds of the poets and the nature of their compositions suggest that *Hir-Ranjha* circulated among people of different classes and religious persuasions. Hari Das Haria was a member of the Sikh *panth* (community). Shah Husain was a Sufi mystic of humble background, who enjoyed renown in elite social and political circles for his *kafis*. These *kafis* were composed to musical ragas and meant to be sung, making them accessible beyond literate circles. Bhai Gurdas was a companion of the Sikh gurus and a learned scholar who served as amanuensis for the first copy of the *Adi Granth*, Sikhism's most sacred text. His compositions were written in a relatively simple style, suggesting accessibility, and expounded on concepts raised in the *Adi Granth*.[17] Finally, Gang Bhatt was a poet at the Mughal court in Lahore, who presumably wrote for an elite audience comprised of royal householders and the Mughal nobility. Importantly, all four poets took their audiences' knowledge of the romance for granted, which allowed them to allude to a broader narrative context without needless elaboration. In sum, the earliest existing literary texts of *Hir-Ranjha* point to a narrative that was already widely known to people of different classes and religions. We can surmise that *qissa* poets adopted the narrative in part, therefore, because of its widespread popularity.

Damodar's rendition of *Hir-Ranjha* is the earliest extant Punjabi-language *qissa*. Over the course of the seventeenth and eighteenth centuries, the *qissa* genre acquired a dominant position in Punjabi literature. Certainly other genres of Punjabi literature were produced through these centuries, but the *qissa* came to be associated with high literary status. One sign of this is the ornate and costly *qissa* manuscripts produced during the seventeenth and eighteenth centuries, such as Minar Kamar al-Din Minnat's *Hir-Ranjha* (c. 1750s), today housed in the British Library (figure 1). Court patronage also marks the genre's status. Punjabi poet Hafiz Barkhurdar wrote in his *Qissa Yusuf-Zulaikha* (1679) of the land he received at the pleasure of his patron Nawab Jaafar Khan, who was in all likelihood the Mughal governor of Lahore:

> I picked up these unparalleled pearls with my eyes
> To produce this necklace in the time of Almgir [*sic*].
> This *qissa* came to be composed on the suggestion
> Of Nawab Jaafar Khan, who was pleased openly and
> heartily to hear it read. He gave to me a piece
> of land, of seven *bigha*s [approximately 1.75 acres]; and a robe and horse in addition to
> a hundred rupees in cash.[18]

If the seventeenth century marked the arrival of the *qissa* as a genre in Punjabi literary culture, then the eighteenth century saw what most literary critics agree was its apogee with Waris Shah's *Hir* (1766). Today almost universally acclaimed as the greatest achievement of Punjabi literature, Waris Shah's *qissa* appears to have enjoyed immense popularity in the Punjab from at least the early nineteenth century. Numerous manuscripts of *Hir Waris* in both the Indo-Persian and Gurmukhi scripts (Punjabi can be written in both) attest to its popularity. The earliest dates from the 1820s.[19]

In the early nineteenth century a new development in *qissa* literature took shape, as the genre became the site for a self-conscious literary historicity. Poets now squarely placed themselves within a Punjabi literary tradition. Hamid Shah Abbasi's *Hir-Ranjha* provides perhaps the earliest example of this.[20] Abbasi (b. 1748) was a Muslim cleric in the princely state of Nurpur and a member of the Nurpur court. He was fluent in Punjabi, Persian, and Arabic, and also studied Hindi and Sanskrit. Abbasi's *qissa Hir-Ranjha*, composed in 1805, opens with a stanza that placed him within a genealogy of poets. He wrote:

> I have asked for my rice from Muqbal,
> and have added some of Ahmad's salt.
> I have taken the oil from Gurdas' shop,
> putting together a *khichri* which will be relished throughout the land.[21]

Khichri literally means mixture or medley. It also refers to a dish made with rice, lentils, oil, or clarified butter (*ghee*), and spices.[22] Abbasi mentions three poets' compositions as the ingredients for his own: Muqbal, Ahmad, and Bhai Gurdas. Each had either referred to or composed *Hir-Ranjha* in Punjabi before him.

Abbasi's use of khichri as a metaphor was not itself unique. Imam Baksh, a contemporary of Abbasi, also used this metaphor, though to different ends. Baksh used it to draw his Punjabi compositions into the ambit of Indo-Persian literature:

> I took rice from Nizami and pulse from Hatif
> from Khusraw came the butter, the salt I added myself to make this mixture.
> People have composed Persian books [*divan*], intoxicated with love.
> This book is Imam Baksh's, in the Punjabi language.[23]

Baksh's poetry provides an interesting contrast to Abbasi's. Baksh referred to Persian poets, two from Iran itself (Nizami and Hatif), and one from India (Khusraw). Abbasi's genealogy of poets, in contrast, placed him squarely and self-consciously within a Punjabi literary tradition. Throughout the nineteenth and into the twentieth centuries, Punjabi poets self-consciously participated in a local literary tradition, often marking this overtly in their texts.

The mid-nineteenth century is a watershed in Punjab's political history, marking the transition to formal colonial rule in the province. From a literary perspective, the midcentury is equally significant, since this is when commercial printing commenced in the Punjab. Although Punjabi publishing was somewhat slow to get off the ground, Punjabi *qisse* were among the earliest texts printed (Punjabi

FIGURE 1. Title page of *Hir-Ranjha*, by Minar Kamar al-Din
Minnat, c. 1750s. © The British Library Board (Or. 6633, IV).

FIGURE 2. Title page of *Qissa Hir te Ranjhe da,* by Kishan Singh 'Arif (Amritsar: Bhai Vasava Singh Juneja Pustak Wale, 1889). Text (from top): "The Qissa of Hir and Ranjha | by the writer of the *kalianwala* verse, Kishan Singh | 'Arif | by permission of Bhai Vasava Singh | Juneja, bookseller, who | had it printed at the Chashm-i Nur Press in Amritsar."

publishing is discussed in detail in chapter 2). By the 1870s, Punjabi print culture was thriving and *qisse* were being composed by scores of people and printed in the thousands. There was a good deal of continuity between precolonial and colonial-era *qissa* production. The corpus of romance stories largely remained the same, and their narratives did not dramatically change with the onset of colonialism. Poets continued to place themselves within a specifically Punjabi literary tradition. Kishan Singh 'Arif (1836–1900) is typical of the period. A publisher and bookshop owner in Amritsar, 'Arif authored numerous poetic texts. His most famous was *Qissa Hir te Ranjhe da* (The *Qissa* of Hir and Ranjha), published in 1889 (figure 2). In his opening pages 'Arif writes: "Poets have given their thoughts on Hir's condition before. . . . Those that I remember I'll tell you, my friend. Hamid, Hasham, Fazl Shah, Waris, Muqbal . . . Hir Husain, Roshan . . , Jog Singh and Kahan Singh, Nar Singh have spoken. Ratan Singh and Krishan Singh Gobind . . . then Bhagwan Singh and Singh Gopal told [it]. There are countless others I have not given attention to."[24] Christopher Shackle has identified such genealogies in late nineteenth-century *qisse* (for there were many, the earliest dated to 1855) as "the first significant records of the Punjabi poetic past," and as a "manifestation of the increased self-consciousness" with which *qissa* poets were participating in a Punjabi literary tradition.[25]

By including authors from the eighteenth and early nineteenth centuries, as well as his contemporaries, 'Arif, like Abbasi before him, was participating in a literary tradition with a clear sense of its own contours and history. This continuity is significant since it points to the enduring salience of a vernacular literature through a period of immense change. But there are also important, if subtle, shifts embedded in 'Arif's text itself and in the context of its production.

THE *QISSA* AND COLONIALISM:
THE LITERARY-HISTORICAL CONTEXT

One of the most significant shifts for literary culture in nineteenth-century India came with the colonial state's designation of official vernacular languages for provincial administration. In much of precolonial India, the official language of administration was Persian. The East India Company, too, used Persian for administrative and judicial purposes at the provincial level until 1837, when it instituted the change from Persian to Indian vernaculars.[26] Across Company territories, the colonial administration debated then established which vernacular language(s) was appropriate for each province. In the Punjab the colonial state designated Urdu—as opposed to Punjabi—as the official language (how this decision was reached is detailed in chapter 1). This circumstance makes the colonial history of Punjabi significantly different from that of other Indian vernaculars, particularly those that were designated official vernaculars, including Urdu, Hindi (not until 1900), Bengali, Tamil, and Telegu.

With the designation of official vernacular languages for provincial administration, the state both formally and informally sponsored the production of materials that would assist officers in learning those languages. Grammars, dictionaries, and primers facilitated this task and helped bring about standardization, which was thought essential to their use in government.[27] The Company also patronized vernacular writers whose poetry and fiction could be used for teaching Company officials and natives alike. This colonial patronage for modern literature written in officially recognized vernacular languages played an important role in the process of creating modern standard Indian languages.[28]

Perhaps even more significant an influence, however, was Company patronage for the translation of English texts, so that "Western" subjects—science, mathematics, and so on—could be taught in a vernacular medium. Particularly important to the development of scholarly prose in Urdu, for example, was the translation work undertaken at Delhi College (est. 1825).[29] The introduction of higher education and the extension of mass education through vernacular languages—invariably the same languages earlier designated as the official languages of provincial government—provided new opportunities for colonial patronage. These included incentives for the production of vernacular materials that could be used for mass education and jobs, both in government bureaus dedicated to translation and in education departments for teachers and administrators. In the Punjab, all such patronage was extended to Urdu projects and personnel. Punjabi poets—*qissa* poets among them—had to seek their sustenance elsewhere. One source of their remuneration was the print market.

In addition to designating official languages, British colonial rule also promoted the Indian adoption of print. Print technology had been available in India since at least the sixteenth century, but it did not flourish as a medium for disseminating texts there until the nineteenth century. Texts that had previously circulated orally and in manuscripts were reproduced in the thousands and sold alongside publications of contemporary writing. In many Indian languages, new genres and new publics emerged with the circulation of periodicals and journals, and with a rise in literacy through education.[30] Despite the creation of Indian reading publics, however, the market in the late nineteenth century did not sustain publishing in Indian languages. Most publishing ventures were not profitable, and colonial state patronage often accounted for the difference between solvency and insolvency. Sanjay Joshi has shown, for example, that in late nineteenth-century Lucknow, only Urdu newspapers with state support were profitable.[31]

Perhaps the clearest indication of the state's role in sustaining vernacular publishing comes from Ulrike Stark's work on the Naval Kishore Press, which was established in 1858 and went on to become the largest Indian-owned printing press and publishing house of the late nineteenth century.[32] An important element of Naval Kishore's success was his appointment in the 1850s as the government's publisher of Hindi and Urdu textbooks for the Northwest Provinces (NWP).[33] This was an extremely lucrative contract for the press, and made the colonial state its biggest client.

The history of Bengali publishing provides another context in which the state's role was extremely significant. Bengali publishing began at the turn of the nineteenth century with books produced by missionaries and the Company, including William Carey's *Grammar of the Bengalee Language* (1801). Carey was a missionary who alongside his missionary work taught Indian languages to Company officials at the Fort William College. It was the efforts of individuals such as Carey, whether for missionary or administrative purposes or both, that sustained Bengali publishing for the first half of the century. A commercial press was not established in Bengal until after 1857. Anindita Ghosh's work on the late nineteenth-century "Battala" or popular press suggests that commercial presses were not successful until the 1860s, and although she describes a vibrant popular market, "educational literature" would remain one of the most important genres, commercially speaking: "school textbooks sold very well and formed a staple of the trade."[34] These same developments applied to all the Indian vernaculars designated as official languages. In other words, in most contexts, the rise of vernacular print cultures in nineteenth-century India relied significantly on the colonial state.

The history of early Punjabi print culture is similar to that of other Indian vernaculars in some regards, and markedly different in others. Missionaries developed the first type fonts for Punjabi printing, as they had for other vernaculars (see chapter 1). Similarly, the rise of Punjabi popular publishing in the 1860s and 1870s is coterminous with other north Indian print cultures, including Bengali, Hindi, and Urdu. Unlike these latter print cultures, however, Punjabi printers and publishers did not enjoy the patronage of the colonial state. This had tangible consequences. As chapter 1 explains, the absence of state support for Punjabi in conjunction with its promotion of Urdu resulted in Urdu becoming the principal language of Punjab's print public sphere. Indeed, as shown in chapter 2, Punjabi newspapers were unable to get any kind of traction in the late nineteenth century.

Punjabi book publishing nevertheless thrived. Punjabi works were published on a range of subjects and sometimes in staggering numbers: print runs ranged from one hundred to twenty-four hundred, and many texts were published in multiple editions. Both religious books (representing all of the Punjab's religious traditions) and secular books found publishers. For all their variety, however, Punjabi books published in the late nineteenth century shared one essential feature: they were composed entirely in classical poetic genres, which was another distinction between Punjabi literary production and that of officially recognized vernacular languages, in which new genres such as the novel began appearing as early as the 1870s. *Qisse* were among the earliest-published Punjabi books, and among the most popular late in the century.[35] Some of these late nineteenth-century texts had been composed earlier but were now disseminated through print—Sultan Bahu's (1629–91) *Majmu'a Baran Mah* and Muqbal's *Hir Muqbal* (c. 1740s) are examples.[36] Others were first written during the colonial period. The overall scale of Punjabi book publishing was considerable: thousands of texts were produced and circulated into the market each year. Unlike the other vernacular print cultures mentioned above, which enjoyed state patronage, Punjabi publishing as an industry was sustained entirely by market forces.

Although the colonial state provided no patronage for Indian-owned Punjabi publishing enterprises, Punjabi print culture necessarily entailed entanglements with the state. The printing press was introduced in the Punjab as a colonial technology, and authors and publishers were subject to censorship and reporting rules. But the state's official neglect of the development of Punjabi literature produced unintended effects. It allowed this literature and print culture to develop largely free from colonial influence and intervention. The colonial state did not, for example, sponsor the creation of new prose traditions through contests and translation projects, as it did with Urdu. Indeed, my analysis of Punjabi publishing points to a level of continuity between the precolonial and colonial periods not seen in other vernacular literary cultures, a continuity made possible only because of the relative autonomy that colonial language policy itself produced for Punjabi literary and print cultures.

In addition to developments in the context in which Punjabi literature was produced, circulated, and consumed, one significant change emerged from within the *qissa* tradition itself. From the early seventeenth century, Punjabi *qissa* texts had been epic-length compositions. These works ran into hundreds of stanzas, and manuscripts contained hundreds of folios. Epic-length renditions related a tale in its entirety and followed conventions of the *qissa* genre, such as use of the *masnavi* rhyme scheme. Many such texts entered Punjabi print culture in the late nineteenth century. Some had been composed generations earlier, such as *Hir Waris Shah* (1766; first published 1851). Others were contemporary compositions, such as Bhai Sant Bajara Singh's *Qissa Hir te Ranjha* da (The *Qissa* of Hir and Ranjha; 1894). Late nineteenth- and early twentieth-century printed texts also included "episodic" versions of *qisse*. These related only one or at most a few scenes or episodes from a larger narrative, taking for granted their audiences' knowledge of the entire narrative. These shorter texts expanded the bounds of what was traditionally considered a *qissa*. Episodic texts in existing collections of colonial-era Punjabi printed books include six genres or subgenres of composition: *si harfi* (thirty letters), *baran mah* (twelve months), *sawal-jawab* (question and answer), *faryad* (plea), *jhok* (abode), and *chitthi* (letter). The first two, which can be traced to classical Persian or Sanskrit prosody, derive from Punjabi precedents before the nineteenth century and usually relate the broad contours of a romance in somewhat condensed form. The latter four, however, have no exact precedents in Punjabi literature. They focus on particular moments within a narrative. Given their various genres, episodic texts are not, strictly speaking, *qisse,* but their authors presented them as part of the *qissa* tradition. *Qissa Hir wa Ranjha,* by Muhammad Shah Sakin, a text explored in more detail in chapter 5, is one example.[37] Although composed in the *si harfi* genre, this text was published as a *qissa.* Beyond its title, it opens with an invocation carefully styled after those of Punjabi *qisse,* suggesting a self-conscious attempt to draw the composition into the ambit of the *qissa* tradition. Not only did authors (and publishers) present episodic texts as part of the *qissa* genre, people seem to have accepted them as such.

Kishan Singh 'Arif's genealogy of poets brings that acceptance into sharper focus. The excerpt above from his *Qissa Hir te Ranjhe da* contains the names of fourteen poets, including the most famous exponent of the Punjabi *qissa,* Waris Shah. It includes poets who composed epic-length *qisse* in the eighteenth century (Muqbal and Waris Shah), the early nineteenth century (Hamid Shah Abbasi, Hasham Shah, and Jog Singh), and the late nineteenth century (Fazl Shah and Bhagwan Singh). Interestingly, it also includes two poets who composed in other genres—Husain and Roshan, who both composed *si harfi*s, not *qisse* proper. Their inclusion in this genealogy, however, which comes at the head of an epic-length rendition, suggests that for 'Arif their work constituted a legitimate part of the *qissa* tradition.

Episodic texts are of special interest because they highlight particular issues and themes from a larger corpus. My analysis in chapters 4 and 5 shows that late nineteenth- and early twentieth-century episodic texts cohered around a limited number of themes, including the significance of *zat* (caste, kinship group) and locality, gender relations, and the proper performance of piety. Given that Punjabi print culture was market driven, its coherence around specific themes suggests that they held particular salience for both poets and their audiences at the time.

THE *QISSA* IN PERFORMANCE

Punjabi *qisse* circulated through manuscripts and printed books, but they were appreciated much more widely through oral performance. *Qisse* are meant to be performed, usually (but not necessarily) to musical accompaniment. During the colonial period, the *qissa* was therefore simultaneously a textual and an oral literature—a fact that is critical to understanding its historical importance. For the historian, it means that the *qissa* relates information about writers and reading publics as well as about performers and listening publics. Chapter 3 will examine the performance contexts of Punjabi literature, focusing on the institutional sites where performances took place, those institutions' locations within a colonial landscape, the performance groups involved, and the composition of audiences. Each of these aspects of performance helps to explain how and why Punjabi and its literature remained vibrant through the colonial period.

Punjabi literature was performed in varied contexts in the late nineteenth and early twentieth centuries. Each of the contexts explored in chapter 3 is significant, but I pay particular attention to institutional sites, because institutions provided important patronage for Punjabi poets and performers. Some of these institutions, such as theaters, were secular. Others were religious sites, such as Sufi shrines and Sikh *gurdwaras* (places of worship), where the recitation or performance of Punjabi literature was central to ritual practices. All of these sites, situated within a colonial landscape, managed to operate with a degree of independence in their internal affairs. In both religious and secular contexts, the performers of Punjabi literature were trained or apprenticed in some way. Many belonged to occupational groups associated with music, dance, and singing. For these groups, the performance of Punjabi literature was the foundation of their livelihoods. Punjabi literature therefore functioned as a nexus of occupational, religious, social, and cultural practices.

Colonial descriptions of *qisse* performances record something otherwise difficult to capture in the historical record: the pleasures of listening to and performing these texts. One may perhaps take for granted that pleasure is inherent to literary culture. However, an analysis of the performance of Punjabi literature points to particular kinds of pleasure—for example, the pleasure taken in listening to tales already known and in interacting with a singer during a performance. Pleasure derived from specific textual content is surely part of the story as well, including the artful turn of phrase, witty banter, love play between characters, and the portrayal of filial relationships.

THE PUNJABI LITERARY FORMATION

The Punjabi literary formation is the rubric I use to analyze the diversity of *qisse* contexts and their historical significance. As mentioned above, this formation was comprised of those individuals who shared practices of producing, circulating, performing, and consuming Punjabi literary texts. Access was open to anyone within the linguistic community, but the literary formation and the linguistic community are not coterminous. That is, simply being a Punjabi speaker did not make one a participant in the formation. Belonging was secured by active participation in the literary tradition. The threshold for belonging was quite expansive, however—the formation was far more inclusive than exclusive. The Punjabi literary formation was not class-, caste-, religion-, or gender-specific, and it encompassed both reading and listening publics. One could engage and gain experience in this activity by composing or performing a Punjabi text, by patronizing a public performance, or by participating in highly refined listening practices. The broad-based nature of this literary formation makes it a particularly compelling new site of historical inquiry since colonial Punjab's historiography has largely focused on specific class, caste, and, most significantly, religious formations.

THE SPECTER OF PARTITION

Histories of modern South Asia invariably underscore the centrality of the 1947 partition for understanding postcolonial India and Pakistan.[38] Partition informs not only the post-1947 history of the subcontinent; its specter is discernible in histories of late nineteenth- and early twentieth-century north India as well. This specter is particularly pronounced in histories of colonial Punjab, not only because the region was partitioned between India and Pakistan but also because it was the site of particularly intense and brutal religious violence. Most of the one million people who died in partition violence were killed in the Punjab, and most of the killing took place over the course of only a few weeks.[39] Communal violence (antagonism along religious lines) precipitated and accompanied the almost wholesale migration of religious minorities from one half of the province to the other. An estimated twelve million refugees were on the move in Punjab in the summer of 1947, Muslims moving westward to Pakistan and Sikhs and Hindus moving eastward to India. In order to account for the violence of partition, historians have sought to understand why, when, and how Punjabi society became so communalized. There are no simple answers. The most viable strands in the historiography suggest two different contributing factors: the colonial state's role in communalizing formal political arenas, and religious-reform organizations that produced new, modern, and increasingly communal religious identities.

The colonial state's role in communalizing Indian politics from the mid-nineteenth century onward has been well documented. Scholars have pointed to the impact of introducing religion as a category in the decennial census, for example.[40] Sudipta Kaviraj has argued that this resulted in an epistemological transformation in Indian society from a "fuzzy" social world to an enumerated one, with significantly sharper contours of differentiation.[41] With the introduction of limited Indian participation in government in the final decades of the nineteenth century, the enumeration of religious communities took on new significance in political arenas as these communities now staked claims to representation according to their strength in numbers. The creation of separate electorates for Muslims in 1909 only formalized a process that the colonial state had already put in place. Hindus and Muslims would henceforward have separate political processes, and dispensations to government were often made on a communal basis.

All of this is well known. But what impact did this have on the incipient public sphere of colonial Punjab? As already mentioned, the print public sphere in colonial Punjab used Urdu as its linguistic medium. If the print public sphere sought to influence the government and impact formal political arenas, then communicating in the designated administrative language was an obvious choice. Following the structures put in place by the state, one finds an increasing communalization of politics in colonial Punjab's Urdu-language press, a phenomenon much less evident in Punjabi print culture. The Punjabi-language press may have leaned in that direction but, as I argue in chapter 2, Punjabi periodicals were never able to establish a firm footing.

That the major sector of Punjabi print culture—book publishing—shows less evidence of communalism is not to deny that religious antagonisms increased over the course of the colonial period; rather it suggests we must reconsider the extent of that communalism and its periodization. Examination of the Punjabi literary formation reveals that the communalism articulated in formal political arenas did not extend to all realms of experience. Through at least the early decades of the twentieth century, the robustness and inclusiveness of that formation provides a necessary corrective to a historiography that has largely focused on communal antagonisms.

The colonial state's political agenda and the advent of democratic politics both contributed to increasing political antagonism between religious communities, and so did the activities of Hindu, Sikh, and Muslim reformers active in colonial Punjab, who had an immense impact in fomenting a more communalized society.[42] Such reformers were prompted to action both by intellectual currents within their traditions and by changes in society brought about by colonialism.[43] An important aspect of the latter was the Punjab government's tacit support for Christian missionary activity in the province. Although missionaries were not immediately successful in gaining converts, their presence, methods, and the state support they received made them particularly alarming to activists among the other religions.[44] Christian missionary activity was one of a host of factors that precipitated religious reform, something that others have documented in impressive detail.[45] What is important to note for the present argument is that although Hindu, Sikh, and Muslim reform programs varied, they shared a common agenda: to produce a modern religious subject whose identity and religious practices were completely distinct from those of any other religion.

Socioreligious reform activity in colonial Punjab was particularly pronounced because of the significant presence of all three major religious communities—Muslim, Hindu, and Sikh—as well as Christian missionary activity. According to the 1901 census of India, British Punjab had a population of approximately twenty million people. Muslims were in the majority (53 percent), followed by Hindus

(39 percent) and Sikhs (7 percent).[46] Although Christian missionaries were very active, as of 1901 Christians numbered only about sixty-five thousand, accounting for less than one-half of one percent of the population. In the ensuing decades, however, their numbers would climb into the hundreds of thousands.[47]

The Punjab was an important site for two varieties of reform movement. The first variety was that of movements founded elsewhere, active throughout north India—if not in all of India—that had a marked impact in the region. These would include movements such as Deoband, the Barelwi, the Brahmo Samaj, and most importantly the Arya Samaj.[48] The Arya Samaj, a Hindu reform movement started by Dayanand Saraswati in Bombay in 1875, took hold not in Bombay but in Punjab, where it became one of the most active organizations of this kind, with a pronounced presence among the urban middle classes.[49] The other variety was that which had its genesis in the Punjab and was most active there. The most significant of these were the Singh Sabha and the Ahmadiyah movements. The Singh Sabha was a Sikh organization founded in Amritsar in 1873. In the following decades, branches were set up across the Punjab. Mirza Ghulam Ahmad inspired the Muslim Ahmadiyah movement, whose adherents recognized Ahmad as a prophet and a regenerator of Islam. This movement is thought to have officially commenced in 1889 in Ludhiana, where Ahmad took on his first initiates. Each of these organizations had their particularities, but what is relevant to us here is the social and political impact of their activities.

These reform organizations' activities focused principally on impacting the beliefs and practices of their coreligionists. In each case the reformers believed that their religion had been corrupted and that people were steeped in "superstitions" and "accretions"—often indications of the influence of other religions—that had weakened the faith. At the same time, these organizations participated in interreligious debate. Rather than interfaith dialogue (in the contemporary sense) or reconciliation, religious debate focused on arguments about the superiority of a given religious tradition over others. Religious reformers often engaged one another in public, and some of their debates seem to have been public spectacles. In one famous example, when Mirza Ghulam Ahmad accepted the Christian missionary Henry Martin Clark's invitation to debate, Ahmad held Martin in extended dialogue for fifteen days.[50] While the Christian mission may have spurred many Indian religious reformers to action, their attitudes toward the church were temperate compared to their vitriolic interactions with one another. Debates between the Ahmadiyah and the Arya Samaj were particularly bitter. While relations between the Singh Sabha and the Arya Samaj were initially cordial, by the turn of the twentieth century they, too, were engaged in charged disagreements. The exchanges between organizations took place not only through public debates but also in print. Their use of the latter has left historians a particularly rich archive, which has in turn led to the special prominence of socioreligious reformers in late nineteenth-century Punjab's historiography.

The reform organizations all employed print to promote their own movements, and print served as a particularly fertile medium for attacking other communities as well. From the 1880s tract wars raged, with reformers publishing short but acerbic pamphlets or tracts attacking one another's faiths. One such exchange occurred between the Arya Samaj and the Ahmadiyah. In 1887 a leading polemicist for the Arya Samaj, Pandit Lekh Ram, published one of his many anti-Muslim– anti-Ahmadiyah tracts, entitled *Takzib-i Barahin-i Ahmadiyah* (Accusing as False the Claims of the Ahmadiyah). An Ahmadiyah leader responded in 1890 with *Tasdiq-i Barahin-i Ahmadiyah* (Verifying the Proofs of the Ahmadiyah), and the next year Mirza Ghulam Ahmad himself responded to Lekh Ram with *Ta'id-i Barahin-i Ahmadiyah* (Confirming the Proofs of the Ahmadiyah). Not to be outdone, Ram retorted in 1892 with a treatise condemning not just the Ahmadiyah but Muslims in general: *Risala-i Jihad ya'ni Din-i Muhammadi ki Bunyad* (Jihad, or the Basis of Muhammadan Religion).[51] The bitterness of such debates should not be underestimated: in 1897, an unknown assailant assassinated Pandit Lekh Ram for his polemical activities and writings.[52]

The Arya Samaj also found itself in contentious debate with Sikhs. Its founder, Dayanand Saraswati, held that Sikhism was merely a cult of Hinduism that would be eradicated through the reform he advocated. This attitude prompted a leading Singh Sabha intellectual, Kahan Singh Nabha, to publish a tract entitled, *Ham Hindu Nahin* (We Are Not Hindus; initially published in Hindi, c. 1879, and in Punjabi in 1899).[53] The Arya Samaj countered, unsurprisingly, with *Sikh Hindu Hain* (Sikhs Are Hindus).[54] While the explicit subject of this debate was religious identity, the subtext was political. If the colonial state counted Sikhs as Hindus then Hindus could claim that much greater a share of any spoils the state distributed. Kahan Singh Nabha's refutation was grounded in this political context; Sikhs had to establish a distinct religious identity if they were to have an independent share of state patronage.

Tracts such as these were part of a massive publishing drive, and the reform organizations established separate wings expressly to oversee these efforts. In 1894, for example, the Singh Sabha established the Khalsa Tract Society, which by 1911 had come out with over four hundred tracts, exceeding one million copies. The Sikh Book Club, the Panch Khalsa Agency, and the Sikh Handbill Society paralleled the Khalsa Tract Society's efforts.[55] With Hindu and Muslim reform organizations equally active in this regard, colonial Punjab's society became virtually saturated with reformers' claims and counterclaims.

Scholars have long agreed that socioreligious reform activities in the Punjab contributed to increasingly rigid religious identities. The careful distinctions drawn between religious communities in the wake of reformers' agitations were not simply about difference, but included an attitude of opposition: religions pitted themselves against each other as they competed for adherents and patronage from the colonial state. This contentious atmosphere bled into the formal political arena where, increasingly after the turn of the twentieth century, Hindus, Muslims, and Sikhs clashed. It is easy to see how this narrative leads to India's—and Punjab's—partition along religious lines in 1947. Kenneth Jones, a historian of the Arya Samaj and socioreligious reform more generally, captures concisely both the commonalities of these organizations and a common view of their net effect:

> They [socioreligious reformers] adopted western organizational techniques with which they created a wide variety of institutions. Each possessed missionaries, tract societies, parochial schools, centres of worship, systems of fund-raising, bureaucracies, and central associations. Lines dividing one religion from another and one socio-religious movement from all others were defined, and aggressively defended. By the end of the nineteenth century . . . this newly strengthened communal consciousness was exported from the Punjab by such movements as the Arya Samaj and the Ahmadiyahs. . . . In the four decades before Independence the attitudes, strategies and organizations predominant in the Punjab spread to other areas of the subcontinent, carrying with them forms of aggressive religious competition.[56]

For Jones, late nineteenth-century Punjab served as an incubator for communalism, which matured there and then spread across India. The specter of partition is not directly raised in Jones's work, but it is readily apparent.

If the colonial state and socioreligious reformers emphasized distinctions, differences, and a sense of religious competition, language activists also did their part to contribute to that discourse. Activists worked throughout the late nineteenth and early twentieth centuries toward the identification of languages and scripts with specific religious communities: Hindi in the Devnagari script with Hindus; Urdu in the Indo-Persian script with Muslims; and Punjabi in the Gurmukhi script with Sikhs. The association of particular languages with particular religions was neither new nor unique to the subcontinent. From their earliest experience of India, for example, colonial officials had correlated language and religion, but such correlations were between religions and their liturgical languages. Sanskrit was associated with Hinduism, Arabic with Islam, and Punjabi with Sikhism (though, as I will show, this last association was only partially correct). What was new about the late nineteenth-century association of language and religion was that it linked vernacular languages and religious communities.

The earliest movement of this kind, the Hindi-Urdu controversy, began in the NWP and Oudh and spread to other provinces. Historian Christopher King has succinctly described the dynamic of the controversy: "At the beginning of the nineteenth century Indo-Persian culture dominated in north India, and the equation,

Urdu equaled Hindus plus Muslims, was widely accepted. . . . By the 1860s, however, this equation began to be challenged . . . and two newer equations emerged,
namely, Urdu equaled Muslim and Hindi equaled Hindu."[57] The stakes involved in
this shift were tangible. In 1837 the colonial state adopted Urdu as the official language in the NWP and, from 1858, in Oudh. From the 1860s, the partisans of Hindi
argued that Urdu was a Muslim language and Hindi was the language of Hindus.
Since Hindus constituted a majority in the area, their logic went, Hindi should
be the official language in these provinces. Partisans of Urdu argued its merits as
the official language, suggesting that Hindi would be ill suited to government use.
Advocates from both camps petitioned the colonial state and tried to sway public opinion through literary journals and societies.[58] Hindi agitators succeeded in
gaining official recognition for Hindi in 1900, but this was only a partial victory
because Hindi did not replace Urdu. Rather, it was recognized alongside Urdu as
an official language in NWP and Oudh.

The impact of the Hindi-Urdu controversy, much like that of socioreligious
reform, would draw ever clearer boundaries between people of different religions.
This impact was not limited to the NWP and Oudh. From its inception there, the
Hindi-Urdu controversy quickly spread to other provinces, including the Punjab,
which, however, proved to be an even more complicated and contested linguistic
terrain as activists there associated specific religious communities not only with
Hindi and Urdu but with Punjabi as well. The Singh Sabha's objectives included
the promotion and recognition of Punjabi (in the Gurmukhi script) as a distinctly
Sikh language. To this end, Singh Sabha intellectuals such as Bhai Vir Singh and
Kahan Singh Nabha wrote extensively in Punjabi on Sikh themes, and the organization established its own printing press, the Wazir Hind Press (est. 1892), and
petitioned the government for official recognition of Punjabi in schools and the
government. Partisans of Hindi such as the Arya Samaj similarly petitioned the
state to make Hindi the language of provincial education and government. Muslim groups such as the Anjuman-i-Hamdardi Islamiya, for their part, countered
with petitions asking the state to maintain its support for Urdu (see chapter 2).
Together, socioreligious reform and language advocacy, often mutually implicated,
were indigenous movements with political, religious, and cultural implications.
While creating new awareness within their communities—of proper religious conduct, the role of women, or the language to use, for example—they also worked
assiduously to mark distinctions between communities in such a way that they
slipped easily into antagonisms.

THE SOCIAL SPACE OF LANGUAGE

Socioreligious reform, language activism, and the communalism to which they
and the colonial state contributed are undoubtedly crucial aspects of north India's

late nineteenth-century and early twentieth-century history. However, shifting focus away from these sites to the Punjabi literary formation and its texts introduces a number of crucial questions about how these have been emphasized in existing historiography. To what extent did communalism penetrate Punjabi society in the late nineteenth and early twentieth centuries? Socioreligious reformers' tracts reveal the positions they advocated, but to what extent did people adopt their attitudes? Similarly, the publishing activity of language activists reveals how they worked to categorize languages, scripts, and literary production into communally demarcated boxes, but how successful were they? For example, did Punjabi become a language of Sikhs alone through the advocacy and activities of the Singh Sabha?

The analysis of Punjabi literary culture presented in this book suggests that important realms of activity in Punjab's society remained relatively unaffected by the communal discourse of the day. Stated briefly, this book argues that the Punjabi literary formation reveals a different history of social and cultural relations than that suggested by socioreligious reformists' tracts, language activists' propaganda, and the Urdu press. Given that the Punjabi literary formation cohered around the popular *qissa* tradition, was driven in its print manifestation almost entirely by market demand, and was sustained by the continuing significance of the relationships and practices through which *qisse* were produced and circulated, the vitality of the formation through the early decades of the twentieth century provides an important additional layer to our understanding of late colonial India. Communalism was promoted, wittingly or unwittingly, by state and civil society, but not to the extent that other community affiliations disappeared. Indeed, through the early decades of the twentieth century the Punjabi literary formation demonstrates important cultural continuities in colonial Punjab and suggests that older ways of being remained immensely important to its inhabitants.

The Social Space of Language examines the survival of the Punjabi language and its print and performance cultures, and reveals the religious, class, caste, and gender diversity of the Punjabi literary formation. A detailed discussion of the content of Punjabi *qisse* in chapters 4 and 5 presents particular themes that animated the literature at the core of this formation: *zat* (caste or kinship group), the significance of locality, the conduct of women, and the proper performance of piety. My analyses in these chapters are based on a number of different renditions of a single narrative, *Hir-Ranjha*. This narrative not only has special historical resonance as the first Punjabi *qissa* (Damodar's *Hir,* c. 1605), it has a well-documented history of composition over the following three hundred years, during which it was among the most popular texts taken up for composition within the *qissa* tradition. This temporal depth allows me to read colonial-era renditions as part of a richly sedimented and evolving literary tradition.[59] The narrative continued to be popular through the colonial period, as evidenced by the density of its print production.

My analysis, thus, emerges from consideration of an archive of seventy-five late nineteenth- and early twentieth-century editions, which enables a particularly deep and well-grounded analysis.

While each rendition examined is unique, together they share a core set of narrative elements. *Hir-Ranjha* is always set in a particular Punjab landscape: the village of Takht Hazara, Jhang, on the banks of the Chenab River, and Tilla Jogian in the Salt Range mountains. Its protagonists are always Dhido, who is referred to by his *zat* (Ranjha), and Hir, the daughter of a prominent Sial (*zat*) landowner of Jhang. While in Damodar's seventeenth-century *qissa* the romance ends with Hir and Ranjha reunited and living happily ever after, from the early eighteenth century it has more often been portrayed as a tragedy in which the two lovers die.

The themes that surface in *Hir-Ranjha* texts elaborate a historical imagination that contributes in important ways to our understanding of colonial Punjab. They mark *zat* as a critical determinant of self and community, not religious community. They represent women in ways that defied the conservative reformist discourse of the day. They point to a relationship between individual, community, and territory that emphasizes the local, with a discernible lack of association with or affect for the nation or even the region. They point to notions of religious identity that could accommodate multiplicity, such that individuals could participate in shared notions of piety without distancing themselves from being Hindu, Muslim, Sikh, or Christian. These are the ways of being that I explore, in contrast to the communalism that is the mainstay of historiography on late nineteenth- and early twentieth-century Punjab and north India.

Ultimately, the moorings of these ways of being were challenged by a transformation of politics in British India, particularly after 1919, that structurally promoted communal political claims within a representative and increasingly democratic framework. As the twentieth century progressed, organizations such as the Singh Sabha would have an increasing impact, particularly when the state tacitly supported their positions. But analysis of the Punjabi literary tradition, its print culture, and the *qissa* tradition in particular, suggests that such organizations' impact dramatically increased only after 1920, and that they never held absolute sway across society. Udham Singh's and Amrita Pritam's uses of *Hir-Ranjha* make this evident. For Singh and Pritam—and for Ganesh Das before them, and countless others since—the story of *Hir-Ranjha* was far more than a fictional romance; the tale's most revered poet, Waris Shah, was far more than a name from the distant past. *Hir-Ranjha* and the *qissa* tradition embodied the historical imagination of a broad cross-section of the Punjab, and that imagination, as we will see, was far more open-ended and complex than a narrowly communalist interpretation can account for.

1

Forging a Language Policy

The East India Company's half-century of vigorous territorial expansion in India began with the marquess of Wellesley's governor-generalship in 1798 and culminated in the annexation of the Punjab in 1849. The Punjab's Sikh kingdom of Lahore (map 3), established by Ranjit Singh in 1799, had proved a particularly capable adversary, and the Company conquered the region only through a combination of political intrigue and military might. The new colonial administrative unit that resulted from this conquest—Punjab province—encompassed all or parts of what had been the Mughal *subas* (provinces) of Lahore, Multan, and Kabul before they had been wrested by the Sikhs. Colonial Punjab as established in 1849 was thus composed of the area's five *doabs*, or inter-riverine tracts, the territory immediately to their east and west (the trans-Indus and the cis-Sutlej territories), and the frontier areas of Peshawar, Leia, and Hazara. In 1858 Delhi and its environs were added to the province, and in 1901, the frontier areas were separated to form the Northwest Frontier Province (map 4). As these transformations suggest, the Punjab has been variously constituted throughout the modern period. The waxing and waning of its administrative borders notwithstanding, the Punjab has a geographic-cultural core, as this book demonstrates, whether conceived as an axis connecting the region's major cities, Amritsar, Lahore, and Multan, or more broadly as the five *doabs* and the cis-Sutlej territory.

The annexation of the Punjab in 1849 has for historians of modern South Asia always marked an important moment in India's colonization, for with Punjab's inclusion Company territories spanned the length and breadth of the subcontinent, albeit with Indian-administered states interspersed. With the transition to Crown Rule in 1858, the map of India (or the political realities it represented) did not

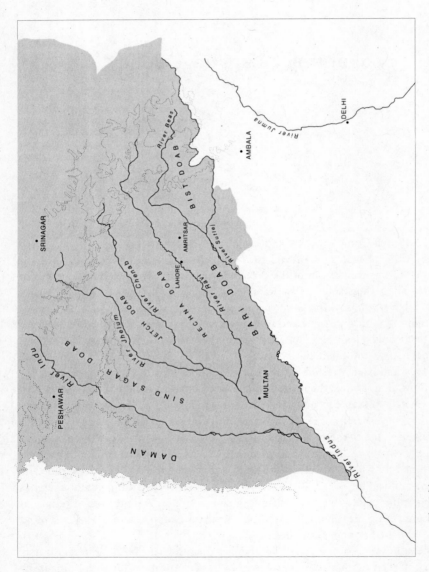

MAP 3. The Sikh empire, 1839.

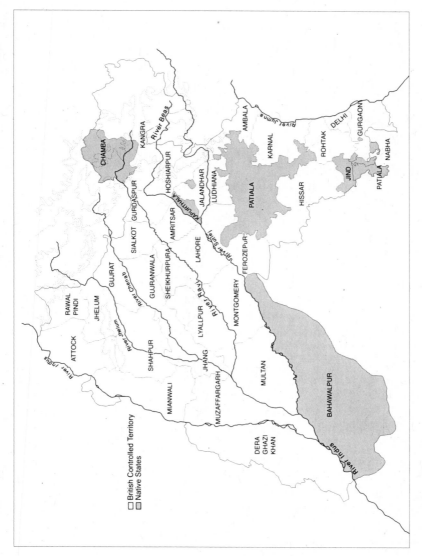

MAP 4. Colonial Punjab.

change dramatically, though the subcontinent was now refigured as British India and Native States. Whether focusing on the Company period or that of Crown Rule, generations of scholars have documented the impact of British colonialism on Indian political, economic, legal, social, and cultural life. Indeed, the Punjab provides especially fertile ground for such study. One can plausibly argue, for instance, that the effects of colonialism were more pronounced in the Punjab than elsewhere, since by the time of its annexation the Company was already well practiced in administering Indian territories to its own advantage. Additionally, the Company instituted a more authoritarian administrative structure in the Punjab, one that was largely retained after 1858. Historians have dubbed this the "Punjab school" of administration and have singled it out for its marked authoritarianism, paternalism, and Christian evangelism. The administrators of this Punjab school were primarily responsible for the province's vigorous incorporation into the greater British enterprise during the late nineteenth-century "high noon" of colonialism, when Indian state and society were unabashedly manipulated to Britain's economic and political ends. Together, these factors contributed to colonialism's tangible, indelible impact on Punjabi society.

Language is undoubtedly a critical arena for the operation of colonial power, and this was as true in colonial India as in other colonial contexts.[1] C. A. Bayly has argued further that language is central to establishing colonial power. In his *Empire and Information,* a study of late eighteenth- and nineteenth-century India, Bayly eloquently argues that the colonial state's ability to access indigenous networks of information and adapt them to its own ends was critical to its success. This access rested on colonial officials' linguistic abilities in Persian, Sanskrit, and local vernacular languages. These were linguistic skills they did not by and large possess, however, forcing them to rely on native intermediaries and interpreters, a situation most administrators found disconcerting.[2] Given the obvious advantages of their own linguistic competence over their reliance on intermediaries, Company officials took pains to learn, codify, and ultimately teach Indian classical and vernacular languages in colonial institutions, in both England and India.[3] Bernard Cohn has persuasively argued that such institutions helped officials gain the "command of language" that was crucial to the consolidation of colonial power in India.[4] If language (competency) was critical to the colonial enterprise, as Bayly and Cohn contend, then so was language policy—that is, which language(s) to adopt for administration. The history of language policy in colonial Punjab, where the language of administration was carefully considered for its ability to integrate the province into broader structures of colonial authority, bears out this important relationship between language and empire.

The policy established by the colonial state in Punjab designated Urdu as the language of provincial administration. This had a number of consequences, the most evident of which is that this designation—which initially applied only to the administration of revenue collection and justice—led to the adoption of Urdu in other branches of government. Less evident is the impact of colonial language policy beyond state arenas to influence Indian society in new and important ways. Most significantly, language policy had a decisive influence on literary production in the Punjab, on its print public sphere, and its print culture more broadly. That the state's language policy impacted print culture is perhaps not surprising given the role of colonial actors in promoting print in nineteenth-century India. As in many other parts of India, it was Christian missionaries who first introduced print in the Punjab (in the early nineteenth century). At first, Indians had exhibited little enthusiasm for the technology, and Indian publishing ventures were few and far between. However, once the region was annexed, its colonial administrators saw potential benefit in an active "native" press and helped to spur Indian publish- ing enterprises by promoting the establishment of presses and purchasing much of what they produced. This publishing industry would in twenty years become the foundation of an incipient indigenous public sphere, though this was surely an unintended effect of colonial policy and patronage. By the 1870s, newspapers were increasing in number and circulation, and book publishing was thriving, with thousands of volumes produced each year, representing together an array of Indian opinion.

Almost all of these newspapers, and certainly all the commercially viable ones, were published in the Urdu language, as were a majority of the books published in Punjab. Given India's robust indigenous literary traditions and colonial efforts to cultivate and modernize vernacular languages across India, it is no surprise that the principal language of publishing in Punjab was an Indian vernacular. But the dominance of Urdu requires explanation. Elsewhere in India, vernacular pub- lishing reflected the principal vernacular language(s) of each province, but Urdu was not prominent in the Punjab. Most of the region's inhabitants spoke Punjabi, the main colloquial language of people from different class, caste, and religious backgrounds, and a language with a rich literary tradition. Urdu, by contrast, had no significant spoken or literary history in the Punjab prior to the establishment of the colonial state. In colonial Punjab, then, the almost complete dominance of Urdu in certain genres of literary production and in the print public sphere, and its preponderance in print culture more generally was an outcome of the state's language policy. Marking this considerable impact of colonialism on indigenous practice is not my chief aim, however.

The more significant aspect of the history of language, literary production, and print culture in late nineteenth- and early twentieth-century Punjab is not that of colonialism's impact, but rather of its limits. The "success" of the colonial state's language policy, documented in this chapter through Punjabis' adoption of Urdu as the language of certain literary genres and the print public sphere, was only partial. Thus, for example, at no point during its rule in Punjab could the colonial

state govern without recourse to Punjabi, colloquially at least. This resilience of the
Punjabi language, despite a colonial policy clearly aimed at replacing it with Urdu,
marks an important limit to colonialism, as does Punjabi literary production, and
Punjabi print and performance cultures. Indeed, this resilience—recovered in this
chapter from the margins of the colonial archive—presents a first indication of
the vitality of the Punjabi literary formation during the late nineteenth and early
twentieth centuries.

EARLY PRINTING IN PUNJAB

Before turning to language policy, it is helpful to examine the state of publishing
in early and mid-nineteenth-century Punjab, since colonial policy had a decided
impact in this arena. Print technology had been available in India as early as the
sixteenth century, but it was not until the nineteenth century that printed texts
were widely disseminated. Across India, Christian missionaries were among the
first groups to use printing presses, since they saw publishing as an effective evan-
gelizing tool. This was true in the Punjab as well, where the American Presbyterian
Mission established the first printing press, in 1836 in Ludhiana.[5] The press initially
had only two type fonts: roman font, used primarily for Romance languages, and
Indo-Persian, with which texts could be produced in Arabic and Persian, as well as
in a number of Indian vernacular languages, including Urdu, Kashmiri, and Punjabi. With these two fonts, the mission published Christian scripture in English,
Urdu, Persian, and "Indo-Roman" (Urdu in roman characters). Subsequently the
mission designed two more fonts: Gurmukhi, used principally for Punjabi, and
Devnagari, used for Sanskrit and Hindi, which it used beginning in 1838 to produce publications in Punjabi and Hindi. Choices about what languages the press
should publish in, and what scripts to use, appear to have been grounded in missionary (and colonial) conceptions about the links between languages, scripts, and
religious communities, discussed below. Be that as it may, the Ludhiana Mission
Press is significant to the history of publishing in the Punjab because it was the
region's first printing press and, perhaps more importantly, because of the sheer
volume of materials it produced and distributed. Despite numerous setbacks, in its
third year (1838) the Mission Press published seventy thousand volumes of twenty-
four titles, comprising well over a million pages. In 1840 the press printed fewer
volumes (just over thirty thousand), but these accounted for a total output of some
two million pages. These were in English, Urdu (in Indo-Persian script), Hindi
(in Devnagari script), Punjabi (in Gurmukhi script), and also Kashmiri (in Indo-
Persian; due to a sizable migrant Kashmiri community in the Punjab).

The American Presbyterian Mission may have brought a new technology to the
Punjab, but this did not spark a revolution in indigenous publishing there. It took
almost fifteen years before an Indian-owned press was established, and then only

in response to the provincial administration's invitation to do so.[6] Hursookh Rai, an experienced printer from the Northwest Provinces (NWP), accepted the government's invitation and in early 1850 established the Kohinoor Press in Lahore. Rai then launched *Kohinoor*, an Urdu-language newspaper whose editorial slant was, not surprisingly, decidedly sympathetic to government concerns.[7] The Kohinoor Press was not the first press the Company government had helped establish in the Punjab, however. As early as the 1840s the British Resident at Lahore facilitated and financed the city's first English-language press, the Chronicle Press. For the Chronicle Press, too, the Company had turned to an experienced printer, in this case Muhammad Azim, who had been associated with the *Delhi Gazette*. Once established, the press published *The Lahore Chronicle*, a journal meant explicitly to further British policy.[8] Although its exact date of inception is unknown, the reminiscences of Lahore resident H. R. Goulding reveal that *The Lahore Chronicle* was available in the late 1840s.[9]

Through such Company initiatives, an Indian-owned-and-operated press was slowly established in the Punjab, and after 1850 presses were launched with increasing frequency. Through the latter half of the nineteenth century, presses were founded in Lahore and Amritsar, and also in smaller cities such as Multan, Sialkot, Jhelum, and Rawalpindi. These engaged in two kinds of publishing: newspapers and periodicals, and books, both in a variety of languages.

Urdu publications dominated, however. According to a survey of late nineteenth-century Punjab newspapers, while periodicals were published in Urdu, English, Punjabi, Hindi, Persian, Arabic, and Sindhi, and some newspapers were composed in more than one language, Urdu was the predominant language of the press.[10] In 1876, for example, of the thirteen most important newspapers and periodicals, seven were in Urdu, four in English, and two in Arabic.[11] In 1883 Urdu was the language of eleven of the thirteen vernacular newspapers published in Lahore.[12] By 1901, 186 vernacular newspapers and periodicals were being published in the province, of which 137 were in Urdu.[13] Taking an aggregate view, of the 413 periodicals published in the Punjab between 1880 and 1905, 343, or about 82 percent, were in Urdu.[14] While some of these Urdu newspapers were short-lived or had limited circulations (sometimes only a few hundred), others were among the Punjab's most important commercial newspapers. The most significant were the *Akhbar-i Am*, started in 1870, and the *Paisa Akhbar*, started in 1887. Both were published in the capital city of Lahore and both had healthy circulations; in 1903 the *Paisa Akhbar*'s weekly edition reached 13,500,[15] an astonishing number for the time, given that the 1901 census documented the literacy rate for Lahore district (with a population of approximately 1.162 million) as a mere 4.4 percent.[16]

Alongside newspaper publishing in the Punjab, book publishing, which remained overwhelmingly lithographic rather than typographic until well into the twentieth century, also commenced in the late nineteenth century. Government

TABLE 1 Publications registered in Punjab, 1867–96

Year	Total number of books	Urdu books (percent of total)	Second most popular language
1870–71	426	150 (35%)	Hindi, 76 (18%)
1875–76	911	319 (35%)	Arabic, 77 (9%)
1879–80	926	395 (43%)	Punjabi, 170 (18%)
1885–86	1,566	806 (51%)	Hindi, 230 (15%)
1889–90	2,206	923 (42%)	Punjabi, 499 (23%)
1895–96	1,304	617 (47%)	Punjabi, 298 (23%)
1902–3	1,233	521 (42%)	Punjabi, 350 (28%)

records indicate that books published there were even more linguistically diverse than the newspapers. Between 1867 and 1896, publishers produced books in Arabic, Hindi, Kashmiri, Marwari, Pahari, Pashto, Persian, Punjabi, Sanskrit, Sindhi, and Urdu, with Urdu publications again outnumbering the others. Numbers give some indication of Urdu's dominance vis-à-vis other publication languages (table 1).[17]

Although precise information about titles and content is unavailable, anecdotal evidence based on surviving texts suggests that Urdu publishing encompassed a range of genres and subjects, from poetry and fiction, to history, religion, and science.

The preponderance of the Urdu language in late nineteenth-century Punjab's newspaper and book trades is an anomaly given that Urdu was not widely spoken in the province. Few indigenous sources detail the Punjab's spoken languages, whether in precolonial or colonial times, but those few that do show that people there did not by and large speak Urdu. Colonial records for the late nineteenth century concur. Similarly, the Punjab does not appear to have been a prominent site of Urdu literary production. This begs two questions: what were the norms of spoken and literary language in precolonial Punjab? And why did Urdu come to dominate the latter arena, at least, in the late nineteenth century?

PRECOLONIAL LINGUISTIC AND LITERARY PRACTICES

A sketch of precolonial language use and literary production in the Punjab provides an important context for understanding the changes wrought by colonialism in these arenas. While charting the latter is possible through the survival of manuscripts, charting the former is challenging since few sources of the kind later available for this purpose—ethnographic surveys and censuses, for example—exist for the Sikh period, or the Mughal and Sultanate periods before it. These difficulties notwithstanding, a composite picture suggests that there were a "diverse collection of languages, different languages for different people on different occasions," in David Lelyveld's words.[18] Lelyveld was writing of the Mughal court, but his words resonate here as in precolonial Punjab, like in much of India historically, there were colloquial, liturgical, sacred, court, and literary languages, some of which overlapped and some of which did not.

The earliest indication of the language(s) spoken in the Punjab is derived by inference from the poetry of the Sufi saint Shaikh Farid (1173–1265). Farid's poetry is among the earliest in the Punjabi literary canon, and we can infer that it represented the contemporary vernacular language of Pakpattan in central Punjab, where he established a Sufi *khanqah,* or hospice. This inference is based on broader patterns of Sufi practice in South Asia, where Sufis are known to have composed poetry in local spoken languages as a means of disseminating Sufi ideas to largely uneducated, lay, local populations.[19] The next available indication of spoken language in Punjab—or its central districts—comes some centuries later from *janam-sakhi* literature, traditional biographies of Guru Nanak (1469–1539), Sikhism's founder and first guru.[20] Composed from the sixteenth century on, in an anecdotal style, many *janam-sakhi*s contain dialogue between individuals who speak in Punjabi (albeit what we would today consider medieval Punjabi), though Persian dialogue is occasionally recorded as well. The *Dabistan-i Mazahib* (School of Religions), a mid-seventeenth-century Persian treatise on India's religions whose author spent time in Punjab, makes reference to the language of the Sikhs, which is referred to as "Jataki." Jataki is identified in nineteenth-century sources as both the language of the Jats, an important caste group in the Punjab (see chapter 4) and as a "corruption" of Multani, spoken in southern Punjab and closely related to Punjabi, if not a dialect of the language.[21] Sujan Rai Bhandari's *Khulasat ut-Tawarikh,* a late seventeenth-century Persian-language history of India, also describes Punjabi as the spoken language of the area.

Punjabi was only one language in use in the region, however, as the reference to Persian in the *janam-sakhi*s suggests. Persian had been the official court language—and thus the language of administration—for precolonial regimes from the turn of the second millennium. Introduced as a court language by the Ghaznavids when they established control over the Punjab during Mahmud's reign (997–1030), Persian remained the court language through the reigns of the Delhi sultans and the Mughals, and even during the era of the Sikh kingdom of Lahore. The status of Persian as a court language helped ensure that with the expansion of Muslim rule in the subcontinent, Persian was widely adopted as a language of letters. Indian elites were thus educated in Persian, both as a means to employment in state apparatuses (as was the case with Guru Nanak) and to partake in a high culture that emanated from courts and was emulated in society more generally.

This process unfolded in Punjab from the Ghaznavid period onward. From approximately 1000 C.E. through the era of Sikh rule, Persian remained an important language of literary production, used for poetry and prose, including nonfiction works such as histories, memoirs, and court chronicles. Beginning with the poetry of Mas'ud Sa'd Salman of Lahore (d. 1121),[22] countless Persian literary works were produced in Punjab, many of them significant to India's Persian canon. Focusing on the immediate precolonial period makes the point adequately, however. Almost all major extant or known historical works produced in early nineteenth-century Punjab were composed in Persian, including Khush-Waqt Rai's *Ahwal-i Firqah-i Sikhan* (1811, a history of the Sikhs from their origins); Diwan Amar Nath's *Zafarnama-i Ranjit Singh* (c. 1830s, a court chronicle of Ranjit Singh's reign); Sohan Lal Suri's *Umdat ut-Tawarikh* (c. 1830s, a history of the Sikhs) and *Ibratnama* (c. 1840s, a poem on political events at the Sikh court from 1840–43); Ghulam Muhi-yuddin's [Bute Shah] *Tarikh-i Punjab* (c. 1842, a general history of the Punjab); and Ganesh Das's *Char Bagh-i Punjab* (1849, a political history and geography of the Punjab).[23] What little we know of the newspapers or protonewspapers produced in the years just before annexation suggests that these, too, were written in Persian.[24]

Persian may have dominated certain genres of precolonial literary production in the Punjab, including history, but other languages also had a presence. Certainly, Sanskrit and Arabic were used in religious rituals and for religious scholarship. Their significance is suggested by a tradition of learning in these languages that extended into the late nineteenth century through indigenous schools.[25] Precolonial Punjab also had a vibrant vernacular literary culture, though not in Urdu. While some see the Punjab, and Lahore in particular, as the cradle of Urdu literature because of the reputed (but now lost) vernacular *divan* (collection) of Mas'ud Sa'd Salman of Lahore, most scholars agree that Urdu's roots lie in the Dakani compositions of Sufi and court poets from the fifteenth- and sixteenth-century Deccan.[26] In north India, classical Urdu literature (principally poetry) came into its own only in the mid-eighteenth century. From then until the disruptions caused by the rebellion of 1857–58, Urdu's major literary centers were Delhi and Lucknow.[27] While Urdu literati also settled in other north Indian cities, including Murshidabad, Patna, Banaras, and Calcutta, neither Lahore nor any other city in the Punjab's central districts figures prominently in Urdu literary history until the colonial period.[28]

A vibrant Punjabi literary culture flourished in precolonial Punjab, however, one that can be traced back to the eleventh century. Most scholars agree that Punjabi's literary foundations were laid in the eleventh and twelfth centuries, with the compositions of religious figures such as the Nath saint Gorakhnath (c. eleventh century) and the Sufi Shaikh Farid. Mohan Singh Uberoi, an influential literary historian writing in the 1930s, sees Gorakhnath and Farid as the first participants in a Punjabi literary era that spanned the eleventh to the fifteenth centuries, which he calls "Old Punjabi." He includes the compositions of the bhakti saint Kabir

(1440–1518), and argues that the period is marked by heavy use of a dialect known as Western Punjabi or Lahnda. Punjabi compositions during this era used a range of poetical forms and genres, some indigenous and some adopted from Persian and Sanskrit. Uberoi identifies thirty-eight such genres, among the most significant being *dohra* (rhyming couplet), *kafi* (couplet), *var* (lay or war ballad), *shloka* (stanza of four parts of equal length), *chaupai* (four-line stanza), and *kabit* (quatrain comprised of thirty-one or thirty-two syllable lines).[29]

Not all historians of Punjabi literature would anchor the tradition as definitively in the eleventh century or include bhakti poets such as Kabir. Christopher Shackle, for example, acknowledges the importance of Shaikh Farid, but suggests that the discernible literary roots of what he calls modern standard Punjabi are much more recent, dating from the sixteenth century. In contrast to Uberoi, who wants to see Guru Nanak's compositions as squarely in the Punjabi literary canon, Shackle suggests that the *Adi Granth* (which includes the writings of Nanak and other *sants*) and other Sikh sacred texts are better described as being in "the sacred language of the Sikhs," which he argues draws many of its elements from a local source (vernacular language—Punjabi, presumably), but is "certainly not 'Old Punjabi.'"[30] These distinctions may seem overly academic, but they point to the contested history of Punjabi literature, including contests over the place of the Punjabi language in twentieth-century politics.

While scholars may thus disagree about whether Sikh sacred scriptures such as the *Adi Granth* and the *Dasam Granth* are central to a Punjabi literary canon, as Uberoi would have it, there is more scholarly consensus on the inclusion of a number of sixteenth-, seventeenth-, and eighteenth-century poets who wrote in a range of verse forms. Among these are Bhai Gurdas Bhalla (c. 1550s–1635), Shah Husain (c. 1530s–1600), Sultan Bahu (1629–91), Damodar (c. early seventeenth century), Muqbal (c. mid-eighteenth century), and Waris Shah (c. mid-eighteenth century). While Bhai Gurdas and the Sufis Shah Husain and Sultan Bahu all composed in traditional genres, *vars* and *kafis*, respectively, the three latter poets composed *qisse*, at the time a new verse genre of Punjabi composition. All these poets used existing folklore or popular tales in their poetry, whether composing Sikh, Sufi, or "secular" poetry. The earlier part of this early modern period also saw the first Punjabi prose compositions, though these were limited to the single genre of *janam-sakhis*. The latter part, the eighteenth century in particular, is marked by a proliferation of Punjabi literary production (though we can also surmise that more manuscripts from then have survived). Uberoi argues that during these centuries a stylistic change is also discernible, as we see more compositions in the language of the Punjab's central districts as opposed to Western Punjabi. One text that employed this new register was Waris Shah's *qissa Hir-Ranjha* (1766). Universally acclaimed as the greatest achievement of Punjabi letters, this text alone explains why the eighteenth century is recognized as an unequivocal high point in the history of Punjabi literature.

Most scholars date Punjabi literature's modern period to the turn of the nineteenth century. A focus on Punjabi literary production in the early nineteenth century helps provide a richer picture of literary conventions on the eve of colonial rule. Punjabi compositions from this era use a number of verse genres, the most significant being the *qissa* and the *var*. The most celebrated poet of the period, Hashim Shah (1735–1843), like many of his contemporaries composed in a variety of genres. He is best remembered, however, for his Punjabi *qisse*, among them the romances *Sassi-Punnun, Shirin-Farhad, Sohni-Mahival,* and *Hir-Ranjha*.[31] Ahmad Yar (1768–1842) also enjoys renown for his Punjabi *qisse*. Indeed, he may be this period's most prolific poet, having produced some forty different Punjabi *qisse* during his lifetime.[32] A teacher of Arabic and Persian and a member of the Sikh court, Ahmad Yar provides particular insight into the polyglot and varied literary production of the day. He composed in Arabic, Persian, and Punjabi, and his subject matter ranged from medicine (*Tibb-i Ahmad Yari*) to history (*Shahnama*, a Persian chronicle of Ranjit Singh's court), Islam (*Jang Ahmad*), and romance (*Hir-Ranjha, Sohni-Mahival, Laila-Majnun,* among others).[33] A number of Ahmad Yar's contemporaries shared his linguistic breadth, underscoring the fact that many Punjabi poets could work in more than one language.

Hamid Shah Abbasi (b. 1748) was, like Ahmad Yar, both a polyglot and a recipient of court patronage. Abbasi composed Punjabi *qisse* and enjoyed the support of the Raja of Nurpur (a Punjab hill state).[34] Abbasi's most significant literary contribution is the *qissa Hir-Ranjha*, a text in which Abbasi self-consciously places himself within a particularly Punjabi literary tradition. His contemporary the poet Vir Singh also composed a *qissa Hir-Ranjha* (1812), and enjoyed the patronage of Maharaja Karan Singh of Patiala, the most important independent state in nineteenth-century Punjab.[35] Other *qissa* poets of the era were from more humble origins. Jog Singh ([*Qissa*] *Hir Jog Singh*, 1825), for example, was a *sadhu* (mendicant). Although he appears to have enjoyed little literary fame, fortune, or patronage during his lifetime, his text inspired a number of future Punjabi poets who placed him prominently in their own literary genealogies.

*Var*s were also an important genre in nineteenth-century Punjabi literary production. As a genre, they date to at least the era of the *Adi Granth* (sixteenth century), when they were first recorded. The most historically significant *var* of the early nineteenth century is likely *Jang Hind Punjab* (The War of Hind and Punjab), by Shah Muhammad (1780–1862). Muhammad served in the army of the Sikh kingdom of Lahore, and his text describes the Anglo-Sikh war of 1845–46 in which he fought. Other significant *var*s were written in the immediate precolonial period as well, among them Qadir Yar's *Hari Singh Nalwa, Puran Bhagat,* and *Rani Kolkila,* and Sahai Singh's *Hari Singh Nalwa*.[36]

In precolonial Punjab, then, as in much of precolonial north India, Persian served as a literary language and the only language for certain genres (in the Punjab, all prose other than religious exegesis). The Punjabi literary tradition was coeval with this Persian literary tradition, but had its own vitality and lineage. In the second half of the nineteenth century, in other parts of north India, writers increasingly used vernacular languages for genres where Persian had once dominated such as history, chronicle, or memoir. This was also true in the Punjab, but there litterateurs adopted Urdu, not Punjabi, as the language of choice for these genres. The genre of history exemplifies this shift. Whereas in the Punjab history had long been written in Persian, in the late nineteenth century a spate of Urdu histories appeared (to my knowledge, no Punjabi language histories were produced). Some of these histories were produced at the behest of the state, examples being Noor Ahmad Chishti's *Yadgar-i Chishti* (Chishti's Memories; 1854) and *Tahqiqaat-i Chishti: Tarikh-i Lahore Ka Encyclopedia* (Chishti's Inquiries: An Encyclopedia of Lahore's History; 1867). Other examples are the local histories produced in the 1860s at the behest of British district commissioners as they were carrying out their settlements of various Punjab districts. The results, such the *Tarikh-i Jhelum* (A History of Jhelum) and *Tarikh-i Zillah Montgomery* (A History of District Montgomery) were composed in Urdu.[37] A number of the histories of the region from the late nineteenth century were not commissioned by the colonial state, yet they, too, were in Urdu. Kanhayalal's *Tarikh-i Lahore* (History of Lahore; c. 1871), and Mufti Ghulam Sarwar's *Tarikh-i Makhzan-i Punjab* (History and Record of Punjab; 1884) are paradigmatic of this literary shift.

What historical processes account for Urdu's dominant place in Punjab's literary and print cultures? Why did it dominate newspaper publishing to the almost complete exclusion of newspapers in other languages? One important element to consider is the disruption in the literary culture of Delhi (and Lucknow) caused by the colonial response to the rebellion of 1857–58. Frances Pritchett, in her fine work on Urdu literary culture during this period, argues that these events witnessed the destruction of the patronage system—grounded in the *ustad-shahgird* (teacher-disciple) relationship—that was so important to Urdu's literary vitality in Delhi. She goes so far as to suggest that the aftermath of 1857 destroyed not only the patronage system but "in fact the whole [Urdu literary] culture."[38] With the demise of Delhi as a site of Urdu patronage, Lahore became an important center of Urdu literary culture as Urdu poets and men of letters migrated there in search of patrons. The historian of Urdu literature Ram Babu Saxena refers to Lahore during this era as a "resort of the exiled men of letters" from Delhi, largely because the Punjab provincial government was based there, and it was often with the colonial state that men like Altaf Husain Hali (1837–1914), one of Urdu's greatest modern poets and critics, found employment.[39] Notwithstanding the important cultural implications of 1857 and the British response in its wake, it is not the dislocation of Urdu literati from other parts of north India that accounts for the dominance of Urdu in colonial Punjab's world of literary production and print culture. More important were the policies of the colonial state, and the most significant of these was its language policy.

COLONIAL INTERVENTIONS

When the East India Company annexed the Punjab in 1849, it instituted a new and unique administrative structure, perhaps owing to both the difficulty with which the area was conquered and its military-strategic significance as a buffer zone between the Gangetic plain and Central Asia. Rather than incorporating the new territory into one of India's three existing presidencies (Bengal, Madras, and Bombay), the Company created a three-member Board of Administration, whose officers were responsible directly to the governor-general in Calcutta. The Company gave the board extensive and centralized power and worked assiduously to establish its rule and assimilate the province into the broader structures of colonial governance in India. Setting a language policy was crucial to both of these priorities.

By 1849, the Company had both precedent and a policy to follow regarding what language(s) to use in administering Indian territories. Through its initial years of rule in India, the Company had used Persian as the language of local administration, in keeping with precolonial practices. Act 29 of 1837 replaced Persian with Indian vernacular languages. While administration at the highest levels would continue to be conducted in English, the act called for administration at provincial and local levels to be in a local Indian language. The proponents of Act 29 had persuasively argued that Indians should be administered and adjudicated in a language they understood, and therefore Persian, which was only accessible to an educated elite, would no longer suffice. While the act did not specify which languages should be adopted in any given province, it was clearly grounded in the idea that the spoken language of an area should be its administrative language. Given the linguistic complexity of the subcontinent—where, as one Indian proverb has it, spoken languages shift dialects as frequently as every four *kos* (eight miles)—this was hardly feasible.[40] Therefore, in instituting the act, Company officials canvassed administrators about the language practices in their jurisdictions and then adopted the vernacular language they deemed most widely spoken in a province or in a number of its districts. On this basis, it was decided that most of the NWP's inhabitants spoke some variation of Urdu. In contrast, in Bengal three languages were chosen (Bengali, Oriya, and Hindi), since clusters of districts reported different languages as their predominant vernaculars.[41]

Despite the seeming clarity of this policy, a discrepancy emerged between colonial intent and practice when it came to instituting vernacular languages for administration. The intent of Act 29 was to make the language of government accessible to the governed, but in practice this effort was vitiated in at least two ways. First, when the state chose a language for local administration, it necessarily privileged one dialect over others. People's ability to understand and use the administrative language therefore depended on its relationship with their own dialect.[42] Second, the register of vernacular language employed by the government in its courts and administration often remained inaccessible to the majority of people because it was heavily laden with terms and vocabulary far removed from everyday usage.[43] Most relevant to the present discussion, though, is that with Act 29 the Company endeavored to make the vernacular language of a province, or particular districts within it, the official language of these places.

When the Board of Administration considered a language policy for the Punjab, it did as Company administrations had done elsewhere: it canvassed local officers, in this case in each of the province's six divisions, and asked which language was "best suited for the courts and Public Business."[44] Officials in the province's western half, which included the western portions of the Punjab and frontier areas (today the Northwest Frontier Province of Pakistan), suggested Persian. Those in the eastern half suggested a shift to Urdu. In both cases the board concurred and thus instituted a two-language policy for the province in September 1849.[45]

In 1854 the board abruptly changed the two-language policy, motivated by new civil service rules that put certain officials in jeopardy of losing their jobs. In November of that year, a mandatory civil service exam was announced that for the first time required all candidates to pass a test in the official language of the courts in which they were employed. Many court officials in western Punjab were not fluent in Persian and so relied on interpreters; under the new rules they faced dismissal. Officers in districts where Persian was the language of the courts petitioned the board to institute Urdu in its place, in the belief that Urdu could more easily be mastered.[46] The board agreed, designating Urdu the official language of colonial government across the Punjab. This designation survived the transition from Company Rule to Crown Rule in 1858, and remained in place until the end of colonial rule in 1947.

The colonial language policy in the Punjab contrasts with that adopted in other Indian provinces in that there is little evidence that Urdu was used in the province in any meaningful way. Colonial officials were, by their own admission, aware of this. John Lawrence, the board's president, clearly indicated as much in a note written in 1849, just as the Persian and Urdu policy was being implemented. "It should be considered," he wrote, "that the Urdu is not the language of these Districts [and] neither is Persian."[47] That Lawrence knew this is no surprise—colonial knowledge about language and linguistic practices had repeatedly affirmed that Punjabi was the colloquial language of the majority.

COLONIAL KNOWLEDGE PRODUCTION
ABOUT INDIAN LANGUAGES

The production of colonial knowledge about Indian languages had begun in earnest with the Company's transformation in the eighteenth century from a trading concern to a political power. Colonial officials' pursuit of such knowledge and their desire to master Indian languages was in part prompted by the exigencies of rule.[48] The study of Sanskrit and Persian in the late eighteenth century, for instance, was crucial to the colonial project of establishing a legal system in India with distinct laws for Hindus (the Gentoo code) and Muslims (Anglo-Muhammadan law).[49] Thomas Trautmann's work has been crucial to recognizing another important context for the colonial production of knowledge about Indian languages: European intellectual preoccupations with the origin and significance of languages, nations, and races. This broader intellectual context is critical for understanding the work of scholars such as William Jones and F. W. Ellis, the "founders" of the Indo-European and Dravidian language families, respectively.[50] The contributions of such early Orientalist scholars notwithstanding, it was missionaries—and those of the Serampore Mission in Bengal, in particular—who produced what is perhaps the most significant information about the languages spoken in India in the early nineteenth century.[51]

Missionaries devoted themselves to the study of Indian languages in order to communicate directly with Indians, to translate the Bible into what they deemed to be the appropriate languages for targeting specific communities, and to produce philological materials that would help other missionaries—and often Company employees—to learn Indian languages.[52] Indeed, missionaries played a significant role in producing knowledge that linked together languages, scripts, and religious communities in India in definitive ways, though not always explicitly. Reconsidering the early publishing efforts of the Ludhiana Mission Press makes these associations evident. Recall that the press initially had only English and Indo-Persian type fonts. Finding themselves in a predominantly Muslim locale—somewhat to their surprise since they thought they were going to the "land of the Sikhs" only to find that Sikhs were a mere 10 percent of Ludhiana's local population—the missionaries' first publication, *A Sermon for the Whole World*, was published in Persian, based on the assumption that this was a Muslim language and that it was the best language by which to proselytize, in print, to local Muslims. They would subsequently publish tracts in Hindi, aimed at the local Hindu population, and in Punjabi, aimed at the local Sikh population, but only with the arrival of Devnagari and Gurmukhi fonts, respectively.

Missionary associations of language with religious community are most clear in their conception of Punjabi, which for them was so closely associated with Sikhism that the two terms—"Shikh" and Punjabi—had by the 1830s long been interchangeable in missionary discourse. The *Seventh Memoir Respecting the Transla-tion of the Sacred Scriptures into the Languages of India, Conducted by the Brethren at Serampore,* published in 1820, provides an example. In a section titled "Languages in Which the New Testament is Published," one finds alongside references to "Pushtoo" (Pashto), "Telinga" (Telegu), and a number of other languages, "the *Shikh* language," clearly a reference to Punjabi.[53] Any doubts about the correlation between the two are dispelled by the writings of William Carey (1761–1834), a Serampore missionary and significant figure in the history of Punjabi, who often referred to the language as "Shikh or Punjabi."[54] That the language was in turn associated with a specific script is clear from the fact that the Serampore missionaries, like the Ludhiana missionaries after them, only published Punjabi in the Gurmukhi script even though it was possible to record the language in Indo-Persian script, a practice that was clearly quite common based on existing Punjabi manuscripts (figure 1, for example). But the missionaries singularly associated Punjabi with the Gurmukhi script and Sikhs. The Gurmukhi script had been created by the Sikh gurus in the sixteenth century to record their Punjabi compositions. Because the gurus created the script expressly for Punjabi it is most closely associated with that language, though it can be used to record any South Asian language.

For missionaries, targeting any religious community necessitated using *their* language and *their* script. Based on their publishing, missionaries correlated the Indo-Persian script and initially Persian and then increasingly Urdu with Muslims, the Devnagari script and Hindi with Hindus, and the Gurmukhi script and Punjabi with Sikhs. Later in the century, language activists in north India would use precisely such (singular) conceptions of language, script, and religious community—put in place by the missionaries and influential among colonial officials—to their own advantage. They, too, would argue that Urdu in the Indo-Persian script was the language of Muslims and that Hindi in the Devnagari script was the language of Hindus. Sikhs would ultimately follow suit with the Gurmukhi-Sikh-Punjabi triad, the groundwork having largely been laid for them by colonial knowledge of Punjabi, knowledge first produced by the Serampore Mission.

The Serampore Mission in Bengal plays a particularly important role in the history of Punjabi because it was the first European institution to produce and disseminate knowledge about the language, a process in which William Carey played a significant part. In pursuit of his missionary work, Carey produced the first modern grammar of Punjabi in 1812, which laid the foundation for all future philological studies of the language.[55] Carey's interest in Punjabi stemmed from his knowledge that it was spoken in large tracts of India's northwest. Indeed, the Serampore missionaries were keen to know which languages were spoken where in India so as to achieve the linguistic competence necessary for their work. Their efforts in this regard were nothing short of remarkable. In 1822, the Baptist Missionary Society published a language map of India based on information compiled by the Serampore missionaries (map 5). The map, the earliest of its kind to my knowledge, contains relatively detailed information about languages then spoken in the Punjab. It divides the Punjab into linguistic zones, and shows "Punjabee" as the language of central Punjab, "Mooltanee or Wuch" as spoken in southern Punjab, and "Hurriana" in eastern Punjab (map 6). As a representation of the earliest existing European data on languages spoken in the Punjab, the map documented two facts immediately relevant to the colonial language policy implemented some twenty-five years later: first, neither Persian nor Urdu was spoken there; and second, the languages identified as spoken in the Punjab were closely related. They can be understood as being on a continuum comprised of a single linguistic field: Punjabi.

The Serampore missionaries were not the only ones to create and circulate knowledge about Punjabi in the early nineteenth century. Missionaries of the American Presbyterian Church, who arrived in India in 1833 as the British were expanding into the Punjab, also took a keen interest. Although the East India Company would not formally annex the region for some years, the cis-Sutlej states (between the Sutlej River and Delhi) had already come under British "protection."[56] William Reed and John Cameron Lowrie, the first American Presbyterian missionaries to arrive in India, decided to establish a mission in British-controlled Punjab because there was as yet no missionary presence there and because they thought it to be the land of the Sikhs, whom they considered particularly susceptible to conversion. The Punjab also appealed because they thought its location would afford an opportunity to spread the gospel into the heart of Central Asia through Kashmir and Afghanistan.[57] By 1834 Lowrie had established a mission in Ludhiana, which, as already noted, established the region's first printing press. In addition to its publishing activities, the mission produced grammars, dictionaries, and guides to the language that would be the standard works for their generation, including Rev. L. Janvier's *Idiomatic Sentences in English and Punjabi* (1846), Rev. J. Newton's *A Grammar of the Panjabi Language, with Appendices* (1851), and Revs. J. Newton and L. Janvier's *A Dictionary of the Panjabi Language, Prepared by a Committee of the Lodiana Mission* (1854).[58] Through these works, in part, the mission played an equally important role in sustaining a colonial conception of Punjabi as the Sikh language.

The colonial state's idea that Punjabi was the Sikh language had been established early in the nineteenth century as the Company, spurred by both security and pecuniary interests, turned its attention to India's northwest. This was an area that the British identified with the "Sikh nation" due to Sikh political control there under the leadership of Ranjit Singh (r. 1799–1839). As Lt. Col. John Malcolm stated explicitly in his 1812 *Sketch of the Sikhs,* information about this community was now vital to Company interests. "Although the information I may convey in such a sketch may be very defective," he wrote in what can only be regarded as false

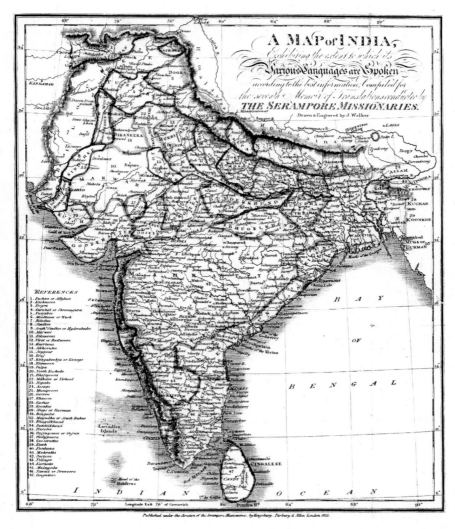

MAP 5. A map of India exhibiting the extent to which its various languages are spoken according to the best information compiled for the seventh Memoir of Translations conducted by the Serampore Missionaries, 1822. Courtesy of the Center for Study of the Life and Work of William Carey, D.D. (1761–1834), William Carey University.

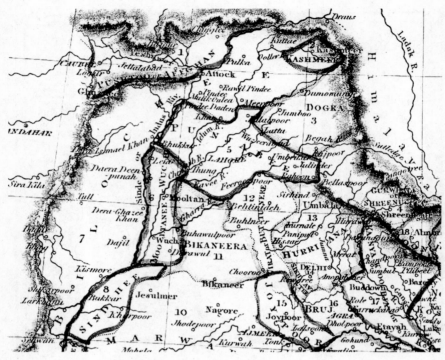

MAP 6. Detail of map 5.

modesty given the tenor of the work more generally, "it will be useful at a moment when every information regarding the Sikhs is of importance."[59] Malcolm's was not the first colonial study of the Sikhs, but he claimed special authority for his work: access to the *Adi Granth*. As with many of his Orientalist contemporaries who deemed texts critical to understanding India's religious traditions,[60] Malcolm thought the *Adi Granth* was a key to understanding the Sikhs, that it would provide insights about their "history, manners, and religion."[61] Through this emphasis on Sikh textual traditions, an approach embraced by subsequent state actors as well, Punjabi became identified as the Sikh liturgical language, though this was something of a misidentification. Sikh sacred scripture (e.g., the *Adi Granth,* the *Dasam Granth,* the *janam-sakhi*s) comprises writings in a number of different Indian languages but is always recorded in the Gurmukhi script. As noted above, although Gurmukhi was created specifically to record Punjabi, it can be used to record any language, and was adopted for Sikh sacred literature during its period of canonization in the sixteenth, seventeenth, and eighteenth centuries. Thus, while not all Sikh sacred literature is in the Punjabi language, it is (almost without exception) recorded in the Gurmukhi script. This distinction was lost on most colonial observers in the early half of the nineteenth century, however, and in both Company and missionary understandings of the Sikh textual, linguistic, and script terrain established at that time, a binding association of the Gurmukhi script with the Punjabi language emerged. This, in turn, contributed to the identification of Punjabi in colonial discourse as the sacred language of Sikhs.

In addition to being understood as the Sikh sacred language, Punjabi was also identified as their colloquial language. While the former was only partially correct, the latter was more firmly grounded in fact since the overwhelming majority of Sikhs were native Punjabi speakers. For the colonial state, as well as the Christian missionaries who tried to convert Sikhs, this confluence of sacred and spoken language produced an abiding belief that Punjabi was specifically a Sikh language. The tenacity of this belief in colonial discourse is striking given the contemporary production of knowledge that made it plainly evident that Punjabi was spoken and written by a much broader spectrum of the population; it was hardly the language of Sikhs alone.

While in the first half of the nineteenth century missionaries had principally gathered and produced knowledge about Punjabi, in the latter half of the century colonial officials and ultimately the colonial state itself produced philological studies on languages used in the province. One important study was *Outlines of Indian Philology* (1867), based on the firsthand experience of colonial officer and amateur philologist John Beames.[62] Beames served in India for thirty-five years (1858–93) and was sent to the Punjab for his first tour, arriving in the town of Gujrat in 1859.[63] His language map confirmed the information published in the Serampore Mission's map earlier in the century: Punjabi was the language of much of the colonial province (map 7). Although Beames had pursued his philological interests as an amateur—his texts were published not by the colonial government but by private publishers in Britain—his work was well respected by contemporary scholars. No less a figure than George Grierson, the leading philologist of his age, wrote at Beames's death (in 1902): "Oriental scholarship has lost one of its most eminent interpreters."[64]

In time, the colonial state also developed an active interest in mapping Indian languages. Although the first censuses of the Punjab (1855 and 1868) contained no information on language(s), statistical information on indigenous language practices began to be collected by various colonial departments in the 1870s. For example, the administration report of the Punjab for 1873–74 recorded spoken vernaculars. A district-by-district breakdown from this report identified Punjabi as the spoken vernacular in every district of central and southern Punjab, and in a number of other districts as well.[65]

As the colonial state's reporting on linguistic practices became more detailed over time, Punjabi was time and again confirmed as the region's primary spoken

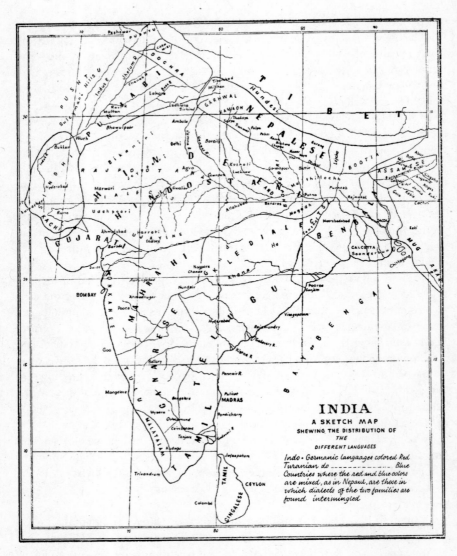

MAP 7. Linguistic map of India, by John Beames, 1867. From John Beames, *Outlines of Indian Philology and Other Philological Papers* (Calcutta: Indian Studies Past and Present, 1960 [1867]).

language. In the first comprehensive census of the Punjab, conducted in 1881, an overwhelming majority in central and southern Punjab returned Punjabi as their vernacular. Subsequent district gazetteers, citing figures on language drawn from this census, show that the Punjabi-speaking population of districts in central and southern Punjab ranged from 85 to 98 percent.[66]

The most comprehensive linguistic study undertaken during the colonial period, George Grierson's *Linguistic Survey of India,* conducted and published between 1903 and 1928, corroborated the information collected by the Serampore missionaries, by John Beames, and by various administrative reports and gazetteers. Grierson reorganized the Punjab into two linguistic zones: east and west. In the east he identified Punjabi and a series of its dialects (one of which was the "Mooltanee" cited in the Serampore Missionaries' language map as a separate language) as the spoken language(s). In the west, Grierson referred to the spoken language as Lahnda.[67] While he argued that Lahnda was distinct from Punjabi, most linguists today agree that Lahnda is best described as a Punjabi dialect. *Dialect* was something of a pejorative term compared to *language* in the philological discourse of the late nineteenth century (and perhaps to this day for language activists). Irrespective of the shifting terrain of *language* and *dialect,* the significant point is that in the early nineteenth century the Serampore missionaries identified Punjabi or closely related idioms, and not Urdu or Persian, as the spoken language of the Punjab, and throughout the late nineteenth and early twentieth centuries colonial surveys repeatedly concurred.

DECONSTRUCTING COLONIAL LANGUAGE POLICY

Knowledge about the Punjabi language produced by both missionaries and colonial employees, then, had two somewhat contradictory aspects, both of which help us to contextualize and explain colonial language policy in the region. The first is that from the early decades of the nineteenth century, missionaries knew that the region's inhabitants spoke Punjabi. This missionary knowledge was accessible to the colonial authorities. William Carey, author of the first Punjabi grammar, taught at the Company's college at Fort William from 1801. The Serampore language map had been published in Britain and would have been readily available to Company authorities. Provincial officials were also in touch with the missionaries of the American Presbyterian Mission at Ludhiana. In 1851 the Punjab government sought out Revs. Forman and Newton of the mission precisely for their expertise in Punjabi.[68] Second, although the Punjab's population was religiously diverse—made up of Muslims, Hindus, Sikhs, and, increasingly from midcentury on, Christians—in colonial perception the Punjabi language was most closely associated with the Sikh community. The language policy adopted by the colonial state in the Punjab suggests that this latter association between language and religious community was more influential than the fact that most of the region's inhabitants spoke Punjabi irrespective of their religious identities.

Given colonial understandings of Punjabi as the language of Sikhs, officials feared that adopting it as the official provincial language might promote Sikh political claims. The nascent colonial state in the Punjab certainly did not want to promote the claims of its defeated rivals, particularly since after annexing the region it found its situation far from ideal. Among the Company's most serious political concerns in the mid-nineteenth century were the military threats it perceived from both within and beyond its borders. From within, the Company feared an uprising by the military of the Sikh kingdom, which had yet to be completely disarmed. Despite its victories in the Anglo-Sikh wars, the Company lacked confidence in its control over the Punjab. That insecurity is evident in a November 1849 report by Charles Napier, commander-in-chief of Company forces: "The Punjaub has been occupied by our troops but it is not conquered," he wrote. "We now occupy it with 54,000 fighting men and it is at present very dangerous ground." Napier's fear was based on his belief that the Punjab still had 100,000 Sikh soldiers, whose "courage has been no way abated by the last struggle," and who he thought "may some day unexpectedly use it" against the Company.[69] These fears bore directly on the language policy implemented by the Company state. To institute Punjabi as the state language could have encouraged Sikh political aspirations, which the state wanted to avoid at all costs. If political concerns about Sikh resurgence suggested that Punjabi should be suppressed, then colonial attitudes about its lack of merit as a language helped justify the implementation of such a strategy.

Colonial officials raised doubts that Punjabi was capable of serving as an administrative language. Such attitudes are most explicit in a series of correspondence from the early 1860s, after language policy had been instituted in the Punjab, but they are hinted at in early archival materials and we can surmise that they formed a continuum with ideas established during the colonial state's earliest experience of rule there. Foremost among officials' opinions about Punjabi was that it was not a language at all, but "merely a *patois* of the Urdu."[70] Unlike classical languages such as Sanskrit or Persian, which were held in high esteem, or vernacular languages such as Urdu, Tamil, or Gujarati, which were used for official purposes, Punjabi was represented as a derivative dialect. Another objection was raised on the grounds that there was no established "standard" Punjabi. "There is no one standard Punjabee to fix as the language of the courts," one official argued, because "there are wide points of divergence between the *patois* of the tribes of the Ravee and that of those of the Sutlej."[71]

Criticism of Punjabi included a perception that it was unsuitable for official uses because it "would be inflexible and barren, and incapable of expressing nice shades of meaning and exact logical ideas with the precision so essential in local proceedings."[72] Some officials based their arguments against Punjabi on its lack of uniformity in its written form. Another erroneously argued, "Punjabee could not be written in the Persian [Indo-Persian] character."[73] Some officials even asserted there was no tradition of writing in Punjabi whatsoever: Colonel Hamilton, commissioner of Multan, wrote, "The Punjabee has never been a written language in the Mooltan division. It is doubtful whether a man could be procured in the division who could write Punjabee correctly in any character."[74]

Such sentiments about Indian vernacular languages had been voiced in other contexts. In the Bengal Presidency, colonial officials had earlier made remarkably similar comments about Bengali, Oriya, and Hindustani (spoken in the presidency's central-eastern, southern, and western portions, respectively). In considering which of these languages should replace Persian as the official language, Company officials had charged that vernacular languages were not standardized;[75] they were "uncouth",[76] "barren," and "unadapted to the conduct of judicial proceedings."[77] They also deemed vernacular languages less efficient than Persian.[78] Officers had also expressed fears that a change from Persian would be extremely detrimental to colonial administration because, in the words of one, finding "competent officers to carry on the business of the courts" would be impossible.[79] Despite these misgivings, all three languages—Bengali, Oriya, and Hindustani—were adopted for use in the Bengal Presidency. The outcome of this earlier debate is helpful in assessing the degree to which the biases and misconceptions of colonial officials in the Punjab figured in colonial language policy there. While such attitudes are sure to have had a role, we can presume they were not decisive. The colonial state would surely have instituted Punjabi as the official language if it had served provincial policy, its "shortcomings" notwithstanding. But it appears that Punjabi did not further colonial officials' political aims. Not only could using Punjabi have helped prompt a Sikh resurgence, but there were decided political and administrative advantages to instituting Urdu instead.

One such advantage was that using Urdu (and initially Persian) allowed the Company to employ a cadre of experienced administrative personnel immediately upon annexation. In the initial years of colonial rule, the Company filled the ranks of Punjab's administration with British and Indian personnel who had served in other Company provinces, principally Bengal and the NWP.[80] The Indians among them were primarily from the Gangetic plains and Bengal, and had no knowledge of Punjabi; their vernacular languages were Hindustani and Bengali. They did have a working knowledge of Urdu and Persian, however, from their service in other parts of north India, and this made their transition to service in Punjab relatively seamless. Similarly, British officers who took up positions in the new colonial province knew no Punjabi, but had a working knowledge of Urdu and, in some cases, a rudimentary knowledge of Persian.[81]

An additional reason for promoting Urdu was that it aided the integration of the new province into the Company's Indian territories. Act 29 had declared

Hindustani the administrative language in Bihar, the NWP, and parts of the Central Provinces.[82] The script officially sanctioned in those provinces was Indo-Persian, and this made the "Hindustani" of much of north India coterminous with the language referred to as "Urdu" in the Punjab. In light of the widespread use of Hindustani, John Lawrence went so far as to refer to it as the lingua franca of India, an idea that had circulated in colonial circles for some time.[83] That the Punjab was included in the area using this lingua franca facilitated the region's integration into the Company's Raj.

Using Urdu in the Punjab provided the colonial state a further advantage, though it is one that does not emerge from the colonial record until some years after the policy was instituted. Correspondence from the early 1860s, in which district officials were asked to judge the merits of replacing Urdu with Punjabi, reveals that some viewed Urdu as the language of Punjab's native elites. The colonial state's policy across India had been to foster native elites as intermediaries with its subjects at large. In the Punjab, the state identified the region's indigenous rural elite—the "Punjab chiefs"—as bulwarks of its power.[84] In return for their support, the state buttressed the power of these elites through honorary titles and, more importantly, land grants. The state's language policy was part of this broader political equation. "If Punjabee is declared the Court language," wrote one official, "what is to become of the Chiefs who almost universally speak very fair Oordoo and the more educated classes who really cannot speak the veritable Punjabee?"[85] The interests of this native elite—the "chiefs" and "educated classes" in colonial parlance—surface repeatedly in considerations of language policy. For instance, in 1863 the commissioner of Rawalpindi Arthur Brandreth argued, "Nothing would be gained by substituting Punjabee for the Urdu. If this were done it would be a retrograde proceeding," particularly because "Urdu is the language of the educated classes."[86] Whether Urdu really was the language of Punjab's indigenous elite is an open question. Colonial linguistic data cited above suggest that is was not, as does an 1855 dispatch from the Court of Directors that stated, "Urdu [should] be made familiar, in the first instance, to the educated classes, and through them, as would certainly follow, to the entire body of the people, to the eventual supersession of inferior dialects."[87] Nonetheless, it appears that officials in the Punjab insisted that Urdu was the language of the elites, and that they saw promotion of the language as a way to protect elite interests, and thereby their own.

Thus a combination of factors explain the colonial state's decision to institute Urdu as the Punjab's official vernacular language. The most important are those related to consolidating colonial rule: using experienced administrative personnel, facilitating Punjab's integration into Company territories, and supporting native intermediaries. British fears of a Sikh resurgence and the conception of Punjabi as a Sikh language surely played their part as well. While this specific set of issues may have influenced the language policy established in the Punjab, the implications of the policy reached well beyond these original considerations.

COLONIAL EDUCATION

The vernacular language policy instituted in 1854 targeted two specific areas of government: judicial proceedings and revenue collection. Once the language policy had been established for these arenas, however, its impact was felt well beyond them. As the colonial government expanded, so did the impact of its language policy. Education was one critical site where this influence was felt. Scholarship on education in colonial India has invariably focused on the Anglicist-Orientalist controversy of the 1830s, which pitted the merits of European subjects of study against the subjects traditionally studied in Indian schools.[88] The Anglicists won that debate. Their victory was reflected in the nature of Indian higher education, which emphasized European subjects and was conducted in English. In the early 1850s, however, the Company decided to extend education to the masses. Colonial officials agreed that for primary education, English was best bypassed for vernacular languages. Which vernacular languages were adopted, and where, appears to have followed established policies about the vernacular language of provincial government.

The East India Company introduced education on a broad scale, on a trial basis, in the NWP in 1850. This scheme of vernacular education was considered successful, and in 1853 the government in Calcutta suggested that the scheme be extended to the Punjab. In response to Calcutta's overtures, Punjab's judicial commissioner Robert Montgomery proposed an education scheme for the province the following year in which he carefully assessed what the language of instruction should be. His minute bears quoting at length because it shows the impact of official language policy on the language chosen for education:

> The language used might be either Punjabee with Goormookhee character, or with the Persian character, or mixed Hindustanee with Punjabee phrases and idioms and written in the Persian or Hindee character; or pure Oordoo or Hindi. The Judicial Commissioner recommends the disuse both of the Punjabee language and of the Goormookhee character. Goormookhee though of sacred origin is rapidly falling into disnature. . . . The currency of Punjabee as a spoken language is also diminishing. It is degenerating into a mere provincial dialect. Hindustanee [Urdu when written in the Indo-Persian script] is the prescribed language of the courts and of the Public Department [and] it is becoming familiar to the Upper and Middle classes and the rural population understand it nearly as well as their brethren of Hindustan though neither perhaps will ever be proficients in this or any other polished language. There is no reason to perpetuate the Punjabee or even check its decondence [sic] at

the expense of the superior Hindustanee. . . . On the whole then the Judicial Commissioner would prefer to adopt the same language as in the N.W.P.'s [*sic*] namely
Oordoo and Hindi and there by to secure uniformity in addition to the advantage
which those languages passes [*sic*] over the less cultivated patois of the Punjab.[89]

On one hand, Montgomery's remarks point to a logic similar to that employed
in earlier considerations about the Punjab's administrative language: continuities
with the NWP and the failings of Punjabi as a language. On the other hand, his
comments reveal something new: Montgomery pointed to the adoption of Urdu
as the "prescribed language of courts and of the Public Department" as part of
his reasoning. With Urdu as the vernacular language of administration, it seemed
prudent to use Urdu in colonial schools.

Chief Commissioner John Lawrence seconded Montgomery's opinion. His sentiments reflected a desire to change indigenous practices in education, in which
children were instructed in "those languages which have been found most popular." Rather, he advocated that "in Government Schools. . . . The Persian Character,
and both the Persian and Oordoo Languages should be adopted . . . they are the
languages of our Courts [the uniform Urdu policy had not yet been instituted] and
of correspondence with the Native gentry. . . . The Punjabi is a barbarous dialect
which if let alone, will gradually disappear."[90] As it turned out, neither Montgomery's education proposal with its language recommendations nor Lawrence's opinion on the matter were implemented due to a parliamentary review of Company
policies. Although never adopted, the Punjab government's education proposals
of 1854 seem to have established that the language of administration—which by
the end of 1854 was Urdu alone—would be the language of government-sponsored
education in the province. When a system of mass education subsequently unfolded under the auspices of "Wood's Despatch," the language of education seemed
a foregone conclusion, not even meriting discussion.

In response to parliament's call for the Company to implement a more comprehensive education policy for India's masses, the Court of Directors sent a despatch to India outlining just such a policy. Commonly known as Wood's Despatch,
it called for a primary education system accessible to Indians of all classes, conducted in vernacular languages. In drawing the education system into broader
networks of colonial rule, the despatch stated: "We have always been most sensitive to the importance of the use of the languages which alone are understood by
the great mass of the population. These languages, and not English, have been put
by us in the place of Persian in the administration of justice, and in the intercourse
between the officers of Government and the people. It is indispensable, therefore,
that in any general system of education the study of them should be assiduously
attended to."[91] The Court of Directors also called for the creation of a separate gov-

ernment department for education. Under its guidelines, the Punjab Department of Public Instruction (DPI) was formally created on 1 January 1856 and an education system set in place.

Under the charge of William Arnold, Punjab's first deputy of public instruction (and brother of famous poet, critic, and educationist Matthew Arnold), a new program of native education was established in the Punjab, with Urdu as its principal medium. From humble beginnings, the education system slowly expanded. In 1860, for example, 33,368 pupils received daily instruction in vernacular schools.[92] As the lieutenant-governor pointed out to the Department of Public Instruction, this was a decidedly small number considering the province's population and the number of potential pupils, estimated at the time to be some 1.5 million.[93] But these numbers steadily increased. According to DPI reports, 84,160 students were enrolled in schools in 1874–75; 105,549 in 1878–79; and 132,993 in 1884–85.[94] The education system the DPI established was hierarchical, with village schools at its base. Then came *tahsili* schools (*tahsil* was a subdistrict, or a collection of villages), then *zillah* schools (which were to be situated at the headquarters of each district), and at the top of the scheme was a college in Lahore, Government College, established in 1864. While increasing enrollments suggest the success of this system, extremely low literacy rates in the Punjab throughout the late nineteenth century—by 1901 it was only 3.6 percent—indicate that the program fell far short of its aims.[95]

While the goal of this scheme was education for the "masses," the system after the 1860s focused on the upper levels of education, not the village schools. Not only did the latter receive little government attention, but the curriculum adopted in them did little to further their popularity. As Tim Allender suggests in his study of colonial education in the Punjab, by the late 1860s, "even the most optimistic British administrator . . . came to doubt the possibility of 'the masses' ever being drawn into government schools and their Western-based curriculums."[96] This was particularly ironic since Punjab's rural masses footed much of the bill for the education system through a one-percent agricultural cess. The system's main beneficiaries in the end appear to have been Punjab's burgeoning middle classes.

The Court of Directors had opted to limit English education in 1854 for fear of creating a class of individuals whose best hope of employment was to work for the state. Instituting Urdu as the language of education and administration had much the same effect, however. As the system of Urdu education became firmly rooted in the Punjab, the colonial state recruited employees from among the graduates. The limited numbers and comparatively well-to-do backgrounds of such individuals provides yet more evidence that education was not serving the "masses" in whose interest the system had been established. Indeed, an 1868 report on education highlights this fact: "[Village schools] teach the Urdu and the Hindi, and many cases the Persian. It is thus seen that the Government schools cannot as yet work among the real Mass of the people, but address themselves more generally to the wants of those who seek for service in the courts of law as *mukhtyars* [attorneys], *mahurirs* [clerks], and *amlas* [the head native officer of a judicial or revenue court]."[97]

That the benefits of the colonial state's education system accrued to a limited and privileged strata of society does not dilute its other significant effects. These were felt not only by those few who enjoyed access to education as students, but also by broader segments of Punjabi society through the manifold activities of the Department of Public Instruction. One of this department's ancillary activities was active patronage of Urdu literary production. Needing Urdu language books suitable for use in the classroom, the DPI set aside resources to produce this literature itself. It took its cue from the Education Committee, an all-India body that had charged provincial education departments with the task of creating a "vernacular literature" for use in schools.[98]

COLONIAL LITERARY PATRONAGE

The Punjab DPI promoted the production of vernacular materials that could be used as texts largely through its subsidiary department, the Government Book Depot. Scholars have documented the impact of government sponsorship on literary production in NWP and the Madras Presidency, but little attention thus far has been paid to the role of the colonial state as a sponsor and patron of Urdu literature in the Punjab.[99] Promotional devices for Urdu literature included such things as rewards for commendable works, the creation of textbook committees to oversee the production of Urdu school books, hiring translators, publishing and translating works suited for use in schools, and publishing and subscribing to Urdu newspapers of various descriptions.

The DPI's activities in 1870 provide a case in point. During this one year, the department undertook the following projects: it hired three translators and compilers (at Rs. 200, 75, and 50 per month) to produce works suited for educational purposes; it spent Rs. 20,820 on rewards and salaries to authors of Urdu books, Rs. 3,264 on subscriptions to vernacular papers and periodicals, and Rs. 5,237 on approved works in English and Urdu.[100] The DPI was not alone in these endeavors. The Punjab government directly assisted in the publication of works of general or special interest, and in some cases bore the entire cost of publication.[101]

The Government Book Depot was particularly important to the DPI's efforts to procure schoolbooks, and the two departments worked in tandem to produce necessary texts. In careful consultation with the DPI, the Book Depot engaged in the production of Urdu texts, the translation of books into Urdu, the purchase of books, and the supply of books to government institutions. Statistics from the report on public instruction for 1860–61 give some indication of the impact the Book Depot's activities had on Punjab's book market. That report states the Book

Depot bought 56,288 vernacular language books that year, of which 11,071 were printed at the government press. The remaining 45,217 were procured from private presses. At a time when the book trade was still in its relative infancy, the purchase of over 45,000 books likely made the Book Depot the biggest purchaser of books in the Punjab.

Precisely because the Punjab government became a patron of Urdu literary production, leading Urdu poets and writers of the day sought their fortunes in Lahore. The government's patronage drew men like Muhammad Husain Azad (b. 1830) and Altaf Husain Hali (b. 1837) in the late nineteenth century, two men whose power "over Urdu literature and criticism has been unequaled ever since."[102] Both men had been based in Delhi in 1857, and found life there untenable after the British crushed the rebellion and with it Delhi's Urdu literary culture. Azad's family had supported the rebels, and when the British retook the city his father was executed and he was exiled. For two years he wandered across India—to Lucknow, Madras, Bombay, and other places—and in 1861 ended up in Lahore, where he was able to obtain a low-level job in the postmaster general's office. For the next three years, Azad actively sought a job in the DPI. He had composed his first book, a textbook for girls, expressly for this purpose. Azad finally secured his desired job and in 1864 was appointed a clerk in the DPI. This became a stepping-stone for him, and he later took employment at Lahore's Oriental College. Hali, too, came to Lahore in 1870 looking for work and secured a job with the Punjab Government Book Depot.

As significant as those government jobs, however, was the attraction of an environment fostered by Lahore's colonial officials that nurtured Urdu literature. The Anjuman-i-Punjab, or Punjab Association, was significant in this regard. Dr. Leitner, a prominent scholar of Arabic, Persian, and Urdu who headed Lahore's Oriental College, started the organization in 1865 to promote Oriental learning and vernaculars. The Anjuman was something of a literary society, and among its many activities it sponsored *mushairas*, or poetry gatherings, for Urdu poets. One series of such *mushairas* in the 1870s provided the occasion for Azad to put forth a stunning critique of Urdu poetry, one that marked a radical break with a literary past and the embrace of a new, modern literary sensibility.[103] Azad's performance at this *mushaira* marks an important moment in the history of Urdu poetry. More significantly, such occurrences underscore the colonial state's efforts to foster Urdu literary production. Alongside providing jobs to Urdu litterateurs, sponsoring the production of a literature for use in schools, and awarding prizes for commendable works, the state also patronized Urdu through civil society institutions such as the Anjuman-i-Punjab. According to Pritchett, the Anjuman-i-Punjab "was actively supported by leading British officials, including the commissioner, the deputy commissioner, officers of the Department of Public Instruction, and even the lieutenant governor himself. . . . Most of its thirty-five original members were directly employed by the government."[104] It was the Anjuman-i-Punjab, and Dr. Leitner's patronage in particular, that encouraged Azad's career.

The promotion of Urdu by the Department of Public Instruction, the Government Book Depot, and other government departments and organizations such as the Anjuman-i-Punjab underscores the impact of official language policy in various arenas of Punjabi society. Once the colonial state established the vernacular language it would use in the Punjab, state institutions used their resources to promote it. The impact of this should not be underestimated, particularly regarding the colonial state's role as a purchaser of Urdu texts and newspapers. Others have noted that the state's purchasing power in the late nineteenth century was a key component in the success or failure of indigenous publishing ventures in other provinces. Ulrike Stark, for example, has examined the role of the NWP government in the fortunes of the Naval Kishore Press in Lucknow, by far the biggest publisher in north India in the late nineteenth century. In the late 1850s, the colonial state commissioned Naval Kishore to produce schoolbooks in Hindi, Urdu, and the classical languages, and, subsequently, became the primary purchaser of those works.[105] Although similarly detailed information is not available for late nineteenth-century Punjab, it is clear from records relating to the Government Book Depot that the Punjab government purchased thousands of Urdu texts per year throughout the late nineteenth century. It is reasonable to assume that the Punjab provincial government played the same critical role in the cultivation of Urdu literature and publishing as provincial governments in other parts of India played in fostering and influencing their designated vernacular literatures. Certainly, given the literary activity in Punjab's incipient public sphere, it seems the colonial state's influence loomed much larger in this regard than previously thought.

PUNJABI ON THE MARGINS

So in fact the colonial state did not "overlook" Punjabi when it established its vernacular language policy for the Punjab, nor was it ignorant of the linguistic practices of the region's inhabitants. Colonial knowledge produced both before and after the language policy was set clearly documented Punjabi as the primary spoken language in much of the province. By instituting Urdu as the official language of provincial administration, the policy's architects were clearly committed to changing indigenous practice. That the state was trying to effect such change in Indians is not surprising; it engaged in similar projects, on a greater and lesser scale, throughout the nineteenth century and into the twentieth century with varying degrees of success. What is compelling about colonial language policy in the Punjab is how it was successful in some arenas and left others largely untouched.

That success can be gauged by Urdu's dominance in the region's print culture. As noted earlier, Urdu dominated commercial newspaper publishing. This is particularly significant because of the key role of the press in constituting the public sphere, even in colonial contexts. Once Urdu was established as the language of government, it became logical to use it as the language of an incipient public sphere. Urdu also accounted for the largest share of book publishing in the region due to the state's patronage of Urdu texts and its purchase of thousands of books a year for use in schools. Yet, the colonial state's purchasing power alone does not explain Urdu's dominance; colonial language policy had a tangible impact on literary production as well. Genres previously composed in Persian were now composed in Urdu. If colonial language policy was meant to influence indigenous practices, then the adoption of Urdu for certain genres of literary production—notably history—is another signal of the policy's success. It even succeeded in marginalizing Punjabi, though perhaps more in colonial discourse than in the everyday experience of Punjab's inhabitants. But if one of the policy's intended effects was to see Punjabi (that "barbarous dialect," in John Lawrence's words) "gradually disappear," then it was largely unsuccessful.[106]

The language policy put in place by Punjab's colonial administrators accorded the Punjabi language no status. In an interesting twist, however, early colonial correspondence suggests that officials in Lahore and Calcutta did not share the same views on this matter.[107] The Governor-General's Office in Calcutta clearly considered Punjabi requisite to effective administration. In the early 1850s, just as the first language policy was being implemented by the Board of Control in Lahore, the Governor-General's Office asked the board to create a committee to test colonial administrators in Punjabi.[108] The board's response illuminates not only the difficulty it faced in fulfilling the governor-general's request, but reaffirms the personnel problems it would have faced (initially, at least) had it tried to implement Punjabi as the official vernacular of government. On behalf of the board, its secretary P. Melville responded to the Governor-General's Office: "I am directed to say that up to the present time there is no officer stationed at Lahore who has passed in Punjabee, but that there are two missionaries well acquainted with the language who are willing in the absence of qualified officers . . . to take part in examinations. . . . A committee consisting of one of the Missionaries referred to, two officers who have passed Interpreter's Examinations and are known to have a good colloquial knowledge of Punjabee . . . may be assembled to examine in Punjabee."[109] The two missionaries were the Reverends Newton and Forman of the American Presbyterian Mission. It was subsequently found that Forman was, in fact, "wholly unacquainted with the language [Punjabi]," and thus Newton was the only European in the province deemed capable of administering a written examination.[110] In response to this news, the Government of India urged the board to constitute whatever committee it could, since it was eager for examinations to be held on a regular basis. That way, it suggested, a cadre of government officers capable of participating in a Punjabi examination committee would be created. By commencing examinations as soon as possible, the governor-general felt confident that "there will soon be no difficulty in finding competent examiners."[111]

Given colonial conceptions of the Punjabi language, it is perhaps no surprise that the format the Governor-General's Office outlined for the exam privileged the Gurmukhi script and Sikh sacred literature. The competency exam it outlined had four parts: translation from Punjabi to English, translation from English to Punjabi, grammatical questions, and conversation. The textual translations prescribed for the exam included selections from the *janam-sakhis*, and the exam was to be administered only in the Gurmukhi script. Whether the board ever constituted the committee or administered exams is unclear, but what we know from the subsequent archival record—that officials constantly wrote of the imminent demise of Punjabi and how Urdu would supersede it—suggests the board did not implement the governor-general's recommendations.

Even if the board was not inclined to accord the Punjabi language official status or to train and test colonial officials in the language, administrators on the ground soon realized that they could not successfully administer justice, collect revenue, or carry on other government functions without recourse to Punjabi. If colonial officials were to communicate with the local population, then Punjabi was critical. Punjab's Police Department, for example, considered Punjabi *the* vernacular necessary for service,[112] and Punjabi proficiency was required of all police officers irrespective of the official language policy. The same was true of Punjab's Department of Public Instruction.[113] Although the DPI had designated Urdu the language of the government's mass education scheme in the province, it required its officers to be proficient in Punjabi so they could communicate and implement DPI goals at the local level.

Colonial language policy in the Punjab thus had two tiers, one official and the other unofficial: Urdu was the official provincial language, serving as the language of record in courts, local administration, and education; Punjabi was necessary to effectively communicate and implement government aims. It is clear that colonial personnel had to learn Punjabi if their jobs involved interacting with the populace. By the century's end, the need for Punjabi proficiency was institutionalized, and members of the Punjab civil service were tested for fluency in spoken Punjabi.[114] But official language policy was never changed to reflect this. Thus, although Punjabi was crucial to the practice of colonial administration, Urdu remained the province's only official vernacular language for the rest of the colonial period, and Punjabi would remain marginal to official discourse.

Colonial language policy that promoted Urdu thus had a decisive impact in the Punjab, on both its print public sphere and its patterns of literary production. But the one impact many colonial officials anticipated as a natural concomitant of their policy—the atrophying or death of Punjabi—did not occur. Punjabi remained the Punjab's principal colloquial language and the language of its literary culture, which thrived in the late nineteenth and early twentieth centuries. Given the nature and intent of colonial language policy in the Punjab, it is tempting to read Punjabi's survival as a form of resistance to colonial rule. This is not borne out by the evidence, however. Rather, Punjabi traditions are better understood through the rubric of resilience, an understanding that foregrounds how Punjabi helped constitute a broader vernacular culture that was relatively independent from, rather than overtly resistant to, colonial power.

2

Punjabi Print Culture

In May 1877, the Punjab University College Senate produced a document entitled "The Punjabi Language, a Memorandum." The memo was the report of a committee constituted to consider the following two questions: "What is Punjabi?" and "Is it a literary language?" These questions had been raised in the senate when a faction of senators called for Punjabi to be included as one of the languages in which students could be examined at the college.[1] The proposal alarmed another faction of senators, who argued that if Punjabi were admitted alongside the more established Urdu, Hindi, Persian, Arabic, and Sanskrit, then other vernaculars such as Pashto and Marathi would soon follow. None of the latter could claim to be literary languages, they asserted, because they were little more than dialects. Punjabi's proponents countered that since the original statutes of the college called for the development of vernacular literatures "where little or none existed," the absence of a recognized literature should not prevent the senate from including Punjabi in the curriculum. Those ranged against including Punjabi asserted that it was "a dialect of limited use in the Punjab" and was "without [a] written literary tradition."

An Indian member of the college senate, Sardar Attar Singh Bhadour, took particular umbrage at this remark and produced in response a list of 389 Punjabi books from his personal library, all written in the Gurmukhi script. That list was appended to the memo mentioned above, and seemed to settle the question: not only did Punjabi possess a written literary tradition, it possessed a body of literature. Beginning in late 1877, Punjabi became one of the languages in which students could be examined at Punjab University.

This debate and its resolution underscore the emphasis on writing as a technology and on books as material artifacts in colonial conceptions of language and language hierarchies. A language—as opposed to a dialect, patois, or pidgin, for example—presupposed a literature, and a literature was something preserved and disseminated through written texts. Some societies had oral literatures, colonialists conceded, but textual traditions (first manuscript, and then print) would replace these oral literatures in due course, as sure a sign as any of a society's progress. When Punjabi literary practices did not conform to this narrow model of progress, colonial officials almost seemed surprised. "Printed books [in Punjabi]," noted the *Lahore Gazetteer* for 1883–84, "have not yet shaken the hold of oral and chanted tradition and legend on the popular mind."[2] Perhaps this surprise was grounded in the fact that Punjabi texts were printed in the thousands in the late nineteenth century, even as colonial officials kept insisting that the language had no tradition of writing.

Bhadour's list proved, however, that there was a tradition of writing and textual production in Punjabi. This textual tradition encompassed both manuscripts, produced and circulated from at least the sixteenth century, and printed materials—periodicals and books—from the mid-nineteenth century. This chapter is focused on the latter, on Punjabi print culture, and will examine Punjabi newspaper and book publishing to understand why a market did not develop for the newspapers despite the attempts of many to establish a Punjabi-language press. This is in striking contrast to the vibrant market that developed in the late nineteenth and early twentieth centuries for Punjabi books in both the Gurmukhi and the Indo-Persian scripts.

Punjabi printed books were one aspect of a late nineteenth-century publishing industry that reflected the polyglot nature of literary and textual production in the province. Persian continued to be an important language of intellectual exchange and literature despite the official shift from Persian to Urdu. A small but substantial body of Arabic and Sanskrit books was also published in the Punjab each year, and the production of Hindi texts increased throughout the period. In all, presses in the region produced books in at least ten different languages. While a multiplicity of languages was a hallmark of Punjab's colonial print culture, it is also clear that some languages were favored in book publishing. Punjabi was among these, and the flourishing Punjabi book trade continued to gain momentum throughout the late nineteenth century.

The timing and momentum of Punjabi print culture mirrored broader trends in print production across India. In the late nineteenth century, presses proliferated and books were produced in ever greater numbers from year to year.[3] Much of this activity was sponsored by the colonial state, but a growing commercial market also played a part. The state vigorously monitored this expanding arena of intellectual and political exchange. In 1867 it passed Act 25, commonly known as the Press and Registration of Books Act. This required presses across British India to register every title they published with the government and required colonial officials in each province to collate information on press activity. Various reports resulted from the act, ranging from lists of every title registered in a province (with a synopsis of each) to statistics on the number of books published and the languages in which they were published. These reports portray Indian print culture through the colonial period. They are particularly instructive for colonial-era Punjabi literary production because they reveal that the colonial state's knowledge of and relationship to the Punjabi language created a space for the language and its literature to thrive largely independent of colonial intervention. Critically, the records from Act 25 document two distinct yet related phenomena that underscore this independence. First, they highlight the uncertainty of, and indeed sometimes the contradictions in, colonial conceptions of the Punjabi language. This is not in and of itself significant, because the same was true of other Indian vernaculars. What is significant, however, is that Punjabi as a linguistic category remained unstable throughout the late nineteenth century, unlike official Indian vernaculars, which reflected the colonial state's absence of will to codify or standardize the language. Even though Punjabi print production was surveyed by the state, Punjabi print (and literary production more generally) was not shaped by colonial interventions. Second, these records point to an astounding degree of continuity in Punjabi literary production, between precolonial literature and colonial-era print, despite the radical changes being wrought on Punjab society. This continuity, too, points to the relative independence of Punjabi literary culture and to the resilience of its practices.

INTERROGATING COLONIAL SOURCES

Act 25 compelled presses to provide the state with a copy of every book published, and officials in each province were required to collate information on press activity.[4] Quarterly reports produced in compliance with the act recorded a wealth of information about books, including title, language, author, subject, place of publication, publisher, date of publication, number of pages, size, edition, print run, type of print (typeset or lithographed), price, and a synopsis of the work. These reports were analyzed on an annual basis to compile aggregate information according to two criteria: language and subject. For the Punjab, this aggregate information was published in annual reports on the province's administration and annual volumes on publications issued and registered across India. The statistical information on publications by language and by subject was accompanied by mention of noteworthy publications in specific subject areas. Annual administration reports also furnished information about the number of presses operating in the region (and the proprietor of each), and the number of newspapers that had circulated.

Both the quarterly catalogs and the annual analyses are treasure troves of information that have served historians of colonial India well, particularly those who study colonial India's book culture.[5] In using this data to reconstruct print activity, however, historians have had to consider its particular limitations. In his essay on late nineteenth-century book production in India, Robert Darnton highlights some of the drawbacks of these colonial reports.[6] He points out that books were classified according to categories that made more sense to British civil servants than to the Indians who produced or read them, and that the catalogs were not necessarily wholly representative of print activity. Certainly, the fifteen categories designated for the organization of Indian book production—biography, drama, fiction, history, language, law, medicine, miscellaneous, poetry, politics, philosophy, religion, science (mathematical), science (natural), and travel—reflected not Indian but British literary understandings, predilections, and classificatory schema. The category "Travel," or "Voyages and Travels" as it appeared in some reports, exemplifies this. As the report on publications registered in the Punjab in 1892 makes clear, Indian authors—or at least Indian authors in the Punjab—had little interest in this genre. Ram Kishen, registrar of Punjab's Education Department and the report's compiler, noted: "*Voyages and Travels*—Of the two books received [of the 1,483 books registered that year] the following deserves mention as being the only instance approaching the requirements of this important but neglected department of literature."[7]

Even categories that were later added to the original fifteen hardly reflected indigenous literary categories, tastes, or publishing trends. "Arts" (often referred to as "arts and crafts") was one such category that failed to reflect indigenous literary or vocational practices. As the 1893 report points out: "ARTS. Books on arts are unknown in this country, as all handicrafts and industries are here learnt, almost exclusively, without any books, in shops and manufactories. In the few technical schools that exist, scholars receive instruction from books imported from foreign countries. The following [just two of the 1,452 books registered that year] are the only publications received, and even these cannot claim to touch the indigenous arts of the Province."[8]

As the colonial publication reports themselves underscore, categories such as arts and travel had little resonance for Punjab's litterateurs, irrespective of the language in which they composed. Instead, the categories that accounted for Punjabis' literary efforts were "religion," "poetry," and "miscellaneous," and the distinctions between these depended on the whims of the official producing the report. Together, these three categories accounted for most of the publications produced in the Punjab throughout the late nineteenth century and into the twentieth.

If the categories used for documenting Indian print production were flawed, so too were the data on the number of books India's presses produced each year. The colonial record itself suggests that the reports generated under Act 25 were hardly comprehensive. A government memorandum from 1868, for example, indicates that one year after the act's inception returns on books were only partial. It noted that the Government of India had received catalogs of books for Bengal, the Northwest Provinces, and the Central Provinces, but that for Bengal they included neither the publications of government presses nor adequate returns for the commercial popular press: "At *Burtollah,* the Grub Street of Calcutta . . . innumerable books, &c., of various sorts are printed every month. In the catalogues, however, submitted . . . a very few books, only, say, five or six, issued from some one or two of the Burtollah Presses have been shown."[9] One reason the returns were partial was that officials relied on presses to voluntarily submit relevant information. Although unregistered publications were deemed illegal, and their publishers were subject to prosecution, many presses nevertheless chose not to report their publishing activity or did so inaccurately. One reason that Indian presses failed to comply fully with Act 25 may have been that they often received no payment for books they deposited with the state.

Act 25 called for publishers to supply three copies of each book they produced, to be paid for at market price.[10] But in practice (and, as the quotation below points out, in some cases with the sanction of the law), publishers often went unpaid. In the 1894 report on publications registered in the Punjab, Ram Kishen (the compiler) noted a rather substantial decline in the publications registered that year (967) compared with the previous year (1,452). He attributed this to a change in the registration rules under the revised act of 1890, and to pecuniary concerns. Kishen wrote that the decrease of about 33 percent was "attributable, to a great extent, to the fact that the Presses in the Province have now come to know that only the first editions have to be delivered for registration. . . . It would seem also that since the law requires the submission of books free of cost, a number of publications are not delivered at all by the Presses."[11] His comments highlight a major obstacle to accurate returns: in an industry where most books sold for annas (one-sixteenth of a rupee) rather than rupees, profit margins were tight. The rule that books must be supplied to the government for free would obviously discourage publishers' willing cooperation with the state.

The deficiencies Darnton highlights, especially the reports' categorizations and accuracy, are common to the data of every region—the questionable comprehensiveness of returns was as true for Bengal and the Northwest Provinces as for Punjab and Madras. Other limitations of the colonial record are specific to the Punjab, where colonial officials' lack of linguistic competency in Punjabi presents a special problem. This limitation was particularly acute in the early decades of colonial rule in the province, and perhaps longer, since it is unclear how many colonial officials ever attained proficiency, and this calls into question the accuracy of reports that organize books by language. When analyzing the Punjab returns we must also consider colonial officials' conflation of the Gurmukhi script and the Punjabi language.

The returns for 1869–70 provide one example of the difficulties encountered in analyzing these colonial records for information on Punjabi language texts. That year, 425 books were registered with the Punjab government; as the act required, this aggregate number was broken down by language.[12] The return divided the books into eleven (apparently linguistic) categories, one of which was Punjabi (with only one book) and another Gurmukhi (with twenty-two). In this case, one could infer that "Gurmukhi" referred to Punjabi language books in the Gurmukhi script. But given the paucity of colonial officials' skills in Punjabi, and the single Punjabi publication (presumably not in the Gurmukhi script, given the existence of that category), one might also presume that some of the books recorded as Urdu (202, which were almost surely in the Indo-Persian script) were actually Punjabi. The 1874–75 returns present a similar conundrum.[13] They record a total of 911 titles, of which only nine are given as "Gurmukhi." Again, one might infer that these books were in the Punjabi language. But what is one to make of the fact that there is no entry for "Punjabi" but that an entry for "Hindi and Punjabi" accounts for 174 books?

In chapter 1, I argued that colonial officials developed a strong, almost absolute association between the Gurmukhi script and the Punjabi language. The Indo-Persian script (sometimes referred to as Persian or Arabic script) was associated principally with Urdu, Persian, and Arabic, despite being commonly used for Punjabi, and the Devnagari script was connected to Hindi and Sanskrit. The returns for the first quarter of 1868 show how such assumptions about language-script relationships were inscribed in the colonial record.[14] The returns included books published in the following languages: Urdu, English, Persian, Arabic, Sanskrit, and Gurmukhi. The text contains no comment on the incongruity between these terms, Gurmukhi being a script and all the others languages. In this context, Gurmukhi was almost certainly a reference to Punjabi language texts. This inference is reinforced by a single entry in the returns for "Panjabi in Persian character."

While colonial officials may have used Gurmukhi and Punjabi interchangeably, and associated particular languages with particular scripts more generally, print production in the Punjab did not follow suit. This is evident from the 1882 report on books registered in the Punjab. In addition to the usual tables organizing book production by subject and language, it contained a table enumerating the various scripts of publication (table 2). This 1882 tabulation is the only such account found in reports issued between 1867 and 1900. Although similar information on script

TABLE 2 The various scripts of publications in Punjab, 1882

Language	In character type	Occurrence
Urdu	Gurmukhi	2
	Nagri	10
	Roman	5
	Persian	466
	Total	483
Punjabi	Gurmukhi	81
	Persian or Arabic	108
	Nagri	1
	Total	190
Hindi	Gurmukhi	38
	Persian	22
	Nagri	93
	Total	153

SOURCE: *Report on Publications Issued and Registered in the Several Provinces of British India.* Calcutta: Office of the Superintendent of Government Printing, 1883, 193.

and language had been recorded in earlier quarterly returns, such data was partial and uneven—some reports referred to publications' scripts, others did not. It alerts us to the fact that while specific scripts may have dominated the writing of particular languages (i.e., Gurmukhi: Punjabi; Indo-Persian: Urdu; [Dev]Nag[a]ri: Hindi), this was not absolute, and each script was used for multiple languages. Thus, while texts identified in colonial records as Gurmukhi were likely in the Punjabi language, this was not necessarily the case. As this table containing data from 1882 suggests, Gurmukhi was used for a number of Indian languages (the *Adi Granth* is a good example), and Punjabi texts were printed in not only the Gurmukhi and Indo-Persian scripts, but in some cases even in Devnagari.

The uncertainties of linguistic classification have two implications. First, they mean that these reports must be used with extreme circumspection, since they more accurately record colonial classification, codification, and epistemology than they do Punjabi print activity. More importantly, they expose ambiguities in colonial understandings of the Punjabi language and its literary practices. The kinds of instabilities, uncertainties, and contradictions found in the examples above were slowly eradicated in the "official" vernaculars. While similar problems crop up with regard to early records of publication in Urdu and Hindi, as vernacular languages used by the state were standardized, so were the scripts in which they were written and published. For example, a quarterly return for books in 1877 included in its "language of publication" column entries such as "Hindi, in Gurmukhi character" and "Urdu, in Nagri character," but by century's end both languages had been codified and standardized, by both Indian activists and the colonial state, making redundant these pairings of language and script.[15] By this time, Hindi was by definition written in Devnagari and Urdu in Indo-Persian script. Indians were at the forefront of producing this distinction and the resulting clearer classification. But they did so because both languages were adopted as official vernaculars—first Urdu, and then, through the agitation of its partisans, Hindi. The solidifying of language and script was one outcome of their adoption as official languages; another was that Urdu and Hindi—like other "official" vernaculars—became standardized and modernized.[16] By contrast, the record of books published in the Punjab, with its shifting conceptions of what constituted Punjabi texts, underscores the absence of concerted colonial interventions in the Punjabi textual-literary tradition, intervention which elsewhere produced standardized, "modern" languages the state could use in its bureaucracy, courts, and schools. In other words, the data generated by Act 25 documents, albeit obliquely, the relative independence of Punjabi literary practices in the late nineteenth century.

This data also suggests another conclusion: namely, that the effects often assumed to emerge from print cultures are rooted in something other than print itself. Print may not be the harbinger of intellectual and political change that scholarship on print culture and nationalism often presume it to be. Studies ranging from the rise of European print cultures to work on nineteenth-century India argue that print produces standardized, and in most cases dominant, forms of languages, in terms of both orthography and dialect.[17] This was not the case with Punjabi, despite its vibrant print culture, as we will see below. The history of Punjabi book publishing thus suggests that print, by itself, cannot exact these changes. The Punjabi case indicates the critical role states can play in the standardization and "modernization" of languages. Similarly, print culture alone does not lay the foundation for nationalism. The colonial period in India did not bring about an ethnolinguistic nationalism based on Punjabi in the way vernacularization processes in Europe did.[18] Nor did it operate in the ways that Benedict Anderson suggested in *Imagined Communities,* where he describes how print cultures in vernacular languages produce nationalist sentiment.

If the relation of script to language was one instance of slippage in the returns produced in the Punjab, then another was the instability of Punjabi as a linguistic category in the early years of colonial rule. Although some late nineteenth-century studies of Indian philology included the Punjab and Punjabi,[19] the most comprehensive linguistic study of the region was George Grierson's *Linguistic Survey of India,* which did not include the Punjab until 1909. Prior to this, what precisely constituted the Punjabi language was clearly in flux. Colonial records on book production reflect its unsettled linguistic classification (and that of related dialects and languages) throughout the late nineteenth century. The inclusion of "Multani" as a category alongside "Punjabi" in some returns but not in others, for example, suggests not only Punjabi's instability as a linguistic category, but also that its definition was subjective, contingent on the perceptions of officials compiling the reports.[20]

Using the reports produced under Act 25 to gauge Punjabi-language print culture poses one other predicament: the boundaries of colonial provinces reflected administrative imperatives, not linguistic communities. In Punjab, like every other province, inhabitants belonged to various linguistic communities, a fact that is reflected in any province-wide assessment of publishing. Punjab's annexation to the East India Company created an administrative unit that included, moving from west to east: Peshawar, the trans-Indus territories (Dera Ghazi Khan and Dera Ismail Khan); the trans-Sutlej territories (central Punjab); Multan (southern Punjab); the cis-Sutlej states (eastern Punjab); and, from 1858, Delhi and its environs (Delhi, Gurgaon, Hissar). The Punjab returns on presses and publishing included all of these areas. The language primarily spoken in Peshawar was Pashto and in Delhi, Urdu, while Punjabi was the spoken language in the trans-Indus territories of Dera Ghazi Khan and Dera Ismail Khan, central Punjab, Multan,[21] and eastern Punjab. The inclusion of returns from Delhi and Peshawar thus skew returns for the Punjabi-speaking areas of the province.

The inclusion of Delhi in the Punjab in 1858 has a critical bearing on how one interprets data about Urdu publishing in the region. The preponderance of Urdu books and newspapers in the province in the late nineteenth century in part reflects that incorporation. If the returns are isolated to literary production in areas where Punjabi was the principal spoken language, Urdu would still account for the majority of books published, but Punjabi books would account for a greater percentage of all books printed. Similarly, the consistent returns for Pashto books in the Punjab reports reflect the print culture of Peshawar more than that of the province's Punjabi-speaking areas. In forming an accurate picture of Punjabi-language publishing in the late nineteenth century it is critical to extrapolate, as far as possible, from the returns for the Punjabi-speaking areas of British Punjab.

THE MATERIALITY OF PRINTED TEXTS

The difficulties posed by the colonial record are mitigated somewhat when we examine late nineteenth-century printed texts themselves. Much of the literature produced for the print market during that period, in Punjabi as in other Indian languages, was ephemeral—largely pamphlets and chapbooks. Nevertheless, copies of many of these books survive in libraries and archives in India, Pakistan, and Britain.[22] Access to them is critical for gaining a more nuanced understanding of Punjabi print culture than colonial reports alone provide. For one thing, they allow one to corroborate information on print runs, prices, and so forth for those works registered with the colonial state. Since some of the surviving books were never registered, they point to the limits of colonial surveillance of Indian print culture. Through reference to and analysis of Punjabi printed books, one can also move beyond colonial judgments on the merits and (far more often) failings of Punjabi literature, of which the 1881 report offers an example: "*Poetry*—Under this head are comprised a large number of publications, amounting to 265 against 232 in the previous year. . . . Though the number of [Punjabi] publications under this head is large and the writing of poetry is very generally cultivated, yet there are few works of real merit."[23]

The materiality of surviving books provides clues about print culture impossible to discern from colonial reports. Late nineteenth-century Punjabi printed books were invariably lithographed, whether in the Indo-Persian or Gurmukhi scripts. While this information is recorded in the quarterly book reports, those reports do not relate the extent to which Punjabi books represent a continuity with an earlier scribal and manuscript tradition. The format of many books mimics that of manuscripts, with geometric or floral designs as borders on their title pages (figures 2 and 5). In others, the scribe is noted on the title page or at the end of the text, suggesting that calligraphy, too, was an important aspect of book production (figure 3). Like manuscripts, these printed texts contain variations in calligraphic style and orthography. One example is Jog Singh's *Hir-Ranjha*, composed in 1825 and published in at least seven editions.[24] If we examine four editions (1877, 1880, 1882, 1887) we find the narrative content is the same, and all show stylistic similarities. Yet each was prepared by a different scribe and contain differences in orthographic systems.

Many late nineteenth-century Punjabi printed texts contain images, most of them on title pages, but some books also include illustrations in the text. These are often rudimentary but are nonetheless significant to understanding Punjabi books. Again, Jog Singh's *Hir-Ranjha* provides a compelling example of this phenomenon, with an illustration that appears in slightly modified form in numerous 1870s and 1880s print editions of the romance (figures 4 and 5). It depicts the lovers Hir and Ranjha seated in the shade of a tree before five holy men. A buffalo or cow alludes to both the story's rural setting and Ranjha's vocation as a cowherd. The inclusion of a cow is perhaps not enough, by itself, to allude to the Hindu deity Krishna, but in some images Ranjha carries a flute, underscoring his connection with the flute-playing cowherd God. The five holy men, known as the *panj pir,* are associated with Sufi Islam. The imagery of the tree, which acts as a *chhatri* (literally umbrella, but in this context better translated as "shade"), engages Sikh iconography in which the religion's founder, Guru Nanak, is portrayed sitting beneath a *chhatri* (figure 6). While the *chhatri* imagery is borrowed from Hindu iconography for royalty, in the Sikh context it serves as a visual reference to Guru Nanak's exalted status, both religious and temporal. What these illustrations point to, then, is the multiplicity of religious motifs engaged by this Punjabi text.

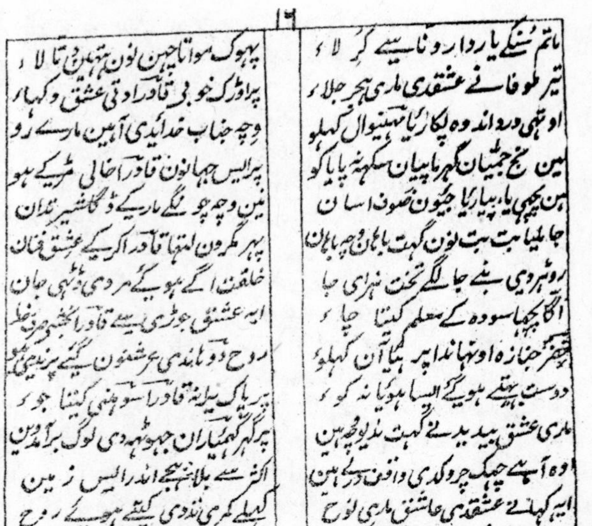

FIGURE 3. Excerpt from Qadir Yar, *Qissa Sohni Mahival M'a Tasvir* (The Qissa Sohni-Mahival with Illustrations) (Lahore: Chiragh al-Din Tajar Kutab, 1877), 16. In the bottom left corner of the final page of this text is reference to the scribe: "From the pen of Qadir Baksh."

FIGURE 4. Title page of *Hir Jog Singh* (Lahore: Mian
Chiragh al-Din Siraj al-Din Tajran Kutab, n.d.). Text (from
top): "Hir Jog Singh | At the request of Mian Chiragh al-Din
Siraj al-Din, booksellers, Kashmiri Bazaar, Lahore | Print
run 750, by Maulvi Karim Baksh | Printed at the Victoria
Press, Lahore."

FIGURE 5. Title page of *Qissa Hir Jog Singh* (Lahore: Malik
Hira Tajar Kutab, 1882). Text (from top): "Qissa Hir Jog
Singh | At the request of Malik Hira Bookseller, Kashmiri
Bazaar, Lahore | Print run 700, 1882 [C.E.] by Haji Karim
Baksh printer | Printed at the Mustafai Press, Lahore."

Although neither the colonial archive nor contemporary collections of late
nineteenth-century Punjabi books and newspapers are comprehensive, together
they give a representative view of print production. At minimum, these sources
allow us to track general trends such as the advance of print as a technology in
the province. Tracing the annual administration reports on presses, we find that

FIGURE 6. Guru Nanak under a *chhatri*, c. 1828–30. © The British Library Board (D.4.f.2).

print technology became relatively widespread after 1850, most of it apparently concentrated in Punjab's major cities. The reports, together with surviving texts, also allow us to gauge the subjects of books published and their print runs.

The methodological problems of colonial records and the limits of existing collections notwithstanding, it is possible to reconstruct broad trends in colonial-era Punjabi print production. These sources together reveal that Punjabi print had a somewhat tentative beginning at midcentury but that by the 1870s a vibrant market for Punjabi books had clearly developed. Punjabi newspapers fared less well—though many were started and supported by interested organizations, they never developed a viable market. A closer examination of the mechanics of newspaper publishing in colonial Punjab will help us understand why.

PUNJABI NEWSPAPER PUBLISHING

As discussed in the last chapter, Christian missionaries brought the printing press to the Punjab in the 1830s. In the late 1840s, the nascent colonial state saw in the press an important tool for promoting its interests, and established its own presses and encouraged vernacular ones. With the state's support, the province's first vernacular newspaper, the Urdu-language *Kohinoor,* was established in 1850. Colonial backing did not extend to Punjabi-language publications, however, and this may be one reason why it was seventeen years before the first Punjabi newspaper, *Akhbar Shri Darbar Sahib,* was launched.

Akhbar Shri Darbar Sahib, established in 1867 in Amritsar, espoused Sikh religious concerns and sought to win British good will. The paper never became very popular in Amritsar or beyond and so was short-lived.[25] The next Punjabi periodical of note, *Gurmukhi Akhbar,* was launched in Lahore in 1880. This weekly aired the concerns of the Lahore branch of the Sikh socioreligious reform organization, the Singh Sabha, and its editor was Bhai Gurmukh Singh, a leading member of the organization and a Punjabi teacher at Punjab University. Historian N. G. Barrier describes the paper's scope as parochial: "The *Gurmukhi Akhbar* . . . reviewed Singh Sabha activities and provided space for dialogues on history, scripture, and the personal views of its subscribers."[26] Its circulation never topped 325 (compared to the Urdu *Paisa Akhbar'*s high of 13,500), and it is clear that, like *Akhbar Shri Darbar Sahib,* it never achieved widespread popularity. Still, the *Gurmukhi Akhbar* was among the longest-running Punjabi periodicals of the late nineteenth century, consistently published from 1880 to 1887 and briefly resuscitated in the 1890s. This longevity reflected the paper's role as the organ for the Lahore Singh Sabha, which was particularly active in the century's last decades.[27]

Only two other Punjabi papers had similar runs during this period: the *Khalsa Akhbar* and the *Khalsa Parkash.*[28] The former was established in 1889 in Lahore and soon failed, but it was resuscitated from 1893 to 1905 and achieved some success as a weekly, with circulation peaking at 1,172 copies.[29] The paper was initially an organ of the Singh Sabha, but from 1893 it represented the interests of the Lahore Khalsa Diwan, a related but distinct Sikh organization. The *Khalsa Parkash* also enjoyed a long print run (1891–99), but had a much smaller distribution. The paper's maximum circulation was three hundred, and even that was only sustained for a year. The *Khalsa Parkash* contained "general and political news," though from its name it is evident that it was geared to the Sikh community (*Khalsa* refers to baptized Sikhs).[30]

As these examples suggest, Punjabi newspapers served the Sikh community rather than Punjabi speakers generally. An analysis of Punjabi newspapers published between 1880 and 1905 reveals that most were oriented toward Sikhs, and the few that were not had a similarly sectarian base. As appendix B shows, ten of the nineteen newspapers published in the Punjabi language (wholly or in part) were directly associated with a Sikh organization or institution.[31] Others represented Sikh opinion, though they were unaffiliated with any particular Sikh organization, while a few represented caste-based interest groups. The point to note is that Punjabi newspapers during this period served sectarian readerships, sometimes defined by religion (Sikh) and sometimes by caste (e.g., Arora). Only the *Panjab Darpan* sought a broader audience, and it closed within a year "because it did not pay."[32]

The data on Punjabi newspapers from 1880 to 1905 suggest that, like Punjabi-language periodicals from earlier periods, they served a different function than did Urdu papers. Undoubtedly, some Urdu periodicals, too, had sectarian Muslim interests,[33] but Urdu was also the language of a nonsectarian press. Examples are papers such as the *Kohinoor* and the *Akhbar-i Am,* which were directed at a broader reading public (though by no means ever truly broad, given literacy rates in the low single digits). If such newspapers were "secular" ventures, unaffiliated with any religious community or caste, then similar ventures were not taken up by Punjabi journalism, which was largely a Sikh affair. But why was there no market for Punjabi newspapers that spoke to a broader, multireligious readership? Why did the *Panjab Darpan* fail? There are at least three answers.

First, newspapers in this period relied heavily on the state's patronage. Readerships were neither large nor wealthy enough to sustain the circulations needed to turn a profit. The state thus played a key role in their success and failure through its subscriptions. In 1870, for example, the Education Department spent Rs. 3,264 on subscriptions to vernacular (Urdu) papers and periodicals "of different descriptions."[34] No such patronage was extended to Punjabi papers.

Second, Punjabi had not traditionally been the language of this sort of text and the type of information it carried. If we consider newspapers as largely for the dissemination of information, then this tradition in the Punjab had been a Persian one. For example, we know from Bayly's *Empire and Information* that within ten years of Ranjit Singh's conquest of Lahore in 1799, he "put in place an excellent system of newswriters" as part of a sophisticated "information system."[35] Given that Persian was the Sikh state's official language, its newsletters (*akhbarat*) were in Persian. It appears that, like other genres of precolonial textual production where Persian had been the principal language, newspapers shifted from Persian to Urdu in the late nineteenth century. In the absence of a tradition of circulating news and information through Punjabi language documents, it is no surprise that such a tradition did not develop in this period, particularly given the state's lack of patronage.

But we must still account for why the Punjabi publishing that did take place under Sikh patronage failed. For this we must consider a third factor: the agenda of Sikh socioreligious reform. The period of active Sikh publishing began in the

1880s, as the Singh Sabha—perhaps taking a cue from missionaries and officials who saw Punjabi texts in the Gurmukhi script as particularly Sikh—through the 1880s and 1890s actively disseminated the idea that Punjabi was "the distinctive vehicle for the expression of a revitalised Sikhism."[36] One way in which Singh Sabha activists supported this claim, and the assertion that Punjabi should therefore have some official capacity, was to sponsor publications in the language. Newspaper publishing was one aspect of an initiative that included the creation of the Khalsa Tract Society in 1894 and the publication of Punjabi tracts. The sectarian impulse that promoted Punjabi newspapers and periodicals marks a critical distinction between Punjabi newspaper and book publishing: unlike newspapers, books were neither directed at nor sustained by a single religious or caste community.

PUNJABI BOOK PUBLISHING

Punjabi was a marginal language in the world of late nineteenth-century newspaper publishing, but this was hardly the case with commercial book publishing. More books may have been published in Urdu than in any other language in the Punjab, but Punjabi titles were close behind. While there may have been the odd lithographed Punjabi text prior to 1850, the production of commercial Punjabi books began in earnest at midcentury.[37] Publication of Punjabi books started slowly, but by the 1870s and 1880s thousands were flowing into the market annually, in both Gurmukhi and Indo-Persian scripts.

Charting the rise of the Punjabi book trade is complicated by a paucity of information from before 1867, when the state started to issue its reports on vernacular publishing. Anecdotal evidence suggests that production of books began when commercial presses were started in midcentury. Literary critic Muhammad Sharif Sabir, for example, writes of an 1851 edition of Waris Shah's *Hir-Ranjha* produced by the Chashm-i Nur Press in Amritsar.[38] Library holdings also point to the production of Punjabi printed texts in these early years. Unfortunately, only a few dozen of these texts still exist. Despite their small number, these texts suggest that a diversity of material was published from the inception of print in the province. Appendix C shows something of their range, including religious texts (the Quran and the *Adi Granth*), explicitly religious poetry (Sunni, Shi'a, and Sufi), secular poetry (*qissa, si harfi,* and *jangnama*), and geographical works. A variety of genres are represented by authors with diverse religious affiliations. Publishing sites included Amritsar, Lahore, and Delhi, which should not be surprising given these cities' political and commercial importance. But Punjabi books were also published in smaller provincial hamlets such as Bhera, a historic town near Sargodha in northwest Punjab.

A bit more information on Punjabi publishing begins to come to light with the production of government returns. Although those for the late 1860s are clearly preliminary and thin, they provide interesting insights into the fledgling industry. A memorandum inserted into the "Annual Return of Presses Worked and Newspapers or Periodical Works Published in the Punjab for the Year 1866–67" recorded all the books published or printed by the Mercer Press in Amritsar during that year.[39] The list was decidedly small and eclectic (see table 3). The list contains two kinds of publications: government publications (or those solicited by the government), for which there are nine entries, and commercial work, of which there is one. This disparity suggests that what is known about presses in other parts of India at this time, such as those in the NWP, was true of the Punjab as well: the colonial state accounted for most of presses' business and government "job work" was their mainstay through at least the 1850s and 1860s. Indeed, the "remarks" column of the earliest returns in the Punjab has numerous entries that suggest this: "the work executed consists wholly of Printed notices";[40] "no newspaper or periodical[,] only job work for Government";[41] "none but job works, &c.";[42] and "this Press only works for the Settlement."[43] The single work of fiction listed in the memorandum deserves comment. Unlike the other entries, this text (*Sussipoonnoo-ki-kissa*, a tale) does not appear to have been solicited by the government. It provides early evidence of a commercial market for Punjabi literature, particularly given its print run of 625. An examination of Punjabi publishing trends from the 1870s confirms that there was such a market for Punjabi fiction, and *qisse* in particular. The c. 1866–67 *Sussipoonoo-ki-kissa* and the 1851 Chashm-i Nur edition of *Hir-Ranjha* are early manifestations of this market.

Despite the examples of these pre-1867 Punjabi printed texts, the Punjabi book trade during the 1850s and 1860s was apparently limited. While books were published as early as 1851, by the latter half of 1867 only twelve titles had been registered in Lahore, an important center of publishing.[44] By the 1870s, however, the trade in Punjabi books appears to have burgeoned. In 1876, for example, the number of registered titles had increased almost ten-fold from a decade earlier.[45] By 1887, there was nearly a forty-fold increase to 473 titles.[46] What these statistics mask, however, is the actual number of Punjabi books circulating in the province, since each of these titles had a publication run from one hundred to twenty-four hundred copies, and sometimes more. With no exact record, we can only hypothesize numbers, but the print runs do suggest that a sizable number of books were produced from the 1870s through the early decades of the twentieth century. Books ranged in price from two paisas (one-quarter of an anna; one-sixty-fourth of a rupee) for short, eight-page texts to eight annas for significantly longer ones. These figures are based on the prices printed on the texts, a practice that became much more common from the 1890s on. Based on the available data, one can assume that prices were the same or perhaps even less in the 1870s and 1880s when the Punjabi book trade was becoming established. Contemporary wage data helps contextualize these prices. In 1875, for example, the average monthly wage of an

TABLE 3 Books published by Mercer Press in Amritsar, 1866–67

Title	Copies issued
Indent for supplies for Maharaja of Jummoo and camp to Hardwar in English and vernacular	50
Roobakaries [pamphlets] regarding smallpox, its prevention by vaccination / vernacular	200
Synopsis of Act X of 1862 / Stamp Act, vernacular	1,000
Price current / vernacular	80
Statement of Jumabandee [revenue assessment] / statement / vernacular	2,792
Questions on examination papers for examining Putwarees [Keeper of Village Records] / vernacular	350
Warrant, summons, etc. / vernacular	2,500
Geography	700
Sussipoonoo-ki-kissa (a tale)	625
Judicial circular reprinted (from 1849 to 1865, classed according to subjects)	700

SOURCE: "Annual Return of Presses Worked and Newspapers of Periodical Works Published in the Punjab for the Year 1866–67," in National Archives of India, Home Department, Public Proceedings, December 1867, 144–45B.

unskilled or agricultural laborer in Amritsar was six rupees, while that of a skilled laborer, a mason, carpenter, or blacksmith, for example, was thirteen rupees. At the turn of the century (1899), these figures had jumped to eight and fifteen rupees, respectively.[47] With books priced in annas and cheaper ones in paisas, it is evident that even those of humble means could purchase them.

While some books were commissioned and sponsored by Christian missionaries, most were produced at presses without obvious sources of patronage or subsidy, which suggests that they were produced in response to market demand. A system of production and distribution obviously sustained this commercial Punjabi book industry. Production was centered in Amritsar and Lahore, in what were the book districts of these cities. In Lahore, Kashmiri Bazaar was (and still is) the principal site of the book trade, and in Amritsar, the Mai Sevan Bazaar. Although there is only limited information about the specifics of this trade in colonial sources, printed texts alert us to the involvement of at least three distinct entities in publishing: a bookseller or publisher, a printer, and a printing press. Thus, for example, *Qissa Hir Jog Singh* (figure 5), an 1882 text that was typical of the period in design, length, and content, lists Malik Hira Bookseller of Kashmiri Bazaar, Lahore, as the publisher, Haji Karim Baksh as the printer, and the Mustafai Press as the institutional site of its production. Publishers were invariably booksellers, merging the function of the former with that of the latter. We can assume that as in other contemporary vernacular print cultures, publishers had distribution networks that gave them reach beyond their bookshops. Anindita Ghosh's description of book distribution in mid- and late nineteenth-century Bengal lays out the contours of this system:

> Bookshops were still rare and had only begun to be opened in the mid-1850s. But the market networked effectively with its consumers through more traditional means. This was made possible by the operation of peddlers or "hawkers," more than two hundred of whom worked for the Calcutta presses in 1857–58. These crucial messengers of the printed word carried their wares into the rural interior, selling books at fairs, festivals, and even roadside bazaars. Many of them sold books seasonally, for eight months only, and devoted the rainy season to the cultivation of their fields. They bought the books wholesale and sold them in distant towns and villages, often at double the usual price. James Long [a colonial official] estimated their monthly income at about six to eight rupees. It was apparently a common sight to see these men going through the "native" parts of Calcutta and the adjacent towns with a pyramid of books on their heads.[48]

The patterns Ghosh identifies were surely typical of much of north India. Ulrike Stark suggests as much in her study of the Naval Kishore Press, the largest press in north India at the time. "No doubt," Stark writes, "north Indian publishers and booksellers followed their Bengali confreres in resorting to the agency of hawkers for disseminating printed matter in the small town and rural market. Local fairs assumed prime importance in this context." Even for a large-scale commercial publisher such as Naval Kishore, Stark argues, colportage remained the most effective means of reaching a market beyond urban centers.[49] Both Stark and Ghosh rely on colonial sources for their reconstructions of the distribution networks of the Hindi-Urdu and Bengali print industries in late nineteenth-century north India. Although colonial reports on book production in Punjab do not provide similar accounts, there is little reason to conclude that the process of book distribution there—of popular literature, at minimum—was different from that in other parts of north India. Certainly, a 1908 photograph titled *A Bookseller at Amritsar* (figure 7), showing an itinerant bookseller with bundles of books and popular images for sale suggests that colportage was indeed an aspect of Punjab's book culture.

Late nineteenth-century Punjabi books varied in content.[50] Some were translations from other languages. These included translations from Persian literature, including such popular works as Amir Khusraw's *Bagh o Bahar* and Hafiz's *Divan*. Most translations, however, were biblical literature and were published by the American Presbyterian Mission. The mission's translations of Christian literature account for a significant percentage of late nineteenth-century Punjabi publishing overall. Recall that as early as 1838 this mission at Ludhiana published seventy thousand volumes totaling over a million pages.[51] Despite this immense production, the mission published only a limited number of titles; the seventy thousand

FIGURE 7. "A Bookseller at Amritsar," 1908. From the holdings of the Ames Library of South Asia, University of Minnesota Libraries, Minneapolis.

volumes of 1838 represented only twenty-four different works. If gauged in terms of titles rather than print runs, then translations account for a small percentage of Punjabi publishing of the period, and the majority of books were original Punjabi compositions. These represented a variety of genres, and covered topics ranging from grammar to philology, religion, geography, medicine, and romance.

A number of published books served as liturgical texts or were self-consciously (even polemically) religious, such as *Sri Guru Granth Sahib Ji* (or the *Adi Granth*; Lahore, 1864); *Pothi Japji* (a prayer from the *Adi Granth*; Lahore, 1865); *Quran Sharif* (The Quran; Lahore, 1873); *Dharm Pustak Vichun Aad Pothi* (The Book of Genesis; Ludhiana, 1862); *Ramayana Tarjama Munshi Budh Singh* (The Ramayana, translated by Munshi Budh Singh; Lahore, 1876); and *Jangnama Imam Husain* (The Battle of Imam Husain, by Shaikh Muhammad Akbar Ali; Lahore, 1887). As these examples suggest, Punjabi religious texts covered a spectrum of faiths—Christianity, Hinduism, Sikhism, and Islam—and they often included works dedicated to particular sects within these larger formations. Almost all Christian material was published by the American Presbyterian Mission in Ludhiana and its sister institutions in Amritsar, Sialkot, and Lahore. A few commercial presses also published Christian religious texts. For example, in 1893 the Akhtar Press of Amritsar published a primer on Christian prayer entitled *(Isaih) Namaz di Chhoti Kitab Punjabi Boli Vich* (A Small Book of Christian Prayer in the Punjabi Language). Hindu texts were principally translations of the Ramayana. Sikh literature mainly consisted of the *Adi Granth* or sections thereof, though *janam-sakhi*s were also published, for example, Bala's *Pothi Janam Sakhi* (Bala's Book of the *Janam-Sakhi*; Lahore, 1890). This Christian, Hindu, and Sikh religious literature was published both in the Gurmukhi and Indo-Persian scripts.[52]

Muslim literature in Punjabi was also published in great quantity during the colonial period. The Quran appeared in Punjabi translation from the 1860s onward. Within the broader category of Muslim literature, we can identify specifically Sunni or Shi'a texts. Much of the work published was Sunni (and didactic) in orientation, such as *Ajaib al Qusas* (Stories of the Prophets; Lahore, 1877) and *Miraj Namah* (The Night Ascension; Lahore, 1870). Shi'a texts principally focused on the martyrdom of Hassan and Husain at Karbala.[53] There are two interesting facts about Shi'a works. First, while Lahore was colonial Punjab's publishing capital, whether in English, Urdu, or Punjabi, Multan was clearly a center of Shi'a publishing. This is not surprising given the historic link between Shi'ism and southern Punjab.[54] Indeed, almost all the texts I encountered that had been published in colonial Multan were Shi'a in orientation. Second, Punjabi authors employed a variety of genres for their Shi'a religious compositions; some are explicitly Shi'a and used solely for religious ritual, such as *marsiya*.[55] The other genres, however, are poetic forms that could treat any subject, religious or not.

Sufi literature comprised another component of the Punjabi corpus. While many Punjabi texts have Sufi undertones, some are the actual compositions of Sufi saints. In the late nineteenth century works by Shaikh Farid (1173–1265), Shah Husain (c. 1530s–1600), Sultan Bahu (1629–91), and Bulleh Shah (1680–1758) were published along with works of other lesser-known Sufi poets.

No account of late nineteenth-century Punjabi religious publishing would be complete without mention of tract literature. Tracts were pamphlets of one, two, four, eight, or at most sixteen pages and were critical to the endeavors of Punjab's socioreligious reform organizations. Thanks to the careful work of Kenneth Jones and Gerald Barrier, we have some knowledge of publishing's role in the contentious relations between the Singh Sabha and the Arya Samaj, and between the Arya Samaj and the Ahmadiyah, in particular (highlighted above in the introduction).[56] "Tract literature," Barrier writes, "became the favored mechanism for promulgating a point of view and attacking opponents." The Singh Sabha created the Khalsa

Tract Society in 1894 expressly for this purpose; the society had an immense output (four hundred tracts and one million copies by 1911). Sikhs also formed other organizations, and each contributed to the saturation of Punjabi society in tract literature. The Panch Khalsa Society, for example, had by 1910 printed 125 tracts, and the Sikh Handbill Society focused its attention on producing a single broadsheet and distributing it in rural areas. Barrier estimates that Sikh organizations produced approximately twelve hundred tracts in the period between 1880 and 1915, representing a range of interests and positions.[57] While Sikh organizations may have excelled in producing such literature, they were certainly not alone. The Arya Samaj, the Ahmadiyah, and various Muslim *anjumans*, or associations, also played a role. Punjabi tract literature included texts that were anti-Brahmin, anti-Shi'a, anti-Wahabi, pro-*tabligh* (conversion to Islam, presumably Sunni), anti-alcohol, and anti-*bhang* (an intoxicating drink made from cannabis), and against meat eating. The latter, although not explicitly religious, were often associated with religious missions. For example, the Anglo-Indian Temperance Association established in 1888 published Punjabi temperance hymns and maintained strong ties with Christian missionaries.[58]

This religious material was published in both the Gurmukhi and Indo-Persian scripts, which is surprising given that this period produced movements that associated languages and scripts with particular religious communities: Punjabi-Gurmukhi-Sikh, Hindi-Devnagari-Hindu, and Urdu-Indo-Persian-Muslim. Linguistic activists waged their political battles across north India, not only with petitions asking the state to recognize their claims, but also through literary journals and societies that put forth (or appropriated) particular genres and scripts as emblematic of their aspirations.[59] The Singh Sabha in the Punjab is an example of this. Smaller organizations also participated in debates over languages, scripts, and religions. Not only the Arya Samaj, but also the Bhasha Pracharini Sabha, advocated for Hindi as the language of Hindus, and the Anjuman Himayat Urdu (Society of the Strength of Urdu) and the Anjuman-i Hamdardi Islamiya (Muslim Association) advocated for Urdu because for them it was a Muslim language.

Each of these organizations petitioned the colonial state, particularly during the Hunter Commission's mission to the Punjab in 1882.[60] The viceroy had appointed the commission to consider education in British India, and it received ninety-six memorials (or petitions) from interested persons and parties when it visited the Punjab in 1882. Most of these took overtly partisan positions on the proper vernacular language of education. It is clear that the petitioners believed there was more at stake than the language of mass education. They wished to gain state recognition of their particular community's claims regarding languages, scripts, and state patronage.

Despite the memorials to the Hunter Commission, however, analysis of late nineteenth-century Punjabi print production, even one limited to religious literature, does not reveal the sorts of script-language-religious community relation-ships that activists advocated. Through this period, Punjabi texts were published in both the Gurmukhi and Indo-Persian scripts, with only limited correlations between religious orientations of texts and scripts used. In other words, Hindu and Sikh texts were not published solely in Gurmukhi. Between 1871 and 1895, eighteen different editions of the *Adi Granth* (often published under its alternate title, *Guru Granth Sahib*) were published in the Indo-Persian script in Lahore, Gujranwala, and Sialkot.[61] Similarly, between 1872 and 1895, five Punjabi transla-tions of the Hindu sacred text *Ramayana* were published in Indo-Persian script. Despite the concerted activities of religious organizations and the record of me-morials submitted to the Hunter Commission, Punjabi religious publications did not in fact fall within the language-script-religious community equivalences that increasingly dominated north Indian public spheres. The same was true of Punjabi nonreligious literature.

Again, publishing in Punjabi at this time encompassed much more than reli-gious literature. Almost without exception this literature represented classical po-etic genres—*baran mah, doha, dole, jangnama, kafi, qissa, si harfi,* and *var*—and poets and authors did not adopt any new genres until 1898, when the first Punjabi novel was published.[62] Thus, Punjabi printed books remained in traditional genres for the first fifty-odd years of publishing in the area.[63] This is not to suggest that classical genres were static, or "survivals" of a premodern past. Rather, their popu-larity and longevity into the print era suggests their resilience and significance for their audiences.

COLONIAL PUNJABI *QISSE*

Qissa is a genre of storytelling in verse with Perso-Islamic roots that became indi-genized in South Asia during the medieval period, through the adoption of Indian meters and narratives. In the Punjab this literary tradition dates to at least the early seventeenth century. One can compose any tale as a *qissa,* and many late nineteenth-century Punjabi *qisse* explicitly reflected the colonial context of their production. *Qissa Warburton* and *Qissa Nahir Firozpur Panjab* are two examples of this.[64] The former tells the tale of a colonial police officer, Colonel Warburton, and the latter is a comment on the benefits to the people of the colonial state's mas-sive irrigation undertaking in the Punjab (the canal colonies project):[65]

> The produce of the deserts and the wastes has been doubled.
> This very land had remained dry from all time,
> And most of the village lands were uncultivated.
> He [Grey Sahib, a colonial official referenced earlier in the text] took much
>   pains for the benefit of the people,
> And brought the canal after the greatest efforts.[66]

Much more common than explicitly contemporary themes were texts that re-worked existing narratives or themes, most often romances.

Most *qisse*, both before and during the colonial period, were reworkings of one of about a dozen romances, some of which had Arabic roots, others that were Persian in origin, and many that were indigenous Indian tales. In these romances poets worked within the parameters of relatively stable narratives known to their audiences. The object of *qissa* poets was not to produce a story de novo (although some did so), but rather to use the *qissa* as a site to engage issues of contemporary concern. Poets drew from a repertoire of stories, alighted upon one, and through subtle shifts produced a text steeped in a literary tradition with deep roots in Indian society and that, simultaneously, entailed contemplation of the present. The poet Sirani's late nineteenth-century romance *Qissa Hir wa Ranjha* exemplifies this Punjabi genre.[67]

In the introduction to his *qissa*, Sirani included a section entitled "The Poet's Questions of His Own Pen." He indicates the repertoire of stories *qissa* poets chose from, as he described (figuratively) the process of composition.

> Placing paper upon a table, I took a pen to hand,
> Taking a reckoning of my heart, I put pen to paper.
> Tell me, my pen, what topic should I write upon?
> Should I engrave the *qissa* of Laila and Majnun upon my heart?
> Or should I exert my mental energy on the tale of Shirin [and Farhad]?
> Or should I compose the *qissa* of Jogi Ranjha, who led Hir's buffaloes
>   to pasture?
> Or should I amuse with the tale of Sassi [Sassi-Punnun] who roamed the
>   desert, or with that of Sohni [and Mahival]?
> Or should I tell you the *qissa* of Shams and Dhol, or the story of Yusuf
>   [and Zulaikha]?[68]

Sirani included in this list of romances narratives that were Arab (*Yusuf-Zulaikha, Laila-Majnun*), Persian (*Shirin-Farhad*), and indigenous (*Hir-Ranjha, Sassi-Punnun, Sohni-Mahival, Shams-Dhol*). After posing still more possibilities, the text continues:

> *I am going to open the history of the times* and tell us something fresh.
> To the dark mirror of my heart I brought a light at night.
> Taking hold of my habits, I brought my heart to the side of truth.
> Then I jarred some memories of Hir and Jogi Ranjha.
> . . . .
> *Piecing together this qissa in the correct tradition,* I will spread it throughout
>   the land.[69]

Sirani's text reflects, in miniature, a broader pattern of *qissa* composition. As Sirani's text illustrates, the *qissa* allowed a form of social commentary, it was a way of "open[ing] the history of the times." It is perhaps because the *qissa* served this purpose that it was taken up for composition by innumerable poets in the late nineteenth and early twentieth centuries. Unfortunately, we know little about most of these poets, in some cases no more than their names.

In part, there is a paucity of knowledge about colonial-era *qissa* poets because most of them never achieved enough fame through their literary pursuits to warrant the attention of their contemporaries or future generations. Perhaps more significant, however, is the fact that there was no tradition of literary history in Punjabi literary culture until the late nineteenth century.[70] The literary genealogies found in the opening passages of some *qisse* from 1855 were a first move in this direction, but these did little more than name poets. The first texts that can confidently be described as literary histories, providing biographical information about poets and descriptions of their texts, were not produced until the early decades of the twentieth century.[71] Drawing on these early twentieth-century texts, the work of more contemporary literary scholars, and information embedded in texts themselves, I provide here a thumbnail sketch of a few of the period's *qissa* poets.

Maula Baksh Kushta (1876–1954) was the first litterateur to compile a text on Punjabi poets, the *Chasm-i Hayat* (1913), and a renowned poet in his own right.[72] An Amritsar native, Kushta was born into the Bhatti Rajput *zat* (caste or kinship group). His early education began in a government school, from which he was withdrawn by his father for fear that he would be converted to Christianity. He then went to Lahore, where he worked in the publishing industry and developed, in the words of Christopher Shackle, "a precocious poetic reputation as an extempore performer." Ultimately, Kushta returned to Amritsar, where he was active as a poet, publisher, and bookseller. In 1913, he published what might be considered his magnum opus, a sixty-five-hundred-line rendition of *Hir-Ranjha*.

Fazl Shah was among the most prolific and commercially successful Punjabi poets of the late nineteenth century. Born in 1827 in the Nawankot area of Lahore, Fazl Shah remained a resident of that city for the rest of his life. He was a well-educated man, well versed in Arabic, Persian, and Urdu in addition to Punjabi. He was also devout, as suggested by the fact that his contemporaries referred to him as a *hafiz* (someone who can recite the Quran from memory), and knew him to be a disciple of the *pir* Ghulam Mohiuddin of Kasur.[73] Fazl Shah authored ten compositions, five of them *qisse*, which reputedly sold in the thousands.[74] Despite this apparent literary success, he earned his living not from his pen but as a clerk in the office of the Financial Commissioner in Lahore.[75] This is a particularly telling biographical detail, as it reminds us that the world of Punjabi letters functioned alongside that of colonial administration, though the former largely enjoyed independence from the latter.

Fazl Shah's contemporary the poet Bhagwan Singh also exemplifies this. The author of five literary works (three of which were *qisse*), Bhagwan Singh is a somewhat enigmatic figure. All that is known about him is that he was from the Ferozepur district, that he was a farmer, and that he served in the British Indian Army for some time.[76]

Kishan Singh 'Arif, whose *Qissa Hir te Ranjhe da* we encountered in the introduction, was prolific, like many of the period's *qissa* poets. Born to a Sikh family near Amritsar in 1836, Kishan Singh was the son of a bookseller whose bookshop stood in Amritsar's Mai Sevan Bazaar.[77] Singh took over this establishment on his father's death, and thus alongside his own literary ambitions he became a publisher (as was the norm for bookshops at the time) and bookseller. He was a disciple of Gulab Das, the spiritual leader of the Vedantic Gulabdasi sect, whose influence can be discerned in his writings (see chapter 5). Writing under the pen name 'Arif, or "knowledgeable" (particularly in the way of God), Kishan Singh wrote at least seven *qisse*.[78]

Compared to Fazl Shah and Kishan Singh, Maula Shah was a man of limited means and humble background. Born in 1867 in Amritsar into the *qasai* (butchers by occupation) community, he grew up in the Gurdaspur district where he worked as an unpaid laborer. While still in his teens, he became a disciple of a local mullah (Muslim cleric) who provided Shah with a basic education. Once educated, Maula Shah returned to Amritsar where he became both a poet and spiritual guide, as suggested by the religious epithet *sain* (religious devotee), under which he published. Sain Maula Shah composed *kafis*, *si harfis*, and at least three *qisse*. His *Hir wa Ranjha* was published in 1912.[79]

In contrast to Maula Shah, Amir Haider Shah enjoyed a life of great privilege as a courtier of the Nawab of Bahawalpur, a princely state in southern Punjab. Born circa 1809, Shah moved to Bahawalpur at a young age where he became a wrestler. He then joined the government of the Nawab, whose service he left in 1866, though he received a pension for the rest of his life. Writing under the pen name Miran Shah Bahawalpuri, he published his *Qissa Hir-Ranjha* in circa 1898–99, shortly before his death in about 1900.[80]

A number of other poets composed Punjabi *qisse* in the late nineteenth and early twentieth centuries, but we know little about them other than what can be discerned from their texts. These include the following; all are authors of epic-length *qisse*: Bhai Sant Bajara Singh, *Qissa Hir te Ranjhe da* (The *Qissa* of Hir and Ranjha; Amritsar, 1894, 195 pages); Lahora Singh (b. 1865), *Hir Lahori* (Lahora's Hir; Lahore, 1931, 195 pages); Kishore Chand, *Navan Qissa Hir Kishore Chand* (Kishore Chand's New *Qissa* Hir; Amritsar, 1914, 80 pages); Gokalchand Sharma Basianwala, *Qissa Hir Gokalchand* (Gokalchand's *Qissa* Hir; Ludhiana, n.d., 156 pages); Firoz Din Sharaf, *Hir Sial* (Lahore, 1933, 176 pages); and Bhai Lakma Singh, *Qissa Hir wa Mian Ranjha* (The *Qissa* of Hir and *Mian* Ranjha; Peshawar, 1876, 100 pages).[81]

Some poets have faded into obscurity, but were clearly significant in their own time and within this literary tradition. This is evident from the genealogy of poets that opens Kishan Singh 'Arif's *Qissa Hir te Ranjhe da* that names the following poets: Hamid [Shah Abbasi], Hasham [Shah], Fazl Shah, Waris [Shah], Muqbal, Husain, Roshan, Jog Singh, Kahan Singh, Nar Singh, Ratan Singh, Krishan Singh Gobind, Bhagwan Singh, and Singh Gopal (12–13). Waris Shah and Muqbal are well-known eighteenth-century literary figures. Hamid Shah Abbasi, Hasham Shah, and Jog Singh each composed *qisse* in the early nineteenth century, and their texts remained popular in the colonial period. The remainder of Kishan Singh's list are late nineteenth-century poets, his contemporaries. Of these, we have only the briefest sketch of Bhagwan Singh, above. In the cases of Husain and Roshan, their texts have survived, but of the others we have no record of any sort. Bhai Sant Bajara Singh similarly included a genealogy of poets in his 1894 *Qissa Hir te Ranjhe da,* which provides similar references.[82] He too cited Muqbal, Jog Singh, Bhagwan Singh, Fazl Shah, and Roshan, suggesting the contemporary significance of these authors. Indeed, Roshan—about whom no biographical information is available—was known to his contemporaries and was also a popular commercial poet. His *Hir Roshan,* an episodic text of only eight pages, was published in at least eight separate editions (two in the Indo-Persian script and six in Gurmukhi) between 1873 and 1900.[83]

My aim in providing these brief sketches and naming poets is not to be exhaustive. Late nineteenth- and early twentieth-century Punjab had innumerable *qissa* poets, and given the historical record it is all but impossible to produce a comprehensive record. What can be concluded from this sampling, however, is that *qissa* poets were a heterogeneous group that cohered—conceptually, across time, space, class, caste, and religion—around the *qissa* tradition.

Judging from publishing records, the *qisse* these poets composed were among the most popular genres of Punjabi book publishing from the late nineteenth century into the twentieth. They were among the first Punjabi texts to be printed, and continued to be printed throughout the period. A number of narratives were taken up in print, almost all of them romances. In some instances, numerous editions of (purportedly) the same *qissa* were published. For example, at least eleven different editions of the poet Muqbal's *Qissa Hir wa Ranjha* were produced between 1872 and 1898 in the Indo-Persian script (and it was also published in Gurmukhi). Literally hundreds of Punjabi *qisse* were published in the late nineteenth and early twentieth centuries, often in multiple editions, with some print runs numbering in the thousands. The Punjabi *qissa* is an interesting phenomenon: it was written in a language that had no official standing, was not taught in schools, and was at times actively suppressed by the state. It was a literary tradition with roots dating to at least the early seventeenth century, disseminated through the very modern means of the printing press, and with immense popular appeal. The *qissa* as a site for social commentary—with its norms and expectations, its articulation of points of conflict, its representation of forms of sociality and gender relations, its expressions of piety—is historically significant for understanding colonial Punjab. Indeed, the *qissa* tradition was the foundation of the Punjabi literary formation.

3

A Punjabi Literary Formation

Punjabi print culture in the late nineteenth century continued many distinct practices of precolonial Punjabi literary culture. Most significantly, during the first half-century of print production, the overwhelming majority of Punjabi printed books were composed in classical verse genres. As discussed in chapter 2, this continuity provides evidence of the resilience and significance of these literary traditions for their composers and audiences. If the genres of late nineteenth-century Punjabi printed books show the tenacity of classical compositional styles, then they also point to the aural and performative dimensions of Punjabi literature. This is because these genres (the *qissa, var, dole, kafi, doha, si harfi,* and *baran mah,* among others) were all meant for oral performance, either through recitation (a style known as *tahat al-lafz*) or, more commonly, by singing to musical accompaniment. In the late nineteenth century, performances of Punjabi literary texts by an array of specialists and performers took place before diverse audiences in a range of sites and settings.

The rendering of classical Punjabi literary genres in manuscripts and printed texts did not produce a radical rupture with the performance traditions they were part of. While the circulation of physical texts suggests the expansion of Punjabi literature's audience from one comprised solely of listeners to one that included readers, it is clear that Punjabi texts were not meant for silent reading. In their form, Punjabi manuscripts and printed texts underscore the fluid line between written word and oral performance. This fluidity can be located in what I will refer to as protocols of orality embedded in the printed texts, which allude to their oral dissemination by performers and their aural consumption by audiences. The printed texts at the heart of this analysis did not therefore effect a break from a prior oral culture, nor did they necessarily diminish the vitality of oral performances, which from all accounts were robust at the time.[1]

If Punjabi printed texts are intrinsically related to performance practices, then they also gesture toward the continuing significance of the scribal tradition in print culture. While the advent of print in some contexts may signal a transition in which compositors displace scribes, in the Punjab, as in much of north India, scribes remained central to book production.[2] The continuities between Punjabi print and scribal cultures on the one hand, and print and performance cultures on the other, destabilize any notion of a linear progression from oral to scribal to print cultures. At the same time, because of these continuities—or, more accurately, simultaneities—the colonial-era Punjabi printed texts I examine here allude to more than the traditional world of print production—constituted by authors, compositors, publishers, distributors, and readers. Punjabi print culture was intimately linked to scribal, performance, and listening traditions as well.

SIGNS IN PUNJABI PRINTED TEXTS

Chapter 2 described how early printed books often used design elements common to (Indo-Islamic) manuscripts, such as geometric or floral borders on their covers (figures 2 and 5).[3] Scribes remained important to Punjabi printed book culture in part because the historic scribal tradition had been central to precolonial and preprint book production. In his 1871 history of Lahore, Kanhayalal related the importance of scribes in Punjab's preprint book trade. "There are now numerous publishing houses in this city," he wrote,

> In the Sikh period . . . all the booksellers would sell handwritten books. A big bookseller of that time was Muhammad Baksh Sahib and his establishment employed many scribes for writing books. He did thousands of rupees of business. There were also small business houses. . . . During the Sikh period, no published book from Hindustan [a reference to other parts of north India] would come to the Punjab. Scribes would produce handwritten texts and sell them. Vendors would sell common books daily in front of Wazir Khan's Mosque. . . . And it is there that the big bookseller Mian Muhammad Baksh Sahib had an establishment in which twenty-five to thirty scribes wrote books. Books from his workshop would go all over the Punjab. In fact, merchants would buy them and take them as far away as Iran and Khurasan.[4]

Indian books that circulated as far away as Iran were thus valued as material objects as well as for their content. Calligraphy was an art in Islamic and Islamicate contexts, and manuscripts were commonly elaborate and ornamental (figure 1).[5] Scribes were often artists in their own right.

By the late nineteenth century, the book trade in Lahore was transitioning from selling manuscripts to selling printed books. The link between the old and new book trades is underscored by the fact that Kashmiri Bazaar—the area outside Wazir Khan's mosque described by Kanhayalal—became the key site of Punjabi publishing in Lahore. Despite the adoption of print technology, for economic and cultural reasons scribes continued to be essential to the Punjabi book trade. Publishers of Punjabi books did not turn to typeset or movable print until after the turn of the twentieth century, despite its availability much earlier.[6] Largely because typeset printing was more expensive than lithography—the former required importing a press, acquiring type fonts that had to be manufactured, and employing typesetters or compositors who had to be trained—lithography became the technology of choice. It required only a rudimentary press, readily available limestone (for making plates), acid, grease, and a scribe.

The decision to use lithography rather than typeset meant not only a lower initial investment, it also preserved a role for the scribes who, if the shift to typesetting had been rapid, would have suffered social, cultural, and economic dislocation.[7] It appears that there was also an important status economy attached to scribal activity. Scribes' names often appeared on Punjabi manuscripts, and in some cases they adorned lithographed texts by being printed on the title page along with the names of authors and publishers, indicating their importance in a broader economy of book production.[8]

Early Punjabi printed texts also reveal links to performance traditions. The bulk of these texts represent verse genres, a predictable development since no classical Punjabi prose genres existed, excepting *janam-sakhi* literature. More significantly, the genres taken up in print were all better suited to performance—to recitation or singing and listening—than to the private act of quiet reading.

A number of compositional elements within Punjabi printed texts index continuities between print and performance, including the common use of dialogue. Many Punjabi printed texts of this time include a literary device, the *sawal wa jawab* or the "question and answer," as a narrative feature. Punjabi poets adopted this well-established device from Persian literature.[9] In Punjabi printed *qisse*, *sawal wa jawab* allowed poets to insert verse dialogue in a genre that was otherwise ill-suited for its inclusion. Historian Anindita Ghosh suggests that dialogue in early Bengali printed texts appealed to an audience making the transition to literacy and reading culture. "For first-generation readers of print," she writes, "the simple language of literature set out in the form of dialogues was very welcome. . . . The oral tradition shows through in the imitation of speech patterns in the narratives."[10] Whereas for Ghosh, dialogue assisted readers in making the "abrupt and stifling" change to silent reading, in Punjabi works the *sawal wa jawab* can be interpreted as a sign of the texts' suitability for oral performance. Dialogue in texts may have helped Indians adapt to new reading practices, but it also lent itself to the oral performance of print texts, suggesting the simultaneity of print and performance.

Repetition is another compositional element in these texts that may be interpreted as revealing traces of orality. This element was singled out for particular disdain by colonial officials, who condemned Punjabi literature as "puerile or indelicate,"[11] "coarse and witless,"[12] and "full of irritating and uninteresting repetitions."[13] Such colonial criticisms of Punjabi works were grounded in their perceived distance from Victorian norms of good literature. Some of that distance was surely due to their intended enjoyment via singing and listening, rather than by the Victorian habit of silent reading. Passages that seemed full of "irritating and uninteresting repetitions" when read silently made more aesthetic sense when performed. Take Khawaish Ali's *Hir-Ranjha*, a romance in verse couplets. The text opens with a philosophical statement that has little immediate relation to the action of the romance: "Make me your devotee [*faqir*], oh Guru."[14] This line closes each of the poem's first eighteen stanzas, serving as a refrain. The effect of such repetition is apparent if we examine the text's opening passages:

> *Make me your devotee, oh Guru,*
> Put the arrow of separation through my heart, oh Guru.
> He [Ranjha] left Takht Hazara and came, he came to the land of the Sials and
>   settled there.
> In the end, oh Guru, he was enchanted by Hir's love,
> *Make me your devotee, oh Guru.*
>
> When the Jat [Hir] stared at him,
> she put the noose of love around his neck.
> He grazed buffalo for twelve years, oh Guru, in exchange for Hir,
> *Make me your devotee, oh Guru.*
>
> As always, I am taking the buffalo into the fields,
> after grazing them I come home.
> I always take the arrows of separation in my heart, oh Guru,
> *Make me your devotee, oh Guru.*
>
> The love of this Jat [Hir] has tormented me,
> that is why I have come to you.
> The circle of her love has shackled me, oh Guru,
> *Make me your devotee, oh Guru.*
>
> I have earned the rage of her parents,
> all the world is astir.
> They separated me from Hir though I am blameless,
> *Make me your devotee, oh Guru.*[15]

After the opening line repeats for the eighteenth time, another section of the narrative begins by introducing a new verse to be repeated: "Crying, Hir always begs, at some point come to my home, oh Ranjha." This line completes every third couplet, and is repeated nine times in all. In this manner, the entire narrative is strung together as a series of sections, each with its own refrain or verse that completes each stanza. While this repetition may be tedious when read, in performance it functions as a refrain. And such refrains are conventional in a number of Punjabi verse genres, for example in the *kafi* form.

Another example of the same type is found in Fassi Niaz Ahmad's *Hir Niaz Ranjha* (Niaz's *Hir-Ranjha*).[16] This eight-page text conveys the broad outlines of the *Hir-Ranjha* romance. It is divided evenly into two parts, each of which constitutes an independent composition. The first is titled "Faryad Ranjha" (Ranjha's Plea), and the second is "Faryad Hir" (Hir's Plea). The text opens with Ranjha disguised as a cowherd so that he and Hir can meet secretly, and it closes with the lovers separated from and pining for one another. Both compositions employ repetition. The first is in simple verse, and opens with Ranjha's plaint, "Your love, oh beautiful Hir, has made me a sufferer in this world."[17] This line occurs ten times, generally completing each four-line stanza of the composition, and it functions much like the refrain in Khawaish Ali's text. What is striking about this example, however, is that the refrain is prominently printed on the cover of the book, alongside information about the author and publisher. Printing identifying lines from a composition on the cover in this way was relatively common (for an example, see figure 8). There are many possible reasons for this, among them that such lines were something of a "teaser" or advertisement for the composition. Or, their inclusion on the cover may indicate that the text was already in oral circulation. Many Punjabi verse compositions have no title, as such, and are identified by their first lines or refrains. (This is true of other vernacular verse traditions as well, the Urdu *ghazal,* for instance). If Niaz's composition circulated as a performed text, printing the refrain on the publication's cover would allow the publisher to capitalize on its popularity.

The second part of *Hir Niaz Ranjha* changes perspective to foreground Hir's voice. It opens with the refrain, "Your love, oh Ranjha, has me in ecstasy" (5), a line that marks the close of every stanza and is repeated through the rest of the composition a total of fifteen times. Such repetition only makes sense if these texts were published with the expectation that they would be performed. Thus repetition registers the traces of orality embedded in these texts, and their multiple modes of transmission and reception.

Arguing that printed books are both textual and oral forms of literature is not the same as collapsing the distinctions between the two. Indeed, as Roger Chartier writes, "When the 'same' text is apprehended through very different mechanisms of representation, it is no longer the same. Each of its forms obeys specific conventions that mold and shape the work according to the laws of that form and connect it, in differing ways, with other arts, other genres, and other texts."[18] Chartier makes an important point, and the discussion of Punjabi texts in performance below highlights precisely such connections. At the same time, however, Chartier

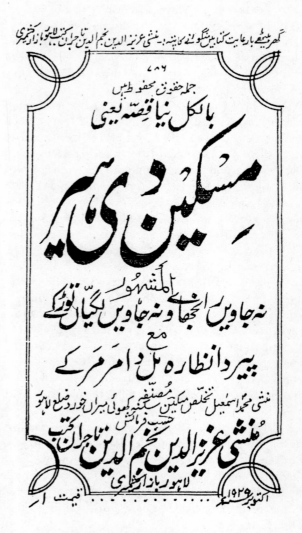

FIGURE 8. Title page of *Maskin di Hir,* by Munshi
Muhammad Ismail [Maskin], 1920. Text (from top):
"786 | All rights reserved | The absolutely new *qissa*—
or | Maskin's Hir | The famous | 'Oh, don't go Ranjha, don't
break our attachment and go | One sees the *pir* only in
death' | By the author Munshi Muhammad Ismail, whose
pen name is 'Maskin' . . . district Lahore | At the request
of | Munshi Aziz al-Din Najm al-Din Booksellers | Lahore,
Kashmiri Bazaar | October 1929 . . . price, 1 anna."

draws too strong a distinction between forms, leaving little room for understanding the ways that different forms interpenetrate one another, or the ways that such interpenetration itself produces what we have come to know as either textual or oral literature. Scholars of Indian literatures Stuart Blackburn and A. K. Ramanujan have elegantly argued this latter point, suggesting that in the Indian context, oral and textual traditions not only coexist but are symbiotic, that they are co-constitutive and engaged in a relationship in which the "borrowing from one to the other has never ceased."[19] Ethnographic work on oral epics in contemporary India provides an interesting example of such interpenetration. In this context, scholars have noted that "some performers are nonliterate and keep the text in front of them for the sake of authenticity. Other performers seem to memorize and repeat parts of the written text in performance."[20] In both cases, albeit in different ways, the written text is integral to oral performance.

Although based on contemporary storytelling practices, the ethnographic insight above and Blackburn and Ramanujan's formulation are both helpful in understanding early Punjabi printed texts because they suggest that the protocols of orality in these texts do not simply index a prior oral tradition being replaced by literacy and reading practices. These protocols in early Punjabi printed texts instead signal a contemporary tradition of recitation and performance. Although easily overlooked—for few indigenous sources elaborate on performance practices and there is little more than passing reference to such activity in colonial archives—performance was central to Punjabi literary culture. It was also central to what I have called the Punjabi literary formation. Before addressing the particularities of late nineteenth- and early twentieth-century Punjabi literary performances, therefore, let us briefly explore just who constituted the Punjabi literary formation and why the notion of a formation helps us understand Punjab's colonial history.

A PUNJABI LITERARY FORMATION

The Punjabi literary formation refers to a group constituted through its members' shared practices of producing, circulating, performing, reading, and listening to Punjabi literary texts, qisse in particular. The concept draws in part on Sheldon Pollock's notion of a "sociotextual community." In his introduction to *Literary Cultures in History: Reconstructions from South Asia*, Pollock defines a sociotextual community as "the community for which literature is produced, in which it circulates, and which derives a portion of its self-understanding as a community from the very acts of hearing, reading, performing, reproducing, and circulating literary texts."[21] Pollock's suggestion that a sociotextual community derives something of its self-understanding from literary practice resonates with my use of "literary formation." The important point—and what is shared with the Punjabi literary formation outlined here—is mutual coproduction: individuals and communities produce texts, and texts, in turn, help constitute both individual and community identity.

In choosing to characterize this group as a literary formation rather than a community, I am drawing on two other critical concepts, each of which elucidates an important facet of this idea. The first is that of a cultural formation, as outlined by Mary Poovey in *Making a Social Body: British Cultural Formation, 1830–1864*. On her choice of title and language, Poovey writes, "The emphasis in the subtitle of this book should fall on *formation* as an active concept—the process of forming— not on *culture* or *formation* as nouns of stasis or realization. I emphasize the active sense of *formation* because . . . culture is never fully formed, never achieved as a unified, homogenous whole."[22] In my use of "formation" I gesture toward Poovey's emphasis, underscoring that the Punjabi literary formation was produced through action—varyingly individual, collective, social, and institutional—and that it was not static. A product of its historical context, it was thus both subject to change and continuously impacted by "newness."[23]

The idea of how "publics" and "counterpublics" are formed and their political function, as discussed by Michael Warner, is the second concept helpful in explaining my use of the Punjabi literary formation.[24] "A public," Warner writes, "appears to be open to indefinite strangers, but in fact selects participants by criteria of shared social space (though not necessarily territorial space), habitus, topical concerns, intergeneric references, and circulating intelligible forms."[25] Warner emphasizes the importance of individual action in constituting a social collective. His argument that publics and counterpublics "select participants" based on the actions of the individuals in question, no matter how limited this action may be, foregrounds the agency of participation. What I take from Warner is the sense that publics and counterpublics do not simply exist but are forged, and that their constitution includes processes of inclusion and exclusion. Participation or belonging rests not in what can be thought of as passive qualities—ethnicity, national origin, and so forth (the kinds of qualities foundational to modern nationalisms)—but rather in more active ones such as intellectual engagement with specific ideas.

Warner's insights into publics and counterpublics are suggestive for thinking about how the Punjabi literary formation constituted a social collective based not only on a shared language (which we might think of as simply a linguistic community) but also on shared literary practices and ideas. Indeed, the *qissa* as a genre was a site not just for aesthetic expression and literary pleasure but also for social commentary. The ideas and attitudes expressed in *qisse*, further, were not just those of literate, middle- and upper-class, and upper-caste groups, but were forged through processes of interaction that included lower castes and classes as well. Notwithstanding the importance of where and among whom *qisse* circulated, their social commentary makes them valuable historical texts; they are expressions

A PUNJABI LITERARY FORMATION   99

of norms and expectations, articulations of points of conflict, representations of forms of sociality and gender relations, as well as expressions of piety.

Access to the Punjabi literary formation was open to anyone within the linguistic community but was not assured by linguistic competence. Belonging was secured by active participation in a tradition that inhabited a shared social space and focused selectively on particular, relevant concerns. While there were criteria for belonging to the Punjabi literary formation, the threshold was actually quite low, and the formation was more inclusive than exclusive. This formation was expansive because it was not class-, caste-, religion-, or gender-specific, and encompassed both reading and listening publics. Belonging entailed engagement and experience: composing or performing a Punjabi text, for example, or knowing how to interact with a singer during a public performance, or participating in (sometimes highly refined) listening practices, such as *sama'*, discussed below.

Although Warner's insights can be used to illuminate some important aspects of the Punjabi literary formation, his notion of publics and counterpublics does not provide the right conceptual model for thinking about the historical significance of people's participation in Punjabi literary culture. The key point of difference lies in different notions of politics. Publics and counterpublics, as described by Warner and others, are intimately connected to the state. While Warner distinguishes publics from Habermas's notion of the public sphere, in practical (as opposed to theoretical) terms, publics and counterpublics "acquire agency in relation to the state."[26] In fact, Warner argues, "It might be that the only way a public is able to act is through its imaginary coupling with the state."[27] The Punjabi literary formation, in contrast, was relatively independent from the state. It was certainly imbued with a politics (articulated, not least, through its choice of language and genre), but these were not directed at the state, nor did the Punjabi formation engage the state as a site of alternative politics. This is perhaps the Punjabi literary formation's most unique feature: while it had amazing traction in Punjabi society, incorporated a diverse range of people around the practices of literature, and represented shared social and cultural values, these values *did not* translate into political action in state arenas.

The Punjabi literary formation emerges in a range of sites where Punjabi literature was performed and in the practices associated with its performance. Three features of the formation were central to its constitution: one, its participants were diverse in religion, caste, class, and gender; two, the literary traditions around which the formation cohered entailed the sustenance of specialists through distinct types of patronage; and three, these literary traditions thrived in institutions or sites that lay outside the zones of greatest colonial influence on Indian society.

What sustained the literary tradition that underpinned this formation? On one hand, the tradition was surely sustained by pleasure. That is, people engaged it as a form of entertainment. Pleasure and entertainment played important roles in the longevity of the literary traditions around which the formation cohered. Locating pleasure in the historical record is a challenge, however, and I found neither indigenous nor colonial sources that allow a sustained analysis of how the formation's participants experienced pleasure. Nonetheless, faint traces of it are there. They can be discerned, for example, in the vignettes of colonial-era performances I discuss below. The role of entertainment and pleasure in sustaining the tradition can also be deduced more obliquely. How else to explain Syad Muhammad Latif's description of Lahore street life in his 1892 history of the city? "Young people in the streets recite epic and other poetry, or sing songs descriptive of love and intrigue," Latif writes. "The ballads most popular are those which describe the love of Mirza and Sahiba . . . the tale of Hir and Ranjha . . . and Sassi and Punnu."[28]

The importance of Punjabi *qisse* as entertainment and sources of pleasure notwithstanding, this chapter will contend that these aspects alone did not preserve this tradition, but rather that it survived because of the devotional practices, social relations, occupations, and commerce through which the Punjabi literary formation was constituted. Punjabi texts circulated in and through a web of complex relationships that gave the formation its coherence, sustained the literary tradition at its foundation, and imbued Punjabi texts with multiple layers of meaning. I turn now to those relationships, as constituted through performance traditions. But first, a brief comment on the sources that undergird the remainder of this chapter.

COLONIAL FOLKLORE

Syad Muhammad Latif's reference above to Punjabi literary performance in his history of colonial Lahore exemplifies the promise and limits of many of the period's sources. His is undoubtedly a tantalizing fragment, one that hints at the ubiquity of Punjabi literary performance, and of *qisse* in particular. Latif, however, does not provide more detail about these performances, the texts performed, the performers, or their audiences. His history therefore remains a very limited source for understanding how Punjabi literature circulated orally in the late nineteenth and early twentieth centuries, whether through recitation or singing. Ironically, it is likely that the ubiquity of such performances, their everydayness, made them unremarkable beyond a passing mention in many of the period's historical sources. Contemporary histories by Indian authors, such as Noor Ahmed Chishti's *Tahqiqaat-i Chishti: Tarikh-i Lahore Ka Encyclopedia* (Chishti's Inquiries: An Encyclopedia of Lahore's History; 1867), Kanhayalal's *Tarikh-i Lahore* (History of Lahore; 1871) and *Tarikh-i Punjab* (History of Punjab; 1877), Mufti Ghulam Sarwar's *Tarikh-i Makhzan-i Punjab* (History and Record of Punjab; 1884), and Latif's *Lahore* (1892) and *History of the Panjab* (1889) provide in rare cases fragments of information about contemporary literary performances, performers, or performance sites, but invariably in a general way that is only marginally helpful. In contrast to the limited utility of indigenous sources, colonial sources provide much useful information. Indeed, due to the enthusiasm of some colonial officials (and their native colleagues) for the relatively new field of folklore, and because much Punjabi literature, including *qisse,* was categorized as folklore, an archive exists that preserves interesting data about colonial-era Punjabi literary performances. But as with any colonial sources on indigenous history, colonial studies of what was deemed native folklore must be read against the grain. At the same time—as is true of any archive, colonial or otherwise—one must be aware of the limits and elisions produced by the collecting practices of colonial folklorists, and the biases that informed their analyses in order to effectively use these texts to different ends.

The goals of late nineteenth- and early twentieth-century colonial folklorists—as opposed to ethnographers—are most clearly laid out in an 1898 address by H. H. Risley, president of the Asiatic Society of Bengal. "Folklore," Risley explained, "has been defined by the English Folk-Lore Society as 'the comparison and identification of the survivals of archaic beliefs, customs and traditions in modern ages.'" India was in his opinion particularly fertile ground for this project, as "in relation to European institutions nearly the whole body of Indian custom, usage and tradition may be regarded as a series of survivals."[29] The goal of colonial folklorists, then, was to identify and document these "survivals," and furthermore to analyze them according to universal schema established by the Folklore Society of England.

In the Punjab, a number of colonial officials were ardent folklore collectors. Unlike contemporary ethnographic studies of Indian society, which were often commissioned by state actors and destined for use by compilers of censuses and gazetteers, the study of folklore was conducted largely outside official duties. Officials were nonetheless able to compile an immense amount of data, publishing much of it in journals and volumes devoted to the subject, including *Panjab Notes and Queries* (later *Indian Notes and Queries*) and *Indian Antiquary.* Richard Carnac Temple (1850–1931) is likely the most important figure in a group—including Flora Annie Steel, J. C. Oman, H. A. Rose, C. F. Usborne, and Charles Swynnerton, among others—who made important contributions to the study of what they deemed to be Punjabi folklore. Temple was the son of a rather illustrious father (Richard Temple),[30] who earned his own acclaim as a soldier and administrator in India. Like his father, Temple joined the British Indian Army and served in the Afghan and Burmese wars before enjoying a succession of important administrative posts across British India.[31] Despite the increasing responsibilities associated with each rise in rank, Temple was an enthusiastic collector of folklore throughout his career. This enthusiasm for his unofficial vocation is suggested by his membership in several societies organized around an interest in the folklore (and anthropology) of India, including: the Royal Geographic Society; the Royal Asiatic,

Philological, and Folklore Societies; the Anthropological Institute; and the Asiatic Society of Bengal. Temple also took an active role in publishing on Indian folklore as a regular contributor to the *Calcutta Review*, founder and editor of *Panjab Notes and Queries* (est. 1883), and editor and proprietor of the *Indian Antiquary* for forty-six years. He wrote on a range of topics, but for our purposes his most significant contributions were on contemporary devotional practices in Punjab (in the *Calcutta Review*) and on what he identified as Punjabi "tales," "ballads," and "legends" collected in his three-volume *Legends of the Panjab*, published between 1884 and 1900. For this text, Temple hired "bards" to perform Punjabi literary texts (many of which were *qisse*), had their texts transcribed, and then translated them for a British audience.[32]

Temple worked closely with Flora Annie Steel (1847–1929), a compelling character in her own right. Steel was the wife of Indian Civil Service officer Henry Steel. The two spent twenty-two years in India (1867–89), chiefly in the Punjab, living in Ludhiana, Dalhousie, and Kasur, near Lahore, where she learned to speak, read, and write Punjabi.[33] She engaged in a number of pursuits while in India (and upon her return to Britain), including spearheading Indian women's educational reform (as Punjab's inspectress of schools at one point, and as a member of the Provincial Education Board at another), collecting Indian folktales, writing on Anglo-Indian domesticity, and producing some twenty works of fiction, among them the highly popular *On the Face of the Waters: A Tale of the Mutiny*. In addition to writing numerous articles for *Panjab Notes and Queries*, Steel published *Wide-Awake Stories* (1884), a collection of Punjabi tales whose 1894 edition, published as *Tales of the Punjab Told by the People*, included illustrations by John Lockwood Kipling (father of the more famous Rudyard Kipling) and notes by Temple.

Much that Temple, Steel, and other folklorists wrote is clearly embedded in their own colonial framework and epistemology. The following example from an essay by Temple is typical. Regarding the performance of a Punjabi text sung in devotion to the Sufi saint Sakhi Sarwar by a group known as the Sansis, Temple wrote the following: "When one takes into account that these bards are completely ignorant of religion and history, sing in the vulgarest Panjabi entirely from memory, and with the calmest indifference as to the proper sequence of the verses, are invariably unable to explain any allusions with clearness—their explanations being all traditional and frequently obviously wrong—it is not difficult to see that it has been no easy task to sift their songs and make sense and sequence out of them."[34]

"The vulgarest Punjabi," "indifference as to the proper sequence of the verses," "frequently obviously wrong": such comments suggest that Temple saw his burden as telling the natives about their literary traditions, not vice-versa. This was a result of Temple's understanding of the contemporary science of folklore, through which he categorized Punjabi tales into universal norms. This is most explicit in his notes to Flora Annie Steel's *Tales of the Punjab Told by the People*, which were published in the form of two essays at the end of the volume. The first of these is titled "Analysis of the Tales on the Plan Adopted by the Folklore Society of England," and includes information about the content of the tales, such as "Dramatis Personae," "Thread of Story," and "Incidental Circumstances," as well as contextual information, such as "Where Published," "Narrator's Name," and "Other Particulars."[35] In the second essay, "A Survey of the Incidents in Modern Indian Folk-Tales," such particulars are reduced to universal categories. This essay organizes the folktales' "incidents," or plots into four classes, each of which has subcategories attuned to an Anglocentric classificatory scheme with universal pretensions. One of these classes, for example, is "Actors," and the categories include: the stepmother, saints and holy personages, witches, ogres, the sleeping beauty, and so on.[36] All of the Punjabi stories in Steel's collection are made to fit one of these categories. My point here is not to exhaustively recount the details of Temple's method, but rather to illustrate how his analysis served to universalize Punjabi "folklore." His project, ultimately, was one of colonial assimilation: colonial in its insistence on the prevalence—indeed, singularity—of a European epistemological framework.[37]

While this interpretive framework may be completely discredited today, the archive produced by Temple, Steel, and others nevertheless remains invaluable for its descriptions of literary performances. These descriptions, notwithstanding their shortcomings, describe specific performances that help bring the constituent elements of the Punjabi literary formation into clearer focus. Indeed, although these folklorists interpreted what they were collecting as "survivals" that confirmed British notions of a static and unchanging India, we can take their descriptions—stripped of their interpretations—as compelling evidence of the vitality of the Punjabi literary formation in colonial Punjab.

PUNJABI TEXTS IN PERFORMANCE

On 16 June 1911, Miles Irving, an officer in the Indian Civil Service, stood before the newly formed Panjab Historical Society in Lahore and described rituals he had observed at a Sufi shrine at Pakpattan in south-central Punjab. The shrine, dedicated to the thirteenth-century saint Shaikh Farid, was and remains one of the most important in the Punjab.[38] Irving conveyed the following:

> The great festival of the year, known as the Urs [death anniversary] of Baba Farid, takes place at the Muharram [the first month of the Muslim calendar]. . . . The Diwan [spiritual heir of Shaikh Farid] enters the courtyard of the shrine at 9 A.M. with his followers, and proceeds to the mausoleum of Baba Farid, outside of which singers and players have been for some time performing. He enters the mausoleum. . . . The use of instrumental music contrary to the rules of orthodox Muhammadan worship deserves remark. From the 1st of Muharram in addition to the above ceremonies the sacred Sufi dance known as the *sama'* is held daily at 3 P.M. . . . It chiefly consists in

the recitation of verses from the works of Farid and others by singers. . . . The dance
is represented by three Sufis dressed in white, who are conducted with the singers
and from time to time as the spirit moves them execute an uncouth dance, rolling
at times in a condition of ecstasy on the ground. At the conclusion of the ceremony
cowries are flung to the crowd by the Diwan.[39]

Although it may not be self-evident, this short description introduces a number of
features central to the Punjabi literary formation. To see the richness of these passages, we must explore what they imply as much as what they explicitly state. As
I show below, Irving's description notes both the musical performance of Punjabi
literature in a ritual context and its audience at a site that can be considered a zone
of limited intervention by the colonial state. At the same time, the description
gestures toward a patronage system that provided sustenance to musicians and
singers.

Irving's account describes musical performances associated with two distinct
activities. The first is a particular set of *urs* rituals that the Diwan carries out: the
opening of Shaikh Farid's mausoleum, the recitation of the Quran there, followed
by the recitation of Farid's genealogy.[40] A musical performance has been in session
for some time when the Diwan initiates his rites, at 9 A.M., and then the music
accompanies these rituals. Although Irving does not use the term, his description
and its context make clear that this was a *qawwali* performance, an important element of Sufi devotional practice (particularly in the Chishti order) and one that at
Shaikh Farid's shrine would have included the performance of his Punjabi literary
texts.[41] The second activity Irving describes, which took place "daily at 3 P.M." during the *urs,* is also a performance of *qawwali,* though in this case as the foundation
for a Sufi devotional practice known as *sama'.* Both of these performances figure
prominently in Irving's account, and both *qawwali* and *sama'* have historically
been important aspects of Sufi devotionalism.

QAWWALI AND SAMA'

Qawwali is a genre of Muslim devotional music related specifically to Sufi prac-
tice; it is the musical presentation of Sufi poetry. Like many practices in South
Asian Islam, *qawwali* takes broad Islamic concepts and localizes them. Regula
Qureshi, the foremost scholar of this genre, suggests that "qawwali follows the
Islamic conception of religious music or chant where music serves text and religious function[s] . . . but it follows the cultural performance norms of South
Asia."[42] In musical terms, this means that *qawwali* is set to Indian musical meters
and ragas (melodic frameworks) and that it adopts Indian instrumentation, specifically the *dholak* (barrel-shaped drum) and harmonium (reed organ). *Qawwali*
functions "to present mystical poetry in a musical setting so as to arouse mystical

love, culminating in ecstasy, in listeners with diverse spiritual needs."[43] The genre is aimed at spiritual ends through the musical presentation of Sufi texts. It is, according to Qureshi, the central ritual of Sufism in South Asia.[44]

As a style of musical composition and performance, *qawwali* is believed to have originated with Amir Khusraw (1254–1325), a disciple of the Sufi saint Nizamuddin Auliya (1238–1325). As a practice, it is associated with Sufi thought and spiritual goals, and with the Sufi shrine, the traditional site of *qawwali* performances. Sufi shrines, or the lineages that control their resources, are the traditional patrons of this artistic form and commission *qawwali* performances for shrine rituals. The performers are hereditary musicians known as *qawwals*. According to Qureshi, *qawwals* have little status within the "ideological and socio-economic setting of Sufism" despite their critical role in Sufi devotional practice.[45] They are not part of the Sufi lineage of a *khanqah* (hospice), though they are usually attached to a particular shrine with which they have a patron-client relationship: "At the shrine of their affiliation they have a hereditary right to the performance opportunities for *qawwali* generated and controlled by their patron, but they are, in turn, obligated to provide their performing services whenever needed; otherwise their patrons can admit outside performers."[46] The texts they perform—highly guarded today and perhaps also in the past—are from "a repertoire sanctioned by [their] patrons and spiritual experts [of the shrine]."[47] In an interesting paradox, *qawwals* have low status within institutionalized Sufism, yet they are key repositories of poetic compositions by the saint to whose shrine they are attached, his descendants, and also verses composed in his honor.

At shrines in the Punjab, many (though not all) of the texts performed are Punjabi. In Punjab as elsewhere in India, using vernacular languages allowed (and allows) Sufis to make theological concepts accessible to a wider public, concepts that previously circulated only in Arabic and Persian texts.[48] Punjabi compositions that emphasized Sufi themes allowed Sufi poets and adepts to "reach out to the common people, share knowledge, observe humility, and eschew arrogance."[49] The immense popular appeal of Sufi saints in the Punjab can be credited in part to their Punjabi poetry, which circulates widely to this day.

Shaikh Farid is particularly significant in the history of this relationship between Sufi thought and vernacular literary production. He is the first Sufi poet known to have composed in Punjabi, and as such was among the earliest Sufi poets to compose in any Indian vernacular language. In addition, his compositions mark the known literary beginnings of the Punjabi language. From Farid's time through the turn of the twentieth century, a number of prominent Sufis made contributions to Punjabi literature, including Shaikh Sharaf (d. 1323), Shah Husain (c. 1530s–1600), Sultan Bahu (1629–91), Bulleh Shah (1680–1757), Ali Haider (1690–1777), Hasham Shah (1735–1843), Fazl Shah (1827–90), Mian Muhammad Baksh (1830–1907), and Ghulam Farid (1845–1901).[50] A saint's poetry reflected his or her spiritual authority and *baraka* (saintly blessings), and was an important element in devotions at the shrines. *Qawwali*, the principal means of disseminating this poetry, was therefore crucial to this devotionalism. Irving's second observation illustrates this. "From the 1st of Muharram, in addition to the above ceremonies the sacred Sufi dance known as the *sama'* is held daily at 3 P.M. . . . It chiefly consists in the recitation of verses from the works of Farid and others by singers."[51] Although Irving does not elaborate further, his reference makes it clear that these were *qawwali* performances. His reference to the ritual *sama'*, however, incorrectly identifies it as a dance. In fact, *sama'* points to the participatory nature of *qawwali* performance, in which audiences were not merely passive listeners; by listening, they were also engaged in a spiritual quest.

   Sama' is the practice of listening to compositions of Sufi mystical poetry set to music. *Sama'* is a highly developed practice that assists the Sufi adept in progressing through the stages of the Sufi path (*tariqa*) to enlightenment and knowledge of God. Its philosophical foundations were established as early as the eleventh century by, among others, Shaikh Ali al-Hujwiri (who settled in Lahore in 1039; d.1073) in his *Kashf-al Mahjub* (The Unveiling of the Concealed), and it has been an aspect of Sufi practice in South Asia since the thirteenth century.[52] While initially practiced in connection with the intimate group singing of disciples of a given Sufi hospice, the practice of musical performance in South Asian Sufism was subsequently professionalized; consequently, professional singers outside the spiritual lineage of a Sufi hospice performed the ritual music of *sama'*.[53] These musicians are *qawwal*s.

   Qureshi argues that the *sama'* ritual can be conceptualized in two complementary ways. The first is the *mahfil-i sama'*, "a 'gathering for listening,' which serves as a context for the Sufi's encounter with the experience of mystical love through listening to mystical poetry set to music and enhanced by powerful rhythm suggesting *dhikr* [repetition of the name of God]."[54] The second is the *darbar-i auliya*, which represents the Sufi's quest for mystical union. I am more concerned here with the *mahfil-i sama'*, in which lay devotees participated alongside Sufi adepts. For both adept and lay devotee, the concept and sense crucial to *sama'* is listening. The emphasis within *sama'* is not on the music as such, but rather on the "musically embellished mystical poetry."[55] Dance is sometimes associated with *sama'*, but only insofar as the *qawwali* performance moves someone to enter *hal*, or a spiritual state.[56]

   While some listeners must have enjoyed *qawwali* as a musical genre without engaging its devotional aspects, the performances Irving described were clearly devotional, engaged through the highly refined listening practices that are central to *sama'*. In the absence of contemporary ethnographic or historical accounts of listening to *qawwali*, or primary sources that touch on the subject, we can only speculate on this aspect of Punjabi literary and devotional experience. Nonetheless, recent anthropological scholarship on listening helps us consider the possible implications of the circulation of Punjabi texts through *qawwali* and *mahfil-i sama'*. In *The Ethical Soundscape: Cassette Sermons and Islamic Counterpublics*, anthropologist Charles Hirschkind considers the circulation of cassette-recorded sermons by Islamic clerics in contemporary Cairo, with a focus on what is entailed in listening to them.[57] He argues that audiences listen actively and ethically to recorded sermons, since listening is part of a process of moral transformation. For Hirschkind, those Egyptians who share the practice of listening to cassette sermons constitute a "counterpublic," one that emphasizes Islamic moral qualities of the self over the political considerations of the state. What is most significant about this work for my purposes is that it alerts us to the importance of listening as both a sense and a practice. Hirschkind characterizes listening as a form of sociality and shows how listening to shared texts fosters affective ties among listeners. This insight suggests how engaging in a highly refined practice of listening such as *sama'* might have similarly produced ties that helped the Punjabi literary formation cohere.

DIVERSITY IN PARTICIPATION: AUDIENCES

The *urs* that Irving described was one of the largest religious festivals in colonial Punjab, both because Shaikh Farid was revered within the Chishti order and because he had a wide following among the lay population generally. Irving's account conveys something of the magnitude of the event. He described how on the fifth of Muharram, Farid's death anniversary, a stream of devotees passed through the precincts of the shrine "all night long . . . till the sunrise." This stream is "only interrupted when some visiting dignitary from another shrine is specially conducted through with his followers. In all some 40,000 pass through during the night."[58] The following evening's participants were fewer, but it was by no means a small crowd, for "about 20,000 pass on this night," Irving wrote.[59] This crowd was made up of people from near and far, since the shrine was a pilgrimage site. Irving noted that the attendees he saw included "a sprinkling of darvishes and pilgrims" who were "attracted from all parts of India as well as from the border," but that "the *vast majority* of devotees come from Montgomery, Multan, and Bahawalpur," the surrounding districts.[60]

Irving commented on the attendees' religious affiliations as well. Although he identified all of them as Muslim, noting that "the shrine has never . . . attracted Hindu devotees," observations by other colonial folklorists contradict this.[61] Indeed, Flora Annie Steel and R. C. Temple wrote about Hindu devotees of Shaikh Farid, which counters Irving's claim directly. Writing in 1882, Steel and Temple described Shaikh Farid as "worshiped by all classes and creeds, Sikhs, Hindus, Musalmans."[62] In addition to his stature as a Sufi saint, Farid holds an eminent

place in the Sikh canon as one of only two Muslim *sants* (saints) whose compositions are included in the *Adi Granth*. Non-Muslims' devotion to Sufi saints in the
Punjab, as elsewhere in India, was not unique, however. Evidence from the period
unequivocally points to Sufi shrines as places that attracted people of all religious
backgrounds, despite being Muslim institutions.[63]

Sakhi Sarwar's shrine was another important site of such multireligious devotion. Unlike Farid, Sakhi Sarwar does not figure prominently in any of South Asia's
major Sufi orders, nor did his shrine in the Dera Ghazi Khan district of southwest-
ern Punjab draw many adherents from beyond the Punjab. He is an important
figure in Punjabi Sufism, however, who enjoyed a large following in the colonial
period. Harjot Oberoi writes in his history of religious reform in colonial Punjab
that "the vast following of Sakhi Sarvar and the importance of the pir [spiritual
guide] in the popular religion of Punjab is evident in the sacred geography of the
Sarvar cult, which covered vast territories in Punjab."[64] That devotion for the saint
cut across religions is documented in a number of colonial and Indian texts. In
recounting the history of the shrine structure, for example, Temple writes: "The
shrine, as it at present stands, was built, they say, by one Isa of Delhi, in Aurang-
zeb's time (1658–1707 A.D.), and improved by the Diwans Lakhpat Rai and Jaspat
Rai of Lahore about A.D. 1730. These names are significant of the general esteem
of the Saint and the mixed religion of his worshippers."[65] Temple made the latter
comment because these patrons' names were not Muslim.

Max Arthur Macauliffe (1841–1913), a colonial officer posted to the Punjab in the
1860s, who is today best remembered for his six-volume work on Sikhism (1909),[66]
documented a similar trend in devotion to Sakhi Sarwar. Writing of the *urs* at
Sakhi Sarwar's shrine in 1875, Macauliffe observed, "Hindus as well as Musalmans
make offerings at the grave, and invoke the divine intercession of God's Musalman
favourite."[67] Mufti Ghulam Sarwar, author of the *Tarikh-i Makhzan-i Punjab* (History and Record of Punjab; 1884), writes that "hundreds of thousands of people,
Hindus and Muslims, from hundreds of miles around, construct caravans and
make a pilgrimage to the shrine."[68] What Macauliffe and others described in the
late nineteenth century appears to have been true into the twentieth century as
well. Major Aubrey O'Brien wrote in 1911 that Sakhi Sarwar was the greatest shrine
in the western region, where "men, women and children, Sikhs, Hindus and Mo-
hammedans alike, come from all districts in the Punjab."[69] Sikh devotion to Sakhi
Sarwar was particularly widespread, it seems; in the 1911 census, 79,085 Sikhs identified themselves as followers of this Sufi saint.[70]

Sufi shrines were not only ecumenical spaces; they were also among the few
institutional sites in colonial society where women were visibly active. In his essay,
O'Brien noted that "men, women, and children" went to Sakhi Sarwar's shrine.
Some shrines were in fact solely the preserve of women, among them the shrine
of Shah Madar in Hoshiarpur district, known to his devotees as Mian Bibi. The

earliest colonial reference to this shrine appears in the *Revised Settlement Report of Hoshiarpur,* published in 1885. A more complete description is given in Lala Dina Nath's essay "The Cult of Mian Bibi in the Panjab."[71] Dina Nath's principal interest was the Punjabi songs about Mian Bibi sung at his shrine, which he published in both the original and in translation. Nath contextualized these songs by providing general information about the shrine and particular information about rituals held there. Nath noted two things in particular: first, the shrine had Hindu and Muslim "votaries," and second, these votaries were all women, since "Mian Bibi . . . is essentially a saint of the female sex alone."[72] Nath's comments point to women's participation in the Punjabi literary formation through their activities at shrines. Delving further into his description, we find that women participated not only as audience members but also as performers.

Nath described rituals at Mian Bibi's shrine that differed markedly from those at either Shaikh Farid's or Sakhi Sarwar's shrines. There was no annual *urs* celebration, for example, and the rituals enacted there actively involved women. The main ceremony at the shrine took place at harvest time, when one of Mian Bibi's devotees would "prepare herself for adoration." As Dina Nath described it, "on such an occasion Mirasi [a musician lineage] women are called in with their instruments, and the woman in a new dress, and adorned as on her wedding day, sits in front of them. They sing songs in praise of Mian Bibi and descant on his manly beauty, his devotion to the Bibis [women] and their love for him, all the while beating on their small drums."[73] Nath's description of this performance and his collection of songs sung reveal that the songs were in the Punjabi language. Indeed, another way of reading Nath's essay is as a description of a musical performance by and for women and of a set of rituals in which Punjabi poetry was central. Nath's renderings include the following two *kafis* (note the repetition of the opening line):

I

When sways the immortal Shah Madar,
Then may I live.
Thy countenance beams with (heavenly) light.
Thy rest is with God.
When sways the immortal, &c.

II

Shah Madar, I am possessed.
See, Shah Madar, I am possessed.
Saint, at thy coming I am a sacrifice.
Thou are the light of both worlds.
I will offer a black goat, a *man* [an indigenous weight measure] and a quarter of
   flour to the kind saint.
Shah Madar, &c.[74]

As these examples suggest, audiences for performances of Punjabi poetry at Sufi shrines were comprised of both men and women of all religions. They also had diverse class affiliations. Contemporary sources point to the plebeian base of mass participation at shrines. Consider the sixty thousand people Irving describes as passing through the precincts of Shaikh Farid's shrine over the course of two nights. Such numbers suggest mass participation that was almost certainly mostly non-elite. Temple elsewhere gives a slightly clearer indication of the class affiliations of those who attended shrines. In his essay on a song about Sakhi Sarwar, Temple writes, "At this shrine is a vast annual fair, attended from all parts of the Panjab by Hindus, Sikhs and Musalmans of the lower sort alike."[75] An understanding of the class composition of the masses that attended shrines is significant because it points to the complex make-up of the Punjabi literary formation. It included elites such as the Diwan, low-status performance specialists such as *qawwals,* and audiences composed of a cross-section of Punjabi society: Hindu, Sikh, and Muslim, rich and poor.

RELIGIOUS SHRINES IN THE COLONIAL LANDSCAPE

The discussion thus far has focused on activities at Shaikh Farid's, Sakhi Sarwar's, and Mian Bibi's shrines because these are among the shrines for which there are late nineteenth- and early twentieth-century descriptions. Other similar depictions could be added, since district gazetteers and memoirs (by British officials) written throughout the colonial period include descriptions of local shrines and their festivals.[76] The important point is that these descriptions reveal that the trends and practices documented for these three shrines were in evidence across colonial Punjab. This landscape was rich with Sufi shrines, ranging from those of significant Sufis such as Shaikh Farid and al-Hujwiri to figures largely unknown outside their most immediate precincts. Sufism had taken hold in the Punjab during the medieval period, in part because of the region's geography. The Punjab was the site of vital north-south and east-west trade routes that carried ideas as well as commerce.[77] The advance of Ghaznavid power into the Punjab at the beginning of the second millennium brought al-Hujwiri, reputedly the first Sufi to come to India, from his native town near Ghazni to Lahore in 1039. Crucially, Punjab was on the overland route from the Middle and Near East to Delhi, the capital of Muslim dynasties from the late eleventh century. This helps account for the location of Shaikh Farid's shrine. Shaikh Farid settled in the central Punjab entrepôt of Ajudhan (known since the sixteenth century as Pakpattan), a nexus point for trade between Delhi and Multan. Multan itself, the commercial and military key to the southern route into India from the Near East, became a major center of Sufi activity.

Sufi shrines in the Punjab historically served a range of functions. More prominent shrines were often complexes that housed other institutions such as *khanqahs* (hospices) for Sufi adepts, *langars* (food halls), and mosques. Those with *khanqahs* were educational sites where adepts in Sufism were trained through the *pir-murid,* the master-disciple relationship central to Sufi pedagogy. They were also sites of conversion. Shaikh Farid's shrine is perhaps a paradigmatic example of this. Richard Eaton has shown how Shaikh Farid (and subsequently his shrine) became for the local, predominantly non-Muslim population a focal point for devotion. Over generations, this devotion slowly transformed into religious conviction, which came to be identified with Islam.[78] Shrines were sites of popular devotion attended by Sufis and laypeople, Hindus, Muslims, and Sikhs.

In terms of their locations within a broader colonial landscape, Sufi shrines remained at some remove from areas and activities most impacted by colonial rule. This was particularly true in rural contexts. Rural shrines across the Punjab were located more in relation to medieval or early modern patterns of settlement, trade, and agricultural production. Even those established in the late eighteenth and early nineteenth centuries (principally those associated with the Chishti *tariqa,* an order that experienced a resurgence in the Punjab at the time) were located in places that did not figure prominently in the colonial landscape—places such as Taunsa in Dera Ghazi Khan district, Sial Sharif in Shahpur district, Jalalpur in Jhelum district, and Golra in Rawalpindi district, none of which were important colonial towns (e.g., Lyallpur, Sargodha, Montgomery, and Khanewal).[79] But these shrines point to the continuing significance of these locales despite lying outside the areas of greatest colonial intervention.

Although located on the periphery of those places most closely associated with the colonial state's power, Sufi shrines nonetheless represented local and sometimes translocal political power.[80] This power was grounded in the devotion of the local populace, as well as the control of wealth. Under Muslim political administration in the medieval and early modern periods, Sufi shrines were by and large recognized as religious endowments and had received land grants for their upkeep. Sufi institutions thus invariably had ample resources at their disposal. Sufi shrines on the whole retained their perquisites and power through the decline of Mughal power in the eighteenth century, as they did during the period of Sikh rule (1799–1849).[81] In the colonial period, the state identified Sufi institutions as centers of political power. Colonial officials saw in them an opportunity to buttress British rule in the region and sought to co-opt the Punjab's shrines and harness their local political authority.[82] The state did this with a light hand, however; it did not revoke all religious endowments and land grants (though it altered some) or take over direct administration of the shrines. By instituting customary rather than Islamic law in the Punjab, the state reinforced the power of shrine lineages, the descendents of the Sufi saint who controlled the resources of the shrine.[83] Sufi shrines may have been co-opted to serve as intermediaries of colonial power in Punjab but, paradoxically, they were also allowed a great degree of internal independence.

There were two notable exceptions, one that involved the state directly in the management of shrines, and one where state involvement was much less direct and invasive.

Barred from direct control over religious institutions, some colonial officials used the courts to influence shrine management, as historians Gregory Kozlowski and David Gilmartin have shown.[84] By intervening in succession disputes, for example, the state sometimes managed to ally shrine lineages to colonial rule, turning the saints' religious mediation into a form of political mediation.[85] Shaikh Farid's shrine provides a good example of this, as Irving relates:

> From Farid to the present incumbent 30 generations are numbered. On Farid's death his spiritual and temporal functions were divided between his two sons, but this arrangement seems to have been the cause of friction, and was indeed only possible when there were two sons. Since then the incumbent, who bears the title of Diwan, has combined both spiritual and temporal functions. Spiritually he as descendant of the Pir partakes in an undefined manner of his ancestor's sanctity, and is alone competent to perform the ceremonies of the shrine. On the secular side he is not only custodian of the shrine but the owner of the large landed estates attached to it, and recipient of the offerings of the faithful. . . . The incumbency of the shrine passes by natural descent, and the last succession was the subject of prolonged litigation, the Privy Council finally deciding.[86]

Shrines may have operated with relative independence in their own internal affairs—outside of succession disputes that were decided in colonial courts—but they fell subject to new initiatives that the state instituted in Punjab at large. For example, colonial officials shared a concern about the sanitary conditions at shrines that was itself part of a broader colonial discourse on public health. This led to state-introduced changes at some shrines. Sakhi Sarwar's shrine, Temple notes, "has been . . . improved in the matter of water-supply under English occupation, probably for reasons of public health."[87] Given these interventions, Sufi shrines were obviously part of a colonial landscape, and not islands somehow exclusive of colonial authority, laws, and administration. At the same time, the impact of colonial rule was not uniform across the Indian landscape. Shrines can be identified as sites in the landscape where colonial control was more muted than interventionist. This was due both to shrines' spatial locations and because the British vested their rule in Punjab to some extent in their relationships with shrine lineages, particularly in rural areas.

Sikh *gurdwaras* (houses of worship) functioned for the Punjabi literary formation much like Sufi shrines: they too were public sites at which ritual specialists performed Punjabi literature for a diverse audience. The main devotional act in a *gurdwara* is to pay obeisance to the *Adi Granth* as the living guru and to listen to his word (*bani,* words, or *gurbani,* the gurus' words). Many of the compositions in the *Adi Granth* are in Punjabi verse. Verse compositions are sung to musical accompaniment by ritual specialists known as *granthi*s, men (almost exclusively) trained in the exegesis of the text and also, importantly, in its performance. The conception of the *Adi Granth* as a sung or performed text was clearly conveyed by Guru Arjan, the text's compiler, who organized the text by raga (each composition is set to a particular raga), rather than author or chronology. All but one of the *Adi Granth's* compositions are composed in and sung to particular ragas.[88] The *gurdwara* as an institution serves as patron of the *granthi*s and provides them remuneration. The singing of, and listening to, the *Adi Granth* in *gurdwara*s is a form of devotional practice known as *kirtan*. In parallel with the importance of listening in the Sufi practice of *sama'*, Sikh devotion, too, centers on listening to literary texts. Indeed, performance of the *Adi Granth* is so important in Sikhism that acoustic considerations are central to Sikh religious architecture; a *gurdwara* must be constructed in such a way that the sound of the *kirtan* is readily accessible to all attendees. Like Sufi shrines (and in contrast to many Hindu temples) *gurdwara*s have historically been open to both men and women and to people of all classes and creeds. As institutional religious sites, Sufi shrines and *gurdwara*s share one other feature: both were zones of limited colonial control.

Prior to colonial rule in the Punjab, political regimes supported the region's religious institutions—Sikh *gurdwara*s and Sufi shrines—through religious endowments. During Mughal times, most endowments went to mosques and Sufi shrines, but Hindu, Jain, and Sikh religious institutions also received support. During Sikh rule in the region, support for Sikh and Hindu institutions increased considerably. When the British came to power in Punjab, their initial impulse was to continue the endowments of previous governments. Governor-General Dalhousie (1848–56) instructed the Punjab Board of Administration to continue all "bonafide" endowments as long as the communities of worshippers kept up the establishments and buildings. The colonial state thus helped fund religious establishments, and in the case of some *gurdwara*s, officials took an active role in their upkeep, much to the disapproval of the many evangelically minded officers. This policy was officially changed by the all-India Act 20 of 1863, which required local governments to transfer management of religious institutions to appointed trustees "who would thereafter be autonomously self-perpetuating." Although the act called for the complete autonomy of religious institutions, there were exceptions to this rule in the Punjab. Most notably, the British continued to interfere in the running of the Golden Temple, Sikhism's holiest religious site.[89]

Notwithstanding its successful and failed attempts to intervene in the management of religious sites, the state never exercised strict control over these institutions. Shrines and *gurdwara*s (and mosques and temples) were not entirely immune from engagement with central authorities, but the state did not have a free hand. These arenas of Indian experience are therefore distinct from certain others—administration and education, for example—in which colonial authority was dominant, if not hegemonic. The relatively free hand granted religious institutions in managing their own affairs was legislated from 1863 until 1920, when the Charitable and Religious Trusts Act of 1920 established a more direct role for the colonial state.[90] For much of the late nineteenth and early twentieth centuries, therefore, the vast majority of religious institutions in the Punjab enjoyed relative independence from the state, a factor rooted both in legislation and in the spatial logic of colonial India's landscape, with its zones of greater and lesser colonial influence.

RELIGIOUS SHRINES: BEYOND RITUAL PERFORMANCES

The state designated Sufi shrines and Sikh *gurdwara*s as "religious" sites, although colonial observers noted that *mela*s, or fairs, often accompanied religious festivals. In their religious function these were sites where literary performance was part and parcel of religious ritual; in the context of fairs, literary performances pertained more to entertainment and commerce than to religious achievement. J. C. Oman, a teacher at Lahore's Government College in the 1880s and 1890s with an interest in Indian social and religious mores and practices, attended a number of such fairs and recorded his experiences in a memoir. One fair he attended was the Chiragan Mela.

The Chiragan Mela is the name of the *urs* held to celebrate the saint Shah Husain. Shah Husain was an important sixteenth-century Sufi whose shrine is on the outskirts of Lahore. The *mela* drew attendees from the city and surrounding areas, and was a destination both for devotees and for locals seeking entertainment. "Three miles of road lie between Lahore and the old Imperial Gardens [the Mughal-era Shalimar Gardens, which were the site of the *mela*]," Oman writes, "and on a Chiragan fair day the whole distance seems for hours to be almost blocked with the traffic. Driving along with the crowd of vehicles of many descriptions, carrying sight-seers or pleasure-seekers from the city to the *mela,* is certainly neither an expeditious nor an exhilarating business, but need not be unpleasant."[91] *Mela*s such as this one provided an array of entertainments, from hawkers selling books and stalls selling food to fortune-tellers plying their trade. They were also occasions for the performance of and listening to Punjabi literature. Oman described the recitation of a Punjabi romance at the fair: "As I made the round of the fair I came upon a man seated on a chair of European pattern at a small table reciting, for the benefit of a small knot of attentive listeners, the story of the loves of Magnoon and Leila [*sic*]."[92] This is a tantalizing fragment, since it clearly points to literary performance as a form of entertainment at Shah Husain's *urs*. Unfortunately, Oman provides no further details, so we learn nothing more about the performer or his audience.

Nor does Oman comment on the *qawwali* performances that surely occurred at the tomb of Shah Husain itself. Notwithstanding these omissions, Oman's memoir is a rich record of life in colonial Lahore and its environs.

Another of Oman's expeditions led him to the Bhadarkali Mela at Thokar Niaz Beg, the largest fair of its day in the environs of Lahore (figure 9). This *mela* was a celebration at the Kali temple at this site, and Punjabi literature was also performed there. It attracted Hindus and Muslims, men and women, the privileged and the impoverished. Oman recounted a "living stream" of people he passed on his way there, most of them on foot, but he depicted the *mela* as particularly significant for Lahore's Hindu elite because it gave them opportunity to mark their social status through philanthropic deeds. Thus, the wealthy commissioned stalls along the route to distribute water free of charge.[93] This is significant because it points to an intersection of Punjabi literary performance (or a site of this literary performance) with the important practice of philanthropy, on the one hand, and with the opportunity to perform one's social status, on the other.

Another aspect of the *mela* that caught Oman's attention was a theater, "where an *opera* was going to be performed."[94] The entrance fee was one anna (one-sixteenth of a rupee), affordable to people of even limited means. The production Oman recounted was a simple one, with four main characters. There was no stage per se, though a painted curtain backdrop provided scenery. The play was performed with the musical accompaniment of a *sarangi* and tabla, and Oman describes "much singing and dancing." The audience numbered no more than "25 or 30 people," but Oman conjectures that there would likely be a "succession of audiences sufficient to provide the players with what would in their eyes be adequate pecuniary reward for their musical and histrionic talent."[95] Oman provides enough contextual information to suggest that this was a Punjabi performance, particularly when coupled with information from another of his excursions. The one anna for this performance was far less that the four annas to three rupees charged for *Indur Sabha*, a play that Oman attended on another occasion.[96] That play was performed by a *nautanki* troupe, the professional theater of the day, and its performance would certainly have been in Urdu.[97] The *nautanki* theater attracted Lahore's upwardly mobile middle classes, who were increasingly conversant in Urdu as a result of colonial language policy. Attendees at a one-anna performance would have been very different, most likely lower class and uneducated, and therefore without access to Urdu. The play at the Bhadarkali Mela, therefore, was almost surely in Punjabi.

Oman describes another play in his memoir, *Prahlad,* which he attended in Lahore in the 1880s. This was also a Punjabi production, though unlike the one at the Bhadarkali Mela, which appeared to be a commercial venture, this performance had a patron. Although Oman was clearly unimpressed by the play, he recorded

FIGURE 9. Attendees at the Bhadarkali Mela at Thokar Niaz Beg, outside Lahore. Photograph by Aurel Stein, 1904. © The British Library Board (Photo 392/6[6]).

it in some detail as "a good sample of the most popular Indian dramas."[98] His description gives important insights into the context and setting of this theater performance:

> The play was acted at the expense of a successful tradesman, who hoped to acquire some religious merit by having a moral drama produced for the benefit of his fellow-townsmen. Admission being free, the audience was by no means select. . . . There was a stage for the actors; but there were no seats for the audience, who contentedly squatted down on a terrace floor before the stage, under an open canopy of a lovely starlit heaven. . . . The play selected, known as "Prahlad," is a good sample of the most popular Indian dramas. I went to the performance at half-past nine and left at midnight, when the play was only half over. . . . As for the acting in this very serious and moral piece, it was enough to make one laugh outright; though the audience, to judge from their almost reverent attention, seemed very much impressed by it.[99]

Prahlad is a popular Hindu devotional allegory celebrating Vishnu typically told at Holi, the springtime Hindu festival. It is both a moral and a religious tale and, as suggested by Oman's description, it is a popular form of entertainment. In addition to religious merit, this performance appears to have been commissioned as a way to sustain, or perhaps gain, social status.

HEREDITARY OCCUPATIONS

Social status could be marked in other ways as well. As the following vignette highlights, sponsoring a Punjabi performance was a means of marking status in rural or urban settings. The passage below points not only to patronage, but also to the significance of hereditary musicians in Punjabi literary performance traditions. It comes from Charles Swynnerton's *Romantic Tales from the Panjab* (1903), a compilation of oral romances collected during Swynnerton's service in the province.[100] The first entry in this volume is "The Love Story of Hir and Ranjha," in which Swynnerton describes how he "picked up" this tale. The description of the performance is one of the most detailed from the period, but at the same time it is laden with the most common colonial tropes about Indian society:

> Riding one day along the mountain road that leads from Abbottabad to the village of Bagnota . . . I turned aside at Damtaur . . . and entered the narrow tortuous streets of the village. . . . As I advanced I could distinguish the rhythmical beating of a tom-tom varied with the strains of a *suringa* [sarangi] and now and then the vociferous singing of some professional bard. . . . When I arrived at the open space in front of the *hujra*, or general guest-house, I found assembled there a company of wedding-guests, all of the nobler sex, who were standing or squatting under a huge *pipal*-tree, listening to the black-bearded minstrel, Sher, son of Mirza, whose fame abounded over all that country side. What was the legend? It was the thrilling adventures of Raja Rasalu, Panjab paladin without a peer, and I was just in time before dismounting to catch the hero's last dying speech, which, being in verse, was duly sung to the scraping of an ancient viol, when his auditors, greedy for more, set up the cry—"Hir and Ranjha! Hir and Ranjha! O excellent *mirasi*, tell us the story of Hir and Ranjha!" . . . The idlers in the rude verandahs around moved nearer to the original group; from the shadows of blank walls and places unknown emerged several grey-beards, casting their cotton togas about their stately forms as they approached; timid-faced girls, darkly-veiled, gazed from house-tops, or peeped from neighboring doors; and some staid matrons, returning home with pitchers of river-water on their graceful heads, shyly came to a halt between sunlight and shade, if so be they might catch fragments of a love-tale.[101]

Swynnerton's description alludes to aspects of the Punjabi literary formation that I have discussed: patronage for performance specialists, diversity of the formation's participants, and performance in marked spaces. His description also alerts us to how sponsoring public performances was a way to articulate social status. What is perhaps most explicit in Swynnerton's description, what he was best able to capture, was people's pleasure in this literary and performance tradition.

The central figure in Swynnerton's description is the *mirasi* performer (figure 10). Before examining other aspects of this ethnographic vignette, let me describe the *mirasi*'s role as a specialist in the performance of Punjabi literature. *Mirasis* were, and remain today, a Muslim hereditary occupational group or lineage. Traditionally, *mirasis* have been genealogists and musicians.[102] Although they have historically commanded a relatively low social status in Punjabi society, they fulfilled an important function as genealogists for the landed elite. Their relationship with the elite was grounded in a patron-client relationship. Mufti Ghulam Sarwar described the group in the following terms in his *Tarikh-i Makhzan-i Punjab:* "Mirasis . . . have memorized the name of every individual in their client's genealogy. Typically, they read the genealogy of the family out at occasions such as betrothals and marriages. Because of this they have established rights with the landed class. They make their living through the patronage of the landed class because it is their hereditary occupation."[103] To give some measure of the value of this social function, during Punjab's partition in 1947, when Punjabi Muslims migrated almost wholesale from east to west Punjab (as did Hindus and Sikhs, from west to east Punjab), many Muslim *mirasis* stayed on in their villages in east Punjab at the behest and under the protection of their patrons.[104]

If *mirasis* were important to local elites, they also played an important role as entertainers. In this latter capacity they served a broader public through performances at popular venues such as fairs. They were one of a number of such groups in the Punjab, many of whom performed in religious contexts as well (e.g., the women *mirasis* at Bibi Mian's shrine, described above). Among these were: *dhadis*—Sikh musicians and singers who performed at *gurdwaras* and as entertainers at large (there are also Sufi *dhadis*);[105] *dums*—musicians and dancers, referred to in colonial ethnography as the Hindu counterpart of *mirasis*;[106] yogis—wandering mendicants of the Nath sect who also functioned as singers, musicians, and popular entertainers;[107] *bhirains*—drummers; *pernas*—known for their female singers; *qalanders*—peripatetic wanderers who served as village entertainers, playing popular tunes, sometimes on bagpipes; *putlivalas*—puppeteers; *na't khwans*—who sang songs in praise of the prophet Muhammad; and *dastangohs* and *qissa khwans*—both groups of storytellers.[108] For each of these, as for the *mirasis*, performing Punjabi literature was intrinsic to their occupation. This relationship between Punjabi literature and hereditary occupations is important for understanding the tradition's survival through the late nineteenth century.

In Swynnerton's description, the *mirasi*'s performance was part of a wedding celebration. It is clear that the performer was there at the behest of a patron who was entertaining wedding guests and other villagers alike, thereby marking his social status. The performance site—by the village pipal tree—gave villagers access to the performance (figure 11). This open-air site in village contexts traditionally served as a space for gatherings and meetings of village elders (the *panchayat*)

FIGURE 10. "Sharaf, a Panjabi Bard [*mirasi*]." From Charles Swynnerton, *Romantic Tales from the Panjab* (London: Archibald Constable, 1903), between xxxii and xxxiii.

and others as well. By performing there, the *mirasi* occupied a space associated with village communal activities. Not only did the performance draw on these communal associations, it also allowed villagers not otherwise invited to the wedding to join the audience alongside invited guests, who likely shared the relatively high social status of their host. The audience, then, was comprised of those gathered around the performer and those who observed from the margins and the shadows. Although those in the shadows were mostly women, women also stood in the main audience (as seen in figure 11). Lastly, we see in this vignette the interactive nature of Punjabi oral performances. The *mirasi* would have performed *Hir-Ranjha*—a tale with which the audience was clearly familiar—in response to popular request.

In sum, Swynnerton's description illustrates how the performance of Punjabi literary texts intersected with important social customs in Punjabi society, how it was embedded in the practices of everyday life. It alludes to the relationship between Punjabi literature and certain hereditary occupations as well as to the connections between *mirasis* and their landed patrons. It shows that performance was deemed a fitting and desirable adjunct to a wedding ritual; how patrons used performance to mark social status and the class and gender diversity of the audience. Of the texts performed, the two that Swynnerton mentions by name are both Punjabi *qisse*. This description also adds an additional layer of diversity to the Punjabi literary formation, one only implicit thus far: people in urban and rural contexts both participated. Indeed, some performance specialists moved between urban and rural clients because of their peripatetic nature. This was true of performers such as *sains*, fakirs, and yogis, all of whom were wandering mendicants. Unlike *mirasis*, these were not hereditary lineage groups but were constituted by those who had chosen to take up a renunciatory ascetic life, often marked by devotion to a religious person or saint. These men (we have few references to women in these groups) performed Punjabi literature as a form of religious devotion. Steel and Temple write of the Faridis, fakirs devoted to Shaikh Farid, and the Sansis and Sultanis, whose "main object of veneration . . . [was] Sakhi Sarwar Sultan," all of who wandered the Punjab singing compositions by and in praise of these saints.[109]

. . .

By reviewing accounts of Punjabi literary performances from the late nineteenth century, this chapter has underscored one of the key features of the Punjabi literary formation: its low threshold of belonging. The people who constituted this formation represent a cross-section of the Punjab's inhabitants. Their diversity makes the literary formation an excellent vantage point for reconsidering the history of late nineteenth-century Punjab. Colonial Punjab has a rich historiography, but one that has largely centered on the examination of religious, caste, and class groups,

FIGURE 11. "Sharaf the Bard Telling His Stories," 1903. From Charles Swynnerton, *Romantic Tales from the Panjab,* xxi.

or particular institutions. For example, there is a rich historiography of religious political formations,[110] and another of religious reform that examines (usually separately) Sikh, Hindu, and Muslim movements.[111] In Sikh and Hindu contexts, reformist movements—principally the Arya Samaj and the Singh Sabha—also had self-conscious (middle-) class ambitions.[112] Other studies have focused on particular caste groups, such as the Jats.[113] And given the Punjab's role as the principal recruiting ground for the British Indian Army in the late nineteenth century, there is also a small but important body of scholarship devoted to this institution.[114] The Punjabi literary formation, in contrast, provides an opportunity for a cross-religious, cross-caste, cross-class analysis of Punjab's late nineteenth- and early twentieth-century political, social, and cultural history.

The literature around which this formation cohered circulated in colonial Punjab through multiple media: manuscripts, printed books, and oral performances in both secular and religious settings. This chapter has focused on its performance at a range of sites. While we cannot know the precise texts performed in each of the contexts presented here, the information available shows that *qissa* texts, such as *Laila-Majnun* and *Hir-Ranjha,* would have circulated in all of these sites. Citing *Hir-Ranjha* as an example, we see that various Sufis took it up in their Punjabi compositions, most notably Shah Husain and Bulleh Shah, and these would have been sung in *qawwali* performances at their shrines. *Hir-Ranjha* would have been performed by *mirasi*s as part of their repertoire, as it was by the *mirasi* Sharaf in Swyynerton's account. *Hir-Ranjha* would have been performed at fairs, just as *Laila-Majnun* was performed at the Chiragan Mela, mentioned above. Similarly, this romance could have been performed as a play, as was *Prahlad* in Oman's account. An audience at any one of these performances would have been aware that the text they were listening to circulated in the other contexts, whether through their own experience, through others' knowledge, or through the content of the text itself. But what are the implications of their awareness of these patterns of circulation?

These patterns of circulation affected how the texts were received. For their audiences, Punjabi texts were imbued with the historical memory of their circulation. If communities can be "fuzzy," as Sudipta Kaviraj has argued so effectively, then perhaps we can think of these texts as "sticky."[115] In other words, a text's significance was constituted by all the various contexts in which it was performed. Punjabi literature's oral circulation was a central part of the literary tradition. Thus, when a text like *Hir-Ranjha* was sung at a wedding celebration, its meaning for its audience in that context was in part constituted by its performance in other times and places—at fairs, at Sufi shrines, as theater—and by the practices and rituals that inhered in each of those contexts. These other performances were known to audiences because they were constitutive of the literary tradition itself. It is the "stickiness" of Punjabi literary texts—their layered accumulated meanings in the Punjabi literary formation—that helps us understand the tradition's durability throughout an era when colonialism was in many ways reshaping Indian society. Not only did texts accrue meaning through their multiple performance sites, they were also open to multiple, simultaneous interpretations.

4

Place and Personhood

In her important book *Fiction in the Archives,* historian Natalie Zemon Davis underscores how, in writing histories from traditional archival records, historians often work with texts that have literary qualities, what Davis refers to as their "fictional qualities" or "their forming, shaping, and molding sentiments: the crafting of a narrative."[1] Despite the influence of the linguistic and cultural turns made by historians in the last twenty years, moving actual fiction to the center of scholarly analysis—as opposed to using government archives with "fictional" aspects—has remained more the purview of literary critics than that of historians.[2]

This book argues that in certain historical contexts historians can find archives in the fiction. By placing Punjabi *qisse* and the Punjabi literary formation at the center of my analysis I engage what I have called, broadly, a vernacular culture. This term is meant to signal both the local rootedness of Punjabi print and performance traditions but also that the patterns of cultural production, circulation, and reception examined here are not isolated to the Punjab. In this chapter, I want to shift the scale of analysis away from broad patterns of literary production and circulation to focus on individual texts; in particular, colonial-era printed renditions of *Hir-Ranjha.* This chapter focuses on three themes in particular, each of which is critical to notions of self and community. The first is *zat* (caste or kinship group), which figures in these texts as the most salient category of social organization. The second is territoriality, which emphasizes the affective attachments people established with the local, and particularly their natal places. The third is gender: *Hir-Ranjha* texts portray female figures, particularly Hir, as having remarkable power given their patriarchal context. Taken together, the way these themes emerge in this literature prompts a reconsideration of what structured and animated everyday life for the Punjabi literary formation in the late nineteenth and early twentieth centuries.

At the same time, each of these three aspects of vernacular culture destabilizes well-entrenched narratives in modern South Asian historiography. That *zat*—which can be a cross-religious formation—was a fundamental marker of individual and community identity undermines perhaps the most significant narrative in modern South Asian history: the rising significance of religious identity and the ascendance of communal politics from the late nineteenth century onward that resulted in the partition of India in 1947. An analysis of *zat* in *Hir-Ranjha* suggests that while the British fundamentally altered how caste operated in Indian society, in late-colonial north India older notions of kinship nevertheless continued to shape everyday experience. Analysis of notions of territoriality in the Punjabi literary formation shows not only the limits of nationalist imaginings at the regional level, but also how region itself was not a stable or self-evident geographic entity. This contrasts with the longstanding focus in the Indian historiography of this period on nationalist imaginings and discourse and an attendant desire to fashion a national state space. Rather, the region emerges in this literature as a territorial unit that is at best difficult for the nation to appropriate.

The representations of gender relations in which women are active agents prompts at minimum a reconsideration of existing historiography's emphasis on the ways socioreligious reformers and nationalists alike reinscribed women's inferior status in society, limited their social roles, and subordinated and subjected them to patriarchal norms and desires. My intention in raising these challenges to the existing historiography is not to be iconoclastic, but rather to show how focusing upon the history of a vernacular culture disrupts the ease with which historians, and scholars of South Asia more generally, have come to accept these historiographical certitudes.

Before turning to colonial-era *Hir-Ranjha* texts themselves, let us revisit the main narrative elements of the romance as they had been established through the eighteenth century. These include Ranjha's epic journey from Takht Hazara to Jhang. Ranjha's self-imposed exile from his natal village is prompted by treatment his brothers meted out to him upon their father's death. The youngest of eight brothers, Ranjha had been his father's favorite and led a carefree life. When his father dies, however, his brothers cheat him of a viable share of their father's land, and his sisters-in-law taunt him. Unable to tolerate his circumstances in Takht Hazara, Ranjha leaves in search of the renowned beauty Hir. His travels take him through daunting terrain, where the *panj pir* (five saints, explained in more detail below) appear both to comfort him and to sanction his search for Hir. Ranjha takes solace in their support and continues his journey through a forest where he finds a mosque and adjoining settlement. Here, he encounters a cleric and villagers before moving on to the final hurdle on his quest to meet Hir: how to cross the

Chenab River, on whose far bank lies Hir's town of Jhang. Ranjha uses his wiles to convince the greedy boatman (Luddan) and his licentious wife to give him passage. In some renditions he meets Hir on this boat, in others only upon arriving on the far bank. In either case, the two immediately fall in love and Hir arranges for Ranjha to become her father's cowherd. Each day Ranjha takes the Sial family buffaloes to pasture on the banks of the Chenab River, where he and Hir meet furtively and their love flourishes.

Hir's scheming uncle Keido learns of the liaison and shatters Hir and Ranjha's idyll by informing her family. Hir's parents refuse to accept Ranjha as a suitor, considering him of low status—gauging by his occupation as a cowherd rather than by his landed heritage—and insist that she marry someone more suitable. They, and community elders, find a more appropriate and advantageous match for Hir in Seido Khera, whom Hir is forced to marry. Hir resolves to remain faithful to Ranjha and refuses to consummate her marriage. Distressed by Hir's marriage, Ranjha retreats to a yogi monastery at Tilla Jogian, where he takes on a yogi's guise in a bid to reunite with Hir. Disguised in the outward trappings of a yogi of the Nath Siddha sect—dress, ornaments, and begging bowl in hand—Ranjha goes to Rangpur, Hir's married home. Here he encounters Hir's sister-in-law, Sehti, who is at first decidedly unsympathetic. As a woman herself separated from her lover, Sehti finally relents and helps Ranjha elope with Hir. Their honor sullied, the Kheras pursue the lovers to the court of Adali Raja (King Adali). Although the raja initially rules that Hir should be returned to her married home, he ultimately decides that the lovers should be reunited. Hir's family then tricks Hir and Ranjha into thinking that they will sanction their marriage, only to kill Hir for her behavior. Ranjha learns of Hir's fate and dies from his grief. Not all *Hir-Ranjha* texts elaborate on each of these narrative elements, but from the eighteenth century on most follow these general contours.

SOCIAL ORGANIZATION

The title *Hir-Ranjha,* along with the many variations encountered in earlier chapters, announces the significance of *zat* in this *qissa* tradition. While Hir is known by her given name, her lover is known by his *zat*: Ranjha. *Zat* operates in two significant ways in *Hir-Ranjha*. First, it is the social category most privileged for defining notions of selfhood and community. Second, it is the root cause of conflict in the narrative's overall plot, which points to a contemporary anxiety about social classifications and, more importantly, to their malleability. Before turning to a reading of *zat* in *Hir-Ranjha* texts, let us attend to the system of social organization it references.

Thus far, "caste" and "kinship group" have been used as synonyms for *zat.* While these terms help approximate *zat,* they do not capture its full complexity.

Both caste and kinship group emphasize social structure, which is an important aspect of *zat*. But another of its meanings—one that is implicated in that social system and important to understanding how it has historically functioned in Indian society—deserves consideration. That meaning is essence, substance, or nature.[3] It is this meaning, for example, that best explains the use of *zat* in Mughal administration for the numerical rank ordering of its nobility. *Zat* as a concept implies the innate qualities individuals possess, but which are, in turn, shared by the group these individuals constitute. In the latter sense, *zat* refers to a corporate social identity, a notion that has been translated into English alternately as caste, tribe, clan, and occupation group. *Zat*'s complexity inheres in the fact that it refers on the one hand to both individual and collective identity, and on the other to multiple, nested identities. In *Hir-Ranjha* texts, for example, *zat* refers simultaneously to different registers of social collectivity. Thus, it is used for the category Jat, a category to which Hir, Ranjha, and Seido all belong, but it simultaneously refers to the social groupings Sial, Ranjha, and Khera, each a discrete subdivision of the category Jat, to which Hir, Ranjha, and Seido respectively belong.

Historically, and into the present, *zat* functions in the Punjab and other north Indian contexts across the Hindu, Sikh, Muslim, and Christian communities. Among Hindus and Sikhs, contemporary and historical evidence suggests that *zat* functioned like *jati*.[4] Indeed, historian Susan Bayly states in her study of caste that *zat* is simply "a regional variant on the word jati."[5] *Jati* refers to a named endogamous kinship group.[6] *Jatis* were usually localized, though some were regional and even transregional, and they were often related to a hereditary occupation. To say that *zat* functioned like (or was) *jati* is also to suggest that it represents a hierarchical system of social status and differentiation.

Zat also operated among Muslims in the Punjab. Historian P. H. M. van den Dungen suggested some years ago that "the egalitarian tradition of Islam had some, though no great influence, on Panjab society," and that nineteenth-century Punjabi Muslims lived in a socially stratified society much like that of their Hindu and Sikh neighbors. "Islam also superimposed its own status concepts on the indigenous Hindu ones," he writes, citing the generally recognized superior social position of the *ashraf* (noblemen): Sayyids, Shaikhs, Mughals, and Pathans, for example.[7] *Hir-Ranjha* texts suggest that during this period *zat* was central to Muslim experience alongside notions of *ashraf* and *ajlaf* (the lower orders). Unfortunately, there have been few studies of how *zat* operated in colonial Punjab. Brian Caton's otherwise informative essay "Social Categories and Colonisation in Panjab, 1849–1920," one of the few recent studies of social systems in colonial Punjab, does not even mention *zat*, for example. He focuses instead on the indigenous terms *misl* ("normally a temporary combination of corroborated claims of descent"), and *qaum* (clan, community, sect or nation, depending on context).[8] Analyses of current social practice, however, help in a broader consideration of how *zat* operates in Muslim communities, if not in precisely how it functioned in colonial Punjab.

Scholars concur that Muslims in the Punjab, and indeed across much of South Asia, employ systems of social stratification. There is little consensus on how best to characterize these systems, however, or on the degree to which Muslim social stratification resembles the Hindu caste system. Sociologist Imtiaz Ahmad argues that kinship structures among South Asian Muslims are "caste-like system[s] of social stratification," though distinct in their functioning without the scriptural authority that in Brahmanical Hindu tradition undergirds caste.[9] Others disagree, arguing that Muslim social stratification is not hierarchical like Hindu caste, and that the concept of *biraderi* (brotherhood, kinship system, or descent group) is a more compelling analytic.[10] Hamza Alavi was one influential proponent of this position, writing that for the Duddhi Rajputs of the Punjab, *zat* "did not indicate a position within any ranked social order. They did not recognize any holistic hierarchical social order to which all *zats* could be said to belong and be classified accordingly. Nor were there any rules, rituals or ceremonies through which any status ranking with other *zats* could be manifested. The essential elements of 'caste' were missing."[11] If Alavi is correct in suggesting that in postcolonial Pakistani Punjab (his field site) there was no "status rank ordering" of *zats*, then *Hir-Ranjha* texts portray *zat* operating differently in colonial Punjab. In their literary representations—always set in a Muslim context—*zat* marked not only solidarities and differences, but also social hierarchies and status. We can turn to *Hir-Ranjha* texts to see how and when hierarchies are invoked, and by whom, to help us better understand how *zat*, and corporate social identity more generally, operated in colonial Punjab.

Zat in colonial-era *Hir-Ranjha* texts operates in two ways: in its relation to the individual, and in its relation to group solidarity. In these texts, *zat* is one of the primary ways in which characters identify themselves and others. The relationship between the individual and his or her *zat* identity is perhaps most closely fused in the character of Ranjha. Similarly important references to *zat* feature in other characters' identities as well. Hir and her family are Sials, and Seido is a Khera, both of which are *zat* names. The association between individual and *zat* is so seamless that these characters are often referred to as Hir Sial and Seido Khera, as if their *zats* were part of their personal names. Particularly telling in this regard are instances when strangers meet. Kishan Singh 'Arif's text provides a typical exchange. In the passage relating Hir and Ranjha's first encounter, Hir's immediate question to Ranjha is: "What is your name, your *zat?*" Ranjha responds, "Dhido is my name, Ranjha is my *zat*, my village is Hazara."[12] Time and again, *Hir-Ranjha* texts exhibit the same pattern.

The importance of *zat* in identifying oneself and using it to locate oneself or another in a broader community is common to *Hir-Ranjha* texts from Damodar's seventeenth-century *qissa*. There we find repeatedly that the first question strangers pose to Ranjha is: "What is your zat?"[13] *Zat* also figures prominently in Damodar's framing of the narrative. His invocation includes the following signature: "My name is Damodar, my *zat* Gulati, I have created this *qissa*."[14] Eighteenth-century texts similarly privilege the importance of *zat*. Indeed, in Muqbal's rendition, we find a line almost identical to that in 'Arif's text. In his recounting of the scene in which Ranjha encounters a mullah, or cleric, Muqbal writes: "He [the mullah] asks him [Ranjha], 'Where have you come from, where are you going?' He answers, 'My name is Dhido, by *zat* a Ranjha, I have come from Takht Hazara.'"[15] From Damodar's era through the colonial period, then, in the *Hir-Ranjha* narrative tradition *zat* remained central to how characters identified themselves and others, and to how they located themselves and others in a social context.

Zat also establishes the narrative's core conflict. That conflict centers on Hir's parents' rejection of Ranjha as a suitor for their daughter because they perceive a gulf between his status and theirs. This issue of status is articulated through the idiom of *zat*. The question of status compatibility is not an entirely straightforward issue in the narrative, however, since Ranjha—both as a Jat and as a Ranjha—is appropriate to the status of the Sials. He, like them, is a landowning Jat, at least by birth. Hir's entreaties to her mother that her love is acceptable in her parents' terms, and that her illicit relationship can be transformed into a socially sanctioned marriage, hinges on this fact of similarly landowning Jat status. The following dialogue between Hir and her mother Malki in Kishan Singh 'Arif's *Qissa Hir te Ranjhe da* demonstrates this. It portrays Malki's anger over Hir's relationship with Ranjha, which has become public. Hir's family refuses to accept Ranjha as her suitor and insists that she give up the relationship. 'Arif reveals the grounds for the family's disapproval through Hir's response to her mother's anger: "Don't put so much pressure on me. I am a Jat, he [Ranjha] is a Jat, what's all the commotion about?"[16] In this example, we find Hir using *zat* differently than in the examples cited above, where it referred to subdivisions of the social collective Jat. Here, it refers to the broader, inclusive category. Hir's statement is an appeal to social solidarity, pointing out that she and Ranjha share a social identity and therefore have the same status. Hir's words further enrage her mother, however, and she responds with violent anger: "We should strangle and kill you, we should cut your nose off!" This statement is immediately followed by Malki's dismay: "Where has this stray come from," she asks, "this cowherd, no-good Jat!" Hir responds to her mother's violence with equanimity, saying: "Ranjha shares our *zat*. Don't call him defiled, a servant, and of lesser *zat* [*kam-zat*]. He grazes the buffalo day and night only for my sake."[17]

Note that *zat* here quite clearly refers to a different kind of social collective than in the earlier examples. Here, the reference is not to a social collective that separates Hir and Ranjha (Sial and Ranjha), but to the broader, inclusive category Jat.

The term *kam-zat* underscores the hierarchical nature of *zat* relationships. *Kam* literally means "less," and in this compound construction translates as "lesser." Hir's parents reject Ranjha because they consider him to belong to a "lesser" or inferior *zat*, a status that is further colored by his occupation. Hir's parents consider Ranjha an unsuitable match for their daughter because they are landowners, a high status in the social economy of Punjab's agrarian society, while Ranjha is a cowherd, a low-status occupation. This gulf in status is complicated by the fact that Ranjha has adopted the guise of a cowherd. The reader or listener knows, as does Hir, that Ranjha was born to a higher social standing. He, too, is from a landowning lineage. This narrative element is critical because it means that Hir is not actually transgressing *zat*-based norms. Interestingly, she does not argue for the rejection of *zat* and its hierarchical structure. Rather, her response to her parents' rebuke is only to argue that her *zat* and Ranjha's are in fact compatible.

This exchange alerts us to an underlying issue at the heart of the *Hir-Ranjha* narrative: the complicated question of whether *zat* is immutable—as a person's essence, substance, or nature, or mutable—as is, say, one's occupation. Hir holds the former position. To her parents, Ranjha's occupation as a cowherd—the ruse that has allowed him access to Hir—demeans his status and makes him unacceptable as a potential son-in-law. Interestingly, Ranjha, too, suggests that he has suffered a loss of status by working as a cowherd. In Muhammad Shah's rendition (c. 1908), Ranjha says, "Falling in love with you has destroyed me, Hir [sexually and socially; *tere ishq mari jat pat Hirey*]. . . . The entire world now knows, oh Hir, that I became a cowherd of the Sials of Jhang."[18]

As a corpus, colonial-era *Hir-Ranjha* texts do not cohere around a single viewpoint on *zat*'s mutability or immutability. On one hand, they can be read as supporting the immutability of *zat* in their positive portrayal of Hir and Ranjha's love; on the other hand, Ranjha's (perceived) loss of status is a key point of tension in the narrative. This treatment of *zat* points to an ongoing anxiety about social classifications and their malleability. Note the continuing centrality of *zat* in the *Hir-Ranjha* tradition from the seventeenth through twentieth centuries.

The tensions around *zat* in colonial India were quite different from those of precolonial India, however. Part of the difference resulted from the colonial state inscribing indigenous social classifications in Indian society, and particularly in the Punjab, in entirely new ways, especially by translating them into the language of caste and tribe. The post-1858 colonial state in India was notable for the renewed vigor with which it sought to "map" Indian society, most obviously through its decennial census but also through the production of gazetteers, glossaries, settlement reports, linguistic surveys, and tribe and caste compendiums. In this "ethnographic state," as Nicholas Dirks has called it, data collection and collation were not passive activities.[19] By mapping Indian society, colonial officials took what they deemed to be Indian "traditions" and transformed them through a range of discursive practices, legal instruments, and alterations in the material environment. In his *Castes of Mind: Colonialism and the Making of Modern India*, Dirks argues that the most significant of these transformations was that of caste, which from the late nineteenth century became "the sign of India's fundamental religiosity, a marker of India's essential difference from the West and from modernity at large." More significant for the present discussion, he argues, "It was under the British that 'caste' became a single term capable of expressing, organizing, and above all 'systematizing' India's diverse forms of social identity, community, and organization."[20]

The privileging of caste marked a shift away from other forms of colonial knowledge about Indian society. Anthropologist Gloria Goodwin Raheja suggests that an earlier emphasis on language changed to an emphasis on caste. In her formulation, early nineteenth-century officials such as H. H. Wilson believed the mastery of India was associated solely with mastering its languages. In the last three decades of the nineteenth century, however, "this mastery of India was coupled, decisively . . . to the mastery of castes as well, and earlier colonial discourses that did not see caste identities as fundamental in Indian society were marginalized and forgotten."[21] Caste may have become preeminent in colonial discourse in the late nineteenth century and the fundamental marker of Indian society for colonial officials, but what precisely did those officials mean by "caste"? Was India uniformly understood through this idiom? Or, to put the question a little differently: to what extent was the "ethnographic state" able to create or even define a coherent vision of caste?

Colonial officer Denzil Ibbetson, who carried out the 1881 census of the Punjab, opens his chapter "The Races, Castes and Tribes of the Panjab" in the following manner: "An old agnostic is said to have summed up his philosophy in the following words: 'The only thing I know is that I know nothing; and I am not quite sure that I know that.' His words express very exactly my own feelings regarding caste in the Panjab."[22] Despite this protestation of particular ignorance, Ibbetson proceeds in the following 169 pages (in the original text) to lay out a very distinct vision of how caste operated in the province, one which differed from the idea of caste that had by then become dominant in colonial discourse. Ibbetson first elaborates on that dominant understanding. "The popular and currently received theory of caste I take to consist of three main articles," he writes:

1. that caste is an institution of the Hindu religion, and wholly peculiar to that religion alone;
2. that it consists primarily of a fourfold classification of people in general under the heads of Brahman, Kshatriya, Vaisya, and Sudra [*varna*];
3. that caste is perpetual and immutable, and has been transmitted from generation to generation throughout the ages of Hindu history and myth without the possibility of change.[23]

Ibbetson then states that he can find very little evidence that social practice in the Punjab corresponds to this definition. In making this claim, Ibbetson reiterates a position established in the early decades of colonial rule in the province, one that broke with the idea that Indian society was best understood through caste (as associated with Brahmanical Hinduism), and with the colonial state's practice of making Indian society legible through its religious communities. As Caton writes, "Although Orientalists and British administrators by 1858 had conceptualised Indian society as fundamentally religious, members of the Punjab Commission believed that Panjabis were measurably different from the rest of India on religious questions. . . . Richard Temple claimed that 'the Punjabees are not so ticklish & bigoted about caste & religion as Hindoostanees.' By the end of the nineteenth century, at least, many British officials had concluded that caste, as enunciated in documents or by Brahmans from Gangetic India, did not exist in Panjab."[24] This is not to say that colonial administrators thought that caste did not operate in Punjab, only that it was particular and discrete from caste elsewhere. Ibbetson's further remarks on the issue make this apparent: "I think that I should still be far nearer to the truth if, in opposition to the popular conception [of caste] thus defined, I were to say," he writes,

1. that caste is a social far more than a religious institution; that it has no necessary connection whatever with the Hindu religion . . . and that conversion from Hinduism to Islam has not necessarily the slightest effect upon caste;
2. [that *varna* is not important in the Punjab];
3. that nothing can be more *variable* and more difficult to define than caste.[25]

Ibbetson saw caste as more of a social than a religious institution, and believed that its mutability was grounded in the fact that occupation, rather than heredity, was its primary basis.

This definition of caste came to inform colonial understandings of social organization in the Punjab. Even though it was broad enough to include non-Hindus, the colonial state nonetheless hesitated to use the term in the case of Muslims. For Muslims, the colonial state alighted upon the language of tribe, though the definition of tribe largely approximated Ibbetson's redefinition of caste. Indeed, in the Punjab "tribe" became the principal idiom for understanding and administering the province. David Gilmartin writes, "From a relatively early date the British attempted, as a matter of policy, to tie their rural administration to the structure of rural kinship as they perceived it."[26] In so-called tribal leaders the state found intermediaries for its rule, "so-called" because the leadership structure the colonial state instituted was "to a large extent artificial, adapted to serve the administrative needs of the British as much as to reflect an indigenous 'tribal' structure."[27] Tribe, then, became a term into which a range of indigenous systems of social classification could be collapsed, including: *zat, qaum, biraderi, misl,* and *jati.* The leadership structure that the state instituted may have been artificial, but having alighted upon tribe as the key to Punjabi social organization (particularly for rural Muslim Punjab), administrators institutionalized this structure in colonial law. Unlike other parts of India, where personal law was based on religious affiliation, personal law in the Punjab was based on the customs of the region's "officially" recognized tribes. Since no compendium of tribal customary law existed, colonial officials were deputed to create one. The *Riwaj-i Ams*—attempts to codify tribal customs at the local level produced in the early decades of colonial rule—were superseded in 1881 by a more "systematic" collection: C. L. Tupper's three-volume *Punjab Customary Law*.[28]

Colonial efforts to regulate how caste operated through the courts, and the recognition (or, perhaps more accurately, creation) of a "tribal" structure, can be read as attempts to fix social practice, to fix social relations as the colonial state understood them. But in one of the ironies of colonial rule, as one arm of the state became invested in social stability, colonial interventions in Punjab's economy caused all manner of social change and dislocation. Van den Dungen shows how, in the late nineteenth century, the colonial context produced changes in status and occupation among low castes such as Malis, Labanas, and Kalals, which resulted in their upward social mobility.[29] If the colonial context provided opportunities for the upward mobility of some, then it also unsettled the social position of others. It produced instability, for example, for certain agricultural groups such as Jats, Gujars, and Rajputs, who increasingly suffered financial distress forcing them to sell their land.[30] The state found this instability in the very group—agriculturalists—to whom they had tethered their rule extremely threatening, so they passed the Punjab Alienation of Land Act of 1900. The act designated official agricultural and nonagricultural castes and tribes, and made alienation of land from the former to the latter illegal.[31] These measures reflected a colonial assumption that caste and tribe were immutable, a position quite different from that espoused by Ibbetson some twenty years earlier.

This was the context in which *Hir-Ranjha* texts circulated in colonial Punjab. What might these texts help us understand about both indigenous notions of social classification and the colonial state's engagement with and manipulation of indigenous social categories? First, it suggests why *Hir-Ranjha* texts were an important site of social commentary in the late nineteenth and early twentieth centuries. The prominence of *zat* in this narrative and the question of its immutability or mutability corresponds to the contemporary significance and reworking of social structures under colonialism. The popularity of *Hir-Ranjha* can perhaps be understood, at least in part, as due to its expression of anxieties produced by the social mobility induced by colonial rule.

Hir-Ranjha texts also underscore the discrepancy between colonial and indigenous understandings of Indian society. What should be evident from the discussion thus far is that a number of social classification systems were operating in the Punjab, among them, *ashraf-ajlaf, zat, qaum, biraderi, misl,* and *jati.* Of these, two—*qaum* and *biraderi*—appear to have captured the colonial administrative imagination more than others. This in turn affected how those categories were deployed by Punjabis' themselves in their own pursuit of power within the colonial state structure. It is worth noting that *zat* goes ummentioned in Caton's essay on social categories in colonial Punjab. This is because *zat* is not a prominent category in the principal text that Caton examines, *Tarikh-i Jhang Sial* (History of the Sials of Jhang), a history by Maulvi Nur Muhammad Chela Sial. This absence in a history of the very place (Jhang) and social collective (Sials) at the heart of the *Hir-Ranjha* narrative is rooted in the history of this text's production and its political purposes. The *Tarikh-i Jhang Sial* was composed at the behest of George Hamilton, deputy commissioner of Jhang in the 1850s. Completed in 1863, its author's primary purpose was to forward his and his kinship group's claims to political power. In the *Tarikh*, the author uses *qaum* to describe his kinship group: the *qaum-i Sial.* Caton's essay shows that in doing so Sial was playing on colonial conceptions of local social relations and appropriating those to his own ends. The language of *qaum*, given its salience to colonial officials, was an effective way to do this. The prominence of the idiom of *zat* rather than *qaum* in *Hir-Ranjha* texts, however, points out the continuing salience in the late nineteenth and early twentieth centuries of the former category in other indigenous understandings of self and community.

The heavy emphasis on *zat* in *Hir-Ranjha* texts foreshadows the fact that idioms which crossed religious boundaries were more significant in the Punjabi literary formation during this period than were those that inscribed religious difference. *Zat* exemplifies this because the concept operated in all religious communities. More important, individual *zats* included people of different religions. Jats, the group portrayed in *Hir-Ranjha,* could be Hindu, Muslim, and Sikh. *Zat* could thus signify a multireligious social collective.

LOCALITY AND REGION

"My name is Dhido, by *zat* a Ranjha, I have come from Takht Hazara."[32] This formulation of name, *zat,* and natal village surfaces repeatedly in *Hir-Ranjha* texts. Ranjha articulates it most often because once he leaves his natal village he is confronted again and again by the question of who he is. But it applies to other characters as well. Hir, for example, is often referred to as "Hir Jhang Sial." Indeed, these three terms are almost interchangeable. The mapping of self and community onto place in *Hir-Ranjha* texts prompts one to ask how place and territory function in colonial-era texts. Three types of representations seem to respond to this question. First is the issue of how the region—Punjab—emerges in these texts. Second is the way these texts treat the relationship between individuals and locality. And finally, how does connection to a locality serve as grounds for group solidarity? Taken together, these three levels of signification articulate a particular "spatial imagination," by which I mean a habit of understanding social relationships as inherently connected to geographic spaces.

The region—as a specific locale—is in many ways pivotal in the *Hir-Ranjha* narrative tradition. It emerges in these texts less as a political geographical entity (the "Punjab" of British colonial administration) than as an imagined ensemble of natal places within a particular topography (rivers, riverbanks, forests, and mountains) and religious geography (Sufi shrines and Hindu monasteries). There are, however, occasional references to "Punjab" in *Hir-Ranjha* texts, and these largely coincide with the colonial political entity or administrative unit. Maula Shah's early twentieth-century text provides a typical example. "The fame of Hir's beauty spread in Punjab, Hind, Sindh, Takht Hazara, Jammu, and Kashmir."[33] Takht Hazara, Ranjha's village, is clearly at odds with the other areas referenced, which can be thought of as separate regions (at least linguistically). Takht Hazara's inclusion was important to the narrative because it is the fame of Hir's beauty that leads Ranjha to Jhang. If we exclude Takht Hazara from consideration, we are left with an interesting list, one that gives us both a relatively accurate political map of northwest India at the time (c. 1912) and insights into how Punjab was conceived in relation to other parts of India.

Each of the areas mentioned is a distinct historic and political unit adjacent to Punjab province. Kashmir is to Punjab's north and Jammu to its northwest. The Sikh court had ruled these areas until 1846 when it ceded them to the East India Company, which sold them to Raja Gulab Singh who subsequently ruled them as a princely state. Sindh is to the south of Punjab. The region was annexed to the East India Company in 1843 and was administered as part of the Company's Bombay Presidency. Hind was not a political-administrative unit of the Company state, but Shah was almost certainly referring to Hindustan or the Indo-Gangetic plain. Irrespective of Punjab's political integration into the north Indian states ruled from Delhi since the twelfth century, the region retained an independent political identity. This identity was more apparent in other literary genres than it was in *qisse*, however. One can see it more clearly, for example, in *vars*, or war ballads.

One of the most renowned Punjabi texts of the nineteenth century is Shah Muhammad's *var* on the Anglo-Sikh war of 1845–46, *Jang Hind Punjab* (The War between Hind and Punjab).[34] This text makes the conception of Punjab as a political unit apparent, though one not necessarily coterminous with precolonial or colonial administrative units. Shah Muhammad had served as an artillery officer in the army of the Sikh kingdom of Ranjit Singh and wrote of the war from his personal experience.[35] Shah Muhammad's composition has a compelling line that is often cited, but little examined: "The battle between Hind and Punjab now raged furiously, on both sides were ranged huge numbers."[36] In the scene that Shah Muhammad describes, the forces of the Sikh kingdom, comprised of Muslims, Hindus, Sikhs, and European mercenaries, were arrayed on one side.[37] On the other side were the forces of the British East India Company, which included Indian soldiers primarily from Bengal, Bihar, and the Northwest Provinces. The former represented Punjab, and the latter Hind, neither of which, however, corresponded to any contemporary administrative units. They represent an important political imaginary, however. Punjab was that territory controlled by the Sikh state and Hind was that territory of north India (Hindustan) controlled by the Company. Shah Muhammad drew a clear distinction—in this case an opposition—between the two. In Shah Muhammad's *var*, then, we see a clear political and geographical entity, just as we do in Maula Shah's text. Maula Shah's *Hir wa Ranjha* is more the exception in *qissa* literature than the rule, however, in naming Punjab explicitly.

Hir-Ranjha texts do not, by and large, name the territory in which the tale is set "Punjab." Yet, fundamental narrative elements and the history of its composition and of its performance ground it in the topography and religious landscape of the five *doabs* and the cis-Sutlej territory of northwest India. If we can refer to this latter area as the region, then it is articulated implicitly through both framing mechanisms and the narrative itself. In framing their texts, authors often made references to their own natal place, and, perhaps more significantly, in their invocations to sources of spiritual authority. Among those sources paid obeisance were Sufi *pirs*, whose shrines were located in the region. These invocations, to be discussed in chapter 5, include the figures Sayyid Jalal ud-din Bukhari, whose shrine is in Multan, and Shaikh Farid, whose shrine is in Pakpattan. And as we have already seen (chapter 3), Sufi shrines also figured as prominent sites of performance, another way in which we might understand the narrative as being inscribed in a religious landscape.

Since the earliest Punjabi *qissa* of *Hir-Ranjha* by Damodar, the inclusion of certain places in the tale has been an unchanging feature of the narrative tradition. Without these locales, *Hir-Ranjha* ceases to be *Hir-Ranjha*. There are five such locations in the story, three of them associated with main characters: Takht Hazara (Ranjha), Jhang (Hir), and Rangpur (Seido). A fourth locale, Tilla Jogian, is the location of Gorakhnath's *dera* (monastery) and the site of Ranjha's apparent transformation into a yogi. Last, though perhaps most important, is the Chenab River. The five rivers of this area, the Jhelum, Chenab, Ravi, Beas, and Sutlej (from west to east), all flow into the Indus and gave rise to the name *Punjab* (Persian *panj* [five] + *ab* [water]). The five *doabs* referred to earlier are the interriverine tracts (five because the tract between the Indus and the Jhelum is included), and the cis-Sutlej area is to the south of this river, up to Delhi. The rivers are a defining feature of the region's landscape and have historically been critical to its economy. They provided irrigation for agriculture and were the foundation of the region's medieval and early modern commercial economy, serving as the main north-south transportation routes moving goods and people.[38] The Chenab is the largest of the five rivers. The town of Jhang on the banks of the Chenab is where the love of Hir and Ranjha flourished. The banks of the Chenab, along with the other four critical locations in the tale, provide *Hir-Ranjha*'s spatial armature. The authors portrayed the region through its constituent parts, and we can be sure that listeners readily recognized their region in the depiction of its secular and spiritual spaces. Thus, although most *Hir-Ranjha* texts, from the colonial period or otherwise, do not describe an administrative region, the narrative is suffused with references to a distinct landscape and a common set of places.

If Punjab is the backdrop for the tale, then the more explicit relationship portrayed in this body of literature is between persons and their natal homes. *Hir-Ranjha* texts provide an opportunity to consider the affective ties between person and place in colonial Punjab. They do so through two different conceptions of this relationship. One concerns the relationship between a person and a territorially bounded entity that is universally accepted—a town, village, or city, for example. The other is the connection between individuals and places that are context-specific and shift in meaning depending upon who uses them. The Punjabi terms for these places are *des* (country), *pardes* (foreign country), and *watan* (homeland).

In *Fluid Signs: Being a Person the Tamil Way,* E. Valentine Daniel discusses the relationship between a person and his or her *ur,* or native village. Daniel argues that "one of the most important relationships to a Tamil is that which exists between a person and the soil of his *ur.*" He defines *ur* as a "spatio-territorial concept" that is: "(1) inhabited by human beings who are believed to share in the substance of the soil of that territory, and (2) a territory to which a Tamil cognitively orients himself at any given time."[39] To elucidate the complex concept of *ur,* Daniel argues that it must be understood in contradistinction to the terms *tecam* and *kiramam,* Tamil for "nation/country" and village, respectively: "Both terms are bounded, standard, universally accepted, and constant spatial units. The government determines what is a tecam and a kiramam, and it is the same for everyone. There is no contextual variation in the use of these terms."[40] Daniel's discussion of the divergence between a defined and constant spatial unit and one that is "defined person-centrically, in terms of its relevance to a given ego" opens up new possibilities for how we might understand representations of place in *Hir-Ranjha* texts.[41]

Sites crucial to the *Hir-Ranjha* narrative—Takht Hazara, Jhang, Rangpur, Tilla Jogian, the banks of the Chenab River—are akin to what Daniel describes as "bounded, standard, universally accepted, and constant spatial units." Affective ties to these places are articulated through the use of terms like *des* or *watan.* Referring to Takht Hazara or Jhang by such terms transforms them from places on a map to places in the heart. This transformation not only points to the affective relationship between individual and place, it also fuses the two so that person and place become inseparable. Or, to put it somewhat differently, place becomes one of the important aspects of a person's identity. The two characters in *Hir-Ranjha* most closely associated with specific sites are Hir and Ranjha themselves. The fact that Ranjha is from Takht Hazara is central to his character; each time he is asked to identify himself, he gives his native place as a form of reference. Ranjha's attachment to this place is best illustrated by his dismay at leaving it. In Khawaish Ali's rendition he laments in an exchange with Hir, "For your sake, I left my beloved homeland [*watan*]."[42] Various renditions portray Ranjha not only lamenting this fate, but also using his lament as an attack against Hir (for marrying Seido Khera). In Fassi Niaz Ahmad's *Hir Niaz Ranjha*, Ranjha says, "I left my beloved Takht Hazara and became your cowherd. I left my parents, my kinsmen [*khawesh*], my clan [*qabila*]; I sacrificed myself."[43] For Ranjha, to be separated from his homeland (*watan*) is distressing because his sense of self is so closely related to this geographic space.

Through the discourse of *des* and *watan,* we also see contours of a sociality in which place forms an important trope. Both terms capture something of what Daniel described in writing of *ur* as a place "inhabited by human beings who are believed to share in the substance of the soil of that territory."[44] Through *des* and *watan,* we see that place is critical to a sense of self but also to a sense of community. Hir's and Ranjha's attachments to place reinforce this: both identified with what I referred to above as universally accepted geographic entities, in this case Jhang and Takht Hazara, respectively; but they also describe that identification in terms of *des* (and its counterpart, *pardes*) and *watan.*[45] Although these terms refer to territory, they are not associated with a fixed geographic entity. They are context-specific terms that demarcate belonging and difference. While *Hir-Ranjha* may have been framed within the geographic confines of the Punjab, the use of these terms suggests that an affinity to locality created a clear sense of group solidarity as well as of difference.

Miran Shah Bahawalpuri's rendition of *Hir-Ranjha* provides an example of the way in which spatial imagery structures the social relationships of individuals in the narrative. Of Ranjha's journey to Jhang, Bahawalpuri writes: "He went to the homeland [*watan*], the land [*des*] of his beloved. And in the process, became a stranger [*pardes*] to his own land [*des*]."[46] One finds a similar sense of demarcating difference later in an exchange between Hir and Ranjha. Hir asks Ranjha, "Where have you come from, where is your hearth[?] Tell me what is your land [*des*], what is your homeland [*watan*]." Locating herself for Ranjha, she says: "My homeland, oh fakir, is Jhang-Sial" (note how place and *zat* together constitute Hir's homeland).[47] This difference in homeland (*watan* or *des*) establishes one of the terms of Hir and Ranjha's social interaction. The spatial imagination in *Hir-Ranjha* texts drew explicit boundaries between Takht Hazara and Jhang, between Hir and Ranjha. An excerpt from *Hir Husain* indicates this unequivocally.[48]

Husain's text opens with Ranjha threatening to leave Jhang, telling Hir to manage her own cattle. As the action ensues, Hir pleads with Ranjha to remain, if for no other reasons than that the cattle will not graze without him and that without him they are "barely capable of taking a breath." The fate of the cattle is the fate of the Sial family's wealth and prestige. Hir implores Ranjha to stay: "Oh, do not exercise your power over the weak and humble. Oh, the lord is severe and uncaring, Ranjha."[49] Ranjha's response reveals the way in which a spatialized understanding informs his relationship with Hir and the community among whom he lives in Jhang:

> Foreigners [*pardesis*] have no power Hir, why do you speak of the strong?
> In truth, this matter is about the powerful [your family], they stand before the
>   strong [the Kheras] seeking a suitor for you.
> I have no wealth, my home is far. I tried to gain wealth, but to no avail.
> Without wealth one does not find refuge. In the end, I am leaving the people of this
>   land [*desis*], I am washing my hands of you all, oh Hir.[50]

By framing himself as a *pardesi* (of a foreign land) and Hir and her family as *desis* (of "this" land), Ranjha points to a conceptual division between the two that is simultaneously social and spatial. It is never specified where, in geographic terms, this line between Takht Hazara and Jhang, between *pardesi* and *desi*, actually falls. What remains important is the way in which this imaginary division contributes to the social relations between individuals from these two localities.

The third type of spatial relationship invoked in the *Hir-Ranjha* narrative is that between locality and group identity. The clearest illustration of this is the way the narrative often refers to Jhang by the spatial metaphor of the Sial community. Muhammad Azim's rendition, for one, uses this metaphor: "[Ranjha] left Takht Hazara, and made his home in Jhang of the Sials [*Jhang sialin*]."[51] Some authors do not even explicitly use the name Jhang for the territory, referring to it instead as the land of the Sials. This is the case in Khawaish Ali's *Hir-Ranjha*, a text that opens with Ranjha leaving Takht Hazara and making his way to Jhang. The author's reference to Jhang is oblique: "[Ranjha] left Takht Hazara, and settled in the land of the Sials [*sialin*]."[52] In this quotation, Ali used the adjective *sialin* without stating the noun that it modifies. That the noun was a geographic entity is nonetheless obvious from the context. Therefore, even without using the geographic name, Ali conveyed Ranjha's migration from Takht Hazara to Jhang by the simple and well-established association of the narrative with specific locales, and of the Sials with Jhang.[53] These examples relate the way in which place, in this case natal place, was associated with specific communities in *Hir-Ranjha* texts. This association was not limited to either this genre or to fiction. The late nineteenth-century history encountered earlier in this chapter, the *Tarikh-i Jhang Sial,* in which *zat* and place are presented as almost synonymous, is another example.

Both individual self-conception and group solidarity in these texts are crucially linked to locality. Indeed, these texts allow us to see how individual, community, and the locality or natal place were mutually constitutive categories of identity in the Punjabi literary formation. It is important to note this emphasis on the locality, rather than the region, even within a vernacular tradition associated with a particular area, an area I have referred to throughout this book as Punjab. I would like to consider this conclusion in the context of two very different contemporary discourses: that of the colonial state and that of Indian nationalism. As Manu Goswami argues, both the colonial state and Indian nationalism were committed to producing a national space in the late nineteenth and early twentieth centuries, though for different reasons.[54] She writes that the colonial production of India as a spatially delimited entity was accomplished through a number of practices in the late nineteenth century that included the creation of "an internally unified market, a spatially centralized monetary system, and an integrated administrative structure."[55] One might add to this the somewhat earlier literal mapping of India through the geographical Survey of India.[56] For the colonial state, sociospatial practices such as these were critical to its economic exploitation of India. An unintended consequence, perhaps, was that these same practices "spawned nationalist imaginings of economy, territory, and culture."[57] "Nationalist constructions of India," Goswami goes on to argue, were "coextensive with the spatial boundaries of the colonial state. Furthermore, these boundaries were associated with a homogenous collectivity defined in economic, historical, and cultural terms and identified as a nation."[58] In this process, "multiple solidarities based on caste, religion, regional differences, and so forth, were progressively and violently sublimated under the unifying rubric of an Indian nationality."[59]

Goswami provides an important analysis of how cultural, economic, and political nationalisms are coproduced, rather than separate aspects of a single phenomenon. Her analysis of Indian nationalism's creation of national space, where territory, economy, and culture merged, draws from "exemplary nationalist writings and practices."[60] This is a nationalist perspective on the process, and we need to examine the creation of national space from other viewpoints. What conception of national space permeated the Punjabi literary formation? Drawing on the "spatial imagination" in colonial-era *Hir-Ranjha* texts, there is little evidence of the idea of nation, much less an affinity for it. Social life, as portrayed in these texts, is highly localized. The implication of this deserves consideration: although India was becoming a "spatially delimited entity" through the discursive and material work of the colonial state and Indian nationalism, important Indian self-conceptions and group solidarities remained associated with spatial concepts that were not national. This is not to suggest these were the only affinities people could have.[61] Rather, the sense of being grounded in a particular relationship to place, one intrinsically tied to group solidarities, was still prevalent through the early twentieth century despite the disciplining mechanisms of state and nationalist agendas. If we examine notions of regional belonging from the standpoint offered by vernacular literature, we can start to grasp the limited extent to which colonial and nationalist spatial reorderings had actually penetrated society. At the same time, this literature provides us with a baseline from which to gauge Indian nationalism's later profound success in bringing the idea of the nation to bear alongside, if not in place of, the affective ties people felt to local places and their regional contexts.

GENDER

Not only do *Hir-Ranjha* texts provide insights about the Punjabi literary formation's notions of social solidarity and spatial imagination, these texts also engage questions of gender in compelling ways. Indeed, while the problem of *zat* poses the narrative's central conflict, that issue is deeply entangled with Hir's parents' desire to control her sexuality. This desire—even insistence—extends beyond her parents to her *zat*, whose members see in her behavior their own dishonor. Ultimately, it is the perceived damage that Hir's behavior does to both family and *zat* honor that leads her family to poison her. This denouement alone suggests the possibilities for *Hir-Ranjha* to have functioned as a morality tale that reinscribed the historically patriarchal norms of Punjabi society, and some critics have interpreted the tale along precisely such lines.[62] Prem Chowdhry best describes Punjab's historically patriarchal norms in her influential essay "Customs in a Peasant Economy," where she documents a "social ethos" that led to female infanticide, purdah (seclusion), total neglect of female education, and "the complete absence of women from any positions of power and decision making."[63] Portrayals of female figures in the *Hir-Ranjha* narrative tradition do not, however, easily lend themselves to the argument that the romance functioned as a morality tale that reinscribed patriarchy. Take, for example, two eighteenth-century renditions, by Shah Jahan Muqbal (c. 1740s) and Waris Shah (1766), respectively. In Muqbal's text, as historian Jeevan Deol writes, Hir is the primary critic of "the nexus between the *shariʿah* and social power," that is, between clerics and landed elites. Waris Shah, in contrast, "creates a markedly subdued Hir who speaks within the bounds of social and literary convention." Interestingly, Deol argues that Muqbal's text eventually subverts Hir's critique, while Waris Shah's text is "ultimately subversive of social ideology."[64]

While early modern texts of *Hir-Ranjha* varied in their portrayals of Hir, renditions from the late nineteenth and early twentieth centuries are remarkably consistent in representing Hir as a spirited woman who defies (or valiantly attempts to defy) the social strictures that stand between her and Ranjha. This fact alone is not what prompts a gendered reading of this romance. More significantly, many of the period's episodic texts—the short, inexpensive texts that treat only a scene or two of the larger narrative—focus on Hir, portraying her exchanges with Ranjha, the *qazi* (Muslim judge), and her mother, respectively. These exchanges invariably highlight the characters' divergent conceptions of Hir's religious and moral duties. That a woman's duties—whether as daughter, sister, or lover-companion—were debated through episodic texts is not surprising given their social, religious, and political context and the nature of *qisse* as social commentary. The decades around the turn of the twentieth century were the heyday of socioreligious reform in the Punjab, as in other parts of north India, and debates on the proper roles for and behavior of women were critical to this discourse, whether Sikh, Hindu, or Muslim.

Late nineteenth-century reformers were openly modernist in bent and self-presentation, but they simultaneously championed the values of indigenous culture and religion (albeit reformed). Crucial to their cause was the "reform" of women's lives. Though many reformers advocated women's education, they did so through a discourse that reinscribed women's inferior status, limited their social roles, and subjected them to patriarchal norms and desires.[65] This is best captured by the idea of the *pativrata* championed by Sikh and Hindu reformers. Anshu Malhotra has shown in her study of colonial Punjab how socioreligious reformers promoted the *pativrata* ideal of a subordinate female companion whose world revolved around devotion to her husband and children (particularly sons).[66] Muslim reformers may have used a different language, but their ideas mapped comfortably onto Sikh and Hindu reformers' ideals.[67]

Although socioreligious reformers were relatively few in number, their advocacy was organized and effective. Their ideas influenced the lives of middle-class and upper-caste women in particular, whose activities beyond the home and family were curtailed during this period. Part of reformers' success derived from their use of modern modes of communication and the media. Reformist organizations produced reams of pamphlets advocating various social and religious positions. For instance, by 1911 the Khalsa Tract Society (est. 1894) had published over four hundred tracts and distributed over one million copies.[68] The Khalsa Tract Society's record is matched by the publications of both sister and rival organizations. The late nineteenth- and early twentieth-century socioreligious reform movement therefore left a substantial archive in its wake. This, in turn, has provided the basis of a rich historiography on reformist ideas in the Punjab,[69] though we know less about their actual impact on society as a whole. Based on this mass of reformist printed materials (including reformist fiction), supplemented by colonial archives, historians have effectively argued that the middle-class, upper-caste moorings of respectability espoused by socioreligious reformers had a discernible impact on women and gender relations both by increasingly circumscribing women to the home and by interfering in what had once been women's relatively autonomous domestic spheres.[70] This "reform" of women reinscribed their subjection to patriarchy, which has become the dominant historical narrative of gender relations in colonial Punjab and north India generally.[71]

Socioreligious reformers did not monopolize late nineteenth- and early twentieth-century discourses about women and their ideal roles in Indian society. The colonial state had its own narrative that represented Punjabis (and Indians at large, particularly north Indians) as having particularly retrograde attitudes toward women. In the late nineteenth century, colonial discourse focused on female infanticide, which for the British epitomized the worst of Indian attitudes toward women. This discourse led, ultimately, to the Act for the Prevention of Female Infanticide, passed in 1870. There are no doubt a number of explanations for British enthusiasm for this "reform" of Indian society. Most obvious is that it provided the state a reason for its "civilizing mission." The condemnation of indigenous society for its attitudes toward and practices affecting women played well with colonial claims that the British were bringing modernity to India. Just as reinscribing the role of women was critical to the articulation of suitably modern religion for socioreligious reformers, so it was for other projects of colonial modernity. But this "civilizing mission" was only one of several reasons for colonial reform, not all of which were as ostensibly laudatory.

In its condemnation of female infanticide, the colonial state was less interested in reforming the nature of gender relations in Indian society than it was with using legislation as a means of reinforcing patriarchy by "pruning its excesses."[72] Earlier laws relating to women had been no different. For example, as Mrinalini Sinha shows, the abolition of *sati* earlier in the nineteenth century was an opportunity to "stake the claims of British colonialism as the modernizers of indigenous patriarchy."[73] It is a sad irony that the practice of infanticide in the Punjab received something of a fillip during the colonial period. In a recent essay, Anshu Malhotra argues that the context created by the British offered Punjabis a "clearer path to social recognition." Taken together with Punjab's changing economy, demands for revenue payments, and "the fixing of land in patriarchal hands [through mechanisms such as customary law] . . . son preference got more strongly established."[74] In the event, colonial discourse and action did little to reform women's lives for the better. Prem Chowdhry, too, argues that many patriarchal customs were "buttressed by the force of law by the colonial state, who became conscious agents in their perpetuation."[75] This is not surprising given Victorian notions of women's role(s) in society, particularly with the middle-class emphasis upon domesticity, which was hardly progressive. Nonetheless, calling for social reform for Indian women was a way for the colonial state to have its cake and eat it too.

Emergent Indian nationalism was at the same time developing its own discourse on Indian women, one equally significant to the context in which *Hir-Ranjha* texts circulated. In defining itself vis-à-vis the colonial state in the late nineteenth century, Partha Chatterjee argues that Indian nationalist thought embraced a split between an "outer" realm of politics, in which the colonial state's superiority was conceded, and an "inner," "spiritual" realm, which remained autonomous.[76]

Women became synonymous with this inner, spiritual realm, and thus central to nationalist ideology. This was undoubtedly an advance in women's ideological prestige, yet they remained well within the confines of a new nationalist patriarchy that "permanently limit[ed] the subject positions available to middle-class women in nationalist discourse."[77] In fact, their new significance circumscribed women's activities in novel and important ways, as they now became the carriers of Indian "tradition." Sinha argues in her *Specters of Mother India* that this "reframing of the women's question was not just part of an anticolonial nationalist politics. . . . It was also a symptom of a growing conservative indigenous backlash against challenges from various quarters in society."[78] This conservative backlash led nationalists to emphasize middle-class, upper-caste notions of domesticity that mapped comfortably onto those of the late nineteenth-century socioreligious reformers (many of whom, incidentally, would become staunch nationalists).

Socioreligious reformist, colonialist, and nationalist discourses presented ideal women as demure, submissive, and devoted to husbands and children, inhabiting a social world prescribed by the norms of a middle-class domesticity. Contemporary *Hir-Ranjha* texts present a very different vision. Rather than their subordination to patriarchal ideals, these texts emphasize women's agency. Some of the forms of legitimate authority held by women in these tales clearly transgress gendered norms of the time. Colonial-era *Hir-Ranjha* texts represent Hir, for example, as confident and even martial in some renditions, as knowledgeable, articulate, cognizant of her rights under Islamic law, outspoken, and defiant of authority. Let us examine such representations by turning to the circa 1880 text *Na'at di Hir* (Na'at's Hir), to explore the implications of these representations for the history of gender in late colonial Punjab and north India.

Na'at di Hir is an episodic text that focuses on a passage where Hir is asked to reject Ranjha and accept her parents' choice of suitor. Hir's refusal to do so prompts her parents to call in the *qazi*, hoping that he will be able to prevail on her in the matter. The exchange between these two opens with Hir's declaration of love for Ranjha, articulated through a devotional idiom: "On the forehead of the cowherd [Ranjha] is written *bismillah* [in the name of God]. Upon seeing it I read out 'Allah, Allah.' God himself has praised him [Ranjha] in the Quran, oh *qazi*."[79] This statement of affection is awkward but telling, for its rhetorical flourish reveals much about Hir's character. Rather than framing her love for Ranjha as corporeal, she portrays it as divinely inspired. For Hir, Ranjha has divine sanction: he carries God's name on his forehead and is praised in the Quran. While the listener and reader know that neither statement about Ranjha is literally true, Hir's depiction of him presents a most effective mode of argumentation with the *qazi*. Hir's enunciation of her love uses precisely those terms supposed to be in the *qazi*'s authority. After all, it is the *qazi*'s role, through his knowledge of scripture and religious law, to determine where divine sanction falls. By using language that places her and

Ranjha's love within the parameters of God's authority, rather than framing it as an illicit affair, Hir limits the *qazi*'s possible arguments.

The success of this tactic becomes clear when the *qazi* resorts to an argument that is not strictly religious to try to convince her to abandon Ranjha. The *qazi* argues that Hir's moral duty is to consent to her parents' will. Unmoved by this position, Hir reiterates her earlier stance: "Open the Quran, oh *qazi,* and see his [Ranjha's] eminence." Hir and the *qazi* are at an impasse, so Hir takes another tack and a sharper tone: "You, oh *qazi,* take bribes. You would perform the marriage rights on the coming day. Every devil goes to hell, oh *qazi.*"[80] The context for her attack is quite simple. Hir knows that under Islamic law she must consent, of her own free will, to her marriage. She senses that despite her protestations, the *qazi* will ignore her rights and perform her marriage to someone other than Ranjha, and this is precisely what happens in the narrative. Although her arguments do not prevail, what is notable in this exchange is Hir's appropriation of a religious-textual tradition interpreted and controlled by men, and her outright abuse of the *qazi,* a character of significantly higher social and religious status.

Qissa Hir wa Ranjha, by Muhammad Shah Sakin, is another late nineteenth-century text in which Hir interacts with religious figures, in this case religious scholars (*'alims*).[81] Unlike her interaction with the *qazi* in Na'at's text, in Sakin's text Hir's encounter with religious scholars is deferential. Hir is assertive, however, in arguing that her relationship with Ranjha is righteous because it is within the dictates of *shari'a* (Islamic law). Hir effectively argues that the marriage that her family has forced on her is illegal by religious dictates. In order to understand the context in which she makes these assertions we must first take note of how the narrative of Sakin's *Qissa Hir wa Ranjha* develops.

The text opens with Hir and Ranjha falling in love, and the *panj pir* immediately sanction their relationship. The term *panj pir* is a cultural signifier across much of north India that historian Romila Thapar refers to as "the five original 'saints' of popular Islam."[82] The precise composition of this icon shifts by region and even within regions; nonetheless, they are a focus of devotion for people of different religious faiths.[83] The *panj pir* appear in Sakin's text to sanction Hir and Ranjha's love by performing their marriage rites. One can think of this as an allegorical spiritual union. In the narrative, therefore, the marriage remains hidden from society, and particularly from Hir's family. The two lovers meet secretly, but their relationship is eventually discovered by Hir's family, who as a consequence forcibly marry her to Seido Khera. From her marriage home Hir escapes with Ranjha, only to be pursued by Khera and his kinsmen. They take refuge at the court of the area's governor and are followed there by the Kheras. The governor inquires about the commotion their arrival causes and is told about the dispute. His immediate response is to throw Ranjha in jail and return Hir to Seido Khera. But these are temporary measures since the governor asks the court's religious scholars to give a ruling on the matter based on the *shariʿa*. At this point a telling exchange takes place.

The governor asks the scholars to: "Examine all that you can on the issue of marriage to find out whether Ranjha or Seido Khera is in the right." The narrator then relates the following: "Muhammad Shah says, look at how Hir answers the religious scholars with reference to the hadith. Hir comes before the scholars, puts her hands together in supplication, and greets them. She tells them that the *panj pir* had performed her marriage to Ranjha [before she was forcibly married to Seido Khera]. She comes before the scholars and shows her [religious] knowledge, saying that to perform marriage upon marriage is not right."[84] Upon her statement, the *panj pir* appear as witnesses and corroborate her story. In light of Hir's testimony and the intercession of the *panj pir*, the court's religious scholars uphold Hir and Ranjha's union and issue a fatwa, or legal opinion, that the Kheras have no claim on Hir, and Hir and Ranjha are reunited.

Though brief, this exchange has many noteworthy aspects. Hir comes before the religious scholars deferential but confident. Importantly, Hir not only advocates her own position—that she should be with Ranjha rather than Seido Khera—but grounds that position squarely in her knowledge of the hadith, one of the sources of the *shariʿa*. As in Naʿat's text, Hir is portrayed as someone with knowledge of religious law. Women in colonial Punjab were expected to attain such knowledge (a grounding in one's religious tradition was a tenet of socioreligious reformers), but it was meant to be wielded only in their domestic space, to allow them to raise their children, particularly their sons, with the proper moral and religious moorings.[85] In this text, however, we see quite the opposite: Hir enters a public forum and uses her religious knowledge to defy the patriarchal norms of her society.

The depiction of Hir as an assertive, agential character is not limited to scenes in which she encounters men with religious authority. Another common motif in colonial-era *Hir-Ranjha* texts is an exchange between Hir and her mother, Malki. These mother-daughter dialogues share certain elements. First, they always entail Malki trying to convince Hir to give up her lover and marry a suitor chosen by her parents. Malki uses a range of arguments to support her position: that Hir is being irreligious in choosing her own lover; that Hir has a moral duty to abide by her parents' wishes; that Hir's behavior has ruined her family's reputation; and that Ranjha cannot keep her in the material comfort to which she is accustomed (this returns us to the issue of status, discussed earlier). The striking aspect of these conversations is Hir's fortitude. While Malki verbally and sometimes viciously lashes out at her daughter, Hir is stoic and provides counterarguments to each of Malki's objections to her relationship with Ranjha. Excerpts from this exchange in Kishan Singh ʿArif's *Qissa Hir te Ranjhe da* provide an example of how Hir is characterized in these dialogues.[86]

Titled "The Answer and Question between Hir and Hir's Mother Malki," this dialogue is comprised of eighteen stanzas of six lines each. The exchange opens with Malki saying, "If only you had drowned in some stream or a well today. Your association with this cowherd [Ranjha] has ruined you; you have no shame. . . . There is no purpose now to your staying in this home."[87] Hir responds:

> You will only be able to send me from this home by marrying me to Ranjha.
> I am his and he is mine.
> I am his disciple, he is my spiritual guide; I am the corpse, he the grave.
> Mother there is no other man for me.
> Hir is like a kite . . . and Ranjha holds the string.[88]

Malki is exasperated by Hir's attitude: "Malki says to Hir, 'Change your ways . . . have you no shame? Should your father and countrymen hear such talk, they will kill you.'"[89] Again, Hir holds firm to her beloved, even in the face of such violent threats:

> Hir says, "The lord is ever constant.
> Without Ranjha, I'd have not a moment of peace.
> With each breath I take his name, I repeat it in my heart day and night.
> My eyes are relieved only at the site of my beloved.
> Ranjha is my beloved; he is my family, my protector.
> Oh, mother, pardon your Hir, and consider her sacrifice like that of Hassan
>   and Husain."
> Kishan Singh says, to be without one's beloved is to sit and wail with grief.[90]

Having failed to sway Hir by threats or reference to the family's ignominy, Malki tries one last tactic: a material argument. "Get out of our house, don't enter it again," she says, "take off our jewels that you wear. . . . We have no need of a salacious daughter."[91] Hir is not swayed by this argument either, and rebuts her mother with a philosophical statement about material concerns. "Hir says, 'Here, keep your jewels. It makes no difference to those in love; for them nothing is the same as *lakhs* [hundreds of thousands]. . . . I won't be swayed from my beloved Ranjha no matter how many times you insist.'"[92]

These mother-daughter dialogues are interesting for a number of reasons. At first glance, they present two rather different representations of women. One is Malki, an upholder of patriarchal authority and custom. Her principal concern is to control Hir's sexuality, the failure to do so having sullied the reputation of Hir's father, and thus of the family. At one point Malki says, "Your father's reputation has been ruined, he who is a *sardar* [headman]."[93] Malki has no interest in her daughter's desires, only in how Hir's behavior breaches decorum. Malki quite clearly abhors Hir's behavior for, in her eyes, it flouts the religious, moral, and social norms prescribed for women.

Hir, on the other hand, is portrayed as a woman of strong conviction, unrelenting in her belief that her behavior is moral. She is able to argue this position by making the pious nature of true love the essence of all of her responses to her mother. This is a subtle argument, and Hir makes it with language that is infused with religious undertones. For example, consider the line "With each breath I take his name, I repeat it [*simran*] in my heart day and night." This language equates Hir's love for Ranjha with devotion, and specifically with the Sufi devotional practice of *dhikr*, or the repetition of God's name. For the listener and reader there is no mistaking this, particularly since she uses the term *simran*, a reference to a rosary. In arguing thus, Hir refuses to concede that Malki's condemnation is in any way justified. While these two positions—Malki's representing patriarchal norms and Hir's flouting them—are opposed, the representations of these female characters share certain attributes. After all, Malki is represented as a woman of some conviction herself. While from a contemporary feminist perspective she may be an unsympathetic figure, it is Malki who confronts Hir, and not her father or brothers, though they too know about her relationship. While the narrative uses Malki to support patriarchal structures, ones that obviously lead to her own subjugation, one must also note her prominent voice. These mother-daughter dialogues are thus exchanges between two intense, passionate women, each convinced that she is right, and each using various rhetorical strategies to try and sway the other to her position.

How is one to interpret these representations of female characters in colonial-era *Hir-Ranjha* texts? What do they reveal about the history of gender in late nineteenth- and early-twentieth-century Punjab? One possibility is offered by studies of late twentieth-century folklore and oral traditions in India. Anthropologists Gloria Raheja and Ann Gold argue that north Indian oral traditions that represent women as "exuberant, resilient, and often refusing degradations by male ideologies or structures of authority" constitute "a moral discourse in which gender . . . identities are constructed, represented, negotiated, and contested in everyday life."[94] The readings of *Hir-Ranjha* texts above suggest that they, too, were a site for constructing, representing, and negotiating gender identities. There are critical differences in both the production and circulation of the texts Gold and Raheja analyze, however, and the colonial-era *qisse* above. The most significant of these is that the former were from a "women's realm." That is, Raheja and Gold analyze texts performed and composed by women, or that circulated solely among women. In contrast, the *Hir-Ranjha* texts above, as is true of all known colonial renditions, were composed and principally performed by men. This undoubtedly complicates the task of historical interpretation, as does the absence of sources on their reception. There is ample material in the texts themselves, taken together with the remarkable consistency of their representations of women, their popularity, and the context of their production and circulation, to suggest that these *qisse* are helpful sources in contemplating the history of gender in colonial Punjab, but not as a mere reflection of social practice or as a simple recovery of women's subjectivity and agency. They are significant because they point to an attitude toward women in the Punjabi literary formation—formed as much, if not more, by men as by women—that fits uneasily with the patriarchal norms outlined above.

The portrayals of strong female characters in colonial-era *Hir-Ranjha* texts point to an attitude toward women not discernible in the traditional archive (that is, the combination of socioreligious literature, state documents, and nationalist literature). The key to interpreting the historical significance of this disjuncture rests not in positing the former as a mere representation and the latter as historical reality, but rather in seeing how both attitudes are constitutive of Punjab's history. Indeed, as Antoinette Burton suggests, we should "understand discourse and reality not as opposing domains but as a vast, interdependent archive."[95] Bringing Punjabi *qissa* literature and the traditional archive into the same frame forces one to reject the binary of a male-produced patriarchy on the one hand and female resistance to it on the other. Instead, *Hir-Ranjha* texts suggest that male-produced patriarchy was not as singular in its attitudes toward women as the existing historiography suggests. Perhaps, as anthropologist Joyce Burkhalter Flueckiger argues in her study *Gender and Genre in the Folklore of Middle India,* this kind of inversion "may reveal an opposition or alternative to 'ideal' norms that is continually present at some level, both in tension with and integrated into the dominant ideology of the society."[96] It is difficult to find traces of this tension in the historiography on gender in late nineteenth- and early twentieth-century Punjab, however. It falls away in Prem Chowdhry's compelling analysis of gender in colonial Haryana, for instance, an analysis applicable not just to Haryana but to colonial Punjab more broadly. "There is a peculiar contradiction in the dominant emergent customs and attitudes of rural Haryana in relation to women in the colonial period," Chowdhry writes. "On the one hand, the agrarian milieu shows the generally accepted indices of high status for women, that is, bride-price, widow-remarriage, polyandry or its own sexual variants and full economic participation in agricultural activities. . . . On the other hand, it shows the region as having indices of women's backwardness."[97] Rather than exploring the nature of the contradiction, however, she unravels it; Chowdhry closes her analysis by showing that there was no contradiction at all, but rather only male patriarchy and female resistance to it: "The indices of high status . . . all emerge as customs evolved, dictated and enforced by the dominant [male] peasantry . . . to suit its own peculiar socio-economic needs. . . . However, even within this tightly controlled peasant culture . . . women's self-assertion and protest [occurred] against a system in which they shared the work but not its fruits."[98]

Hir-Ranjha texts present a history of gender in late nineteenth- and early twentieth-century Punjab that does not fit a simple binary between male patriarchy and female resistance. Rather, these texts portray a world where the role and proper comportment of women was being debated and negotiated. There is a consistent depiction of women in colonial-era *Hir-Ranjha* texts as agential characters armed with conventional forms of authority. In the cases discussed above, this authority was predicated on religious knowledge. Women in these texts behave in ways that confound the prescribed gendered norms of the time, and provide an opening for rethinking patriarchy and gender relations in late colonial Punjab. This is not simply because these representations exist but because these texts had very particular functions in Punjabi society. One function was as a form of entertainment. These narratives were popular among men and women of various class, caste, and religious affiliations. Alongside their entertainment value, these texts served as an arena of social commentary, taking up issues of contemporary concern. These were undoubtedly subversive texts in their presentation of alternative models of womanhood, yet their popularity suggests the salience of these depictions of women in Punjabi society. Representations in renditions of *Hir-Ranjha* differ markedly from the conservative gendered discourses of socioreligious reformers, the colonial state, and India's mainstream nationalism. In doing so, Punjabi *qissa* literature portrays a vernacular culture that could imagine foundations for its late colonial modernity that were at odds with those that depended on the subordinate female subject for their coherence.

5

Piety and Devotion

This chapter will focus on the proper performance of piety and devotion, a theme that figures prominently in both the form and the content of colonial-era compositions of *Hir-Ranjha*. Discourse on piety and devotion in this literature was no new phenomenon; it is discernible in precolonial texts as well. Important differences emerged, however. First, many colonial-era texts highlight precisely those moments in the narrative where the proper performance of piety is at issue. This is done in one of two ways. In epic-length texts, poets elaborated such scenes, adding depth to their treatment by inserting additional narrator commentary, dialogue between characters, or both. It was also done through episodic texts. These short and inexpensive print versions, which typically consider only one or two episodes from a larger narrative, often focused on proper pious conduct and devotion. As examples below will illustrate, episodic texts tended to involve a mullah (Muslim cleric) or a *qazi* (Muslim judge), characters that help elaborate attitudes about proper conduct prevalent at the time.

A second difference between colonial and precolonial texts is the context in which late nineteenth- and early twentieth-century Punjabi literature circulated, an environment steeped in socioreligious reform. In addition to north-India-wide movements such as Deoband, the Barelwi, and the Arya Samaj, colonial Punjab was the site of Sikh socioreligious reform, the Muslim Ahmadiyah movement, and particularly ardent Christian missionary activity. One effect of this, as discussed in the introduction, was a new contentiousness produced by religious communities redefining themselves in increasingly antagonistic terms vis-à-vis one another. A discourse on pious conduct and proper devotional practice became central to this redefinition. Given this historical context, the centrality of piety and devotion in the corpus of Punjabi episodic *qisse* underscores the point that these texts were sites of social engagement and commentary.

Shifting from the perspective of reform organizations to the Punjabi literary formation, or its intellectual history via *qisse*, has important implications for how Punjab's socioreligious culture is understood during this dynamic period. To date, scholarship on socioreligious activity in particular, and religion in colonial Punjab more generally, has emphasized the agendas and activities of Hindu, Muslim, and Sikh reformers. Almost all the indigenous sources historians have used to interpret colonial Punjab's history—tracts, treatises, newspapers, and modern genres of literature—were produced by religious reformers and circulated among an elite reading public. The dominance of reformist narratives has left an indelible imprint on the history of piety and devotion, and indeed religious practice at large, in colonial Punjab. Because the literary texts considered in this chapter are neither sectarian nor solely elite, they afford a different perspective on religious practice and notions of piety.

Hir-Ranjha texts reveal that Punjabis shared notions of pious behavior irrespective of their affiliations to different religions. These texts present a vision of late nineteenth-century sociality and religiosity in which religious community, be it Hindu, Muslim, Sikh, or Christian, was not of paramount importance. Their literary representations do not map comfortably onto contemporary notions of discrete religious communities, yet neither do the practices represented exclude those notions. These texts point to the multiplicity of religious practices in which Punjabis participated while also delineating the importance of shared devotional practices. This complexity has been difficult to integrate into colonial Punjab's history, not only because of the historiographical emphasis on religious reform, but also due to the 1947 partition of India and the Punjab along religious lines. While political difference based on religious community is surely an important aspect of Punjab's late colonial history, political contestation along religious lines did not seep into or inform every aspect of Punjabi society. The texts examined in this chapter indicate that in the late nineteenth and early twentieth centuries an ethos of piety and devotion continued to be both salient to and shared by those who participated in the Punjabi literary formation.

GENRE AND DEVOTION

Colonial-era *Hir-Ranjha* texts were an integral aspect of the Punjabi *qissa* tradition. The *qissa* genre was adopted by India's Persian literati as early as the late thirteenth century. In the following centuries, it was taken up by Punjabi poets, and poets in other vernacular traditions, who indigenized it not only through their choice of language but also by their use of Indian meters and narratives. Punjabi poets retained certain elements of the Persian *qissa* tradition, among them the invocation. While invocations of some sort are familiar in a variety of South Asian literary genres, the particular form employed in Punjabi *qisse*—one that appears to derive from a model presented by Persian *qisse*—is a literary convention constitutive of the *qissa* as a Punjabi genre.[1] Beyond their literary function, invocations serve another purpose: they announce a devotional intent that is amenable to multiple interpretations, secular and religious.

Invocations in early Punjabi *qisse* followed the form of their Persian precursors relatively closely. The mid-eighteenth-century poet Waris Shah's opening to his *Hir-Ranjha* is typical:

> Let us first repeat praise for the Lord . . .
> . . . .
> The second praise is for the Prophet . . .
> . . . .
> Also I praise the four friends of the Prophet . . .
> Abu Bakr and Umar, Usman, Ali . . .
> . . . .
> They are exalted, they are the Lord's slaves.
> Next I must sing praise with love for that *pir* [Sufi spiritual guide], who counts holy
>   men among his followers.[2]
> . . . .
> Maudud's beloved, the Chishti *pir,* Masood Shakar-Ganj, is plenitude itself.[3]
> . . . .
> When one takes up the job of love, first meditate on the name of the Lord.
> Then, with each breath provide praise to the messenger of God and the prophets.
> Friends came to me and asked, will you make a new composition on the love
>   of Hir?
> . . . .
> Bringing together exotic and beautiful poetry, I have written of the union of Hir
>   and Ranjha.[4]

As in Persian invocations, Waris Shah's stands outside the narrative itself, framing it with the poet's obeisance to spiritual powers and the purported circumstances of the text's composition. The particulars of this invocation also epitomize a Punjabi norm: opening with praise for God, followed by praise for the prophet Muhammad, the first four caliphs, and more local spiritual figures, represented by *pirs*.

Not all colonial-era Punjabi *qisse* open with invocations, but the practice was common enough to suggest that it remained a literary convention of the genre. The use of an invocation closely styled on the template described above was one way to link a composition to the *qissa* tradition. The following examples from late nineteenth-century texts highlight this similarity. The first is from Muhammad Shah Sakin's *Qissa Hir wa Ranjha*. This text is comprised of four *si harfis*. *Si harfi* (thirty letters) is a genre adopted into Indian vernacular languages from Persian poetry; it is composed in couplets, each beginning with a successive letter of the Persian alphabet. Sakin's first two stanzas form an invocation:

> First is praise for God and then the prophet, the certain friend of the Lord.
> . . . .
> Then one must praise the companions of the prophet, whose names roll off the tongue as is the custom.
> Muhammad Shah says, "My *pir* is Muhammad Shah Ghaus al-Azam.
> Just taking his name drives away all pain."[5]

The second example is *Faryad Hir* (Hir's Plea), by Khaksar al-Baksh of Lahore, who wrote under the penname Munir. This text opens:

> First praise for the Lord, who is the bestower to all.
> . . . .
> Then let me say praise for the beloved friend of the Lord [Muhammad].
> . . . .
> [Let me praise] Abu Bakr, Umar, and Usman, the fourth exalted one being Ali.
> . . . .
> [Let me praise] Ghaus Azam Shah Jilani, whose benevolence is present in all the world.[6]

These invocations are to some extent formulaic. They do not belabor their point. Their inclusion, no matter how truncated the form, suggests that these poets saw invocations as a convention of the *qissa* genre. Indeed, they are one of the literary elements through which this genre cohered. This is not to suggest that *qisse* had rigid parameters or were not open to literary innovation. Sakin's and Munir's texts exemplify the flexibility of the form, since both were episodic rather than more traditional epic-length renditions. Although episodic texts may have been composed before the early nineteenth century, we have no record of any.[7] They were likely an innovation spurred by a print culture in which short eight- or sixteen-page texts could be readily mass produced and sold for a pittance, many for as low as a few paisas. Sakin's text highlights another kind of flexibility in late nineteenth-century *qisse*, since it was composed in *si harfi* rather than *masnavi*, the traditional *qissa* meter. Yet through the invocation, Sakin clearly located his text within the *qissa* tradition. Its title, *Qissa Hir wa Ranjha*, was obviously aimed at doing the same thing.

The inclusion of different poetic forms and meters was not the only way Punjabi poets shaped *qisse* to local sentiment and context. The invocation proved adaptable in other ways as well. From the earliest existing Punjabi *qisse*, poets opened their texts by invoking spiritual authorities other than those associated with Islam. If the invocation stemmed from an Islamic milieu, as is suggested by the praise for Allah, Muhammad, and the first four caliphs, then invocations that praised alternate genealogies or praised God without using an idiom associated with a particular religion indicate how this literary tradition reflected the Punjab's religious plurality. As far as we know, the Hindu poet Damodar was the first person to compose a Punjabi *qissa*. His early seventeenth-century *Hir-Ranjha* includes the following invocation:

> First let us take the name of the Lord [*sahib*], who created this world.
> Who made land and sky, the heavens and evil with his divine power.
> Who created the moon and the sun, that in every place should be his shadow.
> My name is Damodar, my *zat* Gulati, I have created this *qissa*.[8]

Damodar drew on a source of spiritual authority in his use of *sahib*, described as the creator. Although the word has an Arabic etymology, its use in the Punjabi language is not associated with Islam alone; it serves as a term for God that is not particular to any one religious community or denomination. Similar examples abound, particularly from the late nineteenth century. Kishan Singh 'Arif's *Qissa Hir te Ranjhe da* provides a good example. The text opens with an invocation that self-consciously avoids using any one religious idiom:

> In the beginning, the end, and throughout time, there is only one true one
>   [*sucha subhan*] to be praised.
> Without that grace [*subhan*], all the world would be false.
> He has not one name alone: either Ram, Rabb, or Bhagwan.
> Under God's writ, all the world exists,
> The sun, the stars, the moon, water, land, and sky,
> The life within each thing, each life, and the soul within each body.
> Kishan Singh says, there is one God [*Brahm*], the Vedas and Quran speak the truth.[9]

In his reference to a divine power or God, 'Arif self-consciously avoided using the language of a single religious genealogy or tradition. Instead, he praised a supreme deity (*sucha subhan*) in terms equally accessible to people from all of the Punjab's religious faiths and used terms associated with each of the Punjab's major religions (Ram, Rabb, Bhagwan).

Hindu and Sikh authors were not limited to praising a generic deity in their invocations. In his *Navan Qissa Hir* (A New *Qissa* Hir), Bhai Rann Singh adopted a Sikh idiom:

> Repeat the name of the Lord.
> Who has made the whole world.
> . . . .
> Who has brought us the land and water.
> He who is in every soul.
> He is the ruler of all the world.

Then let us take the name of the fifth king [*Guru Arjun*].
He who made the corpus, the Guru Granth Sahib.[10]

While Damodar's, 'Arif's, and Rann Singh's invocations differ in style and content—Damodar's and 'Arif's drawing on a generic deity and Rann Singh's on a Sikh genealogy—all three texts exemplify the use of invocations as a literary convention, while also showing how that convention was molded to reflect the cultural and religious context in which *qisse* were composed and circulated.

That poets employed invocations to identify specific sources of spiritual authority, underlining their own religious identity in the process, raises the question of whether Punjabi *qisse* were understood as specifically Muslim, Hindu, or Sikh texts by their authors and audiences. The answer can only be speculative, given the limited sources on authorial intent, performers' perspectives, or audience reception, either as readers or attendees at oral performances. On the basis of the *qissa* texts themselves, it appears that while authors used invocations to reflect their religious affiliations, their religious affiliations had little impact on how they recounted the narrative. For example, *Hir-Ranjha* has remained remarkably consistent in tellings across many centuries by authors with diverse religious affiliations. Representations of the love story and the motifs at the heart of this narrative tradition—specific villages, towns, landscapes, rivers, and recognizable figures such as the greedy boatman, his licentious wife, or the immoral mullah—were not informed by a religiously communitarian perspective. In framing the text authors were able to reflect on or include their own class, caste, sectarian, religious, and geographic affiliations and predilections, even though such self-referentiality is barely discernible in the narrative itself. Rather than suggesting the division of the Punjabi *qissa* tradition into Hindu, Muslim, and Sikh segments, invocations that move beyond an Islamic idiom suggest that invocations were an important literary convention, one flexible enough to allow the Punjabi *qissa* to reflect local beliefs and aesthetic and cultural practices. In addition to announcing a text as part of a literary tradition, they also announced its devotional intent. This could be voiced in multiple idioms, Muslim, Sikh, and Hindu, as the examples just given illustrate. The same was true of certain Punjabi *qissa* narratives, among them *Hir-Ranjha*. That is, the narrative could serve as religious allegory—Muslim, Hindu, and Sikh—while at the same time functioning as secular romance.

ROMANCE AS RELIGIOUS ALLEGORY

Most scholarly interpretations of *Hir-Ranjha* have considered the tale as a Sufi allegory. This is true of both Punjabi literary criticism and scholarship on Sufism in South Asia: from Lajwanti Rama Krishna's *Punjabi Sufi poets* (1938), to Annemarie

Schimmel's seminal work on Sufism, *Mystical Dimensions of Islam* (1975), to Sant Singh Sekhon's *A History of Panjabi Literature* (1996), scholars have analyzed the narrative principally through this lens.[11] This is in part due to the fact that two of Punjab's most prominent Sufi saints—Shah Husain (c. 1530s–1600) and Bulleh Shah—adapted the tale to explicitly Sufi ends in their poetry. Additionally, the most critically acclaimed text in *qissa* literature,[12] if not in Punjabi literature writ large—Waris Shah's *Hir-Ranjha*—has distinct Sufi overtones. Neither Shah Husain, Bulleh Shah, nor Waris Shah had to labor to transform *Hir-Ranjha* into a Sufi allegory. This romance, like many in the *qissa* tradition, lends itself well to a Sufi rendering.

Sufis adopted *Hir-Ranjha* for both practical and philosophical considerations. On the practical side, they employed popular narratives in their Indian vernacular poetry as a means of spreading Sufi ideas.[13] By using motifs already familiar and in wide circulation, Sufi poetry became that much more accessible. On the philosophical side, the narrative was useful because in Sufi thought love itself is a central concept. Indeed, as the literary critic and scholar of South Asian Islam Christopher Shackle puts it, in Sufi thought divine love is "the core organising principle of the universe."[14] He explains further: "In the Sufi ideology of love . . . [there is a] central notion of a hierarchy extending upwards from the interpersonal loves of the phenomenal world to the transpersonal connexion with the Divine." Sufis thus embraced the idea that "the phenomenal appearance of the physical world is simply a means to the apprehension of the higher divine reality from which it derives."[15] Sufis elaborated this idea by conceiving of two kinds of love: *ishq-i majazi* (phenomenal love) and *ishq-i haqiqi* (real love). The interplay between these and the related idea of *fana,* or annihilation, are central to the composition or reading of *Hir-Ranjha* as Sufi allegory.

Ishq-i haqiqi is true love for God. Sufi thought and practice revolves around achieving this true love, articulated through the notion of union with the divine. All Sufi adepts are on a spiritual path (*tariqa*) in which Sufi practices such as *dhikr* (the remembrance of God) and *sama'* (listening; see chapter 3) help the adept traverse a hierarchy of states (*hal*) on his or her way to gnosis, "after which," writes Islamicist Frederick Denny, "comes the unitive life in God."[16] *Ishq-i haqiqi,* and ultimately union with God, is a Sufi's driving motivation; separation from the divine leaves a Sufi in a constant state of yearning.

A related concept is *fana,* annihilation in the beloved-God. *Fana,* a doctrine developed by Al-Junayd (d. 910), is conceived as union with God, during which a Sufi is absent from this world and the self. This state can be achieved through the rigorous practice of one's *tariqa,* or spiritual path, but is not permanent. Upon returning to himself or herself and this mundane world, the Sufi experiences great suffering and sadness.[17] This pain is reflected in Sufi writings as akin to that of separated lovers yearning to be united. Yearning is thus a sign of one's true love for the divine, one's desire for union with God, and desire for annihilation of the self in this union.

Sufi poets found in the tale of Hir and Ranjha a broadly accessible and popular idiom through which to circulate these complex and fundamental ideas. In Sufi renditions, their love is symbolic of the Sufi's love for the divine. Ranjha represents the figure of God and Hir the Sufi who yearns to be united with God. The intensity of their love, their yearning for each other, and their union (whether in life or in death) are each symbolic of the Sufi's quest. Shah Husain (whose shrine in Lahore is the site of the Chiragan Mela, examined in chapter 3) is credited with the earliest known Sufi compositions to use *Hir-Ranjha* as an allegory; his *kafis* illustrate the Sufi appropriation of this tale. "Main bhi Jana Jhok Ranjhan di" (I, Too, Want to Go to Ranjha's Solitary Hut) relates ideas about love for the divine, the yearning of lover and beloved, and the path to achieving union. This *kafi* is written in Hir's voice:[18]

> Travelers, I too have to go; I have to go to the solitary hut of Ranjha.
> Is there anyone who will go with me?
> I have begged many to accompany me and now I set out alone.
> Travelers, is there no one who could go with me?
> The river is deep and the shaky bridge creaks as people step on it.
> And the ferry is a known haunt of tigers.
> Will no one go with me to the lonely hut of Ranjha?
> During long nights I have been tortured by my raw wounds.
> I have heard that he, in his lonely hut, knows the sure remedy.
> Will no one come with me, Travelers?[19]

Husain here elaborates the depth of emotion that Hir feels for Ranjha. Hir will throw off the yoke of convention that prohibits her from traveling alone, just as Sufis turn their backs on convention to pursue their love for God. Although part of society, Sufis reject the worldly in their pursuit of spiritual fulfillment. In Husain's composition, Hir begs for assistance. None is forthcoming, however, so she sets out alone on the treacherous and difficult path to her beloved. The dangers of the river not only locate the text in the Punjabi landscape (see chapter 4), but are also symbolic of the difficulty of Hir's pursuit. As Najm Hossain Syed writes in his exegesis of this *kafi*: "The river for centuries has flowed between desire and fulfillment."[20] Hir's physical journey, too, has parallels in Sufi thought and practice. If her journey to Ranjha is a metaphor for the Sufi's journey toward God through his or her *tariqa,* then that, too, will be a difficult path. For the Sufi, overcoming the challenges presented by each successive stage of the *tariqa* is only possible through a true and intense devotion.

Rejecting convention is a motif that appears in another of Shah Husain's compositions, "Ni Mai Menoon Kherian di Gal naa Aakh" (Mother, Do Not Talk to Me of the Kheras). In this *kafi*, Hir tells her mother not to speak to her of the family to which she has been betrothed:

> Do not talk of the Kheras to me, oh mother, do not.
> I belong to Ranjha and he belongs to me.
> And the Kheras dream idle dreams.
> Let the people say, "Hir is crazy; she has given herself to the cowherd."
> Oh mother, he alone knows.
> Please mother, do not talk to me of the Kheras.[21]

In this poem, Hir rejects the conventions of society, those in which a daughter accepts her parents' choice of husband. By rejecting the Kheras, she is flouting both convention and a future that will provide her wealth and status. Hir cares little for either and has told her mother to let the world think she is crazy. Here, Shah Husain uses *Hir-Ranjha* to relate the Sufi ideals of rejecting status, wealth, and material comforts for a life of spiritual achievement.

Bulleh Shah, the eighteen-century Sufi saint whose shrine is in Kasur (today in Pakistan), also engaged Sufi concepts through *Hir-Ranjha*. His *kafi* "Ranjha Ranjha Kardi" (Remembering Ranjha, Ranjha), for example, is among the clearest elaborations of the idea of *fana* in Punjabi poetry. It, too, is written in Hir's voice:

> Remembering Ranjha day and night,
> I have myself become Ranjha.
> Call me Dhido Ranjha,
> No more should I be addressed as Hir.
> I am in Ranjha and Ranjha is in me,
> There is no distinction left.
> I am nowhere; he himself is there.[22]

Hir's state is the goal of all Sufis: to be united with the beloved-God and to be annihilated in him-her. It is an ecstatic state and Bulleh Shah conveys this through both the tone of the *kafi* and through the use of repetition: "I've become Ranjha," "I am in Ranjha, he is in me," "There is no distinction left." As this *kafi* illustrates, Hir's union with Ranjha is an ideal vehicle for conveying the Sufi doctrine of *fana*.

Without doubt, many processes were at work in the historical composition and circulation of Sufi poetry in vernacular languages. Through Richard Eaton's scholarship, in particular, we encounter a sophisticated understanding of why Sufis adopted vernacular languages and local stories and folk literature for their literary compositions.[23] Less considered, however, is what Sufis' adoption of vernacular stories like *Hir-Ranjha* tells us about these narratives. At least two conclusions can be drawn from the examples above. First, by the time Shah Husain and Bulleh Shah composed their poetry (in the mid-sixteenth and early eighteenth centuries, respectively), *Hir-Ranjha* was already well known and popular among the local populations of Lahore and Kasur. This is suggested by the way both Shah Husain and Bulleh Shah took their audiences' knowledge of the narrative for granted in their compositions. The power of a single *kafi,* even a single couplet, to convey complex Sufi ideas rested partially in the use of metaphors that their audiences could relate to. Punjabis were clearly familiar with the arc of the story: Hir and Ranjha's intense love for one another, the conflict this led to within Hir's family, the lovers' anguish at separation, and their final union, often depicted as occurring in death (note that the term used for a Sufi saint's death anniversary—*urs*—literally means "marriage" with God). Second, in appropriating *Hir-Ranjha* to Sufi ends, these poets made an indelible impact on the narrative tradition itself. Once the narrative had been appropriated to Sufi ends in the sixteenth century, it was thereafter always available as a Sufi text.

Some poets were explicit in their composition of the *Hir-Ranjha* story as Sufi allegory. As already mentioned, Waris Shah's 1766 rendition is generally accepted as a Sufi rendering of the romance.[24] Many colonial-era *qissa* poets took this approach also, among them Maula Shah (b. 1867), Hadayatullah (1838–1929), and Fazl Shah (1827–90). Maula Shah not only took a Sufi approach in his *Hir-Ranjha,* published in about 1912, but was himself a spiritual guide (*pir*) in the city of Amritsar where he resided.[25] Hadayatullah's *Hir-Ranjha* was something of a novelty. Published in 1887, the text was comprised of Waris Shah's rendition in its entirety, with original couplets embellishing this text. Of these three poets, Fazl Shah is perhaps the most interesting. A disciple of Hazrat Ghulam Mohiuddin of Kasur, he was well versed in Arabic, Persian, and Urdu as well as in Punjabi, and worked as a clerk in the office of the Financial Commissioner in Lahore.[26] He was one of the most widely published *qissa* poets of the late nineteenth century. His *Qissa Hir wa Ranjha* (1867), published in at least ten separate editions,[27] resembled his other writings symbolic of divine love.[28] Many other compositions explicitly Sufi in their orientation can be adduced, even when their authors did not explicitly draw connections between the narrative and Sufi concepts. Therefore, *Hir-Ranjha* always remained available to be read, heard, interpreted, and understood as a Sufi allegory.

SIKH AND HINDU DEVOTIONAL IDIOMS

The *Hir-Ranjha* narrative is open to more than Sufi interpretation alone. Just as it served as Sufi allegory, this narrative also worked allegorically in Sikh and Hindu devotionalism. An early nineteenth-century text by Vir Singh exemplifies how the narrative served as a Sikh devotional text. It opens with the following invocation:

My supplication to Guru Gobind Singh, who is the master of all beings.
I would sacrifice myself for Gobind Singh, my strength, my spiritual guide is
    Gobind Singh.
The Guru is ever my refuge, as water is the refuge for fish.
Vir Singh, the Guru will support you as you compose this *qissa* of Hir and Ranjha.[29]

In Vir Singh's work, Ranjha is a symbol of the tenth Sikh guru, Gobind Singh, and Hir represents the author. Hir's yearning thereby became the poet's yearning for Guru Gobind Singh. Much more common than Sikh allegory, however, were texts that represented *Hir-Ranjha* as an allegory of bhakti devotion, specifically bhakti that centered on the Hindu god Krishna. Bhakti evolved as a form of devotionalism first in south India in the sixth century. The result, writes literary critic Francesca Orsini in *Love in South Asia: A Cultural History,* "was a whole new universe of expression that centred around the person of the devotee and the loving relationship between the devotee and his or her God."[30] From south India, bhakti devotionalism spread throughout India, including the Punjab, where it had a profound impact in the medieval period. One can read the teachings of Sikhism's founder, Guru Nanak (b. 1469), as stemming from this intellectual and religious milieu.

The strand of bhakti most relevant to *Hir-Ranjha* texts is that which focuses on Krishna. In *Hir-Ranjha* texts, Ranjha represents Krishna, and Hir his consort, Radha. Krishna is an incarnation of Vishnu in the Hindu pantheon. He appears prominently in the *Bhagavad Gita* (a part of the *Mahabharata,* c. 200) as a charioteer who offers critical counsel on dharma, or proper action. More relevant to the present discussion is how Krishna is depicted in the "Harivamsa," an appendix to the *Mahabharata.* In this text, Vishnu incarnates himself as Krishna to destroy a tyrannical demon. The "Harivamsa" portrays Krishna as born of royal parents but raised among a tribe of cowherds on the banks of the Yamuna River.[31] Being a cowherd is one of the three critical elements of Krishna's identity, for our purposes. The others are his flute playing and his sexual appeal to the *gopis,* or cowherdesses. The *gopis* have an intense love for Krishna, for which they will sacrifice anything. Literary texts present these women as abandoning their homes, husbands, and families as they follow the flute-playing god into the forest.[32] Krishna's flute, too, has important symbolism. On one hand it, or its music, is a symbol of God. As cultural historian Denis Matringe writes, the flute's "music symbolizes the pervading immanence of God."[33] But the flute also has a more mundane symbolism, representing human carnal desires. Sanskritist Barbara Stoler Miller argues, "the sexual freedom enjoyed by the adolescent cowherd is symbolized by Krishna's simple bamboo flute. . . . Krishna's magical flute is an adolescent instrument for arousing and sustaining sexual desire."[34] Krishna's sexual desire and appeal is most strikingly portrayed in his relationship with Radha, the most affecting of the *gopis* (figure 12).

FIGURE 12. *Krishna Playing the Flute*, c. 1770. © The British Library Board (J.45, 39).

The first full and datable evidence of the legend of Radha and Krishna occurs in the twelfth-century *Gitagovinda,* a Sanskrit text by the poet Jayadeva.[35] This text provides the first elaborate portrayal of Radha, who until that time had appeared only in stray verses of Sanskrit poetry.[36] In the *Gitagovinda,* however, Radha comes to life as "neither a wife nor a worshiping rustic playmate," as Miller puts it, but "an intense, solitary, proud female who complements and reflects the mood of Krishna's passion. She is Krishna's partner in a secret and exclusive love."[37] While many longer and more recent compositions describing Krishna and Radha's passion exist, literary renderings of these two figures have remained relatively consistent since the *Gitagovinda.*

From the Sanskrit treatments of this divine love story, the image of Krishna is one of a humble cowherd, though a royal scion, and a flute player who from an early age intoxicated the women around him. "This lover of others' wives" had many consorts, among whom Radha held special favor.[38] Krishna and Radha's was a divine love, of course. Thus, alongside their depiction of carnal passions, representations of Krishna, Radha, and the *gopis* also carry religious significance. Krishna represents the divine and Radha and the *gopis*, in their desire for sexual union with Krishna, represent the human soul's desire for the divine. As Hinduism scholar Glen Hayes writes, "In the loyalty of the cowherd girls [especially Radha] for [Krishna], we have a representation of the human search for the sacred."[39] Much like the Sufi search for the divine, then, the story of Krishna, Radha, and the *gopis* addresses spiritual yearning and devotion for the beloved-God.

Given the tale of Krishna and Radha as rendered in Sanskrit literature from the twelfth century on, and from which it was widely disseminated in vernacular languages, one can see the facility with which *Hir-Ranjha* could serve as an allegory for this tale of divine love. Ranjha, a cowherd, though of high birth, is a fluteplaying lover and easily assimilable to the figure of Krishna. Hir, the enamored lover who secretly cavorts with her beloved each day on the banks of the Chenab (as Radha did with Krishna on the banks of the Yamuna), and who pines for her beloved when they are separated, is easily assimilable to the figure of Radha. And in Hir's friends, who accompany her to the riverbank each day in many renditions of the narrative, we see the *gopis*. Through these parallels, *Hir-Ranjha* offers, in Denis Matringe's words, "an ideal repertory of . . . [Krishnaite] . . . symbols, as well as the allegorical framework of a mystical parable."[40] The possibilities of interlacing these two narratives was not lost on Punjabi poets, and many of them composed the tale of Hir and Ranjha explicitly as a metaphor for Krishnaite devotion.

Literary renderings of *Hir-Ranjha* from the eighteenth century onward are replete with images that draw parallels between Ranjha and Krishna, Hir and Radha, Hir's friends and the *gopis*, and, more broadly, with the story of Krishna and Radha's relationship as a whole. In some cases, the comparison is explicit, as in Kishan Singh 'Arif's *Qissa Hir te Ranjhe da* (1889). In this rendition, while on his way to Jhang, Ranjha mesmerizes a mullah and a group of townspeople by playing his flute. Here, 'Arif underscores the likeness between Ranjha and Krishna:

> When Ranjha picked up his flute and played a tune,
> Kishan Singh, everyone's spirit was calmed by listening to his song.
> The people said to Ranjha, "Why don't you stay for some days,
> You have a pleasant (divine) appearance and your virtue is boundless,
> You play the flute well, just like the Lord Krishna."[41]

But Krishna need not be mentioned by name for the allusion to the story of Krishna and Radha to operate. The most consistent confluence between the two stories is in the characterization of Ranjha as a cowherd and a flute player (Manjit Bawa captures this elegantly in his paintings *Krishna with Cows* and *Heer;* figures 13 and 14). It is important to note that Ranjha is always represented with these attributes, no matter how short or cursory a *Hir-Ranjha* text might be.

The late nineteenth-century poet Niaz, for example, opened his text with reference to Ranjha's vocation as a cowherd: "Your love, oh beautiful Hir, has made me a sufferer in this world. I have grazed cows for twelve years and ultimately been disappointed."[42] The reference to Ranjha's tenure as a cowherd, which allowed for their intimacy—both emotional and physical—is critical to Ranjha's literary rendering and surfaces repeatedly. It figures prominently in the opening verse of Khawaish Ali's *Hir-Ranjha,* for example: "I [Ranjha] left Takht Hazara and came, I came to the land of the Sials and made it my home. . . . In exchange for Hir, oh Guru, I was a cowherd for twelve years."[43] The important parallel with Krishna here is not only the fact that both were cowherds but that they were both born to a higher status. Muhammad Shah Sakin's *Qissa Hir wa Ranjha* makes Ranjha's loss of status clear. In an opening exchange with Hir, Ranjha says: "I have worked for you for twelve years, oh Hir, and all my energies have gone to waste. . . . I have wasted an era in the forest to no avail, oh Hir. . . . I am the beloved son of Moju Meher of Takht Hazara, over your love I have given up my status, oh Hir. . . . The entire world now knows, oh Hir, that I became a cowherd of the Sials of Jhang."[44] By drawing attention to his status by birth, Ranjha underscores that, like Krishna, his tenure as a cowherd was a stark departure from the status he was born into as the son of a landowner.

Another crucial aspect of Ranjha's literary representation was his depiction as a flute player. Poets had to reference not only his flute playing, but as in Kishan Singh 'Arif's text above, where Ranjha mesmerizes a group of strangers, draw attention to its power. Sometimes references to this power are passing, as in Munir's *Faryad Hir,* a late nineteenth-century episodic text. Munir's account opens with Hir lamenting her separation from Ranjha after her marriage to Seido Khera. She recounts her love for Ranjha, forced marriage, subsequent unhappiness and yearning, all expressed and emphasized by a line repeated at the end of every verse:

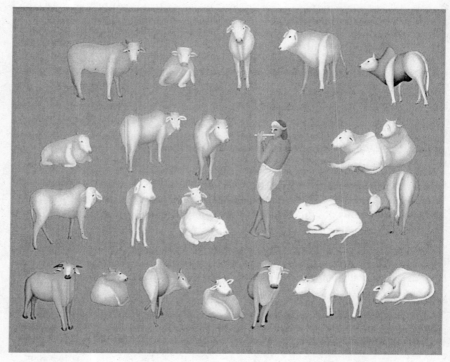

FIGURE 13. *Krishna with Cows*, by Manjit Bawa, n.d. Courtesy of Bhavna Bawa.

"Lamenting, I, Hir, call out, I yearn to see you, oh Ranjha."[45] In this text, Ranjha's flute playing is a prominent device. At one point, Hir says to him, "The sound of your flute has greatly charmed my heart. Your love has entranced me."[46] By drawing attention to the effect and power of Ranjha's flute over Hir, even in the limited space of this composition (which is only seven pages in length), Munir included an accepted—and perhaps expected—aspect of Ranjha's character and, simultaneously, drew allusion to the image of Krishna.

Kishore Chand's *Navan Qissa Hir Kishore Chand* (Kishore Chand's New *Qissa* Hir) offers a more elaborate example of this. His narrative begins in Takht Hazara with the death of Moju Meher (Ranjha's father) and Ranjha's subsequent neglect. Dejected by his treatment, Ranjha goes to meet a group of fakirs (mendicants) camped on the outskirts of his village. While he sits with them the narrator interjects, alternating between giving Ranjha commands and narrating his actions: "'Enchant them [he says to Ranjha] by playing your flute.' He plays *raga* Bhairavi for them. He plays other *raga*s for them. He sings *thumri*s and other musical com-

FIGURE 14. *Heer,* by Manjit Bawa, n.d. Courtesy of Bhavna Bawa.

positions for them. 'Enchant them by playing your flute.' With his flute he played other *ragas* for them."[47] In the larger passage from which this excerpt is taken, the refrain "enchant them by playing your flute" is repeated four times, suggesting the importance of this aspect of Ranjha's character and its power to sway others to his favor. In his highlighting Ranjha as a flute player Chand was surely drawing a strong parallel with that most definable of Krishna's features.

That *Hir-Ranjha* overtly referred to Krishnaite devotion is evident in compositions from the eighteenth to the twentieth centuries. Importantly, poets did not have to self-consciously underscore the parallels for the symbolism to operate. *Hir-Ranjha* as a literary text was infused with Krishnaite symbolism. Any poet who undertook his own composition of the tale operated in a narrative tradition that drew parallels between the tales of Hir and Ranjha and Krishna and Radha in multiple ways, both explicit and implicit. After all, the literary figure of Ranjha was constituted by precisely those elements that made him a figure for Krishna: his relatively high-status birth, his vocation as a cowherd, his flute playing, and his love play with Hir. The decision to compose *Hir-Ranjha* meant that allusions to Krishnaite imagery were a necessary concomitant of the process, whether they were overt or not. No matter what particular emphasis a poet chose, Krishnaite symbolism was embedded in the *Hir-Ranjha* narrative tradition.

It is important to remember that *Hir-Ranjha* operated in these multiple registers simultaneously. It was always a Sufi text, a Sikh text, a Hindu text, and yet was never limited to any one of those interpretations or easily appropriable to sectarian interests. To present an example of this multiplicity, consider the composition by eighteenth-century Sufi saint Bulleh Shah. Bulleh Shah, as noted above, appropriated *Hir-Ranjha* to Sufi ends. Here I want to draw attention to a composition that highlights most explicitly how *Hir-Ranjha* could be appropriated to serve simultaneously as both Sufi and Hindu allegory. In the following *kafi*, Bulleh Shah alludes to the Sufi concept of *fana*, annihilation in the divine, while at the same time he portrays Krishnaite devotion, using the epithet Kahan for Krishna:

> Kahan plays the flute wonderfully.
> . . . .
> Flute-player, cowherd Ranjha,
> Your melody unites with everything,
> Your pleasures are in me,
> Our appearances themselves have mingled.
> Kahan plays the flute wonderfully.[48]

In this case, Ranjha ceases to exist as he becomes one with the divine. And how did the poet accomplish this in literary terms? By representing Ranjha as a flute player and cowherd. In this composition, through *Hir-Ranjha,* Sufi and Krishnaite symbolism operate within a single text, indeed within a single *kafi*. What Bulleh Shah's *kafi* does explicitly was implicit in all *Hir-Ranjha* texts. *Hir-Ranjha* could always operate in multiple registers. It was for poets, performers, and audiences to decide how they chose to compose, perform, read, listen to, and interpret the text. No one had to adopt a single framework for composition, performance, or analysis, or render the text in a single devotional idiom.

REPRESENTATIONS OF PIETY

Given the particular configuration of the production and circulation of *Hir-Ranjha* texts—their autonomy from colonial intervention, their popularity, their dissemination through print and performance, their function as a site for social commentary, their devotional idiom, and, most significantly, their engagement with piety as a central theme—colonial-era *Hir-Ranjha* texts present an excellent source for assessing contemporary religious beliefs. They are replete with "religious" characters: mullahs, *qazis*, and yogis, all of whom figure prominently in a theme that emanates from this literature: the critique of false piety. The first two—the mullah and the *qazi*—are Muslim figures of local and sometimes translocal authority, but in *Hir-Ranjha* texts they function as representatives of religious authority in general. The critique in these texts is not therefore limited to Islam or to Muslim society, but is a broader sociological and religious critique. Yogis, associated specifically with the Nath Siddha (Hindu) tradition in *Hir-Ranjha* texts, contrast with mullahs and *qazi*s in having low social status. Nevertheless, all three characters are portrayed in much the same light: as individuals whose piety is insincere. This is less a critique of religion as such than a reflection on the gulf between right intention and action.

Mullahs, also known as *maulvi*s, hold an important position in South Asian Muslim communities even though their title does not indicate a particularly rigorous religious education or any formal religious office. At minimum, mullahs must be able to read the Quran in its original Arabic and lead congregational prayers, because they serve as custodians of mosques. They are also often entrusted with the religious education of children, teaching them to read the Quran in Arabic. Mullahs can also perform other religious functions, such as reading funeral rites or performing marriages. Their religious authority and social status is grounded in their religious learning, however limited, their stewardship of mosques, their function as preceptors for the community's young, and their role in Muslim rituals.

A *qazi* is a judge with state authority to adjudicate matters subject to Islamic law on the basis of his religious education and study of *fiqh*, or Islamic jurisprudence. Under Muslim states in South Asia, *qazi*s were appointed to adjudicate both religious and secular issues. According to historian J. S. Grewal, their duties could include the following: to uphold and execute penal laws, to adjudicate and keep records of lawsuits, to ensure that Friday prayers and congregations in general were properly held, to perform Muslim marriages, to determine the distribution of inheritance and look after unclaimed property and the property of orphans, to appoint legatees, and to induce men to piety.[49] Although it is commonly assumed that *qazi*s' authority related to Muslims alone, in the Punjab and likely elsewhere across north India, they often adjudicated the disputes of Muslims and non-Muslims alike. Grewal has published documents indicating that in certain contexts *qazi*s continued to adjudicate non-Muslim and even secular affairs into the Sikh period (1799–1849).[50] During the late nineteenth century this secular role was summarily circumscribed by the colonial state.[51] *Qazi*s continued to enjoy authority within the Muslim community, however, principally due to their educational and ritual roles.

In *Hir-Ranjha*, mullahs and *qazi*s figure in two crucial episodes, one that takes place in a mosque and the other at Hir's marriage. In the first, Ranjha stops at a village mosque on his way from Takht Hazara to Jhang. Ranjha had left home with little or no provisions and had, therefore, to rely on the generosity of the mosque's custodian. Although mosques are supposed to extend refuge and hospitality to travelers, in many *Hir-Ranjha* texts this custodian—sometimes referred to as a mullah, sometimes a *qazi*—refuses Ranjha this courtesy. The marriage episode comes later in the narrative, when Hir is forcibly married to Seido Khera. By Islamic law, a woman must consent to marriage of her own free will. It is the responsibility of the person performing these rites—in the texts considered here, always a *qazi*—to ensure that a woman's rights and Islamic law are upheld. In these stories, however, the *qazi* colludes with Hir's family and makes her marry under duress. As we will see in these two scenes, the mullah and the *qazi* are portrayed as self-righteous, immoral, greedy, and self-serving.

Maula Shah's *Hir wa Ranjha* provides a paradigmatic example of how the mosque scene was depicted in colonial-era texts.[52] His Ranjha is a sympathetic figure, a young man frightened by and exhausted from his journey through alien territory. As night falls, Ranjha comes upon a mosque where he encounters a *qazi* who has just finished his evening prayers. This image of quiet contemplative religiosity is a far cry from the *qazi*'s subsequent behavior. Upon seeing Ranjha, the *qazi* accosts him: "'Without any intention of saying your prayers why have you entered the mosque. Where have you come from, what is your place? . . . Tell me who you are,' he said with passion and anger, scaring Ranjha."[53] Met with hostility rather than hospitality, Ranjha verbally attacks the *qazi*, ridiculing and belittling him. "Don't babble such trifling and absurd words, you idiot," Ranjha retorts, adding, "Don't sit in the mosque and fart, don't defile its purity by causing the dust to fly!"[54] Besides being witty, the imagery captures a distinct contempt for the *qazi*.

Maula Shah's text is particularly interesting because of its rather lengthy invocation, which includes extensive praise for God, the prophet Muhammad, the first four caliphs, and numerous *pirs*. Given this reverence for the divine and for these most important figures within institutional Islam, and for more local figures of spiritual authority (*pirs*) and religious institutions (their shrines), it is difficult to read Shah's opprobrium for the *qazi* as contempt for Islam, religious institutions, or organized religion more generally. Rather, Shah's text presents a critique of the false piety of the *qazi*, a man who engages in prayers one moment and abuses a traveler who enters his mosque the next. Indeed, considering the figures Shah praised at the beginning of his text, all of whom were models of pious action, one can see how, in the shadow of these men, the *qazi*'s behavior toward a bedraggled traveler could hardly seem less virtuous.

While the mosque scene appeared in many colonial-era renditions of *Hir-Ranjha*, criticism of figures of religious authority centered more often on the wedding scene, a focal scene in many of the *Hir-Ranjha* texts of the period. *Hir Niaz Ranjha* provides one example. This episodic text is a mere eight pages in length, and had two distinct compositions: "Faryad Ranjha" (Ranjha's Lamentation) and "Faryad Hir" (Hir's Lamentation). The first, written in Ranjha's voice, reveals his agony at Hir's marriage to Seido Khera. He is tormented by their separation: "Without you [Hir] I have no peace; in the pangs of separation each breath is like fire. Crying, I writhe in anguish; this separation from you has made me sick."[55] Ranjha presents himself as a hapless victim crushed by the turn of events, and accuses Hir of faithlessness.

> You reside blissful in Rangpur, laughing and playing with Seido.
> I cry walking in alleys, separation from you has crippled me.
> Your love, oh beautiful Hir, has made me a sufferer in this world.
> . . . .
> If you weren't going to fulfill your commitments, why did you love me?
> Mistakenly I came to your abode, and you made this cowherd your lover.
> Your love, oh beautiful Hir, has made me a sufferer in this world.[56]

Hir's defense in "Faryad Hir" rests on one critical argument: that she had been forced to marry Seido Khera, an act in which the *qazi* was complicit. Hir repeatedly states her love for and commitment to Ranjha, but for Ranjha her statements are meaningless because she has married another man. His suspicions and hurt are succinctly captured in the closing lines of his lament: "Getting into your palanquin, you didn't seem fazed. What is this that has come over your heart? Don't speak to me as you are leaving, having rejected me."[57] Hir's response, in one line, clears her of aspersions as she argues that the *qazi*'s immoral behavior was to blame. "The *qazi* forcibly read the *nikah* [Muslim marriage contract]," she says, "he did a dishonest thing." With this statement, Hir exonerates herself as she indicts the *qazi* for his corrupt behavior. Although his corruption is not detailed, pointing to it obliquely suggests that this representation of the *qazi* drew on prevalent attitudes toward figures of religious authority, who could be viewed as self-serving and corrupt.

Abd al-Karim Na'at's rendition of the tale contains a more direct assault on the *qazi*.[58] Published in about 1880, Na'at's text is similar to *Hir Niaz Ranjha* in length (eight pages) and form. It, too, is comprised of two sections, in this case each a *sawal-jawab* (question and answer). One is a dialogue between Hir and the *qazi*, and the other between Hir and Ranjha. I will focus upon the former, a scene encountered in chapter 4 in which the *qazi* tries to convince Hir to marry Seido Khera. Earlier I focused on the representation of Hir as an active agent who challenges a figure of significantly greater social and religious status. Here I focus instead on the representation of the *qazi*. Each of his remarks in this exchange are punctuated with the pronouncement: "Accept the Khera [Seido], he is your equal, oh Jat [Hir]. Accept this dictate from your parents' heart, oh Jat."[59] Hir is not persuaded, yet the *qazi* persists. Losing patience with his platitudes, Hir explodes, "You, oh *qazi*, take bribes. You would perform the marriage rites on the coming day. Every devil goes to hell, oh *qazi*."[60] Hir's suspicions about the *qazi*'s integrity are quickly validated when he responds with equal hostility: "You have no witnesses. The order for your wedding has come down like an axe. You will go on the path that leads to the Kheras with Seido, oh Jat."[61] The *qazi*'s threat reveals his treachery, making clear that Hir's contestations will go unheard. And indeed, the *qazi* marries her against her will, in violation of the Islamic law he is bound to uphold.

Criticism of figures of religious authority like that of mullahs and *qazi*s is found in other colonial-era vernacular traditions (both other genres of Punjabi literature and literature in other Indian vernacular languages, such as Urdu), as it is in precolonial texts of *Hir-Ranjha*. Perhaps no work of Punjabi literature dissects the character of the mullah as mercilessly as Waris Shah's *Hir-Ranjha*.[62] What makes the colonial-era portrayals historiographically significant, however, is the context of their production and circulation. Why might the mosque scene or the marriage scene, in particular, have been focuses of literary production in the colonial period? One answer is that at this time the behavior of local figures of institutionalized religious authority was under scrutiny and subject to reform, whether they were local mullahs, *qazi*s, *mahant*s (caretakers of *gurdwara*s), or Brahmins (as caretakers of temple rituals). A good example can be seen in the simplification of rituals, particularly temple rituals, that was central to the Arya Samaj's agenda. The emphasis on the reform of temple rituals emerged partly out of a concern that the Brahmins who ran these institutions had lost sight of the deeper values and core of the Hindu faith. In simplifying religious ritual and focusing on a supposedly "pure" Vedic past, the Arya Samaj was surely reinscribing the importance of Brahmins; but it was simultaneously insisting on their earnest commitment to right action through their own example.

Similarly, a Sikh movement that would emerge in the twentieth century as the Gurdwara Reform movement was already targeting the *mahant*s of Sikh *gurdwara*s in the late nineteenth century. In the eyes of their critics, these caretakers were corrupt and had turned *gurdwara*s into personal fiefdoms. *Mahant*s were well ensconced in their positions, so extracting control of these sites was a drawn-out and bloody process. In the end the reformers prevailed, their success marked by the creation of the Shiromani Gurdwara Prabhandak Committee in 1919 to oversee Sikhism's religious sites.[63] At this time in the Punjab and north India generally, Islam too was in the throes of religious reform. The actions of the local mullah and *qazi* were also of central concern. The Deoband movement provides a case in point. The Dar-ul Uloom, the religious seminary at Deoband (United Provinces), was started by a group of *ulema* (religious scholars) in the 1860s as a response to the perceived fall of the Muslim community. Spurred to action by the political overthrow of Mughal sovereignty by British colonial rule, the *ulema* associated with Deoband saw moral decline in the demise of Muslim political power. These *ulema* decided that the remedy was to reeducate Muslims about the proper ways of their faith, a process that would be spearheaded by the *ulema* themselves. Although Deobandis were concerned with the moral welfare of the Muslim community at large, working through local clerics was central to their method. Thus, the school at Deoband educated a new generation of *ulema* in a reformed Islam. From this base in Deoband, trained *ulema* fanned out across the Indian subcontinent (and beyond) to propagate Deoband's interpretation of Islam, through their own example as much as through their teachings. The Deoband movement took root in the Punjab not only through the activities of *ulema* trained at the Dar-ul Uloom but also at two affiliated schools established there by the end of the century, one in Lahore and another in Gujranwala.[64]

By focusing attention on characters with religious authority, the various *Hir-Ranjha* texts engaged broader social and religious currents. Their representations suggest a popular and widespread disaffection with the corrupt behavior of local religious figures. These texts were not of a piece with socioreligious reform literature, however; they were neither propagandistic nor didactic. What they contribute to the historiography of colonial Punjab is a window into the nature of popular attitudes toward such figures as mullahs and *qazis*. These attitudes clearly dovetailed with the agendas of socioreligious reformers, which in part addressed the corruption and moral decay of such individuals. This confluence may help explain why socioreligious reformers found the Punjab such fertile ground for their efforts.

Mullahs and *qazis* were not alone in being singled out for opprobrium in colonial-era *Hir-Ranjha* texts. Yogis, particularly those associated with the Nath Siddha sect, were portrayed with similar contempt, as parasites feeding off society. Before turning to their representation in this literature, let us consider the historic presence of yogis, specifically Nath yogis, in Punjabi society. The Nath yogis, alternately known as Nathpanthis, Gorakhnathis, or Nath Siddhas, have a historic relationship to the Punjab. In the Salt Range mountains sits Tilla Jogian, the oldest Nath yogi *dera*, or monastery, which is associated with the sect's much-revered founder, Gorakhnath. Some even suggest that this site is "undoubtedly one of the oldest religious establishments in Northern India."[65] The yogi *dera*s that cropped up across north India in the medieval period claimed connections to this site. Emanating from the Punjab, this movement influenced both its immediate environs and much of north India.

The Nath Siddha sect associated with Tilla Jogian is thought to have originated in the twelfth century.[66] Members worshipped Shiva above all other incarnations of God and claimed to imitate him in their religious practice. David Gordon White, a scholar of Hindu Tantra traditions, argues that the sect represents an important strand in Indian religious thought. "In very broad terms," he writes, "the siddha traditions . . . emphasized the perfectibility of the human body as a means to dominating the forces and laws of nature, including life and death. Present in every siddha tradition was a body of techniques for physical transformation called *hatha yoga* (the 'yoga of violent force')."[67] The creation of the system of hatha yoga, or at least its revelation, is credited to Gorakhnath and Matsyendranath, the legendary founders of the sect, both of whom are revered as India's greatest hatha yogis. They are also likely responsible for instituting the visible initiation practices of the sect, which include having the ear torn (*kan pharna*) and wearing wide hoop earrings (called *mundra*s or *darsan*s).

Although Nath Siddhas were devotees of Shiva, they were censured by Hindu society for three principal reasons, according to White. Probably most important of these was their interaction with Sufism. "Perhaps no Hindu religious sect has interacted on as profound and sustained a level as have the Nath Siddhas with exponents of . . . Sufism. Over the centuries, a great number of the religious virtuosi of Sufism, called fakirs, *pir*s, and *wali*s have come to be identified with various Nath Siddhas, and vice versa." Second, the emphasis within the sect on hatha yoga displaced dependence on a god or goddess, an aspect of the sect that "did not sit well with the more mainstream devotional cults of medieval India." This led to yogis being accused of "arrogance and material self-sufficiency" by "sants [holy persons] from a broad array of traditions." Third, the Nath Siddhas did not evolve in their theology and they continued to emphasize their hatha yoga principles, leading to their being "branded by their critics as frauds and conjurers, deceivers both of themselves and of their followers."[68] While institutional Shaivism may have shunned Nath yogis, they found a place in Punjabi society through popular appeal: "Like the fakirs and pirs who are their Muslim counterparts—and this much to the chagrin of the more elite sectarian followers of medieval and contemporary Hinduism—they have always been the chosen holy men and wonder workers of the Hindu masses. . . . And so it is that down the ages, it has been Nath Siddhas who have healed ailing cows, provided barren women with sons, and brought down the mighty in favor of the poor."[69]

Hir-Ranjha texts suggest that this may be a somewhat idealized vision of the relationship between yogis and the population among which they lived. Nath elements are important to the *Hir-Ranjha* narrative through the inclusion of certain characters and sites. Most significant of these is Balnath Yogi, the spiritual preceptor of the *dera* at Tilla Jogian. Precolonial texts established Tilla Jogian as an important site in the unfolding of the narrative. Upon Hir's marriage to Seido Khera, Ranjha retreats to the *dera* where he is inducted into the Nath yogi sect with the ear-cutting ceremony. He subsequently uses his yogi's attire as a disguise so that he can visit Hir in her married home. Here, Ranjha's initiation into the sect is a sham—he joins for his own ulterior motives. On the other hand, Ranjha takes on an ascetic's garb out of devotion to his beloved. With this "conversion," *Hir-Ranjha* texts incorporated one more metaphor of devotionalism: that of the desire of the *yogini* (female yogi) to be subsumed in the yogi; a relationship of deep longing between the divine and the mortal that finds parallels in Sufi and Krishnaite devotionalism. The following Bulleh Shah *kafi,* written in Hir's voice, illustrates this particular idiom:

> Ranjha has come, having made himself a yogi,
> The actor has played his role!
> . . . .
> When I saw his face, misery and pangs of separation went away.
> . . . .
> Ranjha is the yogi and I am his *yogini*.
> I shall fetch water for him.
> I have wasted my past life,
> But now he has enchanted me.[70]

Bulleh Shah's *kafi* portrays the devotion of *yogini* for yogi. Yet in colonial-era texts of *Hir-Ranjha,* the yogi's appearance causes revulsion, at least initially.

Miran Shah Bahawalpuri's *Qissa Hir-Ranjha* (1898–99) provides a complex portrayal of the yogi. Bahawalpuri took poetic license with the chronology of the tale and thus his text begins with Ranjha's adoption of a yogi's guise. In portraying this transformation, the text emphasizes Ranjha's devotion:

> Ranjha left Hazara, in the cause of his love for Hir.
> Thus he found the land of the saffron-clad yogis.
> He put ash on his forehead and picked up his flute.
> He put a ring in his ear and a sign on his forehead.
> He accepted the mendicancy of his friend.
> And headed for the land of his beloved,
> becoming a stranger to his own land.[71]

Miran Shah presents a new twist on Ranjha's self-imposed exile from Takht Hazara. It was not because of his difficulties with his brothers or his material circumstances (having been essentially reduced to penury by their land grab), but rather in the cause of love for Hir. And his transformation into a yogi is motivated by this commitment to love. Initiated into the sect and taking on the outward appearance of a yogi, Ranjha makes his way to Rangpur, the home of the Kheras. There he seeks a meeting with Hir. Not recognizing Ranjha in his yogi disguise, Hir voices her disdain:

> Yogis and ascetics roam the land.
> . . . .
> . . . having no wisdom whatsoever.
> They loot the people disguised behind the signs of asceticism.
> Hastily they move about, spreading their deception and poison.[72]

Hir's remarks reveal a strong resentment. Her comments impugn the sincerity of yogis and ascetics, suggesting that instead of enlightenment, they spread deception. Of course, in this case Ranjha is not genuinely a yogi; this is a guise to particular ends. And yet his motivation is presented as noble-hearted. The critique suggested is of intentions and practice, as underscored by Hir's comment that yogis and ascetics "loot the people disguised behind the signs of asceticism." It is a critique of false intentions and false piety.

Khawaish Ali's *Hir-Ranjha* includes a similar criticism of yogis, this time voiced by Sehti, Hir's sister-in-law. In their first encounter, she says to Ranjha (who is in his yogi disguise):

> Oh new yogi, where have you come from?
> . . . .
> Immediately upon entering you made such noise, oh strange yogi.
> Your appearance isn't that of fakirs [mendicants], neither is your gait.
> . . . .
> There are many fakirs like you,
> I've seen them making rounds from home to home.
> Trying to incite as many women as they can.
> Your appearance isn't that of fakirs, neither is your gait.[73]

Preying on women, Sehti suggests, the yogi is really involved in a self-interested deception.

While the initial reaction to yogis is scorn, fakirs are presented as having an important social function. This is illustrated by an exchange between Ranjha and a wandering fakir in Kishan Singh 'Arif's *Qissa Hir te Ranjhe da*. In this text, after his father has died and his brothers have cheated him of his inheritance, Ranjha, despondent, leaves home and retreats into the forest. A fakir he meets there gives him a long disquisition on the merits of disavowing worldliness. Ranjha is so moved by the discourse that he wants to become an ascetic himself. In a passage that intermingles the narrator's and Ranjha's voices, 'Arif writes:

> Ranjha's heart [upon hearing the fakir] was immediately converted to that of a dervish.
> . . . .
> I am going to become a naked fakir, leaving behind all religions.
> Let us become yogis, oh Kishan Singh, and make the world our land.[74]

Although Ranjha does not ultimately give up his worldly aspirations, the exchange reveals a respect for the philosophic tradition of renunciation in which the fakir was grounded.

A similar attitude is conveyed in Kishore Chand's *Hir*. Here, upon being disinherited by his brothers, Ranjha goes to visit a group of fakirs encamped outside Takht Hazara. There, he shares with them his many sorrows: that his father has passed away, that his brothers have cheated him of his inheritance and his sisters-in-law taunt him. The fakirs are portrayed as benign figures. Upon hearing Ranjha's woes, they make a prophecy. They tell him that he will be protected by the *panj pir* (see chapter 4), that these saints will always be there to assist him.[75] This representation, in which the fakirs provide Ranjha solace, suggests that fakirs—in this text as in society—functioned as a sort of social safety valve allowing individuals to vent their problems; they provided an ameliorative mechanism.

Hir-Ranjha texts, then, present a complex mix of attitudes toward yogis and fakirs. Representations that on first glance appear contradictory are in fact quite consistent with other aspects of these texts. Religious figures, whether clerics, judges, or mendicants, are consistently subjected to withering criticism if their actions are deemed hypocritical. Those who are considered genuinely pious fulfill an important social function.

SHARED PIETY

If religious hypocrites are singled out for ridicule in colonial-era *Hir-Ranjha* texts, these texts also portray more positive assertions of piety. Positive representations of fakirs vis-à-vis yogis are one example. Still, while fakirs are portrayed as serving an important social function, there is no indication that this form of piety or religiosity should be widely adopted. After all, in Kishan Singh 'Arif's text, Ranjha wants to become an ascetic, but does not. Fakirs were not the only characters or figures associated with piety, however. Another parallel discourse on proper and true pious conduct privileged the practices of saint veneration. Rather than understanding saint veneration as solely symbolic of adherence to Sufi values (though that meaning, too, is important), in these texts such veneration suggests a form of piety in which all Punjabis could participate. This "shared piety" did not conflict with an individual's nominative religious identity but constituted a sphere of religiosity and devotion that cut across the boundaries that distinguished the Punjab's major religious traditions.

Piety as discussed thus far has drawn on one definition of the term: personal devotion to religious observance (and thus moral conduct). In extending the discussion of representations of piety here, we must consider another of its meanings: that of dutifulness, often articulated as duty to one's parents or elders. While these meanings may appear unrelated, both senses of piety are imbricated in the *Hir-Ranjha* narrative, as its characters, Hir in particular, struggle over the proper forms that piety should take.

The discourse on piety in *Hir-Ranjha* texts is inextricably linked to the practice of saint veneration, particularly of Sufi *pirs*, a practice in which Punjabis of diverse religious and class affiliations participated during the colonial period (see chapter 3). The practices associated with Sufi *pirs* and their shrines in the Punjab have been the focus of excellent studies that have demarcated their religious, social, and political functions. David Gilmartin has shown that Sufi *pirs* held considerable political power within their locales and played an instrumental role in connecting local religious practices to broader conceptions of Islam.[76] Richard Eaton's work on Sufism generally, and on the shrine of Shaikh Farid of Pakpattan in particular, argues that Sufi *pirs* acted as intermediaries between individuals and God, and that they made Islam accessible to many of the non-Muslims among whom they lived.[77] While Gilmartin and Eaton emphasize different aspects of the various roles Sufi *pirs* and their shrines played in Punjab's history, they share a focus on the Sufi *pir* and his or her shrine as the locus of study.

In contrast, Harjot Oberoi examines the veneration of Sufi saints in colonial Punjab from the perspective of non-Muslim participation in this form of devotion. In *The Construction of Religious Boundaries,* he argues that in the late nineteenth century Sikh reformers advanced an increasingly rigid definition of Sikhism, one that sought to cleanse the community of devotional practices they deemed unacceptable as proper Sikh conduct. To provide a context for this reformist activity, Oberoi describes the religious practices of late nineteenth-century Punjab's "subordinate social sector," one that participated in an "enchanted universe" of popular religion marked by miracle saints, malevolent goddesses, village sacred sites, evil spirits, and witchcraft.[78] The veneration of saints (Sufi *pirs* in the Punjabi context) is one among the myriad aspects of "popular religion" that he analyzes. As Gilmartin, Eaton, and Oberoi all point out, the veneration of Sufi *pirs* was not limited to individuals who considered themselves adherents of the Sufi way, or even of Islam more generally. Hindus, Sikhs, and Christians participated in the veneration of Muslim saints in the Punjab with as much vigor as their Muslim contemporaries. Seeking to understand such non-Muslim participation, Oberoi suggests that it was grounded in a syncretic tradition of shrines that drew on Hindu, Muslim, and Sikh normative traditions as well as on "cognitive frameworks of illness and healing."[79]

These interpretations, even if taken together, do not adequately explain the widespread Punjabi participation in shrine activities, or in the veneration of saints. At issue is Oberoi's reliance on syncretism as an analytic. He writes: "The cultural space of the shrine, its architectural fusion, and the icons it enshrined contained elements from the 'great' religious traditions of Punjab, enabling it to generate popular devotion."[80] This argument suggests that participation in shrine activities was a result of the elements of the "great" religious traditions embedded therein. The foundation of his analysis, then, remains an individual's "normative" religious identity, whether Hindu, Muslim, or Sikh. Oberoi is, of course, not alone in relying on syncretism as an analytic for understanding religious practices that incorporate people from multiple religious traditions.[81] Syncretism has invariably been used in the context of South Asian religious practices to suggest a simple mixture of two or more otherwise distinct religious traditions. I have detailed elsewhere why this is a flawed analytic with which to interrogate certain religious practices in South Asia.[82] Among its flaws are the presupposition that religions in India (primarily Islam and Hinduism, but also Islam and Sikhism) are, a priori, in conflict. Another is that it relies on purity or coherence in the traditions that combine, and thereby elides the diversity of thought, opinion, and belief within South Asian Islam, Hinduism, and Sikhism. Furthermore, the analytic of syncretism limits the conceptual possibilities through which we might understand such religious practice on its own terms. This last point is particularly germane to the present discussion. In considering religious practices in colonial Punjab such as the veneration of Sufi saints in which Hindus, Muslims, Sikhs, and Christians participated, my concern is to move beyond the centrality of Hindu, Muslim, or any other preexisting religious identity, to grapple with locally specific relationships, local social and religious values. This allows one to consider what was being constructed and affirmed in such practices not in terms of their relation to Islam, Hinduism, or Sikhism, but rather on their own terms. *Hir-Ranjha* texts, given the centrality of saint veneration in their discourse on piety, are particularly valuable sources because they allow for such an analysis.

Let us turn to colonial-era texts themselves to consider what forms of piety they affirm. Abd al-Karim Na'at's *Na'at di Hir* offers a good vantage onto this question, specifically in its portrayal of the conversation between Hir and the *qazi*. As we have seen, this conversation was really more of a dispute, as Hir and the *qazi* argue about her conduct. The *qazi* maintains that Hir should marry her parents' choice of suitor. Although the *qazi*'s argument here does not explicitly draw on Islamic law, he was clearly urging Hir to acquiesce to her parents' wishes on the grounds that this would fulfill both her religious and moral duties. In contrast, Hir argues that her position—being faithful to Ranjha—is truer to the spirit of Islam. What we find here is not a denial of the religious law upon which the *qazi*'s authority was grounded, but a discourse on the proper interpretation of that law, with the question of pious conduct at its very core.

In this text, the *qazi*'s authority is taken for granted; there is no need for any elaboration of it. By virtue of being a *qazi* he has the sanction of Islamic law behind him. Hir nevertheless does not cower before his authority and insists on her right to marry a man of her choice. Realizing that his religious authority alone is not bending Hir to his (and her parents') will, the *qazi* adds a moral tenor to the discussion, arguing that it is Hir's moral duty to abide by her parents' wishes. The weight of religion and familial duty—or one might say the patriarchal structure—come together when the *qazi* tells her: "Where the parents are willing, and the *qazi* is also willing, only by accepting that same place will you be happy." Hir rejects this argument, responding, "I will not be separated from my beloved. My body and soul are his." The *qazi* chastises Hir for this comment: "Do not forego your shame," he tells her, "protect your parents' honor." Hir's reply underscores the strength of her convictions: "I would sacrifice my life as well as my faith [for Ranjha]."[83] In the course of the *qazi*'s attempt to persuade her by invoking the obligation of duty to one's parents, Hir changes the terms of the debate altogether.

In her rebuttal Hir reinterprets the concept of piety in which filial and religious duty are entwined. The description of her devotion to Ranjha points to another view of proper conduct: "Every day like a slave I take Ranjha's name, without him, oh *qazi,* to eat or drink would be forbidden [*haram*]."[84] The language Hir uses, especially the term *haram,* co-opts a language associated with doctrinal Islam in which actions are deemed *halal* or *haram,* sanctioned or forbidden. Hir is being subversive in her use of the same language to very different ends. Instead of adhering to an order of behavior as sanctioned or forbidden under Islamic law and social custom, she defines a code of behavior, anchored in her devotion to her lover, which has its own set of principles. Hir alludes to these principles in her conversation with the *qazi.* She first rejects the *qazi's* moral universe for its corruption and suggests that to abide by her parents' wishes would bring her into conflict with her own beliefs, her own sense of pious conduct. "I asked for Ranjha from the shrine, from true belief and purity itself," she tells the *qazi.*[85] Given that earlier in the text Hir had conflated her devotion to Ranjha with devotion to God, this reference to the shrine as the source for Ranjha suggests that the shrine was also the source for Hir's understanding of pious action and that it was the locus of her devotion. While one might interpret the conflict between the *qazi* and Hir as representing a duality between doctrinal Islam and Sufi Islam, this would be a misreading of this text. Rather, Hir anchors her beliefs in an institutional site with deep foundations in the Punjab and simultaneously deploys the language and concept of the Sufi shrine to challenge the authority, social norms, and notions of duty sustained by the *qazi.*

This point becomes clearer in the poet Roshan's rendition of *Hir-Ranjha.*[86] Entitled *Hir Roshan* and published repeatedly between 1873 and 1900, his episodic text focused on a conversation between Hir and her mother, Malki. At issue, as in Na'at's text, is Hir's resistance to the marriage arranged by her parents. Malki's role is to convince Hir to abide by her parents' wishes. Malki frames their debate around religious obligation; she argues that in order to behave in ways that coincide with honor, right conduct, and religious duty, Hir is obligated to marry the man her parents have chosen for her. The conversation between the two opens with Malki admonishing Hir to behave in accordance with Islamic law, or *shari'a.* "Abide by the *shari'a,* Hir," Malki tells her daughter, "do not go the way of the devil, oh my daughter." Hir's response both prevents her mother from pursuing this line of argument further and introduces Hir's own notion of right conduct and religious duty: "If I were to turn my face away from Ranjha, I would die an infidel [*kafir*], oh mother. I hold the dictates of religious law dearly, I would not take one step outside of them, oh mother."[87] As in Na'at's use of the term *haram* in the earlier example, Roshan's use of *kafir* brings with it a wealth of meaning.

In this exchange, Roshan sets up a duality with concepts that initially appear to be opposed. One is *shari'a,* Islamic law, the other is the notion of a *kafir,* or an individual who does not believe in, or does not abide by the tenets of Islam. While Malki argues that Islamic law prescribes that Hir obey her parents in order to be a good Muslim, Hir's response follows the same logic, only reversing its terms. Her rebuttal argues that to give up Ranjha, precisely what her parents desire, would make her an infidel, one who turns her back on God. Hir's response also suggests that her interpretation of Islamic law results in very different ends than does her mother's. In challenging Malki's interpretation of what behavior is in accordance with *shari'a*, what constitutes a *kafir*, Hir challenges her mother's interpretation of pious conduct. Hir's actions in this text suggest that the religious law she adheres to defines pious conduct in very different ways than does Malki. While Roshan did not go on to describe the parameters of this alternative, parallel realm of belief, other renditions of *Hir-Ranjha* bring some of its associations into clearer focus.

Hir Husain, a text comprised of two *si harfis,* was extremely popular throughout the late nineteenth century. First published in 1871, *Hir Husain* was republished at least a dozen times through the late 1880s.[88] The first *si harfi* is a dialogue between Hir and Ranjha and the second is a dialogue between Hir and Malki. This text neither introduces events from the earlier parts of the narrative, nor treats the narrative in its entirety. Instead, it explores two points of conflict in detail: the conflict between Hir and Ranjha over her betrothal to Seido Khéra and that between Hir and Malki over the former's relationship with Ranjha. Both exchanges portray Hir as a woman firm in her convictions as she defends herself against Ranjha's accusations of infidelity, and counters her mother's laments about her immorality. *Hir Husain* also reveals, in very subtle shades, Hir's piety and its heavy emphasis on saint veneration.

Husain's first *si harfi* opens with Ranjha leaving Jhang, accusing Hir of being unfaithful to him. Agitated by her betrothal to Seido Khera, Ranjha exclaims, "Get up and manage your cattle, Hir, Ranjha is laying off this yoke. . . . Your thoughts are always with the Kheras, you have no consideration for Ranjha, oh Hir."[89] Through the rest of the *si harfi*, Hir defends herself against Ranjha's accusations. Her strength of character is underscored in the last lines she utters to Ranjha, in which she urges him to remember her faithfulness and that she "broke the bonds of family and religion" for his sake.[90] What religion had Hir broken from, and to what form of piety did she turn? The text's second half alludes to the answers to both questions.

In Husain's second *si harfi,* Malki implores Hir to give up what society deems to be her shameful behavior. Hir's response shows that her mother was using more than the pressure of social norms to sway her daughter's behavior; Malki was relying on religious concepts as well. The response to her mother's censure is telling: "Stop mother, don't tell me any more, I have understood your meaning. You are making me turn my back on the Kaaba, by speaking of the hadith and the Kheras in the same breath."[91] Hir's comment clearly indicates that Malki was relying on arguments about proper religious conduct to persuade Hir to marry Seido Khera. Hir does not reject those religious symbols but rather the associations upon which her mother's argument rested. In rejecting her mother's dictates, Hir does not wish to literally "turn [her] back on the Kaaba" and the hadith. Instead, Hir challenges the very structures upon which her mother's arguments are based. This is evident from a comment directed at Ranjha. The following line indicates where, and in what, Hir vested her piety. Cognizant of the challenges facing them both, in a poignant closing line to Ranjha, Hir exclaims, "I, Hir, am your slave, keep your trust and hope in the *panj pir*, oh Ranjha."[92] As discussed in chapter 4, the *panj pir* is a cultural signifier across much of north India and an icon of devotion for people of different religious faiths. In urging trust in the *panj pir*, Hir's words are full of hope and faith. By asking Ranjha to keep his faith in them she signals her belief in an order symbolized by the archetypal saints of the Punjab.

These representations of piety in *Hir-Ranjha* texts have thus far been taken from texts by Muslim authors, and the discourse on religion and piety in these texts is decidedly in a Muslim idiom. But the *Hir-Ranjha* narrative was part of a vernacular literary tradition participated in by poets of all religions; what representations of piety are found in texts by Sikh and Hindu authors? Are those representations markedly different from the ones just discussed? Or do they also represent participation and belief in an order symbolized by saint veneration? Analysis of a series of texts by Hindu and Sikh authors suggests that, in these texts as well, the privileged form of piety was that associated with saint veneration.

Consider the episode in which Ranjha, dejected by his disinheritance, visits the fakirs camped on the outskirts of Takht Hazara as portrayed in *Navan Qissa Hir* by the Hindu poet Kishore Chand.[93] Ranjha shares his sorrows with the fakirs and they in turn console him by referring to the intervention of the *panj pir*. Upon hearing his tale they say, "The *panj pir* will always help you. We have given our solemn pledge."[94] With these words, Ranjha's fears are assuaged and, under the protection of the *panj pir*, he leaves Takht Hazara on his epic journey in search of Hir.

The importance of saints also surfaces in the rendition of *Hir-Ranjha* by Kishan Singh 'Arif.[95] Here again, saint veneration is a privileged form of devotion. This initially comes through in the intervention of the *panj pir*. In 'Arif's text, the *panj pir* come to Ranjha in a dream as he travels from Takht Hazara to Jhang. The reader or listener is told, "Along the way he came in contact with some *pirs*. The *panj pir* themselves came to him in a dream, a wondrous miracle. Kishan Singh says, to meet the *panj pir* is to know God's essence." Ranjha's respect for and devotion to these individuals is represented in his behavior during this encounter. "Ranjha put his two hands together as he prostrated himself in salutation," 'Arif writes, "saying to them, I am your . . . slave."[96] Although the *panj pir* initially chastise Ranjha for leaving home at too young an age, upon hearing of his devotion to Hir they support his endeavor: "Go now and meet Hir, for this we pray. We will meet you again in Jhang. If you encounter any difficulty, remember us in your heart. Kishan Singh says, with each breath focus your soul's attention on the Lord." The exchange between Ranjha and the *panj pir* ends with this injunction: "Kishan Singh says, to live without one's beloved is forbidden [*haram*] in this world."[97]

That 'Arif, a Sikh (though a follower of the Gulab Dasi sect which emphasized Vedantic thought), should use *haram*, a word steeped with Islamic connotations, suggests that the Islamic idiom of *Hir-Ranjha* texts was just that—an idiom— rather than a discourse specifically on Islam. 'Arif's use of *haram* not only indicates that an Islamic idiom was the literary norm for this narrative, but also that, irrespective of idiom, the sentiments depicted in *Hir-Ranjha* texts were relevant beyond the Muslim community. Given the multivalence of the language used in these texts, *haram* connoted both that which was forbidden under *shari'a* in an Islamic context and that which was forbidden under the tenets of religion more broadly. The Islamic idiom used in *Hir-Ranjha* texts was thus employed for a discourse on piety that was not, at the levels of either production or consumption, limited to Muslims alone.

. . .

In an essay on the *Ramayana* narrative tradition, A. K. Ramanujan wrote that its plot, like that of many Indian popular narratives, including *Hir-Ranjha*, is "always already there."[98] Audiences did not read or listen to *Hir-Ranjha* to learn what happens; they read or listened out of an appreciation for the art of poetic composition or artistic performance. The audience of Kishan Singh 'Arif's text, then, knew from the outset that the relationship between Hir and Ranjha would be in conflict with an interpretation of religious obligation used to buttress the authority of Hir's parents. Thus, to suggest that Ranjha's living without his beloved was *haram* reveals an interpretation of Islam different from that put forth by Hir's family. In short, what the brief meeting between Ranjha and the *panj pir* in 'Arif's text illustrates is both the privileging of saint veneration above other forms of religiosity and the allusion to forms of piety that opposed the injunctions of religion as practiced by the dominant forces in society. *Hir-Ranjha* texts privilege an understanding of religious obligation and piety that challenges authority structures and a vision of piety distinct from the religiosity of characters such as the *qazi* and Hir's parents. That piety is articulated by reference to Sufi saints and shrines, institutions and institutional sites that were prominent across the Punjab and patronized by people from all walks of life. *Hir-Ranjha* texts thus point to saint veneration as the prominent form of piety in the Punjabi literary formation.

That saint veneration is central to these texts is clear. It is also clear, however, that these depictions of saint veneration make little reference to Punjab's major religious traditions. Characters' participation in this world of devotion and devotional practice bears no direct relation to Islam, Hinduism, Sikhism, or any other religion. The way saint veneration is presented in these texts points to an independent set of beliefs that are neither in direct conflict nor coterminous with Punjab's major religious traditions. *Hir-Ranjha* texts portray a religious world—with remarkable consistency—that operates as a parallel arena of belief. Hir, after all, does not want to be in conflict with the *shari'a;* she does not want to be a *kafir.* But she is also not satisfied with the religious world of her parents and the *qazi.* The relationship between the spheres of religiosity presented in *Hir-Ranjha* texts is ill represented by the notion of syncretism. Hir's belief is not an amalgam of Hindu and Muslim practice; nor does her participation in the religious world of the shrine appear to be in any way predicated on her religious identity as a Muslim.

What are the implications of this reading for understanding Punjab's colonial history? Most important is that it points toward a notion of piety shared by Punjabis of different religions. Although existing historiography emphasizes increasing communalism in colonial Punjab, a shared ethos of piety continued to animate Punjabi social and religious life. This is not to suggest that the two—communalism and shared piety—are mutually exclusive. Certainly, for reasons discussed in the introduction, Punjabis were increasingly positing political claims through the prism of religious community during the colonial period. But this political history is only one facet of the history of colonial Punjab. Equally significant, though until now muted, are the shared beliefs and practices that continued to be relevant throughout this period. These texts help recover the kinds of everyday practices that bound people together across the increasingly divisive lines of religious community to constitute the Punjabi literary formation. *Hir-Ranjha* texts thus open an alternate history of religion and culture in colonial Punjab. In the history they relate, normative religious identities—Hindu, Muslim, Sikh, Christian, and so on—were neither reinscribed by being made a constant point of reference nor abandoned. These texts suggest that participants in the Punjabi literary formation were less invested in specifying who was a Hindu, who a Sikh, who a Muslim, than in the question of what constituted pious action. The answer to that, perhaps not surprisingly given the multivalence of this narrative tradition, was not vested in a single religion's path, but in a path to which members of any religion could adhere.

Conclusion

It should now be evident that when Amrita Pritam wrote her elegiac poem "To Waris Shah," in the wake of India's partition in 1947, she was invoking something like the ethos of the Punjabi literary formation. "Today corpses lie in the thickets and full of blood is the Chenab [River]," Pritam wrote. "Somebody mixed poison into the five rivers, and those waters watered the earth. . . . Lost is the flute where once sounded the pipings of love. Ranjha and his kind have forgotten how to play."[1] Indeed, through the rest of her life (she died in 2005), Pritam would have been hard pressed to find evidence of the formation's presence in either India or Pakistan, at least in the political histories of those countries. Given my emphasis throughout this book on the longevity of the *qissa* tradition and on its durable presence through at least the 1930s, one may wonder why the relevance of this tradition seemed, to Pritam and others, to wane at the cusp of independence and diminish further during the postcolonial period. How do we reconcile the history of a vibrant vernacular culture anchored in shared practices and sentiments that cut across religious lines with the history of India's partition, an event that epitomized religious rupture? Similarly, given the evidence of the Punjabi literary formation's affective attachments to the Punjabi language and its literature during the colonial period, why has Punjabi proved unviable as a ground for ethno-linguistic claims in Pakistan and India, claims that the literature on language politics would lead us to expect?

In closing, I would like to push beyond the late colonial period to consider these questions. Obviously, the postcolonial era is a dramatically different context from the period focused on in this study, and each of the themes raised above—the partition and language politics in postcolonial India and Pakistan—has been the subject of numerous studies. My aim is therefore modest: to consider how the history I have narrated can contribute to our understanding of postcolonial South Asia, and its language politics in particular.

Any historian traversing the temporal threshold from the colonial to the postcolonial period must contend with the partition of India. For a historian of the Punjab the partition looms especially large, both in history and historiography. Its political, economic, social, and cultural impacts were immense. Communities were torn apart at the local, regional, and subcontinental levels.[2] Given my arguments in the preceding chapters, along with the sentiment that Pritam's poem underscores, the partition may seem to negate all that the Punjabi literary formation stood for. Partition and its communal violence suggest that the sentiments shared across the Punjabi literary formation disintegrated under the pressure of religio-political identities and the divisive politics of empire's endgame. Indeed, it is tempting to conclude that affection for the Punjabi language was insufficient to challenge the politics of religious difference that cohered in the run-up to independence. Such a conclusion would surely help reconcile the colonial history of the Punjabi literary formation with the history of the partition. It would also help explain the religious fractures that undermined the Punjabi Suba movement (discussed below), and the absence of a sustained politics around the Punjabi language in Pakistan. But the Punjabi literary formation did not collapse in the years leading up to independence. Punjabi literary trends no doubt shifted during the early decades of the twentieth century in ways that sometimes challenged the formation's previous ways of functioning.[3] But these shifts did not signal the end of the formation; the shared practices and sentiments that held it together did not simply vanish.

How, then, do we explain the apparent paradox between the shared sentiments and practices around which the formation cohered and the politics exercised in state arenas? One answer can be found by stepping back from these particular histories to examine the assumptions of historical scholarship on language. In an engaging essay on the subject of historians and language, Penelope Corfield writes that the study of language is in many ways at the core of historical method, most significantly because "as a subject for investigation in its own right all language in history . . . is of potential interest to historians."[4] Corfield may be right, but there has been little impetus within the discipline of history to take up language as a subject of historical analysis in its own right. Foundations were laid in the late 1980s and early 1990s for a social history of language but, linguistic and cultural turns notwithstanding, the dominant paradigm within historiography has been and remains to study language primarily in its relation to nationalism or nationalist-subnationalist politics.[5]

The historic role played by language in forming political identities in modern Europe, and indeed in modern South Asia, is surely part of the story.[6] The centrality of linguistic nationalism to the political reshaping of Europe in the nineteenth century is a well-known story.[7] So, too, is the story of how linguistic movements prompted the reorganization of states in India largely along linguistic lines in the decades following independence.[8] To be sure, these processes are not entirely commensurate, and historians of language movements in modern India have been highly sensitive to the distinctions that must be drawn between the two. Sumathi Ramaswamy, in particular, highlights these distinctions in her *Passions of the Tongue: Language Devotion in Tamil India, 1891–1970*, where she interrogates the poetics and politics of *tamilparru* (Tamil devotion) and analyzes the "discourses of love, labor, and life that have coalesced around Tamil in this [the twentieth] century."[9] Lisa Mitchell, like Ramaswamy, is sensitive to these distinctions in her study of the Telegu language movement, where she traces the cultural and political changes that contributed to the rise of a discourse around mother tongues in twentieth-century India.[10] Both of these excellent studies also historicize how affection (or indeed devotion, in Ramaswamy's case) for language translates swiftly into a state-oriented politics. The Tamil and Telegu movements, after all, are the two most politically significant language movements of twentieth-century India. The histories of Tamil and Telegu display cases of affection for language being mobilized for state-centric political aims, and the same can be said of other languages in late twentieth-century India and Pakistan, including Marathi, Assamese, Bengali, and Sindhi, among others.[11] The history of Punjabi, however, is different.

Punjabi historically functioned in Punjab society as one of a number of languages, each with particular functions and political possibilities. Like many other Indian vernacular languages, Punjabi had not historically been prominent in state arenas. We have seen that when colonial language policy drew vernaculars into the state apparatus in the early nineteenth century, Punjabi continued to function largely as it historically always had, at the margins of state discourse. Through the colonial period, the language and its literary traditions were sustained by their popularity and by the patronage of indigenous institutions. Given this history, it is perhaps not surprising that public affinity for Punjabi language and literature evident in the colonial period did not produce an attendant movement in political arenas. Similarly, the language did not readily present possibilities for a politics that could counteract the divisive and communal politics that led to the partition of India. That we look to the language to do so is a product not of its history but of the scholarly tendency to causally link affective ties to language with state-oriented politics. This tendency also informs perspectives on the postcolonial fate of Punjabi in India and Pakistan. By its logic, we are compelled to read Punjabi's failure to serve as a ground for a religiously plural linguistic identity in postcolonial India or as a linguistic identity of any political impact in Pakistan as an absence of its affective power. Grounded in the colonial history of the Punjabi literary formation, however, which unequivocally shows us that affective ties to language and state-centric politics need not be linked, I will argue instead that we question the assumptions that undergird the story of language politics in modern South Asia.

THE PUNJABI SUBA MOVEMENT

Punjabi operated only with difficulty as a vehicle for a state-oriented politics. This was true in 1947, and in the ensuing decades. The evolution of a Punjabi language movement in India in the 1950s and 1960s thus deserves some discussion. The demand for a "Punjabi Suba," or Punjabi state, was spearheaded by Sikh politicians in the immediate postpartition period. Initially, they made the demand on the basis of religious identity and only subsequently, from the early 1950s, did they present it as a demand based on language. Despite making that demand on behalf of all Punjabi speakers, Sikh and Hindu, the movement ultimately fractured along religious lines. This was made manifest in the movement's 1966 denouement, when the Union government reconfigured Punjab's boundaries by considerably reducing its size, a move that enlarged Himachal Pradesh and produced the new state of Haryana. Paul Brass' *Language, Religion, and Politics in North India* studies this movement from genesis to fruition, so I relate only the broad contours here.[12] I will focus less on the movement's details than on historicizing it in light of the history presented in this book.

Most significantly, the colonial history of Punjabi highlights the novelty of the Punjabi Suba movement in making claims on the state on the basis of linguistic identity. In this sense, the movement was decidedly *not* building on colonial foundations. As we have seen, neither the Punjabi language nor its literature had ever served as a basis for cross-religious political action in state arenas. Even the Punjab Unionist Party, a regional party representing the interests of Muslim, Sikh, and Hindu landlords and landed gentry that dominated Punjab's provincial politics through the 1930s and into the 1940s, never used Punjabi as a political rallying point.[13] Since Punjabi had historically operated at a remove from state institutions, it was less easily appropriable as a ground for political mobilization in these arenas. By arguing for Punjabi as the basis of a territorial and political identity, the Punjabi Suba movement linked the language to political action in entirely new ways. In part, this shift was the result of the immediate postindependence political context in India, which fostered demands for statehood based on linguistic identity.

Immediately after independence, a variety of linguistic and political activists called on India's Union government to reconstitute states along linguistic lines. No such demand emanated from the Punjab, however. Sikh politicians, who were dominant in state politics, initially made a demand for a Sikh-majority state, clearly operating under older political assumptions. By the late nineteenth century, religious identity had become a legitimate ground for political mobilization in India, particularly in negotiations with the colonial state. In the wake of partition, however, political claims based on religious identity were no longer considered valid. This shift in the political climate posed a particular dilemma for the Akali Dal, the political wing of the Sikh reformist organization, the Shiromani Gurdwara Prabandhak Committee. Established in 1920, the Akali Dal became prominent in Punjab politics over the ensuing decade. In the following decades, the party participated in the colonial political arena as the representative of Sikh interests.[14] As India's partition grew imminent, the Akali Dal agitated for a sovereign Sikh state.[15] It was unsuccessful, however, and at partition the party could do little more than seek to consolidate power for Sikhs in the new political context of independent India.

For the Akali Dal, the postcolonial political context brought both advantages and challenges. On the one hand, partition's radical demographic shifts provided the party a firmer political footing since Sikhs, due to their exodus from Pakistan, were now more geographically concentrated. Following partition, Sikhs were a majority in six of Punjab's districts, and a large minority in another five. On the other hand, despite these strengths at the district level, Sikhs constituted only about one-third of Punjab's total population, with most of the rest being Hindus. In these circumstances, the Akali Dal attempted to consolidate its position by demanding a Sikh-majority state from the Indian Union in October 1949. The Union government refused, leading the Akali Dal to launch a major agitation in August 1950.[16]

While demands based on religious identity were untenable in independent India, demands based on linguistic identity were not. The Union government may not have been receptive to linguistic demands as it faced the challenges of consolidating the new republic, but they were not deemed illegitimate.[17] Prompted by this political context, the Akali Dal approached the 1953 States Reorganization Commission and asked for a Punjabi Suba based on linguistic rather than religious grounds. Linguistic identity became the expedient by which to realize the political and territorial ambitions of the Akali Dal constituency, the vast majority of Punjab's Sikh population. But Punjabi had shallow foundations with which to enable this kind of political appropriation, and it proved difficult to fashion a cross-religious political identity on the basis of the language. In part, Sikh socio-religious activism itself undercut this possibility. Since the early twentieth century Singh Sabha activists had tried to associate the language specifically with Sikhs, an agenda that the Akali Dal had supported. As Paul Brass has noted, "Sikh political leaders value Punjabi in the Gurumukhi script as a means for transmitting a sense of separateness to Sikhs. . . . [Their purposes] have been the promotion of a Sikh, not a Punjabi identity."[18] My earlier chapters have shown, however, that no matter how vociferous Sikh efforts were to appropriate Punjabi as singularly Sikh in colonial Punjab, they were unsuccessful. Nonetheless, those efforts made it difficult for the Akali Dal to convincingly claim in 1953 that Punjabi was the foundation of a political identity shared by Hindus and Sikhs. Certainly, the States Reorganization

Commission remained unpersuaded and did not concede the demand for a Punjabi Suba when it recommended in 1956 that most of India be reorganized on linguistic grounds.[19]

The Akali Dal continued its campaign, but an already difficult task was made more arduous when the Arya Samaj and other Hindu organizations began mobilizing people against the Akali Dal demand, in part by promoting and advocating for Hindi. Critically, the Arya Samaj organized a campaign for the 1961 census that urged Punjabi Hindus to return Hindi as their "mother tongue," irrespective of what their first or primary language actually was. Using the trope of Sikh domination of Hindus in a future Punjabi Suba, the Arya Samaj was remarkably successful. The Punjabi-speaking Hindu population almost uniformly returned Hindi as their mother tongue, leading to an unprecedented situation: for the first time since census records had begun recording language information in the nineteenth century, Hindi—and not Punjabi—was returned as the majority language in the Punjab!

The Akali Dal continued to agitate for its political and territorial goals under the banner of linguistic identity through the 1960s, despite the apparent cleavages between Hindus and Sikhs made manifest in the 1961 census. In the mid-1960s, however, two events made the political context more favorable for their achieving those goals. First, in 1964 Prime Minister Jawaharlal Nehru, who had remained staunchly opposed to the Punjabi Suba, passed away. Second, in 1965 India and Pakistan went to war over Kashmir. The war highlighted Punjab's strategic position as a border state, making political unrest there a threat to India's broader security, and in 1966 the Akali Dal's demand for a Punjabi Suba was finally met. In granting the demand, the Union government trifurcated the province. Its eastern hill districts were amalgamated into Himachal Pradesh. The southern districts, all of which had been returned as majority Hindi-speaking in the 1961 census, became the new state of Haryana. The remaining districts constituted the new Punjabi Suba (maps 8 and 9).

The Punjabi Suba movement provides an example of how, given the language's colonial history, Punjabi was difficult to appropriate as the foundation for a linguistic identity in formal political arenas. The movement also provides an opportunity to consider some specific scholarly assumptions about language, society, and politics. If the existing scholarly framework posits that affect for language can produce a nationalist politics, then a subtle assumption of this same scholarship is that the absence of a nationalist politics based on linguistic identity marks a corresponding absence of affect for language. The Punjabi Suba movement provides an interesting illustration of this assumption. The implicit suggestion in existing historiography is that Hindus' mass disavowal of Punjabi in the 1961 census—despite the fact that for many of them Punjabi was their "mother tongue"—is a sign that they felt no attachment to Punjabi. Baldev Raj Nayar helped establish this

MAP 8. Punjab state, India, 1947.

PAKISTAN

HIMACHAL PRADESH

CHINA

PUNJAB

Chandigarh

HARYANA

UTTAR
PRADESH

RAJASTHAN

MAP 9. Punjab state, India, 1966.

perspective in his foundational history of the Punjabi Suba movement, *Minority Politics in the Punjab,* where he wrote:

> The Hindu opposition to the demand for the Punjabi Suba went beyond the mere expression of objection to the formation of such a state. To the Akali emphasis on Punjabi language as the basis for the formation of Punjabi Suba, the Hindus in the Punjab reacted by disowning the Punjabi language itself. They declared that . . . Punjabi is not their language. . . . The Hindus argue that their attachment to Hindi is of no recent origin. . . . Thus long before the present conflict Hindus seem to have shown a marked preference for Hindi.[20]

This absence of affection for their mother tongue is naturalized by reference to the colonial-era activities of the Arya Samaj, which since the 1880s had been promoting Hindi as the language of Hindus in the region. The conclusion seems to be that the Arya Samaj was successful in its aims.

While affection for a language can often authorize state-centered political claims, the latter are a poor measure of the affective relations people establish with their linguistic and literary traditions. We have seen that despite the activities of the Arya Samaj, the Singh Sabha, and Muslim organizations in the colonial period, each advocating that particular languages and scripts represented the aspirations of their respective communities, Punjabi continued to thrive. In interpreting Hindus' mass disavowal of Punjabi in the 1961 census, we should bear in mind the distinction between affect for language and political action, and recall that Punjabi had historically been the object of the former—as exemplified by the tenacity of the Punjabi literary formation under colonialism—and had only of late been implicated in the latter, and then only by the Akali Dal. Bringing the colonial history of the Punjabi literary formation to bear on our understanding of the Punjabi Suba movement unsettles the ease with which scholars have naturalized Punjabi-speaking Hindus' disavowal of Punjabi in official state arenas. This undoubtedly complicates the picture of the Punjabi Suba movement, particularly its inability to gain traction with Punjab's Hindus. Given the continuing relevance of Punjabi among Hindu communities in today's Punjab and Haryana (and beyond), an absence of Punjabi Hindu support for the Punjabi Suba does not translate into an absence of affect for the Punjabi language.

PUNJABI IN PAKISTAN

The postcolonial fate of Punjabi in Pakistan has long been considered something of an anomaly in the language politics of postcolonial South Asia. In a country where language was an important site of political contestation in the latter half of the twentieth century, Punjabi seems to defy this trend.[21] Language has been crucial to both national and regional political identities in Pakistan.[22] While Pakistan's architects thought Urdu would help consolidate national identity, vernacular languages have been critical to regional political assertions, particularly in Bengal and Sindh. Bengalis and Sindhis, among others, have agitated at different times for the use (or retention) of their languages in state arenas, declaring such recognition as essential to group status and legitimacy, and to a share in state power.

In contrast, Punjabi has never formed the basis for a popular movement in Pakistan, despite its being the only regional language that has never enjoyed an official status. In a context where language groups have mobilized to demand or ensure that their vernacular languages enjoy official status, that Punjabi speakers have been quiescent in demanding an official role or recognition at the state or national level makes Punjabi an anomaly. Indeed, since 1947 Punjabis have dominated the Pakistan state's two most powerful agencies: the bureaucracy and the military. Given their predominance, a movement by Punjabi speakers to establish Punjabi as a regional language in 1947—or at any point since that year—would surely have gained momentum. But such a movement has never materialized: Urdu remains the official language in Pakistani Punjab, just as it was in colonial Punjab.

Tariq Rahman, whose *Language and Politics in Pakistan* has been the standard reference on the subject since its publication in 1996, argues that Punjabis have subordinated their affinity for Punjabi in order to secure political dominance of the state and its resources.[23] Rahman uses the same logic to interpret the Siraiki language movement, which although marginal in the early years of the Pakistani state has been more active since the 1970s.[24] The Siraiki movement seeks recognition for Siraiki as a language independent of Punjabi, and as the foundation of a Siraiki ethnicity. In making claims on the state for recognition of Siraiki's independence from Punjabi, the movement has also advocated a territorial division of Punjab province to provide it with greater access to resources. While Punjab is by all indicators the wealthiest province in Pakistan, the Siraiki belt in the south lags behind the province as a whole. Christopher Shackle describes the movement as "a classic illustration of the association between most modern language movements and a sense of oppression."[25] With the absence of a broad-based politics based on Punjabi, and with exactly the opposite in the case of Siraiki, a materialist reading such as Rahman's would seem to provide an adequate explanation for how language has operated in Pakistani Punjab. However, given the history of the Punjabi literary formation presented in this book, the postcolonial fate of Punjabi in Pakistan appears in striking continuity with the ways the language functioned historically.

In recent years, however, a language movement calling for state recognition of Punjabi has developed in Pakistan. The movement is not widespread and has yet to develop a popular base, but it has been increasingly assertive since the late 1980s.[26] Alyssa Ayres, historian of language and nationalism in Pakistan, provides a compelling analysis of this "Punjabiyat" (Punjabiness) movement in her essay,

"Language, the Nation, and Symbolic Capital: The Case of the Punjab."[27] Ayres describes the movement as being animated by Punjabi's marginal status vis-à-vis both Urdu and English. Being marginal to the Urdu-language official sphere is, of course, nothing new for Punjabi. And although since the colonial period English has always held an important role at the most elite levels of society, English has become increasingly prevalent in recent decades across a broader spectrum of society. In this linguistic context, Ayres argues that "Punjabi is doubly marginal." "Given this context," she writes, "it is indeed surprising that the Punjabi language . . . perdures in Pakistan."[28]

For readers of this book it should *not* be surprising that the Punjabi language survives without state support or an official status. But what is interesting about the Punjabiyat movement is that in seeking to secure an official status for Punjabi, the movement may mark an important historical discontinuity (much like the Punjabi Suba movement) in the role the Punjabi language is seen to play in mediating people's relationship to the state. One can go so far as to say that the Punjabiyat movement is inverting the historical role of the state in relation to Punjabi. As Nadir Ali, a leading short story writer and prominent proponent of Punjabi, said some years ago in reference to the language having no official status: "The state in not saving the Punjabi language is actually destroying Punjab and its people."[29] The movement has had little success in swaying the state thus far, however. Ironically, the movement's institutions, such as *sangat*, a weekly gathering to read and interpret Punjabi literature, and its initiatives, such as Huma Safdar's late-1990s theater production of Damodar's seventeenth-century *Hir* in Lahore, precisely recall the kinds of institutions and initiatives that have historically sustained Punjabi.

The postcolonial histories of Punjabi in India and Pakistan are comparable in that in neither case has Punjabi proved a viable ground for (cross-religious, in India) ethno-linguistic claims. The absence of such politics, particularly among Hindus in India and among the vast majority of Punjabis in Pakistan, should not be taken as an absence of affection or affinity for the language. Punjabi remains vital today, with approximately a hundred million speakers in the subcontinent and millions more in the diaspora.[30] Punjabi literary production thrives and is today a transnational phenomenon with critically acclaimed authors and poets in India (i.e., Surjit Patar), Pakistan (Najm Hossain Syed), Britain (Amarjit Chandan), and Canada (Surjeet Kalsey), and other countries. There are transnational publications (i.e., *Sanjh*), Web sites (i.e., http://uddari.wordpress.com), and organizations (i.e., the Academy of the Punjab in North America). Punjabi music circulates globally, in traditional forms such as *qawwali* and hybrid forms such as British *bhangra*. All of which suggests that Punjabi continues to be significant to life-worlds, both in the Punjab and beyond.

The absence of a state-centric Punjabi politics, then, in the postcolonial as in the colonial period, does not diminish the historical significance of the Punjabi literary formation, or of the language and literary traditions around which it co-hered. Rather, the Punjabi literary formation provides an important case study of a language that has elicited passionate attachments—as evidenced by the way it and its literary traditions were kept vibrant under colonialism and remain so today—but that nonetheless defies the narrow definition of politics routinely associated with language. Punjabi may not produce a nationalist politics, but the language remains the site of sustained and political engagement by its speakers.

Colonial-Era *Hir-Ranjha* Texts Consulted

Author	Title	City	Publisher	Date	Print Run	Pages	Script
Ahmad, Fassi Niaz	*Hir Niaz Ranjha (Niaz's Hir-Ranjha)*	Lahore	Munshi Aziz al-Din wa Najm al-Din	n.d. [c. 1914]	n/a	8	I-P (Indo-Persian)
Akbar, Muhammad Sadiq Sahib	*Ranjhe di Faryad (Ranjha's Plea)*	Lahore	Shaikh Zafar Muhammad	n.d.	n/a	8	I-P
al-Baksh, Khaksar [Munir]	*Faryad Hir (Hir's Plea)*	Lahore	Munshi Aziz al-Din Najm al-Din	n.d.	n/a	8	I-P
Ali, Khawaish	*Hir-Ranjha*	Lahore	Pandit Labo Ram and Sons Tajran Kutab	n.d. [c. 1933]	n/a	44	I-P
Ali, Mian Sher	*Chitthi Ranjhe di (Ranjha's Letter)*	Amritsar	Vazir Hind Press	n.d. [c. 1915]	n/a	8	I-P
'Arif, Kishan Singh	*Qissa Hir te Ranjhe da (The Qissa of Hir and Ranjha)*	Amritsar	Bhai Vasava Singh Juneja Pustak Wale	1889	n/a	245	G (Gurmukhi)
Azim, Muhammad	*Hir Azim Ranjha (Azim's Hir-Ranjha)*	Lahore	Munshi Aziz al-Din Najm al-Din	1914	n/a	8	I-P
Azim, Muhammad	*Hir Azim Ranjha (Azim's Hir-Ranjha)*	Lahore	Munshi Aziz al-Din Najm al-Din	n.d. [c. 1922]	n/a	8	I-P
Bahawalpuri, Miran Shah	*Hir Miran Shah Mukamal (The Complete Hir Miran Shah) (Includes Qissa Hir-Ranjha)*	Multan	Maulvi Khuda Yar wa Nur Ahmad wa Nur Muhammad wa Faiz Ahmad Tajar Kutab	1316 h. [1898–99]	2,000	28	I-P
Basianwala, Gokalchand Sharma	*Qissa Hir Gokalchand*	Ludhiana	Allah Baksh Maula Bakhsh	n.d.	n/a	156	G
Chand, Bhagat Diwan	*Si Harfi Hir*	Gujranwala	Prem Bilas Press	1916	n/a	16	I-P

Author	Title	Place	Publisher	Date			
Chand, Kishore	*Navan Qissa Hir Kishore Chand* (Kishore Chand's New Qissa Hir)	Amritsar	Bhai Harnam Singh Karam Singh	1914	2,000	80	G
Chand, Kishore	*Navan Qissa Hir Kishore Chand* (Kishore Chand's New Qissa Hir)	Amritsar	Bhai Harnam Singh Karam Singh	1918	2,000	79	G
Das, Pandit Gopal	*Faryad Hir* (Hir's Plea)	Lahore	Bhatia and Co. Tajran Kutab	n.d. [c. 1933]	n/a	16	I-P
Din, Hafiz Muhammad	*Ranjhan Par* (Ranjha, the Distant Shore)	Amritsar	Munshi Muhammad Ismail Sahib Mushtaq	n.d. [c. 1920]	n/a	8	I-P
Farshi, Munshi Muhammad Baksh Sahib	*Farshi di Hir (hissa chaharam)* (Farshi's Hir [the Fourth Part])	Lahore	Munshi Aziz al-Din Najm al-Din	1929	n/a	8	I-P
Hadayatullah	*Baran Masa Hadayatullah* (Hadayatullah's Baran Mah)	Amritsar	n.p.	1876	n/a	8	G
Haider, Mian Ali	*Si Harfi Ali Haider*	Lahore	Chiragh al-Din Kutab Farosh	1879	2,400	16	I-P
Haider, Mian Ali	*Si Harfian Maʿanah Hir* (Si Harfis on Hir)	Lahore	Shaikh al-Baksh	1885	n/a	28	I-P
Husain	*Hir Husain*	Lahore	Gulab Singh and Sons	1898	n/a	n/a	G
Husain	*Hir Husain, Si Harfi Ashraf, Si Harfi Arora Rai, Si Harfi Ghulam*	Lahore	Shaikh Barkat Ali Mohsen Ali	n.d.	n/a	16	I-P

continued

Author	Title	City	Publisher	Date	Print Run	Pages	Script
Husain	Hir Husain, Si Harfi Ashraf, Si Harfi Arora Rai, Si Harfi Ghulam	Lahore	Matbah Sultani	1873	2,100	16	I-P
Husain	Hir Husain, Si Harfi Ashraf, Si Harfi Arora Rai, Si Harfi Ghulam	Lahore	Chiragh al-Din Siraj al-Din	n.d. [c. 1888]	2,100	16	I-P
Husain	Hir Husain, Si Harfi Ashraf, Si Harfi Arora Rai, Si Harfi Ghulam	Lahore	Munshi Gulab Singh	1891	n/a	16	I-P
Husain	Hir Husain, Si Harfi Ashraf, Si Harfi Arora Rai, Si Harfi Ghulam	Lahore	Munshi Aziz al-Din Najm al-Din	1928	n/a	16	I-P
Husain, Munshi Ghulam	Jhok Ranjhe di (Ranjha's Abode)	Lahore	Munshi Nawab Ali Brothers	1322 h. [1904–5]	n/a	16	I-P
Ismail, Munshi Muhammad [Maskin]	Maskin di Hir (Maskin's Hir)	Lahore	Munshi Aziz al-Din Najm al-Din	1929	n/a	8	I-P
Khadam, M. M. Y.	Mukamal Drama Hir-Ranjha (The Complete Drama Hir-Ranjha)	n.p.	N. D. Haskal and Sons	n.d. [c. 1923]	1,000	36	I-P
Malik, Salim	Qissa Hir-Ranjha wa Sehti-Murad (Qissa Hir-Ranjha and Sehti-Murad)	Lahore	Munshi Aziz al-Din	n.d.	n/a	n/a	I-P

Author	Title	Place	Publisher	Date		Pages	
Muqbal, Shah Jahan	*Hir Muqbal*	Lahore	Haji Chiragh al-Din Siraj al-Din	n.d.	n/a	92	1-P
Muqbal, Shah Jahan	*Hir Muqbal*	Lahore	Chiragh al-Din	n.d. [1873]	1,050	48	1-P
Muqbal, Shah Jahan	*Hir Muqbal*	Lahore	n.p.	1875	n/a	n/a	1-P
Muqbal, Shah Jahan	*Hir Muqbal*	Lahore	Chiragh al-Din Siraj al-Din	1890	700	48	1-P
Muqbal, Shah Jahan	*Hir Muqbal*	Lahore	Rai Sahib Munshi Gulab Singh and Sons	1912	n/a	103	G
Muqbal, Shah Jahan	*Hir Muqbal Punjabi*	Lahore	Haji Chiragh al-Din Siraj al-Din	n.d.	n/a	92	1-P
Naat, Abd al-Karim	*Naat di Hir (Naat's Hir)*	Multan	Hafiz Muhammad al-Din Aziz al-Din Bashir al-Din Tajran Kutab	n.d. [c. 1880]	n/a	8	1-P
Nath, Amar	*Hir-Ranjha Natak (Hir-Ranjha, a Play)*	n.p.	Amar Press	1900	n/a	119	1-P
Qureshi, Mian Muhammad Fazil	*Hir Viragan (The Mendicant Hir)*	Jhelum	n.p.	n.d. [c. 1923]	n/a	8	1-P
Ram, Kirpa	*Qissa Hir-Ranjha*	Nawan Shahr (Jalandhar)	Lala Nand Lal Basanta Mal Zaini	1927	n/a	30	G
Roshan	*Hir Roshan*	Lahore	Mian Chiragh al-Din	n.d. [c. 1873]	1,900	8	1-P
Roshan	*Hir Roshan*	n.p.	n.p.	1893	n/a	8	G
Roshan	*Hir Roshan*	Lahore	n.p.	1895	n/a	8	G
Roshan	*Hir Roshan*	Lahore	n.p.	1895	n/a	8	G
Roshan	*Hir Roshan*	Lahore	Hafiz Muhammad Din	1895	n/a	15	G

continued

Author	Title	City	Publisher	Date	Print Run	Pages	Script
Roshan	*Hir Roshan*	Lahore	Munshi Gulab Singh and Sons	1896	n/a	15	G
Roshan	*Hir Roshan*	Lahore	Rai Sahib Munshi Gulab Singh and Sons	1900	n/a	15	G
Sakin, [Pir] Muhammad Shah	*Qissa Hir wa Ranjha*	Amritsar	Prem Singh Sachdio and Sons	n.d.	n/a	16	I-P
Sakin, [Pir] Muhammad Shah	*Qissa Hir wa Ranjha*	Lahore	Malik Din Muhammad Tajar Kutab	n.d.	n/a	16	I-P
Sakin, [Pir] Muhammad Shah	*Qissa Hir wa Ranjha*	Lahore	Malik Din Muhammad and Sons	n.d.	n/a	16	I-P
[Sakin], [Pir] Muhammad Shah	*Qissa Hir wa Ranjha*	Lahore	Malik Din Muhammad Tajran Kutab	1924	n/a	16	I-P
[Sakin], [Pir] Muhammad Shah	*Qissa Hir wa Ranjha*	Lahore	Munshi Aziz al-Din	n.d. [c. 1929]	n/a	16	I-P
Shah, Fazl	*Barah Mah Fazl Shah (Fazl Shah's Baran Mah)*	Lahore	Chiragh al-Din Kutab Farosh	1879	2,400	16	I-P
Shah, Fazl	*Majmu'a Si Harfian Fazl Shah (A Collection of Fazl Shah's Si Harfis)*	Lahore	Mir Amir Baksh and Sons	n.d	n/a	36	I-P
Shah, Fazl	*Qissa Hir wa Ranjha Punjabi*	Lahore	Munshi Muhammad Adbul Aziz	n.d. [c. 1911]	n/a	144	I-P
Shah, Fazl	*Si Harfi Hir, Si Harfi Zulaikha, Si Harfi Sohni, Si Harfi Laila, Si Harfi Sassi*	Lahore	Shaikh Muhammad Ashraf	n.d.	n/a	56	I-P
Shah, Fazl	*Si Harfi Hir, Si Harfi Sassi, Si Harfi Sohni*	Lahore	Chiragh al-Din Kutab Farosh	n.d. [c. 1886]	n/a	32	I-P

Shah, Hamid	*Hir Hamid Shah*	Lahore	n.p.	1908	1,000	208	1-P
Shah, Maula	*Hir wa Ranjha*	Amritsar	Imam al-Din Ma'raj al-Din	1330 h. [1911–12]	n/a	n/a	1-P
Shah, Muhammad	*Qissa Hir wa Ranjha*	Rawalpindi	Lala Butamul Sahib	n.d. [c. 1908]	1,000	16	G
Sharaf, Babu Firoz Din	*Hir Sial*	Lahore	Punjabi Pustak Bhandar	1933	1,000	176	G
Singh, Bhagwan	*Hir Bhagwan Singh*	Amritsar	Lala Dhani Ram Sahib	n.d.	n/a	68	1-P
Singh, Bhagwan	*Hir Bhagwan Singh*	Amritsar	Lala Ram Nath Tajar Kutab	1892	n/a	48	1-P
Singh, Bhagwan	*Hir Bhagwan Singh*	Lahore	Rai Sahib Munshi Gulab Singh and Sons	1924	n/a	82	G
Singh, Bhagwan	*Hir-Ranjha*	Amritsar	Bhai Chattar Singh Jivan Singh	n.d.	n/a	157	G
Singh, Bhai Lakma	*Qissa Hir wa Mian Ranjha*	Peshawar	Bhai Lakma Singh	n.d. [c. 1876]	n/a	100	1-P
Singh, Bhai Rann	*Navan Qissa Hir (A New Qissa Hir)*	Amritsar	Gurmat Press	1913	2,000	56	G
Singh, Bhai Sant Bajara	*Qissa Hir te Ranjhe da (The Qissa of Hir and Ranjha)*	Amritsar	Bhai Hari Singh	1951 b. [1894]	n/a	195	G
Singh, Gurbaksh	*Baran Mah Gurbaksh Singh (Gurbaksh Singh's Baran Mar)*	n.p.	n.p.	n.d.	n/a	8	1-P
Singh, Jog	*Hir Jog Singh*	Lahore	Chiragh al-Din Siraj al-Din Tajran Kutab	n.d.	750	56	1-P

continued

Author	Title	City	Publisher	Date	Print Run	Pages	Script
Singh, Jog	*Hir Jog Singh*	Lahore	Mian Chiragh al-Din Siraj al-Din Tajran Kutab	n.d.	750	56	I-P
Singh, Jog	*Hir Jog Singh*	Lahore	Hafiz Muhammad Din wa Ahmad Din Tajran Kutab	1887	700	56	I-P
Singh, Jog	*Hir Jog Singh*	Lahore	Munshi Gobind Singh	n.d. [c. 1888]	n/a	56	I-P
Singh, Jog	*Qissa Hir Jog Singh*	Lahore	Chiragh al-Din Kutab Farosh	1877	1,050	56	I-P
Singh, Jog	*Qissa Hir Jog Singh*	Lahore	Chiragh al-Din Tajar Kutab	1880	n/a	56	I-P
Singh, Jog	*Qissa Hir Jog Singh*	Lahore	Malik Hira Tajar Kutab	1882	700	56	I-P
Singh, Lahora	*Hir Lahori* (Lahora's Hir)	Lahore	Gurdial Singh and Sons	1931	n/a	156	G
Sirani, Malik Ahmad Baksh Toba [Ghafil]	*Qissa Hir wa Ranjha*	Lahore	Matba' Kadimi Lahore	n.d.	n/a	n/a	I-P
Yar, Maulvi Ahmad	*Hir wa Ranjha*	Lahore	Matba' Mufid-i Am	1928	n/a	149	I-P

Punjabi Newspapers, 1880–1905

Name	Place of Publication	Years	Maximum Circulation	Information
Aror Vans Samachar	Lahore	1885–86	Monthly; 350	Deals with local news and caste questions (Arora).
Bhatia Samachar	Lahore	1901	Bimonthly; 400	Contains news about the Bhatia sect.
Gurmukhi Akhbar	Lahore and Amritsar	1880–87, 1893	Initially weekly, but then trimonthly; 325	This paper is the organ of the Singh Sabha.
Indian Khalsa Gazette	Lahore	1899	Monthly; 100	Paper started for the benefit of the Sikhs and contains extracts of the *Adi Granth*, and gives general news.
Khalsa Akhbar	Lahore	1889, 1893–1905	Weekly; 1,172	The object of the paper is to disseminate the religious doctrines of the Sikhs and to promote learning.
Khalsa Dharm Parcharak	Amritsar	1901	Monthly; 300	Treats general and religious (Sikh) news, and exercised small influence.
Khalsa Gazzette	Lahore	1899–1901	Weekly; 300	Religious (Sikh) and general news.
Khalsa Parkash	Lahore	1891–99	Weekly; 300	General and political news (Khalsa in the title suggests that this was a publication geared toward the Sikh community).
Khalsa Samachar	Amritsar	1899–1905	Weekly; 3,000	General and political news. Tone is moderate and treats religious subjects in connection with the Sikh faith. (Published by the Wazir-i-Hind Press, a Singh Sabha organ.)
Khalsa Sewak	Amritsar	1903–5	Monthly; 1,000	Opened by several Sikh gentlemen for the propagation of the Sikh religion. Reprints views of the Sikh Sabha and Chief Khalsa Diwan.
Lyall Khalsa Gazette (Urdu and Punjabi)	Sialkot	1891–93	Weekly; 150	Political and religious news. Professes to have as its chief object the promotion and advancement of Sikhs, morally and socially.
Monthly Circular	Lahore	1903–5	Monthly; 500	Accounts of the Punjab Mutual Hindu Family Relief Fund affairs, and contains notes on science.

Nirgunyara	Amritsar	1902–5	Bimonthly: 2,000	Religious news (proprietor given as Khalsa Tract Society, an organ of the Singh Sabha).
Panjab Darpan	Amritsar City	1885	Weekly; 350	Paper was closed because it did not pay. Religious and secular matters were discussed in its columns. Generally used to extract news from Urdu papers.
Ramgharia Patrika	Lahore	1903	Monthly; 500	Organ of the Ramgharia community.
Shudi Patr Khalsa Dharm Prakashak	Lahore	1899	Monthly; 650	Religious (Khalsa in the title suggests that this was a publication geared toward the Sikh community).
Singh Sabha Gazette	Amritsar	1893	Weekly; 500	Politics and religion; support of the Singh Sabha.
Siri Gaihar Gambhir Gazette	Rupar (Amritsar district)	1903	Monthly; 100	Religious (proprietor given as Swami Bishan Das, Udasi).
Vidyark Panjab	Lahore	1881	Monthly; no circulation figures	Published by the Singh Sabha of Lahore.

Information collated from colonial reports on newspapers by N. G. Barrier and Paul Wallace, *The Punjab Press, 1880–1905* (East Lansing: Michigan State University, 1970).

APPENDIX C

Punjabi Books Published Prior to 1867

Date	Author	Title	Place of Publication	Press
1274 h. [1857–58]	Muhammad Jaan Mir	Jangnamah Zaitun (The Battle of Zaitun)	Lahore	
1277 h. [1858–59]	Ilakim Devidayala	Qissa Laila wa Majnun	Lahore	
1278 h. [1861–62]	Maulvi Muhammad Muslim	Ajaib al Qasas (Stories of the Prophets)	Jullundur	Matba' Muhammadi
1862	Fazl Shah	Qissa Sassi wa Punnun	Delhi	
1280 h. [1863–64]	Hamid Shah	Shahadat Namah (The Story of Martyrdom)	Bhera	Maulvi Imam al-Din Tajar Kutab
1864		Adi Granth	Lahore	
1864	Muhammad Barak Allah	Anwa' Barak Allah		
1864	Allah Baksh	Baran Mah	Lahore	Haji Mahmood Matba'
1864	Muqbal	Jangnamah Imamein (The War of the Imams)	Lahore	Ameer al Din
1281 h. [1864–65]	Fard Faqir	Baran Mah	Lahore	Haji Muhammad Matba' Tajar
1281 h. [1864–65]	Arora Rai	Baran Mah	Lahore	Haji Mahmood Matba' Nazar
1281 h. [1864–65]	Ganpat Rai Lahore	Baran Mah	Lahore	Haji Muhammad
1281 h. [1864–65]	Khawaja Nur Muhammad	Jama' al Wajahat	Lahore	Matba' Lares Press
1281 h. [1864–65]	Sultan Bahu	Majmua' Barah Mah (A Collection of Baran Mah)	Lahore	Haji Muhammad Matba' Nazir
1281 h. [1864–65]	Maulvi Muhammad Din	Pakki Roti (Muslim traditions and religious precepts)	Meerut	Matba' Nasir Shahdarah
1281 h. [1864–65]	Syed Fazl Shah	Sohni Mahival	Lahore	
1865	Syed Bulleh Shah	Baran Mah	Lahore	Haji Mahmood Sahib Matba' Tajar
1865	Sanwal Yar	Barah Mah	Lahore	Haji Mahmood Nazar
1282 h. [1865–66]	Shah Muhammad	Qissa Shah Muhammad	Lahore	Ilahi Baksh
1866 (2nd edition)	Nanak	Japji Pothi	Lahore	
1284 h. [1867–68]	Isa (Jesus)	Dar Ashfai Matba' Punjabi	Lahore	
1284 h. [1867–68]	Bute Shah (trans. Munshi Bahlol)	A Geographical Description of the Punjab, in Panjabi	Ludhiana	
1284 h. [1867–68]	Syed Fazl Shah	Si Harfi Hir, Si Harfi Sohni, Si Harfi Sassi	Lahore	Khair al-Din Chiragh al-Din

INTRODUCTION

1. Although it literally means "the four gardens of the Punjab," *Char Bagh-i Punjab* is better translated as "A History of the Punjab." Historians J. S. Grewal and Indu Banga take literary license with the title of their partial translation of this text, published as *Early Nineteenth Century Panjab.*

2. For a partial translation see J.S. Grewal and Indu Banga, trans. and eds., *Early Nineteenth Century Panjab: From Ganesh Das's "Char Bagh-i-Panjab"* (Amritsar: Guru Nanak Dev University, 1975).

3. On 13 April 1919, a crowd had gathered at the Jallianwala Bagh in Amritsar to celebrate a fair (the Baisakhi Mela), oblivious to the martial law regulation prohibiting mass assembly. The crowd was indiscriminately fired upon, without warning, resulting in 379 deaths and 1,200 injuries. See Sugata Bose and Ayesha Jalal, *Modern South Asia: History, Culture, Political Economy* (New York: Routledge, 1998), 138. The massacre itself was ordered by General Reginald Dyer. Subsequent to the event, O'Dwyer supported Dyer's actions. Udham Singh had gone to England intent on killing either man, whichever opportunity presented itself first.

4. Jyotika Sood and Anuradha Shukla, "Udham Singh's 'Heer' in for a Makeover," *The Tribune* (Chandigarh), 26 July 2007.

5. All translations from Punjabi and Urdu are mine unless otherwise stated. This translation is adapted from Amrita Pritam, "I Call on Varis Shah!" trans. Gibb Schreffler, *Journal of Punjab Studies* 13, 1–2 (2006): 79; and Amrita Pritam, "To Waris Shah," in *Alone in the Multitude*, ed. and trans. Suresh Kohli (New Delhi: Indian Literary Review, 1979), 11.

6. Syad Muhammad Latif, *Lahore: Its History, Architectural Remains and Antiquities, with an Account of Its Modern Institutions, Inhabitants, Their Trade, Customs, &c.* (Lahore:

Sang-e-Meel Publications, 1994 [1892]), 267. The context makes clear the texts performed were in Punjabi.

7. Punjabi is an Indo-Aryan language consisting of a number of dialects, principally spoken in the northwest regions of the Indian subcontinent. Definitions of the language have shifted over the past three centuries, as linguists (and linguistic activists, more recently) have contested which dialects should be included under the general rubric of "Punjabi" and which constitute independent languages. In this book, I use *Punjabi* to denote a range of mutually intelligible dialects spoken in the area from Delhi to Peshawar, including Majhi, Siraiki, Malvai, Puadhi, Kangri, Doabi, Hindko, and Pothohari. The clearest linguistic exposition of the language is Christopher Shackle, "Panjabi," in *The Indo-Aryan Languages,* ed. Dhanesh Jain and George Cardona (New York: Routledge, 2003), 581–621.

8. See, for example, Shafqat Tanveer Mirza, *Resistance Themes in Punjabi Literature* (Lahore: Sang-e-Meel Publications, 1992).

9. Despite my use of "Hindi," "Urdu," and "Bengali," these were not stable categories in the nineteenth century. A range of dialects constituted Urdu and Hindi (as was true with Bengali), such as Khari Boli, Awadhi, and Braj. Only during the nineteenth century, through the careful work of government, litterateurs, and activists, did stable definitions of Hindi and Urdu emerge, and even these continued to be highly contested through the early half of the twentieth century (and remain so, in certain circumstances, even today). For a linguistic analysis of both languages, see: Michael Shapiro's "Hindi" and Ruth Schmidt's "Urdu," in *Indo-Aryan Languages,* ed. Jain and Cardona, 250–85 and 286–350, respectively.

10. Secretary to the Government of the Punjab, letter to the commissioners of divisions. Cited in "Abstract of Opinions Regarding Vernacular of the Courts," Lahore, 21 February 1863, National Archives of India, Home Department Proceedings, Education, no. 30, September 1876.

11. The evolution of the Punjabi *qissa* is examined in more detail in Farina Mir, "Genre and Devotion in Punjabi Popular Narratives: Rethinking Cultural and Religious Syncretism," *Comparative Studies in Society and History* 48, 3 (July 2006): 734–46.

12. Masnavi is "a series of distitchs in rhyming pairs (aa, bb, cc, etc.)." Jan Rypka, *History of Iranian Literature* (Dordrecht: Reidel, 1968), 91.

13. Sunil Sharma, *Amir Khusraw: The Poet of Sufis and Sultans* (Oxford: Oneworld, 2005).

14. Information on these poets is compiled from: Mohan Singh Uberoi, *A History of Panjabi Literature, 1100–1932* (Jalandhar: Bharat Prakashan, 1971 [1933]); Mohan Singh Uberoi, *Punjabi Sahit di Itihas Rekha* (A Timeline of Punjabi Literature) (Chandigarh: Panjabi University, 1962 [1958]); Lajwanti Rama Krishna and A. R. Luther, *Madho Lal Husain: Sufi Poet of the Punjab* (Lahore: Mubarak Ali, 1982); S. S. Sekhon, *A History of Panjabi Literature,* vol. 2 (Patiala: Punjabi University Publication Bureau, 1996); S. S. Sekhon and K. S. Duggal, *A History of Punjabi Literature* (New Delhi: Sahitya Akademi, 1992); Jit Singh Sital, "Hir Waris," in *Hir Waris,* by Waris Shah, ed. Jit Singh Sital (Delhi: Aarsi Publishers, 2004), 10–21; and Pritam Singh, *Bhai Gurdas* (New Delhi: Sahitya Akademi, 1992).

15. Haria, Husain, Bhalla, and Bhatt composed in *shloka*s, *kafi*s, *var*s, and *kabit*s, respectively. A *shloka,* usually associated with Sanskrit literature, is a distich consisting of two sixteen-syllable lines, each of which consists of equal eight-syllable halves. *Kabit* is a

quatrain in which each line has thirty-one or thirty-two syllables. *Kafi* is a lyric of three or four stanzas, each of which can have two, three, or four lines. Each line of a *kafi* can vary in meter and length. *Vars* are "ballads and lays of war and strife [that] have been sung by professional bards for the entertainment of rajas [kings] and jagirdars [landlords] as well as gatherings of common people at fairs and on festive occasions like weddings and birthday celebrations." Sekhon and Duggal, *History of Punjabi Literature*, 91.

16. Husain's compositions are in the language of central Punjab (an area known as the Majha), or a dialect known as Majhi. Haria's compositions are in Siraiki, the language of southern Punjab.

17. Sekhon and Duggal, *History of Punjabi Literature*, 61.

18. I have modified the translation provided by Sekhon in his *History of Panjabi Literature*, 2: 61.

19. The earliest Indo-Persian manuscript that Punjabi literary scholars cite is dated 1834 and is housed at the Bhasha Vibhag, Patiala. Early Gurmukhi manuscripts dated 1821 and 1827 are also housed there.

20. Information on Hamid Shah Abbasi is compiled from Ajmer Singh, *Maharaja Ranjit Singh ate Punjabi Sahit* (Maharaja Ranjit Singh and Punjabi Literature) (Patiala: Punjabi University Publication Bureau, 1982); Damodar, *Hir Damodar*, ed. Jagtar Singh (Patiala: Punjab University, 1987); and Piara Singh Padam, introduction to *Hir Ahmad*, by Ahmad Gujar (Patiala: Punjabi University Publication Bureau, 1960).

21. The Punjabi verse is cited in Padam, introduction to *Hir Ahmad*, 7.

22. John Platts, *A Dictionary of Urdu, Classical Hindi, and English* (Lahore: Sang-e-Meel Publications, 1994 [1911]).

23. Punjabi text in Joginder Singh Ramdev, *Punjabi Likhari Kosh* (A Dictionary of Punjabi Writers) (Jalandhar: New Book Company, 1964), 40.

24. Kishan Singh 'Arif, *Qissa Hir te Ranjhe da* (The *Qissa* of Hir and Ranjha) (Amritsar, 1889), 12–13. For a more detailed description of this and similar genealogies, see chapter 2.

25. Christopher Shackle, "Making Punjabi Literary History," in *Sikh Religion, Culture, and Ethnicity*, ed. Christopher Shackle et al. (Richmond, Surrey: Curzon Press, 2001), 103.

26. I examine the broader political philosophy underpinning this shift in my essay "Imperial Policy, Provincial Practices: Colonial Language Policy in Nineteenth-Century India," *Indian Economic and Social History Review* 43, 4 (2006): 395–427.

27. The College of Fort William was at the vanguard of these efforts, publishing texts such as Ramram Basu's Bengali *Lipimala* (Specimen Bengali Letters) (1802); and William Carey's *A Grammar of the Bengalee Language* (1801), *Dialogues Intended to Facilitate the Acquiring of the Bengalee Language* (1802), and *The Bengalee English Dictionary* (1815). The college also produced and published materials on Urdu, Hindi, Kannada, Marathi, and Oriya.

28. For example, in 1868 the government of the Northwest Provinces sponsored a prize for "the production of useful works in the vernacular [Urdu or Hindi]. . . . The only condition is that the book shall subserve some useful purpose. . . . Books suitable for the women of India will be especially acceptable, and well rewarded. The government will ordinarily be prepared to aid in the publication of any meritorious work." The first prize, of one thousand rupees—a substantial amount for 1869—and a watch, was awarded to Nazir Ahmad for his *Mirat al-'arus*, the first Urdu novel. See C. M. Naim, "Prize-Winning *Adab*: A Study of Five

Urdu Books Written in Response to the Allahabad Government Gazette Notification," in *Moral Conduct and Authority: The Place of Adab in South Asian Islam,* ed. Barbara Metcalf (Berkeley: University of California Press, 1984), 290–314. On the standardization of Hindi, for example, see: Christopher King, *One Language, Two Scripts: The Hindi Movement in Nineteenth Century North India* (New Delhi: Oxford University Press, 1994).

29. Gail Minault, "Delhi College and Urdu," *Annual of Urdu Studies* 14 (1999): 126.

30. Two important studies that elucidate this are: Veena Naregal, *Language Politics, Elites, and the Public Sphere: Western India under Colonialism* (Delhi: Permanent Black, 2001); and Anindita Ghosh, *Power in Print: Popular Publishing and the Politics of Language and Culture in a Colonial Society, 1778–1905* (New Delhi: Oxford University Press, 2006).

31. Sanjay Joshi, *Fractured Modernity: Making of a Middle Class in Colonial North India* (New Delhi: Oxford University Press, 2001), 37–38.

32. Ulrike Stark, *An Empire of Books: The Naval Kishore Press and the Diffusion of the Printed Word in Colonial India* (Delhi: Permanent Black, 2007).

33. Ibid., 229.

34. Anindita Ghosh, "An Uncertain 'Coming of the Book': Early Print Cultures in Colonial India," *Book History* 6 (2003): 28.

35. Other classical genres included: *baran mah, doha, dole, jangnama, kafi, si harfi,* and *var.*

36. *Majmu'a Baran Mah* was published in 1864 and *Hir Muqbal* was published in at least eleven editions between 1872 and 1898, in the Indo-Persian script alone, suggesting its popularity. See Shahbaz Malik, *Punjabi Kitabiyat* (A Bibliography of Punjabi Printed Books Written in Perso-Arabic Script) (Islamabad: Akademi Adabiyat Pakistan, 1991), 464. *Hir Muqbal* was also published in the Gurmukhi script, though in how many editions is unclear.

37. Muhammad Shah Sakin, *Qissa Hir wa Ranjha* (Lahore: Malik Din Muhammad and Sons, n.d.).

38. Two recent examples are: Vazira Zamindar, *The Long Partition and the Making of Modern South Asia* (New York: Columbia University Press, 2007); and Yasmin Khan, *The Great Partition: The Making of India and Pakistan* (New Haven, CT: Yale University Press, 2007).

39. These were the weeks on either side of 15 August 1947, the date of the "transfer of power." Swarna Aiyar, "'August Anarchy': The Partition Massacres in Punjab, 1947," *South Asia* 18, supplement 1 (1995): 13–36.

40. See Bernard Cohn, "The Census, Social Structure, and Objectification in South Asia," in *An Anthropologist among the Historians and Other Essays* (New Delhi: Oxford University Press, 1987), 224–54; and Kenneth W. Jones, "Religious Identity and the Indian Census," in *The Census in British India: New Perspectives,* ed. N.G. Barrier (New Delhi: Manohar, 1981), 73–101.

41. Sudipta Kaviraj, "The Imaginary Institution of India," in *Subaltern Studies: Writings on South Asian History and Society,* ed. Partha Chatterjee and Gyanendra Pandey (New Delhi: Oxford University Press, 1992), 7: 1–39.

42. The most concise articulation of this argument is Kenneth W. Jones, *Socio-Religious Reform Movements in British India* (New Delhi: Foundation Books, 1994 [1989]), chap. 4.

43. See Bob van der Linden, *Moral Languages from Colonial Punjab: The Singh Sabha, Arya Samaj, and Ahmadiyahs* (New Delhi: Manohar, 2008), chap. 1.

44. On Christian missionary activity in colonial Punjab, see Christopher Harding, *Religious Transformation in South Asia: The Meanings of Conversion in Colonial Punjab* (New York: Oxford University Press, 2008); Jeffrey Cox, *Imperial Fault Lines: Christianity and Colonial Power in India, 1818–1940* (Stanford, CA: Stanford University Press, 2002); and Antony Copley, *Religions in Conflict: Ideology, Cultural Contact, and Conversion in Late Colonial India* (New Delhi: Oxford University Press, 1997), chap. 5.

45. The most comprehensive studies of socioreligious reform in colonial Punjab are: Kenneth W. Jones, *Arya Dharm: Hindu Consciousness in 19th-Century Punjab* (New Delhi: Manohar, 1989 [1976]); Harjot Oberoi, *The Construction of Religious Boundaries: Culture, Identity, and Diversity in the Sikh Tradition* (Chicago: University of Chicago Press, 1994); and Yohanan Friedmann, *Prophecy Continuous: Aspects of Ahmadi Religious Thought and Its Medieval Background* (Berkeley: University of California Press, 1989). See van der Linden, *Moral Languages from Colonial Punjab*, for a comparative approach.

46. Government of India, *Census of India, 1901*, vol. 1A, pt. 2 (Calcutta: Superintendent of Government Printing, 1903), 58–62. Harjot Oberoi argues that due to colonial biases, Sikhs were grossly underrepresented in the British census throughout the late nineteenth and early twentieth centuries. Oberoi, *Construction of Religious Boundaries*, 210–12.

47. Christopher Harding puts the number at half a million by the late 1930s. *Religious Transformation in South Asia*, 1.

48. Excellent monographs examine each of these movements. See: Barbara Metcalf, *Islamic Revival in British India: Deoband, 1860–1900* (Princeton, NJ: Princeton University Press, 1982); Usha Sanyal, *Devotional Islam and Politics in British India: Ahmad Riza Khan Barelwi and His Movement, 1870–1920* (New Delhi: Oxford University Press, 1996); David Kopf, *The Brahmo Samaj and the Shaping of the Indian Mind* (Princeton, NJ: Princeton University Press, 1979); and Jones, *Arya Dharm*. On the Brahmo Samaj in Punjab specifically, see Jones, *Arya Dharm*.

49. See Anshu Malhotra, *Gender, Caste, and Religious Identities: Restructuring Class in Colonial Punjab* (New Delhi: Oxford University Press, 2002).

50. Yohanan Friedmann, *Prophecy Continuous: Aspects of Ahmadi Religious Thought and Its Medieval Background* (Berkeley: University of California Press, 1989), 6–7.

51. Jones, *Socio-Religious Reform Movements in British India*, 118.

52. Kenneth Jones, "Communalism in the Punjab: The Arya Samaj Contribution," *Journal of Asian Studies* 28, 1 (1968): 51.

53. Jones, *Socio-Religious Reform Movements in British India*, 288.

54. Kenneth Jones, "Ham Hindu Nahin: Arya-Sikh Relations, 1877–1905," *Journal of Asian Studies* 32, 3 (1973): 457–75.

55. N. G. Barrier, "Vernacular Publishing and Sikh Public Life in the Punjab, 1880–1910," in *Religious Controversy in British India: Dialogues in South Asian Languages*, ed. Kenneth W. Jones (Albany: State University of New York, 1992), 208.

56. Jones, *Socio-Religious Reform in British India*, 121.

57. Christopher King, "Images of Virtue and Vice: The Hindi-Urdu Controversy in Two Nineteenth-century Hindi Plays," in *Religious Controversy in British India,* ed. Jones, 126.

58. Vasudha Dalmia, *The Nationalization of Hindu Traditions: Bharatendu Harischandra and Nineteenth-Century Banaras* (New Delhi: Oxford University Press, 1997); and Francesca Orsini, *The Hindi Public Sphere, 1920-1940: Language and Literature in the Age of Nationalism* (New York: Oxford University Press, 2002).

59. Appendix A provides details of these texts. They are in both the Gurmukhi and Indo-Persian scripts and are composed by some forty different poets.

1. FORGING A LANGUAGE POLICY

1. Johannes Fabian, *Language and Colonial Power: The Appropriation of Swahili in the Former Belgian Congo, 1880-1938* (Cambridge: Cambridge University Press, 1986), continues to be a foundational text on the role of language in colonialism.

2. C. A. Bayly, *Empire and Information: Intelligence Gathering and Social Communication in India, 1780-1870* (Cambridge: Cambridge University Press, 1996).

3. The first such institution was the College of Fort William in Calcutta, founded in 1800. In 1806, the Company established a college at Haileybury, England, for the purpose of educating recruits before they arrived in India. In 1812, a second institution was founded in India: the College of Fort St. George in Madras.

4. Bernard Cohn, "The Command of Language and the Language of Command," in *Colonialism and Its Forms of Knowledge* (Princeton, NJ: Princeton University Press, 1996), 16-56.

5. Information on this press is drawn from Graham W. Shaw, "The First Printing Press in the Panjab," *Library Chronicle* 43, 2 (1979): 159-79. John Lowrie of the mission recorded in his memoir that Ranjit Singh licensed two lithographic presses during his reign, in the hopes of disseminating the *Adi Granth,* Sikhism's sacred text, and later had them closed. See his *Two Years in Upper India* (New York: R. Carter and Brothers, 1850). I have found no other reference to these early presses.

6. Nazar Singh, "Newspapers, Politics, and Literature in the Nineteenth Century Delhi and Punjab," *Panjab Past and Present* 24, 2 (1990): 401.

7. Ibid.

8. Ibid., 392-407.

9. H. R. Goulding, *Old Lahore: Reminiscences of a Resident* (Lahore: Sang-e-Meel Publications, n.d. [1924]), 28.

10. N. G. Barrier and Paul Wallace, *The Punjab Press, 1880-1905* (East Lansing: Michigan State University, 1970), 159.

11. Singh, "Newspapers, Politics, and Literature," 402. Though Singh does not give the titles of the Arabic newspapers, they were likely organs of Muslim socioreligious reform organizations, many of which were then active in the Punjab.

12. "Report on Vernacular Newspapers Published in the Punjab during 1883," in National Archives of India (henceforth NAI), Home, Public Proceedings, nos. 14-15B, June 1884.

13. Singh, "Newspapers, Politics, and Literature," 402.

14. Barrier and Wallace, *Punjab Press*, 159.

15. Ibid., 102.

16. Government of India, *Imperial Gazetteer of India: Provincial Series Punjab*, vol. 2 (Calcutta: Government of India, 1908), 19 and 26. Literacy was defined in the loosest terms: "No attempt was made to record the *degree* of literacy. . . . Hence by 'literate' in the returns of the current Census is meant a person who considers him or herself literate . . . and literacy includes every degree of proficiency." Government of India, *Census of India, 1901*, vol. 17, pt. 1 (Simla: Government of India, 1902), 263.

17. These figures are from Punjab administrative reports for the relevant years.

18. David Lelyveld, "*Zuban-e Urdu-e Mu'alla* and the Idol of Linguistic Origins," *Annual of Urdu Studies* 9 (1994): 66.

19. See Richard Eaton, *Sufis of Bijapur, 1300–1700: Social Roles of Sufis in Medieval India* (Princeton, NJ: Princeton University Press, 1978).

20. See W. H. McLeod, *The Early Sikh Tradition: A Study of the Janam-Sakhis* (Oxford: Clarendon Press, 1980).

21. On the *Dabistan-i Mazahib* see, J. Horovitz, "Dabistan al-Madhahib," *Encyclopaedia of Islam,* 2nd ed., P. Bearman, et al., eds. (Leiden: E. J. Brill, 2009), www.brillonline.nl/sub scriber/entry?entry = islam_SIM-1647 (accessed 20 February 2009). On the later definition of Jataki, see Erskine Perry, "On the Geographical Distribution of the Principal Languages of India, and the Feasibility of Introducing English as a Lingua Franca," *Journal of the Bombay Branch of the Royal Asiatic Society* 4 (1853): 297. I address the relationship between Multani and Punjabi in chapter 2, note 21.

22. Sunil Sharma, *Persian Poetry at the Indian Frontier: Mas'ud Sa'd Salman of Lahore* (Delhi: Permanent Black, 2000).

23. These texts, among others, are cited with brief descriptions in Ikram Ali Malik, *The History of the Punjab, 1799–1947* (Delhi: Low Price Publications, 1993 [1970]), 681–93. There are some important exceptions, such as Ratan Singh Bhangu's Punjabi *Gur Panth Prakash* (completed in 1841) and Ram Sukh Rao's Punjabi biographies of the first three rulers of Kapurthala, produced in the early nineteenth century.

24. Graham W. Shaw, "The Parameters of Publishing in Nineteenth-Century North India: A Study Based Loosely on Delhi," paper presented at the New Literary Histories for the Nineteenth Century Workshop, University of California, Berkeley, 17 September 1999.

25. G. W. Leitner, *History of Indigenous Education in the Panjab Since Annexation and in 1882* (Patiala: Languages Department, 1971 [1883]).

26. On the early history of Urdu, see Shamsur Rahman Faruqi, *Early Urdu Literary Culture and History* (New Delhi: Oxford University Press, 2001).

27. Carla Petievich, *Assembly of Rivals: Delhi, Lucknow, and the Urdu Ghazal* (Lahore: Vanguard, 1992), 13.

28. Faruqi, *Early Urdu Literary Culture and History,* 179.

29. Mohan Singh Uberoi, *A History of Panjabi Literature, 1100–1932* (Jalandhar: Bharat Prakashan, 1971 [1933]), 20–38.

30. Christopher Shackle, "Some Observations of the Evolution of Modern Standard Punjabi," *Sikh History and Religion in the Twentieth Century,* ed. Joseph O'Connell et al. (Toronto: University of Toronto Press, 1988), 105.

31. S. S. Sekhon, *A History of Panjabi Literature*, vol. 2 (Patiala: Punjabi University Publication Bureau, 1996), 108–12.

32. Maula Baksh Kushta, *Punjabi Shairan da Tazkira* (A Dictionary of Punjabi Poets), ed. Chaudhry Muhammad Afzal Khan (Lahore: Aziz Publishers, 1988 [1960]), 148.

33. Piara Singh Padam, *Kalam de Dhani* (The Wealth of Poets) (Patiala: Piara Singh Padam, 1998), 154.

34. Ajmer Singh, *Maharaja Ranjit Singh ate Punjabi Sahit* (Maharaja Ranjit Singh and Punjabi Literature) (Patiala: Punjabi University Publication Bureau, 1982), 53.

35. Ibid., 74.

36. Sekhon, *History of Panjabi Literature*, 123–26.

37. Interestingly, histories produced at the behest of colonial officials in the first half of the nineteenth century were composed in Persian. For example, Khush-Waqt Rai's *Ahwal-i Firqah-i Sikhan* (A History of the Sikhs from their Origins) was written at the request of Colonel David Ochterlony and Ghulam Muhiyuddin's *Tarikh-i Punjab* (History of Punjab) at the suggestion of the political agent at Ludhiana.

38. Frances Pritchett, "Urdu Literary Culture, Part 2," in *Literary Cultures in History*, ed. Sheldon Pollock (Berkeley: University of California Press, 2003), 905. Also see Frances Pritchett, *Nets of Awareness* (Berkeley: University of California Press, 1994), chaps. 1–2.

39. Hali was employed at the Government Book Depot in Lahore, where he revised translations of English books into Urdu for the Education Department. Ram Babu Saksena, *A History of Urdu Literature* (Lahore: Sang-e-Meel Publications, 1996 [1927]), 234. Also see Pritchett, *Nets of Awareness*, chap. 3.

40. The Hindi proverb is "kos kos pai pani badle, char kos pai bani" (the language changes every four *kos*, the water every two). Cited and translated by Norbert Peabody, in *Hindu Kingship and Polity in Precolonial India* (Cambridge: Cambridge University Press, 2003), xii.

41. This process is discussed in more detail in my "Imperial Policy, Provincial Practices: Colonial Language Policy in Nineteenth-Century India," *Indian Economic and Social History Review* 43, 4 (2006): 395–427.

42. Chris King, *One Language, Two Scripts: The Hindi Movement in Nineteenth Century North India* (New Delhi: Oxford University Press, 1994), 7.

43. Vasudha Dalmia, *The Nationalization of Hindu Traditions: Bharatendu Harischandra and Nineteenth-Century Banaras* (New Delhi: Oxford University Press, 1997), 177.

44. Secretary to the Board of Administration Punjab, letter to the Commissioners and Superintendents: (i) Lahore Division; (ii) Multan Division; (iii) Leia Division; (iv) Jhelum Division; and the Deputy Commissioners: (i) Peshawar Division; (ii) Hazara Division, 1 June 1849, in Government of Punjab, *The Development of Urdu as Official Language in the Punjab, 1849–1974*, comp. Nazir Ahmad Chaudhry (Lahore: Government of the Punjab, 1977), 5. This volume includes the Punjab Board of Administration's correspondence on language policy, archived in the Punjab Provincial Archives (Lahore).

45. Urdu was made the official language of courts in the Lahore and Jhelum districts, and in the northeastern reaches of the Multan Division, as well as in southeastern Punjab. Persian was retained as the official language of judicial records in Multan city, as well as in the Leia, Peshawar, and Hazara Divisions. Secretary to the Board of Administration for

Punjab, letter to H. M. Elliot, Secretary to the Government of India with the Governor-General, 17 August 1849, in ibid., 22–24.

46. Lieutenant F. R. Pollock, Officiating Deputy Commissioner, Dera Ghazi Khan, letter to Major D. Ross, Commissioner and Superintendent, Leia Division, 8 June 1854, in ibid., 32.

47. Note by Sir John Lawrence, appended to Secretary to the Board of Administration Punjab, letter to Commissioner and Superintendent, Multan Division, 20 September 1849, in ibid., 28.

48. Bayly, *Empire and Information;* and Cohn, "Command of Language and the Language of Command."

49. See Thomas Metcalf, *Ideologies of the Raj* (Cambridge: Cambridge University Press, 1994).

50. Thomas Trautmann, *Aryans and British India* (Berkeley: University of California Press, 1997); and his *Languages and Nations: Conversations in Colonial South India* (Berkeley: University of California Press, 2006).

51. On the Serampore mission of the Baptist Missionary Society, established in 1800 by William Carey, Joshua Marshman, and William Ward, see E. Daniel Potts, *British Baptist Missionaries in India, 1793–1837* (Cambridge: Cambridge University Press, 1967).

52. The Serampore missionaries were not alone in their philological zeal. On the knowledge of native languages as a critical aspect of missionary activities in the modern colonial world, see Fabian, *Language and Colonial Power;* and Jean Comaroff and John Comaroff, *Of Revelation and Revolution,* vol. 1 (Chicago: University of Chicago Press, 1991), chap. 6.

53. Cited in *American Baptist Magazine and Missionary Intelligencer* 3, 11 (1822): 424–26.

54. See, for example, his letter to Mr. Fuller, 4 August 1814: "Shikh or Punjabi, N.T. [New Testament] printed within a few chapters." Cited in Eustace Carey, *Memoir of William Carey, D.D.* (Hartford, CT: Canfield and Robins, 1837), 401.

55. William Carey, *A Grammar of the Punjaubee Language* (Serampore: Serampore Mission Press, 1812).

56. An 1809 treaty with the Sikh kingdom of Lahore had given the British control of the Cis-Sutlej area.

57. Shaw, "First Printing Press," 159.

58. For a complete listing of nineteenth-century colonial grammars and dictionaries of Punjabi, see George Grierson, "A Bibliography of the Panjabi Language," *Indian Antiquary* 35 (1906): 65–72.

59. Lt. Col. John Malcolm, *Sketch of the Sikhs* (New Delhi: Asian Educational Services, 1986 [1812]), 4.

60. Orientalist scholarship on Hindu scriptures in the eighteenth and nineteenth centuries is another important example of this. See Peter van der Veer, *Imperial Encounters: Religion and Modernity in India and Britain* (Princeton, NJ: Princeton University Press, 2001), 106–33.

61. Malcolm, *Sketch of the Sikhs,* 1.

62. John Beames, *Outlines of Indian Philology and Other Philological Papers* (Calcutta: Indian Studies Past and Present, 1960 [1867]).

63. John Beames, *Memoirs of a Bengal Civilian* (1867; reprint, London: Chatto and Windus, 1961).

64. George Grierson, "John Beames" [obituary], *Journal of the Royal Asiatic Society* (1902): 722.

65. The report cited Punjabi as a vernacular in the following districts: Ambala, Ludhiana, Hissar, Jalandhar, Hoshiarpur, Amritsar, Sialkot, Gurdaspur, Lahore, Gujranwala, Ferozepur, Rawalpindi, Jhelum, Gujrat, Shahpur, Kohat, Hazara, Multan, Jhang, Montgomery, Muzaffargarh, and Dera Ismail Khan. See Government of Punjab, *Report on Popular Education in the Punjab and Its Dependencies, for the Year 1874–75* (Lahore: Government of the Punjab, 1875), vii, which cites figures from the administration report of the Punjab for the previous year.

66. The exact figures are: Amritsar, 96 percent; Dera Ismail Khan, Punjabi, 65 percent; Jataki (a dialect of Punjabi) 20 percent; Ferozepur, 97 percent; Gujrat, 99 percent; Gurdaspur, 86 percent; Lahore, 96 percent; Ludhiana, 98 percent. Statistics based on table 9 of the census report of 1881.

67. George Grierson, *Grierson on Punjabi* [reprint of Punjabi sections of *Linguistic Survey of India*, vol. 9] (Patiala: Languages Department, 1961 [1919]). Grierson's method is detailed in his private papers: Oriental and India Office Collection (henceforth OIOC), British Library (henceforth BL), MS EUR/E223.

68. NAI, Foreign Department Proceedings, Foreign Consultations, nos. 82 and 83, 14 November 1851.

69. Charles Napier, "Report by Lt-Gen Sir Charles Napier," 27 November 1849, OIOC, BL, MS EUR/C123.

70. Secretary to the Government of the Punjab, letter to the Commissioners of Divisions, cited in "Abstract of Opinions Regarding Vernacular of the Courts," Lahore, 21 February 1863, NAI, Home, Education, no. 30, September 1876.

71. Ibid.

72. Captain Maxwell, Deputy Commissioner Googaira, letter to Lt. Col. G. W. Hamilton, Commissioner and Superintendent, Mooltan Division, 23 June 1862, in Government of Punjab, *Development of Urdu*, 61.

73. Ibid., 62.

74. Secretary to the Government of the Punjab, letter to the Commissioners of Divisions.

75. This was said of Hindi in particular. See J. R. Davidson, letter to J. F. M. Reid, Registrar of the Court of Sudder Dewany Adawlut, [Fort William], 7 March 1836, OIOC, BL, F/4/1684.

76. This was said of Oriya in particular. See H. Ricketts, letter to J. F. M. Reid, Registrar of the Court of the Sudder Dewany Adawlut, Fort William, 19 February 1836, OIOC, BL, F/4/1684.

77. This was said of Bengali in particular. See R. Barlow, letter to J. F. M. Reid, Registrar of the Court of Sudder Dewany Adawlut, [Fort William], 23 April 1836, OIOC, BL, F/4/1684.

78. This was said of all three languages.

79. J. R. Davidson, letter to J. F. M. Reid, Registrar of the Court of Sudder Dewany Adawlut, [Fort William], 7 March 1836, OIOC, BL, F/4/1684.

80. Kenneth W. Jones, *Arya Dharm: Hindu Consciousness in 19th-Century Punjab* (New Delhi: Manohar, 1989 [1976]), 13.

81. The Company's colleges at Haileybury and Fort William offered training in these languages.

82. Dalmia, *Nationalization of Hindu Traditions,* 176.

83. Note by Sir John Lawrence, in Government of Punjab, *Development of Urdu,* 28.

84. The colonial state understood the social structure of the Punjab as essentially tribal and identified tribal chiefs as the region's elite. See David Gilmartin, "Customary Law and *Shari'at* in British Punjab," in *Shari'at and Ambiguity in South Asian Islam,* ed. Katherine P. Ewing (Berkeley: University of California Press, 1988), 43–62.

85. P. S. Melvill, Commissioner and Superintendent, Delhi Division, letter to Secretary to the Government of the Punjab, 16 June 1862, in Government of Punjab, *Development of Urdu,* 66–67.

86. Secretary to the Government of the Punjab, letter to the Commissioners of Divisions. Cited in "Abstract of Opinions Regarding Vernacular of the Courts."

87. Cited in H. R. Mehta, *A History of the Growth and Development of Western Education in the Punjab, 1846–84* (Delhi: Nirmal Publications, 1987 [1929]), 29.

88. Gauri Viswanathan, *Masks of Conquest: Literary Study and British Rule in India* (New York: Columbia University Press, 1989). See also, Lynn Zastoupil and Martin Moir, eds., *The Great Indian Education Debate: Documents Relating to the Orientalist-Anglicist Controversy, 1781–1843* (London: Curzon Press, 1999).

89. "Minute by the Judicial Commissioner Punjab [Robert Montgomery; 1854]," in Government of Punjab, *Development of Urdu,* 138–39.

90. Secretary to the Chief Commissioner to the Secretary to the Government of India, 1 May 1854, no. 363, OIOC, BL, P/188/8, cited in Tim Allender, *Ruling through Education: The Politics of Schooling in Colonial Punjab* (Elgin, IL: New Dawn Press, 2006), 94.

91. "Despatch from the Court of Directors of the East India Company to the Governor General of India in Council, dated 19th July, 1854, No. 49," NAI, Foreign, Foreign Consultations, no. 56, 15 July 1859.

92. Government of Punjab, *Report on Popular Education in the Punjab and Its Dependencies, for the Year 1860–61,* by A. R. Fuller (Lahore: Government of the Punjab, 1865), i.

93. Ibid.

94. Government of Punjab, *Report on Popular Education in the Punjab and Its Dependencies, for the Year 1874–75,* by W. R. M. Holroyd (Lahore: Government of the Punjab, 1876), 1; Government of Punjab, *Report on Popular Education in the Punjab and Its Dependencies, for the Year 1878–79,* by W. R. M. Holroyd (Lahore: Government of the Punjab, 1880), 1; Government of Punjab, *Report on Popular Education in the Punjab and Its Dependencies, for the Year 1884–85,* by Denzil Ibbetson (Lahore: Government of the Punjab, 1885), 1.

95. *Census of India 1901,* vol. 17, pt. 1, 272.

96. Allender, *Ruling through Education,* 56.

97. Babu Bhudeb Mukhopadhyay, *Report on the Village Schools of the North West Province and the Panjab* (Calcutta: n.p., 1868), 52. Quoted in NAI, Home, Education, nos. 23–25B, 10 October 1868.

98. Cited in Syed Mahmood, *A History of English Education in India* (Aligarh: Muhammadan Anglo-Oriental College, 1895), 57.

99. For the colonial state's promotion of Urdu and Hindi materials in NWP, see King, *One Language, Two Scripts.* For the Madras Presidency and the promotion of Tamil materials, see Stuart Blackburn, *Print, Folklore, and Nationalism in Colonial South India* (Delhi: Permanent Black, 2003), chap. 4.

100. Lepel Griffin, Under-Secretary to Government, Punjab, letter to the Secretary to Government of India, Home Department, Lahore, 20 October 1870. In the Punjab Provincial Archives, Chandigarh (henceforth PPAC), Education, Science, and Art Department Proceedings, no. 5, March 1870.

101. Ibid.

102. Pritchett, *Nets of Awareness,* 11. Information on Azad's and Hali's Lahore experience is taken from chapter 3 of this work.

103. Ibid., 34–35.

104. Ibid., 32.

105. Ulrike Stark, *An Empire of Books: The Naval Kishore Press and the Diffusion of the Printed Word in Colonial India* (Delhi: Permanent Black, 2007), 229.

106. Secretary to the Chief Commissioner to the Secretary to the Government of India, 1 May 1854, no. 363, OIOC, BL, P/188/8, cited in Allender, *Ruling through Education,* 94.

107. I examine the difference between all-India and provincial imperatives in my essay, "Imperial Policy, Provincial Practices."

108. Henry Elliot, Secretary to the Government of India with the Governor-General, letter to P. Melville, Secretary to the Board of Administration, Punjab. 26 November 1850, NAI, Foreign, Foreign Consultations, no. 44, 1 August 1851.

109. P. Melville, Secretary to the Board of Administration, Punjab, letter to Henry Elliot, Secretary to the Government of India with the Governor-General, Lahore, 2 April 1851, NAI, Foreign, Foreign Consultations, no. 44, 1 August 1851.

110. NAI, Foreign, Foreign Consultations, nos. 82 and 83, 14 November 1851.

111. NAI, Foreign, Foreign Consultations, no. 46, 1 August 1851.

112. NAI, Home, Public, nos. 67–68, 7 August 1869.

113. W. R. M. Holroyd, Director of Public Instruction, Punjab, letter to T. H. Thornton, Secretary to Government, Punjab, 21 March 1870, PPAC, Education, Science, and Art Department Proceedings, no. 6, March 1870.

114. H. J. Maynard, Judicial and General Secretary to the Government of the Punjab, letter to the Secretary to the Government of India, Home Department, 31 July 1899, NAI, Home Department, Examinations, no. 3, October 1899. This document records that the lieutenant-governor of the Punjab no longer thought a colloquial test was sufficient, and petitioned the government of India to sanction "a more severe test, both literary and colloquial" for officers serving in the Lahore, Jullundur, and Rawalpindi divisions. His request was denied.

2. PUNJABI PRINT CULTURE

1. The senate was comprised of both British and Indian members. Charter members included office holders in the provincial government, such as the judges of the chief court, the financial commissioner, and the director of public instruction, and Indian citizens of note. Information on the Punjab University senate and its debate over the inclusion of Punjabi in the curriculum is taken from Jeffrey Price Perrill, "Punjab Orientalism: The Anjuman-i-Punjab and Punjab University, 1865–1888," Ph.D. diss., University of Missouri, 1976, 445–62.

2. Government of Punjab, *Punjab District Gazetteers, Lahore District, 1883–1884* (Lahore: Sang-e-Meel Publications, 1989 [1884]), 55.

3. Stuart Blackburn and Vasudha Dalmia, eds., *India's Literary History: Essays on the Nineteenth Century* (Delhi: Permanent Black, 2004).

4. Officially, the act was entitled "An Act for the Regulation of Printing Presses and Newspapers, for the Preservation of Copies of Books Printed in British India, and for the Registration of such Books." Oriental and India Office Collection, British Library, V/8/40.

5. Although the history of the book is a small subfield of Indian history, a few important works have taken advantage of colonial sources on book production: Anindita Ghosh, *Power in Print: Popular Publishing and the Politics of Language and Culture in a Colonial Society, 1778–1905* (New Delhi: Oxford University Press, 2006); Priya Joshi, *In Another Country: Colonialism, Culture, and the English Novel in India* (New York: Columbia University Press, 2002); and Ulrike Stark, *An Empire of Books: The Naval Kishore Press and the Diffusion of the Printed Word in Colonial India* (Delhi: Permanent Black, 2007).

6. Robert Darnton, "Book Production in British India, 1850–1900," *Book History* 5 (2002): 239–62.

7. Government of India, *Report on Publications Issued and Registered in the Several Provinces of British India* (Calcutta: Office of the Superintendent of Government Printing, 1893), 87.

8. Government of India, *Report on Publications Issued and Registered in the Several Provinces of British India* (Calcutta: Office of the Superintendent of Government Printing, 1894), 84.

9. "Memorandum," National Archives of India (henceforth NAI), New Delhi, Home Department, Public Proceedings, 14 March 1868, 86–87A.

10. Darnton, "Book Production in British India," 245.

11. Government of India, *Report on Publications Issued and Registered in the Several Provinces of British India* (Calcutta: Office of the Superintendent of Government Printing, 1895), 70–71.

12. Government of India, *Report on Publications Issued and Registered in the Several Provinces of British India* (Calcutta: Office of the Superintendent of Government Printing, 1870).

13. Government of India, *Report on Publications Issued and Registered in the Several Provinces of British India* (Calcutta: Office of the Superintendent of Government Printing, 1875).

14. *Catalogue of Books printed in the Punjab during the Quarter ending 31st March, 1868,* in NAI, Home, Public, 22 August 1868, 116A–119.

15. *Catalogue of Books Registered in the Punjab for the Quarter ending 30th June 1877,* in NAI, Home, Public, February 1879, 81–82B.

16. Chris King is particularly informative about how Hindi, and Urdu by default, were distinguished from one another, standardized, and made suitably "modern" for use as colonial official vernaculars. See his *One Language, Two Scripts: The Hindi Movement in Nineteenth Century North India* (New Delhi: Oxford University Press, 1994). On Indian participation in this process, see Vasudha Dalmia, *The Nationalization of Hindu Traditions: Bharatendu Harischandra and Nineteenth–Century Banaras* (New Delhi: Oxford University Press, 1997).

17. Examples of works that explore the standardizing effects of print, whether directly or obliquely, abound. Among them are: Benedict Anderson, *Imagined Communities: Reflections on the Origin and Spread of Nationalism,* rev. ed. (London: Verso, 1991 [1983]); Peter Roberts, *From Oral to Literate Culture: Colonial Experience in the English West Indies* (Kingston, Jamaica: University of the West Indies Press, 1997); Elizabeth Eisenstein, *The Printing Revolution in Early Modern Europe* (Cambridge: Cambridge University Press, 1983); and King, *One Language, Two Scripts.*

18. Eric Hobsbawm, *Nations and Nationalism since 1780* (Cambridge: Cambridge University Press, 1990).

19. John Beames's *Outlines of Indian Philology and Other Philological Papers* (Calcutta: Indian Studies Past and Present, 1960 [1867]) is one example.

20. The returns for 1877–78, for example, had entries for both Punjabi and Multani. Government of India, *Report on Publications Issued and Registered in the Several Provinces of British India* (Calcutta: Office of the Superintendent of Government Printing, 1875), 176.

21. The language spoken in Multan—Multani, or Siraiki—has been the basis of a language movement in postcolonial Pakistan, the Siraiki movement. The movement calls for the recognition of Siraiki as a distinct language (from Punjabi) and for it to be implemented as the official language of the Multan and Bahawalpur areas. Christopher Shackle, who has written on the movement, considers Siraiki a distinct language from Punjabi on linguistic grounds, arguing that Siraiki is "linguistically the most divergent from the central Lahore [Punjabi] norm." See his "Panjabi," in *The Indo-Aryan Languages,* ed. Dhanesh Jain and George Cardona (New York: Routledge, 2003), 640. Also see his "Siraiki: A Language Movement in Pakistan," *Modern Asian Studies* 11, 3 (1977): 379–403; and "The Multani 'Marsiya,'" *Islam* 55 (1978): 281–311. For the purposes of this study, however, I treat it not as a separate language but as a dialect of Punjabi, for two reasons. First, doing so allows me to privilege the cultural continuities between central and southern Punjab, continuities manifest in the genres of literature shared between the two. Second, the Siraiki movement is a postcolonial phenomenon rooted in the particularities of Pakistan's politics. For the colonial period, it seems to me appropriate to recognize that Siraiki differs in linguistic terms from central Punjab, but to recognize it as a distinct language entails political claims not appropriate to this period.

22. The principal repositories in India are Guru Nanak Dev University (Amritsar) and Punjabi University (Patiala); in Pakistan, the Punjab Public Library (Lahore) and the Dyal Singh Trust Library (Lahore); and in Britain, the British Library (London).

23. Government of India, *Report on Publications Issued and Registered in the Several Provinces of British India* (Calcutta: Office of the Superintendent of Government Printing, 1882), 132.

24. Seven texts in the Indo-Persian script are listed in Shahbaz Malik, *Punjabi Kitabiyat* (A Bibliography of Punjabi Printed Books Written in Perso-Arabic Script) (Islamabad: Akademi Adabiyat Pakistan, 1991), 93–94. One Indo-Persian text (1880) not mentioned by Malik is located at the Punjab Public Library, Lahore. Evidence suggests that Jog Singh's composition was also published in Gurmukhi, though in how many editions is unknown. That it was published in Gurmukhi is clear from an announcement at the end of *Hir Jog Singh* (Lahore: Chiragh al-Din Kutab Farosh, 1877) which states that the publishers had the text transliterated from Gurmukhi to the Indo-Persian script, with permission. In light of the discussion in note 21 above about Siraiki, it should be noted that there are Siraiki equivalents to Malik's volume: Muhammad Ubaidurrahman, *Siraiki Kitabiyat* (Bahawalpur: Siraiki Adabi Majlis, 1980); and Tahir Taunsvi, *Siraiki Kitabiyat: Aghaz ta 1993* (Islamabad: Akademi Adabiyat Pakistan, 1994).

25. The *Akhbar Shri Darbar Sahib* receives no mention in the colonial returns on newspapers published in the Punjab, suggesting that it did not survive long enough to be included in those returns, which commenced in 1867. This characterization of the paper comes from Aneeta Rani, "Evolution of Press in the Punjab (1855–1910)," *Panjab Past and Present* 21, 1 (1987): 148.

26. N. G. Barrier, "Vernacular Publishing and Sikh Public Life in the Punjab, 1880–1910," in *Religious Controversy in British India: Dialogues in South Asian Languages*, ed. Kenneth W. Jones (Albany: State University of New York Press, 1992), 206.

27. On the Lahore Singh Sabha, see Harjot Oberoi, *The Construction of Religious Boundaries: Culture, Identity, and Diversity in the Sikh Tradition* (Chicago: University of Chicago Press, 1994), chaps. 4 and 5.

28. Information on both of these papers is taken from N. G. Barrier and Paul Wallace, *The Punjab Press, 1880–1905* (East Lansing: Michigan State University Press, 1970), 73 and 75.

29. *Sources on Punjab History* gives the paper's dates as 1894–1904 and 1912–19. See Kenneth W. Jones and W. Eric Gustafson, comps., *Sources on Punjab History* (New Delhi: Manohar, 1975), 241.

30. *Khalsa* means "the pure" (from the Arabic *khalis*, "to become clear"), and here connotes the community of Sikhs established by Guru Gobind Singh in 1699. Members of the Khalsa keep the five symbols of Sikhism and take the name Singh. See Gurinder Singh Mann, *Sikhism* (Upper Saddle River, NJ: Prentice Hall, 2004).

31. Six were associated with the Singh Sabha, and one each with the Chief Khalsa Diwan (Amritsar), the Khalsa Diwan (Lahore), the Khalsa Diwan (Amritsar), and the Khalsa Tract Society, respectively.

32. Barrier and Wallace, *Punjab Press*, 103.

33. The *Al Hakam,* for example, presented Ahmadiyah views, while the *Anwar-ul-Islam* was a "religious paper in answer to all objections and questions against Islam." Ibid., 19–20, 23.

34. Lepel Griffin, Under-Secretary to the Government, Punjab, letter to the Secretary to Government of India, Home Department, Lahore, 20 October 1870, in Punjab Provincial Archives, Chandigarh, Education, Science, and Art Department Proceedings, 5 March 1870.

35. C. A. Bayly, *Empire and Information: Intelligence Gathering and Social Communication in India, 1780–1870* (Cambridge: Cambridge University Press, 1996), 133.

36. Christopher Shackle, "Some Observations of the Evolution of Modern Standard Punjabi," in *Sikh History and Religion in the Twentieth Century,* ed. Joseph O'Connell et al. (Toronto: University of Toronto Press, 1988), 104–5.

37. In his *Punjabi Kitabiyat,* Shahbaz Malik lists three texts with known publication dates prior to 1857. I came across no commercial texts from the pre-1857 period in India, Pakistan, or Britain, however.

38. Muhammad Sharif Sabir, "Ta'aruf," introduction to *Hir Waris Shah,* by Waris Shah, ed. Muhammad Sharif Sabir (Lahore: Waris Shah Memorial Committee, 1985), 3.

39. NAI, Home, Public, December 1867, 144–45B.

40. This was in reference to the Ambala branch of the Simla Press and the Punjab Trading Company Press, Ambala. Ibid.

41. This was in reference to the Lawrence press, Lahore. NAI Home, Public, 10 August 1866, 88–89B.

42. This was in reference to the Punjabee Press, Lahore. NAI, Home, Public, 17 October 1868, 68.

43. This was in reference to the Gujranwala branch of the Victoria Press. NAI, Home, Public, 17 October 1868, 68.

44. *Catalogue of Books Printed in the Punjab during the Quarter Ending 30th September 1867,* in NAI, Home, Public, nos. 112–20, 11 April 1868; *Catalogue of Books Printed in the Punjab during the Quarter Ending 31st December 1867,* in NAI, Home, Public, nos. 112–20, 11 April 1868. More books may have been produced in Delhi during the 1850s and 1860s. Barring Delhi, however, Lahore was clearly the emerging center of publishing in the Punjab.

45. "Analysis of Publications in the Punjab during the Calendar Year 1876 under Act XXV of 1867," in Government of India, *Selections from the Records of the Government of India, No. 143* (Calcutta: Office of the Superintendent of Government Printing, n.d.).

46. "Publication Issued and Published in 1887," in *Selections from the Records of the Government of India, No. 247.* (Calcutta: Office of the Superintendent of Government Printing, n.d.).

47. Government of India, *Prices and Wages in India* (Calcutta: Office of the Superintendent of Government Printing, 1900), 280.

48. Anindita Ghosh, "'An Uncertain Coming of the Book': Early Print Cultures in Colonial India," *Book History* 6 (2003): 30.

49. Ulrike Stark, *An Empire of Books: The Naval Kishore Press and the Diffusion of the Printed Word in Colonial India* (Delhi: Permanent Black, 2007), 197.

50. My analysis of the themes treated in late nineteenth-century Punjabi printed books is based on collections I examined at the Dyal Singh Trust Public Library (Lahore), the Punjab University Library (Lahore), the Punjab Public Library (Lahore), the Oriental College Library (Lahore), the Punjab University Library (Chandigarh), the Punjabi University Library (Patiala), the Central Library (Patiala), the Guru Nanak Dev Library (Amritsar), and the British Library (London). In addition, I consulted Shahbaz Malik's *Punjabi Kitabiyat*.

51. Graham W. Shaw, "The First Printing Press in the Panjab," *Library Chronicle* 43, 2 (1979): 164.

52. I found evidence of at least twenty-two Christian texts, thirty-two Sikh texts (almost all sections of the *Adi Granth*), and six Hindu texts published in the Indo-Persian script. However, Singh Sabha tracts were invariably in Gurmukhi.

53. They include: *Doha Matam* (Mourning Poetry; Multan, 1899); *Guldasta Marsiya Multani* (A Bouquet of Multani Elegiacal Poetry; Multan, 1897); *Gulshan-i Shahadat* (The Garden of Martyrdom; Jalandhar, 1883); *Gulzar-i Husain* (The Blooming Garden of Husain; Lahore, 1897); *Jangnama Imamein* (The War of the Imams; Lahore, 1864); *Qissa Hazrat Imamein* (The Story of the Holy Imams; Lahore, 1869); *Si Harfi Karbala* (Poems on Karbala; Amritsar, 1879); and *Masnavi Makhzan-i Gham* (A Treasury of Heartrending Poetry; Multan, 1900).

54. See Juan R. Cole, *Roots of North India Shi'ism in Iran and Iraq: Religion and State in Awadh, 1722–1859* (Berkeley: University of California Press, 1989).

55. Generically, *marsiya* is an elegiac poem and can treat any subject. In the South Asian context, however, it almost universally refers to a poem on the battle of Karbala and the martyrdom of Hassan and Husain. For a detailed study of *marsiya* in South Asia, see Syed Akbar Hyder, *Reliving Karbala: Martyrdom in South Asian Memory* (New York: Oxford University Press, 2006), which examines the Urdu tradition.

56. See N. G. Barrier, *The Punjab in Nineteenth Century Tracts: An Introduction to the Pamphlet Collections in the British Museum and India Office* (East Lansing: Michigan State University Press, 1969); Barrier, "Vernacular Publishing"; and Kenneth W. Jones, *Arya Dharm: Hindu Consciousness in 19th-Century Punjab* (New Delhi: Manohar, 1989 [1976]); Kenneth W. Jones, *Socio-Religious Reform Movements in British India* (New Delhi: Foundations Books, 1994 [1989]), 85–121.

57. Barrier, "Vernacular Publishing," 207–8.

58. See Lucy Carroll, "The Temperance Movement in India: Politics and Social Reform," *Modern Asian Studies* 10, 3 (1976): 417–47.

59. Dalmia, *Nationalization of Hindu Traditions;* King, *One Language, Two Scripts;* Oberoi, *Construction of Religious Boundaries.*

60. NAI, Home, Education, July 1883, 52–58.

61. See Malik, *Punjabi Kitabiyat.*

62. This novel was Bhai Vir Singh's *Sundari.* He was an influential figure in the Singh Sabha. Given the Singh Sabha language politics discussed thus far, it should perhaps be no surprise that Singh was invested in Punjabi's literary "modernity," something crucially linked to the genre of the novel.

63. Here, too, Punjabi contrasts in particular with Urdu, in which novels were being composed as early as the 1860s and serialized in Urdu journals. Some of the most important

novels of the late nineteenth century, such as those by Nazir Ahmad, are directly related to colonial patronage (see introduction, note 28).

64. Muhammad Akbar Ali, *Qissa Warburton* (Lahore: n.p., 1891); Mian Fattehu'd-Din's "*Qissa Nahir Firozpur Panjab*" was published in Punjabi in roman font in *Indian Antiquary* 11 (June 1882): 166–67.

65. On the canal colonies, see Imran Ali, *The Punjab under Imperialism, 1885–1947* (Princeton, NJ: Princeton University Press, 1988).

66. Passage translated by R. C. Temple in "The Story of the Ferozpur Canal," *Indian Antiquary* 11 (June 1882): 168.

67. Malik Ahmad Baksh Toba Sirani [Ghafil], *Qissa Hir wa Ranjha* (Lahore: Matba' Kadimi, n.d.).

68. Ibid., 2–3.

69. Ibid., 3; my emphasis.

70. Christopher Shackle, "Making Punjabi Literary History," in *Sikh Religion, Culture, and Ethnicity*, ed. Christopher Shackle et al. (Richmond, Surrey: Curzon Press, 2001), 97–117.

71. The most important figures in this regard are Maula Baksh Kushta and Bava Budh Singh. See ibid.

72. This sketch is drawn from ibid., 104–5.

73. Tarlok Singh Anand, "Sohni Jan Pecchan" (A Critical Introduction to *Sohni*), in *Sohni (Fazl Shah)*, by Fazl Shah, ed. Tarlok Singh Anand (Patiala: Punjabi University Publication Bureau, 1987), 8.

74. Maula Baksh Kushta provides these figures in his *Punjabi Shairan da Tazkira* (A Dictionary of Punjabi Poets), ed. Chaudhry Muhammad Afzal Khan (Lahore: Aziz Publishers, 1988 [1960]), 193. Fazl Shah composed the following *qisse*: *Sohni-Mahival* (c. 1848), *Sassi-Punnun* (c. 1863), *Hir-Ranjha* (c. 1867), *Laila-Majnun* (c. 1871), and *Yusuf-Zulaikha* (c. 1884).

75. Anand, "Sohni Jan Pechhan," 9.

76. Ramdev, *Punjabi Likhari Kosh* (A Dictionary of Punjabi Writers) (Jalandhar: New Book Company, 1964), 245–46. His *qisse* were *Sohni-Mahival, Hir-Ranjha* (1878) and *Mirza-Sahiban*.

77. Kushta, *Punjabi Shairan*, 215.

78. Kishan Singh 'Arif's known compositions are: *Hir-Ranjha* (1889), *Raja-Rasalu, Dula-Bhatti, Shirin-Farhad, Puran-Bhagat, Kishan-Kitar, Raj Niti, Kafian Jiun Siapa*. Pritam Saini, "Kavi Kishan Singh 'Arif: Ik Alochnatmik Adhiain" (Poet Kishan Singh 'Arif: A Critical Study), Ph.D. diss., Punjabi University, n.d.

79. Kushta, *Punjabi Shairan*, 313. The three *qisse* were *Hir-Ranjha, Sassi-Punnun,* and *Mirza-Sahiban*.

80. Ibid., 251.

81. *Mian* is "an address expressive of kindness, or respect." John Platts, *A Dictionary of Urdu, Classical Hindi, and English* (Lahore: Sang-e-Meel Publications, 1994 [1911]).

82. Bhai Sant Bajara Singh, *Qissa Hir te Ranjhe da* (The *Qissa* of Hir and Ranjha) (Amritsar: Bhai Hari Singh, 1951 b [1894]).

83. For information on the Gurmukhi editions, see appendix A. Reference to the Indo-Persian script editions (1873 and 1878) comes from: Malik, *Punjabi Kitabiyat*, 164.

3. A PUNJABI LITERARY FORMATION

1. My argument thus stands in contrast to that of Jack Goody, who argues that, "the process of writing down inevitably tends to eliminate variation [in oral traditions]." See his *The Power of the Written Tradition* (Washington, DC: Smithsonian Institution Press, 2000), 54. Brenda Beck makes a similar argument about the impact of print on oral traditions in India: *The Three Twins: The Telling of a South Indian Folk Epic* (Bloomington: Indiana University Press, 1982).

2. Elizabeth Eisenstein's *The Printing Press as an Agent of Change: Communication and Cultural Transformation in Early-Modern Europe*, 2 vols. (Cambridge: Cambridge University Press, 1979) is a classic study that lays out this transition. Her work was foundational for a generation of scholarship on the history of print and the book, some of which has challenged her assumptions and conclusions. See, for example, Adrian Johns, *The Nature of the Book: Print and Knowledge in the Making* (Chicago: University of Chicago Press, 1998).

3. There are a number of distinct manuscript traditions associated with ancient, medieval, and early modern India. The design elements I refer to here—floral and geometric borders—were most closely associated with Indo-Islamic manuscript traditions.

4. Kanhayalal, *Tarikh-i Lahore* (Lahore: Sang-e-Meel Publications, 1990 [1871]), 43–46.

5. I borrow the term *Islamicate* from Marshal Hodgson, who used it to refer to the social and cultural complex historically associated with Islam. See his *Venture of Islam*, 3 vols. (Chicago: University of Chicago Press, 1977).

6. Producing Punjabi typeset books in the Gurmukhi script had been possible since at least 1838, when the missionaries at Serampore created and sent Gurmukhi fonts to Ludhiana for use by the mission there. Nastaliq type font, used for Punjabi, Urdu, Persian, Arabic, and other languages, had been developed decades earlier. See Graham Shaw, "The First Printing Press in the Panjab," *Library Chronicle* 43, 2 (1979): 164; Francesca Orsini, "Detective Novels: A Commercial Genre in Nineteenth-Century North India," in *India's Literary History: Essays on the Nineteenth Century*, ed. Stuart Blackburn and Vasudha Dalmia (Delhi: Permanent Black, 2004), 435–82.

7. Colonial Administrator James Lyall points to an additional consideration, suggesting that while typeset printing was well suited for alphabets derived from Sanskrit, this ease was not "equally applicable to the flowing and graceful characters of Persian." See his "Hindostani Literature," *Encyclopedia Brittanica*, 11th ed., ed. Hugh Chisholm (New York: Encyclopedia Brittanica, 1910), 12: 490. This may help explain why Gurmukhi texts were predominantly typeset by the early decades of the twentieth century, while Punjabi texts in the Indo-Persian script continued to be lithographed throughout the colonial period.

8. Many Punjabi manuscripts that I examined record the name of the scribe. Two examples are: *Shirin Farhad Hasham*, which names Ram Singh Tapti as the scribe (MSS M/615, Patiala State Archives, Patiala); and *Hir Waris Shah*, whose scribe was Dal Singh, (MSS 11, Bhasha Vibhag, Patiala). Unfortunately, there is no other trace of these scribes in the historical record.

9. *Sawal wa jawab* was a very well established genre in classical Persian literature.

10. Anindita Ghosh, "'An Uncertain Coming of the Book': Early Print Cultures in Colonial India," *Book History* 6 (2003): 40.

11. Government of Punjab, *Punjab District Gazetteers, Lahore District, 1883–1884* (Lahore: Sang-e-Meel Publications, 1989 [1884]), 55.

12. Ibid.

13. R. C. Temple, *Legends of the Panjab* (Lahore: Sang-e-Meel Publications, n.d. [1884]), 1: vi.

14. Khawaish Ali, *Hir-Ranjha* (Lahore: Pandit Labo Ram and Sons Tajran Kutab, n.d. [1933]), 2.

15. Ibid., 2–3.

16. Fassi Niaz Ahmed, *Hir Niaz Ranjha* (Niaz's *Hir-Ranjha*) (Lahore: Munshi Aziz al-Din wa Najm al-Din, n.d. [c. 1914]).

17. Ibid., 2.

18. Roger Chartier, *Forms and Meanings: Texts, Performances, and Audiences from Codex to Computer* (Philadelphia: University of Pennsylvania Press, 1994), 2.

19. Stuart Blackburn and A. K. Ramanujan, introduction to *Another Harmony: New Essays on the Folklore of India*, ed. A. K. Ramanujan and Stuart Blackburn (Berkeley: University of California Press, 1986), 4.

20. Stuart Blackburn and Joyce Flueckiger, introduction to *Oral Epics in India*, ed. Stuart Blackburn et al. (Berkeley: University of California Press, 1989), 11.

21. Sheldon Pollock, introduction to *Literary Cultures in History: Reconstructions from South Asia*, ed. Sheldon Pollock (Berkeley: University of California Press, 2003), 27.

22. Mary Poovey, *Making a Social Body: British Cultural Formation, 1830–1864* (Chicago: University of Chicago Press, 1995), 1.

23. On this latter point, see William J. Glover, *Making Lahore Modern: Constructing and Imagining a Colonial City* (Minneapolis: University of Minnesota Press, 2008), 30.

24. Michael Warner, "Publics and Counterpublics," *Public Culture* 14, 1 (2002): 49–90. Also see his *Publics and Counterpublics* (Cambridge: Zone Books, 2002).

25. Warner, "Publics and Counterpublics," 75.

26. Ibid., 89.

27. Ibid.

28. Syad Muhammad Latif, *Lahore: Its History, Architectural Remains and Antiquities, with an Account of Its Modern Institutions, Inhabitants, Their Trade, Customs, &c.* (Lahore: Sang-e-Meel Publications, 1994 [1892]), 267. Each of these texts was a Punjabi *qissa*.

29. Circular from H. H. Risley, president of the Asiatic Society of Bengal, 4 August 1898, Oriental and India Office Collections (henceforth OIOC), British Library (henceforth BL), MS EUR/E100.

30. Richard Temple's Indian career included appointments as chief commissioner of the Central Provinces, lieutenant-governor of Bengal, and governor-general of Bombay.

31. Temple was appointed a cantonment magistrate in the Punjab (in 1879), then assistant commissioner in Burma, and eventually chief commissioner of the Andaman and Nicobar Islands.

32. Temple described the process in fascinating detail in his notes to the volumes. See his "Memorandum," 14 July 1886, OIOC, BL, MS EUR/F98/4b.

33. Information on Steel is taken from: Ralph Crane and Anna Johnston, "Flora Annie Steel in the Punjab," in *Writing, Travel, and Empire*, ed. Peter Hulme and Russell McDougall (London: I. B. Tauris, 2007), 71–96.

34. R. C. Temple, "A Song about Sakhi Sarwar," *Calcutta Review* 73 (1881): 253.

35. R. C. Temple, "Analysis of the Tales on the Plan Adopted by the Folklore Society of England," in *Tales of the Punjab Told by the People*, by F. A. Steel (London: Macmillan, 1894), 327–55.

36. R. C. Temple, "A Survey of the Incidents in Modern Indian Folk-Tales," in ibid., 356–95.

37. On colonial folklore studies, see Blackburn and Ramanujan's introduction to *Another Harmony*, 1–40. Colonial folklore shared many of the attributes of colonial ethnography, which has been the subject of more sustained analysis. See, for example, Thomas Trautmann, *Aryans and British India* (Berkeley: University of California Press, 1997); and George Stocking, *Victorian Anthropology* (New York: Free Press, 1987).

38. The shrine is significant due to Shaikh Farid's important place in the spiritual lineage (*silsila*) of the Chishti order (*tariqa*) in India. He was the *murid* (disciple) of Qutbuddin Bakhtiar Kaki, himself the *murid* of Muinuddin Chishti, the founder of the Chishti order in India. Farid, in turn, was the *pir* (spiritual guide) of Nizamuddin Auliya, an important Sufi at the Sultanate court in Delhi and a saint in his own right.

39. Miles Irving, "The Shrine of Baba Farid Shakarganj at Pakpattan," *Journal of the Panjab University Historical Society* 1, 1 (1911–12): 74–75.

40. Ibid., 74.

41. Among the prominent South Asian Sufi *tariqas* (orders), *qawwali* is most integral to Chishti practices. It is condemned by Naqshbandis, who see *qawwali* as an ecstatic and therefore impermissible form of devotion.

42. Regula Qureshi, "His Master's Voice: Exploring Qawwali and 'Gramophone Culture' in South Asia," *Popular Music* 18, 1 (1999): 68.

43. Ibid.

44. Regula Qureshi, *Sufi Music of India and Pakistan: Sound, Context, and Meaning in Qawwali* (Karachi: Oxford University Press, 2006 [1986]), 96.

45. Ibid.

46. Ibid., 97.

47. Qureshi, "His Master's Voice," 65.

48. Richard Eaton, "Approaches to the Study of Conversion to Islam in South Asia," in *Approaches to Islam in Religious Studies*, ed. Richard C. Martin (Tucson: University of Arizona Press, 1985), 106–23.

49. Hasan Gardezi, "Sufi Cosmology: An Indigenous Oral Tradition," in *East-West Dialogue in Knowledge and Higher Education*, ed. Ruth Hayhoe and Julia Pan (Armonk: M. E. Sharpe, 1996), 204.

50. Piara Singh Padam, *Sufi Kavidhara* (Sufi Poetry) (Patiala: Piara Singh Padam, 1993).

51. Irving, "Shrine of Baba Farid," 74–75.

52. For a discussion on the early debates around *sama'* and its position within different Sufi lineages, see Bruce B. Lawrence, "The Early Chishti Approach to Sama,'" in *Sacred Sound: Music in Religious Thought and Practice,* ed. Joyce Irwin (Chico, CA: Scholars Press, 1983), 93–110.

53. Qureshi, *Sufi Music of India and Pakistan,* 96–102.

54. Regula Qureshi, "Sama' in the Royal Court of Saints: The Chishtiyya of South Asia," in *Manifestations of Sainthood in Islam,* ed. Grace Martin Smith and Carl Ernst (Istanbul: Isis Press, 1987), 112.

55. Regula Qureshi, "Sufi Music and the Historicity of Oral Tradition," in *Ethnomusicology and Modern Music History,* ed. Stephen Blum, Philip Bohlman, and Daniel Neuman (Chicago: University of Illinois Press, 1991), 109.

56. One can only surmise that Irving misconstrued *sama'* as akin to the practices of the Mevlevi order of Turkey, or the "whirling dervishes."

57. Charles Hirschkind, *The Ethical Soundscape: Cassette Sermons and Islamic Counterpublics* (New York: Columbia University Press, 2006).

58. Irving, "Shrine of Baba Farid," 75.

59. Ibid., 76.

60. Ibid.; emphasis added.

61. Ibid.

62. Flora Annie Steel and R. C. Temple, "Folklore in the Panjab," *Indian Antiquary* 11 (1882): 32.

63. In addition to the evidence below, Punjab's district gazetteers contain many references to Sufi saint's tombs, big and small, as sites that attracted people from all religious communities.

64. Harjot Oberoi, *The Construction of Religious Boundaries: Culture, Identity, and Diversity in the Sikh Tradition* (Chicago: University of Chicago Press, 1994), 147.

65. Temple, "Song about Sakhi Sarwar," 254.

66. On Macauliffe, see Harbans Lal, "The Western Gateway to Sikhism: The Life and Works of Max Arthur Macauliffe," in *Sikh Art and Literature,* ed. Kerry Brown (New York: Routledge, 1999), 129–42.

67. Max Arthur Macauliffe, "The Fair at Sakhi Sarwar," *Calcutta Review* 60 (1875): 80.

68. Mufti Ghulam Sarwar, *Tarikh-i Makhzan-i Punjab* (History and Record of Punjab) (Lahore: Dost Associates, 1996 [1884]), 529.

69. Major Aubrey O'Brien, "The Mohammedan Saints of the Western Punjab," *Journal of the Royal Anthropological Institute* 41 (1911): 519, cited in Oberoi, *Construction of Religious Boundaries,* 147.

70. Oberoi argues that this number likely underrepresents the number of Sikhs who associated with the saint in the late nineteenth century, because by 1911 Singh Sabha reformers were enjoying some success in their attempts to distance Sikhs from devotion to Sufi saints. Ibid., 148.

71. Lala Dina Nath, "The Cult of Mian Bibi," *Indian Antiquary* 34 (June 1905): 125–31.

72. Ibid., 126.

73. Ibid.

74. Ibid., 127.

75. Temple, "Song about Sakhi Sarwar," 254.

76. For a colonial-era description of Al-Hujwiri's shrine in Lahore, for example, see John Campbell Oman, *Cults, Customs, and Superstitions of India* [originally published as *Indian Life, Religious and Social*], rev. ed. (London: T. Fisher Unwin, 1908 [1889]), 298–99.

77. Chetan Singh, *Region and Empire: Panjab in the Seventeenth Century* (New Delhi: Oxford University Press, 1991).

78. Richard Eaton, "The Political and Religious Authority of the Shrine of Baba Farid," in *Moral Conduct and Authority: The Place of Adab in South Asian Islam*, ed. Barbara Metcalf (Berkeley: University of California Press, 1984), 333–56.

79. David Gilmartin, "Religious Leadership and the Pakistan Movement in the Punjab," *Modern Asian Studies* 13, 3 (1979): 490; Akhtar Husain Siddiqi, "Small Town Growth and Development Policy in Pakistan," in Graham Chapman et al., eds., *The Asian City: Processes of Development, Characteristics, and Planning* (New York: Springer, 1994), 184–85.

80. Richard Eaton and David Gilmartin have documented this well. See Eaton's *Sufis of Bijapur, 1300–1700: Social Roles of Sufis in Medieval India* (Princeton, NJ: Princeton University Press, 1978); and, more recently, his *A Social History of the Deccan, 1300–1761: Eight Indian Lives* (Cambridge: Cambridge University Press, 2005), chap. 2. See Gilmartin, *Empire and Islam: Punjab and the Making of Pakistan* (London: I. B. Tauris, 1988).

81. Ranjit Singh (r. 1799–1839) retained most existing religious endowments unchanged. See Indu Banga, *The Agrarian System of the Sikhs: Late Eighteenth and Early Nineteenth Century* (Columbia, MO: South Asia Books, 1978).

82. Gilmartin, *Empire and Islam*.

83. See David Gilmartin, "Customary Law and *Shari'at* in British Punjab," in *Shari'at and Ambiguity in South Asian Islam*, ed. Katherine P. Ewing (Berkeley: University of California Press, 1988), 43–62.

84. Gregory Kozlowski, *Muslim Endowments and Society in British India* (New York: Cambridge University Press, 1985); and Gilmartin, *Empire and Islam*.

85. See Gilmartin, *Empire and Islam*.

86. Irving, "Shrine of Baba Farid," 73–74.

87. Temple, "Song about Sakhi Sarwar," 254.

88. The Japji, the opening hymn of the *Adi Granth*, is not assigned a raga, suggesting that it was meant for recitation without musical instrumentation.

89. Ian Kerr, "British Relations with the Golden Temple, 1849–90," *Indian Economic and Social History Review* 21, 2 (1984): 139–51.

90. Ibid., 140.

91. Oman, *Cults, Customs, and Superstitions*, 211–12.

92. Ibid., 214.

93. Ibid., 204.

94. Ibid., 205.

95. Ibid., 206.

96. Ibid., 191.

97. See Kathryn Hansen, *Grounds for Play: The Nautanki Theatre of North India* (Berkeley: University of California Press, 1992).

98. Oman, *Cults, Customs, and Superstitions*, 195.

99. Ibid., 195–97.

100. Charles Swynnerton, *Romantic Tales from the Panjab* (London: Archibald Constable, 1903).

101. Ibid., xviii–xx.

102. On contemporary *mirasi*s, see Daniel Neuman, *The Life of Music in North India: The Organization of an Artistic Tradition* (Detroit: Wayne State University Press, 1980).

103. Sarwar, *Tarikh-i Makhzan-i Punjab*, 560.

104. Personal communication with Gurinder Singh Mann, 14 February 2007.

105. On the *dhadi* tradition, see Michael Nijhawan, *Dhadi Darbar: Religion, Violence, and the Performance of Sikh History* (New Delhi: Oxford University Press, 2006).

106. Denzil Ibbetson, *Panjab Castes* (Lahore: Sang-e-Meel Publications, 1994 [1883]), 234.

107. Hansen, *Grounds for Play*, 70–72.

108. On these other groups, see Adam Nayyar, "Punjab," in *The Garland Encyclopedia of World Music*, ed. Alison Arnold, vol. 5, *South Asia: The Indian Subcontinent* (New York: Garland Publishing, 2000), 766–71.

109. Steel and Temple, "Folklore in the Panjab," 32.

110. See, for example, Gilmartin, *Empire and Islam*.

111. See Oberoi, *The Construction of Religious Boundaries*; Kenneth W. Jones, *Arya Dharm: Hindu Consciousness in 19th-Century Punjab* (New Delhi: Manohar, 1989 [1976]); Yohanan Friedmann, *Prophecy Continuous: Aspects of Ahmadi Religious Thought and Its Medieval Background* (Berkeley: University of California Press, 1989); and Gail Minault, *Secluded Scholars: Women's Education and Muslim Social Reform in Colonial India* (New Delhi: Oxford University Press, 1998). A recent comparative consideration of three of these movements is Bob van der Linden, *Moral Languages from Colonial Punjab: The Singh Sabha, Arya Samaj, and Ahmadiyahs* (New Delhi: Manohar, 2008).

112. Anshu Malhotra, *Gender, Caste, and Religious Identities: Restructuring Class in Colonial Punjab* (New Delhi: Oxford University Press, 2002). Another class-based movement was the Unionist Party, which represented cross-religious landed interests. See Ian Talbot, *Khizr Tiwana, the Punjab Unionist Party, and the Partition of India* (Richmond, Surrey: Curzon Press, 1996).

113. Nonica Datta, *Forming an Identity: A Social History of the Jats* (New Delhi: Oxford University Press, 1999).

114. One might consider in this light Richard Fox's *Lions of the Punjab: Culture in the Making* (Berkeley: University of California Press, 1985). Also see Rajit Mazumder, *The Indian Army and the Making of Punjab* (Delhi: Permanent Black, 2003); and Tan Tai Yong, *The Garrison State: The Military, Government and Society in Colonial Punjab, 1849–1947* (Thousand Oaks, CA: Sage Publications, 2005).

115. Sudipta Kaviraj, "The Imaginary Institution of India," in *Subaltern Studies: Writings on South Asian History and Society,* ed. Partha Chatterjee and Gyanendra Pandey (New Delhi: Oxford University Press, 1992), 7: 1–39.

4. PLACE AND PERSONHOOD

1. Natalie Zemon Davis, *Fiction in the Archives: Pardon Tales and Their Tellers in Sixteenth-Century France* (Stanford, CA: Stanford University Press, 1987), 2–3.

2. An important exception is Velcheru Narayana Rao, David Shulman, and Sanjay Subrahmanyam, *Textures of Time: Writing History in South India, 1600–1800* (New York: Other Press, 2003), which argues that history writing in early modern South India took place in a number of genres, including folk epics and prose narratives.

3. John T. Platts, *A Dictionary of Urdu, Classical Hindi, and English* (Lahore: Sang-e-Meel Publications, 1994 [1911]).

4. Although Sikhism eradicated caste distinctions in theory, in practice, prior caste (prior to conversion, that is) affiliations continued to effect social practice. *Zat* was an institution through which *jati* continued to inform everyday life for Sikhs as well.

5. Susan Bayly, *Caste, Society, and Politics in India from the Eighteenth Century to the Modern Age* (Cambridge: Cambridge University Press, 1999), 312.

6. Ursula Sharma, *Caste* (Philadelphia: Open University Press, 1999), 5.

7. P. H. M. van den Dungen, "Changes in Status and Occupation in Nineteenth-Century Panjab," in *Soundings in Modern South Asian History*, ed. D. A. Low (Berkeley: University of California Press, 1968), 62.

8. Brian Caton, "Social Categories and Colonisation in Panjab, 1849–1920," *Indian Economic and Social History Review* 41, 1 (2004): 33–50.

9. Imtiaz Ahmad, "Preface to the First Edition (1973)," preface to *Caste and Social Stratification among Muslims in India*, ed. Imtiaz Ahmad (New Delhi: Manohar, 1978), vii.

10. For a discussion of the definition of *biraderi*, see David Gilmartin, "*Biraderi* and Bureaucracy: The Politics of Muslim Kinship Solidarity in Twentieth Century Punjab," *International Journal of Punjab Studies* 1, 1 (1994): 2–5.

11. Hamza Alavi, "The Two Biraderis: Kinship in Rural West Pakistan," in *Muslim Communities of South Asia*, ed. T. N. Madan (New Delhi: Manohar, 1995), 9–10. Imtiaz Ahmad directly refutes an earlier formulation of Alavi's argument, arguing that the social institution of *zat* within Muslim communities is, in fact, akin to the caste system. See his "Caste and Kinship in a Muslim Village of Eastern Uttar Pradesh," in *Family, Kinship, and Marriage among Muslims in India*, ed. Imtiaz Ahmad (New Delhi: Manohar, 1976), 319–46.

12. Kishan Singh 'Arif, *Qissa Hir te Ranjhe da* (Amritsar: Bhai Vasava Singh Juneja Pustak Wale, 1889), 52, and 53.

13. For one example, see Damodar, *Hir Damodar*, ed. Jagtar Singh (Patiala: Punjabi University Publications Bureau, 1987), 118.

14. Damodar, *Hir Damodar*, ed. Muhammad Asif Khan (Lahore: Pakistan Punjabi Adabi Board, 1986), 37.

15. Muqbal, *Hir Muqbal*, ed. Faqir Muhammad Faqir (N.p.: n.p., n.d. [1990]), 8.

16. 'Arif, *Qissa Hir te Ranjhe da*, 74.

17. Ibid., 75, and 76.

18. Muhammad Shah, *Qissa Hir wa Ranjha* (Rawalpindi: Lala Butamal Sahib, n.d. [c. 1908]), 2–3.

19. Nicholas Dirks, *Castes of Mind: Colonialism and the Making of Modern India* (Princeton, NJ: Princeton University Press, 2001), 43–60.

20. Ibid., 5.

21. Gloria Goodwin Raheja, "The Illusion of Consent: Language, Caste, and Colonial Rule in India," in *Colonial Subjects: Essays on the Practical History of Anthropology,* ed. Peter Pels and Oscar Salemink (Ann Arbor: University of Michigan Press, 1999), 144.

22. Denzil Ibbetson, *Panjab Castes* (Lahore: Sang-e-Meel Publications, 1994 [1883]), 1.

23. Ibid., 1–2.

24. Caton, "Social Categories and Colonisation," 33–34.

25. Ibbetson, *Panjab Castes,* 2; my emphasis.

26. David Gilmartin, "Customary Law and *Shari'at* in British Punjab," in *Shari'at and Ambiguity in South Asian Islam,* ed. Katherine P. Ewing (Berkeley: University of California Press, 1988), 45.

27. Ibid., 46.

28. Ibid., 46–47.

29. Van den Dungen, "Changes in Status and Occupation," 63–71.

30. Ibid., 71–77.

31. N. G. Barrier, *The Punjab Alienation of Land Bill of 1900* (Durham, NC: Duke University Press, 1966).

32. Muqbal, *Hir Muqbal,* 8.

33. Maula Shah, *Hir wa Ranjha* (Amritsar: Imam al-Din Miraj al-Din, 1330 H. [1911–12]), 6.

34. P. K. Nijhawan, introduction to *The First Punjab War: Shah Mohammed's Jangnama,* by Shah Muhammad, ed. P. K. Nijhawan (Amritsar: Singh Brothers, 2001), 19. The text is also known as *Var Shah Muhammad* and *Jangnama Sikhan te Firangian da.*

35. Prithipal Singh Kapur, prologue to *First Punjab War,* 7.

36. Translated by Nijhawan in *First Punjab War,* 237.

37. Jean Marie Lafont, *Fauj-i-Khas Maharaja Ranjit Singh and His French Officers* (Amritsar: Guru Nanak Dev University, 2002).

38. Chetan Singh, *Region and Empire: Panjab in the Seventeenth Century* (New Delhi: Oxford University Press, 1991).

39. E. Valentine Daniel, *Fluid Signs: Being a Person the Tamil Way* (Berkeley: University of California Press, 1984), 63.

40. Ibid., 68–69.

41. Ibid., 68.

42. Khawaish Ali, *Hir-Ranjha* (Lahore: Pandit Labo Ram and Sons Tajran Kutab, n.d. [1933]), 23.

43. Fassi Niaz Ahmad, *Hir Niaz Ranjha* (Niaz's *Hir-Ranjha*) (Lahore: Munshi Aziz al-Din wa Najm al-Din, n.d. [c. 1914]), 3.

44. Daniel, *Fluid Signs,* 63.

45. I have defined *pardes* above as "foreign country." It has, however, a richer lexical store of meanings. *Pardesi,* for example, can be defined as: foreign, foreigner, alien, not native; one from another part of the country, or stranger.

46. The title of the text is: *Qissa Hir-Ranjha*. It was published in a compilation of Miran Shah Bahawalpuri's verse: *Hir Miran Shah Mukamal* (The Complete Hir Miran Shah) (Multan: Maulvi Khuda Yar wa Nur Ahmad wa Nur Muhammad wa Faiz Ahmad Tajar Kutab, 1316 h. [1898–99]), 3–20; this passage, 4.

47. Ibid., 9 and 10.

48. Husain, *Hir Husain, Si Harfi Ashraf, Si Harfi Arora Rai, Si Harfi Ghulam* (Lahore: Matbah Sultani, 1873).

49. Ibid., 3.

50. Ibid.

51. Muhammad Azim, *Hir Azim Ranjha* (Azim's *Hir-Ranjha*) (Lahore: Munshi Aziz al-Din Najm al-Din, 1914), 3.

52. Khawaish Ali, *Hir-Ranjha*, 2.

53. Khawaish Ali uses the same technique later in the text to associate the Khera clan with a specific area (Rangpur). He does this by using the adjective *kheran* in a context where a geographic noun is obvious, therefore rendering translation of the term as "the land of the Kheras." Ibid., 5.

54. Manu Goswami, "From Swadesh to Swaraj: Nation, Economy, Territory in Colonial South Asia, 1870 to 1907," *Comparative Studies in Society and History* 40, 4 (1998): 609–36.

55. Ibid., 612.

56. Matthew Edney, *Mapping an Empire: The Geographical Construction of British India, 1765–1843* (Chicago: University of Chicago Press, 1997); and Ian Barrow, *Making History, Drawing Territory: British Mapping in India, c. 1765–1905* (New Delhi: Oxford University Press, 2003).

57. Goswami, "From Swadesh to Swaraj," 612.

58. Ibid., 623.

59. Ibid., 626.

60. Ibid., 611.

61. Indians' insularity and lack of nation-ness was a familiar colonial trope.

62. Najm Hossain Syed points to the work of such critics in his *Recurrent Patterns in Punjabi Poetry*, 2nd ed. (Lahore: Punjab Adbi Markaz, 1978), 3.

63. Prem Chowhdry, "Customs in a Peasant Economy: Women in Colonial Haryana," in *Recasting Women: Essays in Indian Colonial History*, ed. Kumkum Sangari and Sudesh Vaid (Delhi: Kali for Women, 1989), 303. Although this essay concerns Haryana specifically (the southeastern districts of Punjab), the peasant "social ethos" that Chowdhry documents through proverbs and practices—barring the *ghunghat* (veil) custom—is applicable to the Punjab as a whole.

64. Jeevan Deol, "Sex, Social Critique, and the Female Figure in Premodern Punjabi Poetry: Varis Shah's 'Hir,'" *Modern Asian Studies* 36, 1 (2002): 145 and 169.

65. Madhu Kishwar, "The Daughters of Aryavarta," in *Women and Social Reform in Modern India: A Reader*, ed. Sumit Sarkar and Tanika Sarkar (Delhi: Permanent Black, 2007), 1: 298–340; and Gail Minault, *Secluded Scholars: Women's Education and Muslim Social Reform in Colonial India* (New Delhi: Oxford University Press, 1998).

66. Anshu Malhotra, *Gender, Caste, and Religious Identities: Restructuring Class in Colonial Punjab* (New Delhi: Oxford University Press, 2002).

67. Minault, *Secluded Scholars;* and Barbara Metcalf, *Perfecting Women: Maulana Ashraf Ali Thanawi's Bihishti Zewar: A Partial Translation with Commentary* (Berkeley: University of California Press, 1990).

68. N.G. Barrier, "Vernacular Publishing and Sikh Public Life in the Punjab, 1880–1910," in *Religious Controversy in British India: Dialogues in South Asian Languages,* ed. Kenneth W. Jones (Albany: State University of New York Press, 1992), 208.

69. Nonica Datta, *Forming an Identity: A Social History of the Jats* (New Delhi: Oxford University Press, 1999); Kenneth W. Jones, *Arya Dharm: Hindu Consciousness in 19th-Century Punjab* (New Delhi: Manohar, 1989 [1976]); Malhotra, *Gender, Caste, and Religious Identities;* Harjot Oberoi, *The Construction of Religious Boundaries: Culture, Identity, and Diversity in the Sikh Tradition* (Chicago: University of Chicago Press, 1994); and Bob van der Linden, *Moral Languages from Colonial Punjab: The Singh Sabha, Arya Samaj, and Ahmadiyahs* (New Delhi: Manohar, 2008).

70. Ashraf Ali Thanawi's *Bihishti Zewar* is a particularly compelling example of this. Thanawi's views on women's proper comportment were inspired by his commitment to a Deobandi reformed Islam. See Barbara Metcalf, "An Introduction to the *Bihishti Zewar,*" in her *Perfecting Women,* 1–38.

71. Late nineteenth- and early twentieth-century socioreligious reform thus reinforced a broader trend in colonial India's middle-class society. The important volume *Recasting Women,* edited by Sangari and Vaid, argues that the Indian bourgeoisie produced by colonial rule recast women and gender practices to produce a new form of patriarchy that advocated certain reforms for women but always within a framework that ultimately reinforced male domination. This highly influential argument continues to inform dominant understandings of gender in colonial Indian society.

72. Radhika Singha, *A Despotism of Law: Crime and Justice in Early Colonial India* (New Delhi: Oxford University Press, 1998), 136.

73. Mrinalini Sinha, "The Lineage of the 'Indian' Modern: Rhetoric, Agency and the Sarda Act in Late Colonial India," in *Gender, Sexuality, and Colonial Modernities,* ed. Antoinette Burton (New York: Routledge, 1999), 207.

74. Anshu Malhotra, "The Quack of Patran and Other Stories," *Seminar* 569 (2007): 74–78.

75. Chowdhry, "Customs in a Peasant Economy," 302.

76. Partha Chatterjee, *The Nation and Its Fragments: Colonial and Postcolonial Histories* (Princeton, NJ: Princeton University Press, 1993). Many have challenged Chatterjee's formulation in important respects. See, for example, Manu Goswami, *Producing India: From Colonial Economy to National Space* (Chicago: University of Chicago Press, 2004), 23–24.

77. Sinha, "Lineage of the 'Indian' Modern," 209.

78. Mrinalini Sinha, *Specters of Mother India: The Global Restructuring of an Empire* (Durham, NC: Duke University Press, 2006), 44.

79. Abd al-Karim Na'at, *Na'at di Hir* (Na'at's Hir) (Multan: Hafiz Muhammad al-Din, Aziz al-Din, Bashir al-Din Tajran Kutab, n.d. [c. 1880]), 2.

80. Ibid., 4.

81. Muhammad Shah Sakin, *Qissa Hir wa Ranjha* (Lahore: Malik Din Muhammad and Sons, n.d.).

82. Romila Thapar, *Somanatha: The Many Voices of a History* (New York: Verso, 2005 [2004]), 151.

83. Thapar notes that "the symbolism of five is archaic in India, going back to the *Mahabharata*," and suggests this is why the *panj pir* may have resonated with India's predominantly Hindu population. See ibid. The number five is also significant to Islam and Sikhism. Irrespective of sect, Muslims recognize five pillars of their faith and there are five prescribed daily prayers (*salat*). Five is particularly significant to Shi'ism because of the importance of the *Ahl-al Bayt*, often called the *panjitan*: Muhammad, Fatima, Ali, Hassan, and Husain. In Sikhism, there are five practices (the five *K*'s) that define a Khalsa Sikh, for example, and five devotees (*panj piare*) who first accepted initiation into the Khalsa at the hands of Guru Gobind Singh. See Gurinder Singh Mann, *Sikhism* (Upper Saddle River, NJ: Prentice Hall, 2004), 121.

84. Sakin, *Qissa Hir wa Ranjha*, 15.

85. See Minault, *Secluded Scholars*.

86. 'Arif, *Qissa Hir te Ranjhe da*.

87. Ibid., 73.

88. Ibid., 74.

89. Ibid., 74–75.

90. Ibid., 75.

91. Ibid., 78–79.

92. Ibid., 79.

93. Ibid., 78.

94. Gloria Raheja and Ann Gold, *Listen to the Heron's Words: Reimagining Gender and Kinship in North India* (Berkeley: University of California Press, 1994), xv, and 1.

95. Antoinette Burton, *Dwelling in the Archive: Women Writing House, Home, and History in Late Colonial India* (New York: Oxford University Press, 2003), 5.

96. Joyce Burkhalter Flueckiger, *Gender and Genre in the Folklore of Middle India* (Ithaca, NY: Cornell University Press, 1996), 69.

97. Chowdhry, "Customs in a Peasant Economy," 303.

98. Ibid., 327–28.

5. PIETY AND DEVOTION

1. I discuss both Persian and Punjabi invocations in more detail in my essay "Genre and Devotion in Punjabi Popular Narratives: Rethinking Cultural and Religious Syncretism," *Comparative Studies in Society and History* 43, 4 (December 2006): 737–46.

2. Sant Singh Sekhon suggests this is the Sufi saint Sayyid Jalal ud-din Bukhari of Multan. See Waris Shah, *The Love of Hir and Ranjha*, trans. Sant Singh Sekhon (Ludhiana: Punjab Agricultural University, 1978), 264.

3. This is a reference to Shaikh Farid of Pakpattan.

4. Waris Shah, *Hir*, ed. Muhammad Baqir (Lahore: Pakistan Punjabi Adabi Board, 1993 [1988]), 1–2.

5. Muhammad Shah Sakin, *Qissa Hir wa Ranjha* (Lahore: Malik Din Muhammad and Sons, n.d.), 2. The reference is to Ghaus al-Azam, or Abdul Qadir Jilani, the founder of the Qadiri Sufi order.

6. Khaksar al-Baksh [Munir], *Faryad Hir* (Hir's Plea) (Lahore: Munshi Aziz al-Din Najm al-Din, n.d.), 2. This reference is also to Abdul Qadir Jilani.

7. I came across no manuscripts that could be described as episodic texts in the Punjabi manuscript collections I consulted. These included those at: Punjab University, Chandigarh; Punjabi University, Patiala; Bhasha Vibhag, Patiala; Central State Library, Patiala; and Punjab University Library, Lahore.

8. Damodar, *Hir Damodar,* ed. Muhammad Asif Khan (Lahore: Pakistan Punjabi Adabi Board, 1986), 37.

9. Kishan Singh 'Arif, *Qissa Hir te Ranjhe da* (Amritsar: Bhai Vasava Singh Juneja Pustak Wale, 1889), 2.

10. Bhai Rann Singh, *Navan Qissa Hir* (A New *Qissa* Hir) (Amritsar: Gurmat Press, 1913), 2.

11. Lajwanti Rama Krishna, *Panjabi Sufi Poets,* A.D. *1460–1900* (New Delhi: Ashajanak Publications, 1973 [1938]); Annemarie Schimmel, *Mystical Dimensions of Islam* (Chapel Hill: University of North Carolina Press, 1975); S. S. Sekhon, *A History of Panjabi Literature* (Patiala: Punjabi University Publication Bureau, 1996), vol. 2.

12. Christopher Shackle, "Transition and Transformation in Varis Shah's *Hir,*" in *The Indian Narrative: Perspectives and Patterns,* Christopher Shackle and Rupert Snell, eds. (Wiesbaden: Otto Harrassowitz, 1992), 241–64.

13. Richard Eaton, *Sufis of Bijapur, 1300–1700: Social Roles of Sufis in Medieval India* (Princeton, NJ: Princeton University Press, 1978), esp. 135–74.

14. Christopher Shackle, "The Shifting Sands of Love," in *Love in South Asia: A Cultural History,* ed. Francesca Orsini (Cambridge: Cambridge University Press, 2006), 88.

15. Ibid.

16. Frederick Denny, *An Introduction to Islam,* 2nd ed. (New York: Macmillan, 1986), 238.

17. Ibid., 233.

18. For an insightful analysis of the female gendered voice in comparative perspective, see Carla Petievich, *When Men Speak as Women: Vocal Masquerade in Indo-Muslim Poetry* (New Delhi: Oxford University Press, 2007).

19. Translated by Najm Hossain Syed in his, *Recurrent Patterns in Punjabi Poetry,* 2nd ed. (Lahore: Punjab Adbi Markaz, 1978), 7.

20. Ibid.

21. Translated by Najm Hossain Syed, in ibid., 4.

22. Translation adapted from Kartar Singh Duggal, *Sain Bulleh Shah: The Mystic Muse* (Delhi: Abhinav Publications, 1996), 53.

23. In addition to his *Sufis of Bijapur,* see his essay, "Women's Grinding and Spinning Songs of Devotion in the Late Medieval Deccan," in *Islam in South Asia in Practice,* ed. Barbara Metcalf (Princeton, NJ: Princeton University Press, 2009), 87–92; and his "Sufi Folk Literature and the Expansion of Indian Islam," *History of Religions* 14, 2 (1974): 117–27.

24. Literary critic Najm Hossain Syed disagrees with this interpretation, however. See his *Recurrent Patterns in Punjabi Poetry,* 31–46.

25. Maula Baksh Kushta, *Punjabi Shairan da Tazkira* (A Dictionary of Punjabi Poets), ed. Chaudhry Muhammad Afzal Khan (Lahore: Aziz Publishers, 1988 [1960]), 313.

26. Tarlok Singh Anand, "Sohni Jan Pecchan" (A Critical Introduction to *Sohni*), in *Sohni (Fazl Shah),* by Fazl Shah, ed. Tarlok Singh Anand (Patiala: Punjabi University Publication Bureau, 1987), 8–9; and Ratan Singh Jaggi, "Bhumika," introduction to *Sohni (Fazl Shah),* v.

27. Shahbaz Malik, *Punjabi Kitabiyat* (A Bibliography of Punjabi Printed Books Written in Perso-Arabic Script) (Islamabad: Akademi Adabiyat Pakistan, 1991), 305.

28. Sekhon, *History of Panjabi Literature,* 2: 134.

29. Punjabi text cited in Ajmer Singh, *Maharaja Ranjit Singh ate Punjabi Sahit* (Maharaja Ranjit Singh and Punjabi Literature) (Patiala: Punjabi University Publication Bureau, 1982), 73.

30. Francesca Orsini, introduction to *Love in South Asia: A Cultural History,* ed. Orsini, 23.

31. Richard Davis, introduction to *Religions of India in Practice,* ed. Donald Lopez, Jr. (Princeton, NJ: Princeton University Press, 1995), 23.

32. Edward Dimock, *The Place of the Hidden Moon: Erotic Mysticism in the Vaisnava-sahajiya Cult of Bengal* (Chicago: University of Chicago Press, 1989 [1966]), 19.

33. Denis Matringe, "Krsnaite and Nath Elements in the Sufi Poetry of the Eighteenth-Century Panjabi Sufi Bullhe Sah," in *Devotional Literature in South Asia: Current Research, 1985–1988,* ed. R. S. McGregor (Cambridge: Cambridge University Press, 1992), 191.

34. Barbara Stoler Miller, *Love Song of the Dark Lord: Jayadeva's Gitagovinda* (New York: Columbia University Press, 1977), 24–25.

35. Dimock, *Place of the Hidden Moon,* 33.

36. Miller, *Love Song of the Dark Lord,* 26.

37. Ibid.

38. Davis, introduction to *Religions of India in Practice,* 23.

39. Glen Hayes, "The Vaisnava Sahijya Traditions," in *Religions of India in Practice,* ed. Lopez, 337–38.

40. Matringe, "Krsnaite and Nath Elements," 198.

41. 'Arif, *Qissa Hir te Ranjhe da,* 39.

42. Fassi Niaz Ahmad, *Hir Niaz Ranjha* (Niaz's *Hir-Ranjha*) (Lahore: Munshi Aziz al-Din wa Najm al-Din, n.d. [c. 1914]), 2.

43. Khawaish Ali, *Hir-Ranjha* (Lahore: Pandit Labo Ram and Sons Tajran Kutab, n.d. [1933]), 2.

44. Sakin, *Qissa Hir wa Ranjha,* 2–3.

45. Al-Baksh [Munir], *Faryad Hir,* 2.

46. Ibid., 4.

47. Kishore Chand, *Navan Qissa Hir Kishore Chand* (Kishore Chand's New *Qissa* Hir) (Amritsar: Bhai Harnam Singh Karam Singh, 1914), 3–4.

48. Matringe, "Krsnaite and Nath Elements," 191.

49. J.S. Grewal, *In the By-Lanes of History: Some Persian Documents from a Punjab Town* (Simla: Indian Institute of Advanced Study, 1975), 8.

50. Ibid.

51. Ayesha Jalal, *Self and Sovereignty: Individual and Community in South Asian Islam since 1850* (New York: Routledge, 2000), 148–53.

52. Maula Shah, *Hir wa Ranjha* (n.p. [Amritsar]: n.p. [Imam al-Din Ma'raj al-Din], 1330 H. [1911–12]).

53. Ibid., 10.

54. Ibid.

55. Ahmad, *Hir Niaz Ranjha*, 2.

56. Ibid.

57. Ibid., 4.

58. Abd al-Karim Na'at, *Na'at di Hir* (Na'at's Hir) (Multan: Hafiz Muhammad al-Din, Aziz al-Din Bashir al-Din Tajran Kutab, n.d. [c. 1880]).

59. Ibid., 2.

60. Ibid., 4.

61. Ibid.

62. See Syed, *Recurrent Patterns in Punjabi Poetry,* 31–46.

63. J.S. Grewal, *The Sikhs of the Punjab,* rev. ed. (Cambridge: Cambridge University Press, 1998 [1990]), 159.

64. Barbara Metcalf, *Islamic Revival in British India: Deoband, 1860–1900* (Princeton, NJ: Princeton University Press, 1982), 134.

65. *The Gazetteer of the Jhelum District* (pt. A, 1904, 35–36). Cited in J.S. Grewal and B.N. Goswamy, *The Mughals and the Jogis of Jakhbar: Some Madad-i-Ma'ash and Other Documents* (Simla: Indian Institute of Advanced Study, 1967), 41.

66. Information on the Nath Siddha sect is taken from David Gordon White, "The Wonders of Mastnath," in *Religions of India in Practice,* ed. Lopez, 399–411.

67. Ibid., 399.

68. Ibid., 402.

69. Ibid., 402–3.

70. Matringe, "Krsnaite and Nath Elements," 195.

71. Miran Shah Bahawalpuri's *Qissa Hir-Ranjha* was published in a compilation of his work: *Hir Miran Shah Mukamal* (The Complete Hir Miran Shah) (Multan: Maulvi Khuda Yar wa Nur Ahmad wa Nur Muhammad wa Faiz Ahmad, 1316 h. [1898–99]), 3–20; this passage, 4.

72. Ibid., 8.

73. Ali, *Hir-Ranjha*, 28–29.

74. 'Arif, *Qissa Hir te Ranjha da,* 25.

75. Chand, *Navan Qissa Hir Kishore Chand,* 4.

76. David Gilmartin, *Empire and Islam: Punjab and the Making of Pakistan* (London: I.B. Tauris, 1988); and David Gilmartin, "Shrines, Succession and Sources of Moral Authority," in *Moral Conduct and Authority,* ed. Barbara Metcalf (Berkeley: University of California Press, 1984), 221–40.

77. Eaton, *Sufis of Bijapur;* and Richard Eaton, "The Political and Religious Authority of the Shrine of Baba Farid," in *Moral Conduct and Authority,* ed. Metcalf, 333–56.

78. Harjot Oberoi, *The Construction of Religious Boundaries: Culture, Identity, and Diversity in the Sikh Tradition* (Chicago: University of Chicago Press, 1994), 139–206.

79. Ibid., 156.

80. Ibid., 151.

81. See, for example, Derryl MacLean, *Religion and Society in Arab Sind* (Leiden: E. J. Brill, 1989); Asim Roy, *The Islamic Syncretistic Tradition in Bengal* (Princeton, NJ: Princeton University Press, 1983); and M. Waseem, trans. and ed., *On Becoming an Indian Muslim: French Essays on Aspects of Syncretism* (New Delhi: Oxford University Press, 2003).

82. Mir, "Genre and Devotion," 730–34.

83. Na'at, *Na'at di Hir,* 3–4.

84. Ibid., 5.

85. Ibid., 6.

86. Roshan, *Hir Roshan* (Lahore: Mian Chiragh al-Din, n.d. [c. 1873]).

87. Ibid., 4–5.

88. My citations are drawn from Husain, *Hir Husain, Si Harfi Ashraf, Si Harfi Arora Rai, Si Harfi Ghulam* (Lahore: Matbah Sultani, 1873).

89. Ibid., 2.

90. Ibid., 4.

91. Ibid., 5. The hadith are the reputed sayings and actions of the Prophet Muhammad. They are a fundamental component of Islamic law. "Kheras" is a reference to the family to which Hir's parents have betrothed her.

92. Ibid., 4.

93. Chand, *Navan Qissa Hir Kishore Chand.*

94. Ibid., 4.

95. 'Arif, *Qissa Hir te Ranjhe da.*

96. Ibid., 40.

97. Ibid., 43–44.

98. A. K. Ramanujan, "Three Hundred *Ramayanas:* Five Examples and Three Thoughts on Translation," in *Many Ramayanas: The Diversity of a Narrative Tradition in South Asia,* ed. Paula Richman (Berkeley: University of California Press, 1991), 46.

CONCLUSION

1. This translation is adapted from: Amrita Pritam, "I Call on Varis Shah!" trans. Gibb Schreffler, *Journal of Punjab Studies* 13, 1–2 (2006): 79; and Amrita Pritam, "To Waris Shah," in *Alone in the Multitude,* by Amrita Pritam, ed. and trans. Suresh Kohli (New Delhi: Indian Literary Review, 1979), 11.

2. Gyanendra Pandey has written eloquently about the ruptures at these three levels. See his *Remembering Partition: Violence, Nationalism, and History in India* (Cambridge: Cambridge University Press, 2001), chap. 2.

3. Singh Sabha intellectuals initiated the most significant shifts in literary trends by introducing new genres of Punjabi composition. New genres such as the novel helped

untether Punjabi literary culture from the institutions and sites that it previously inhabited. The "new" literature also became a site for different modes of communication, introducing a didactic tone meant to guide and mold the behavior and sentiments of its audience in ways very different from forms such as the *qissa*.

4. Penelope Corfield, "Historians and Language," introduction to *Language, History and Class,* ed. Penelope Corfield (Oxford: Basil Blackwell, 1991), 13.

5. See Peter Burke and Roy Porter, eds., *A Social History of Language* (Cambridge: Cambridge University Press, 1987); Peter Burke and Roy Porter, eds., *Language, Self, and Society: A Social History of Language* (Cambridge: Polity Press, 1991); Peter Burke and Roy Porter, eds., *Languages and Jargons: Contributions to a Social History of Language* (Cambridge: Polity Press, 1995). For a more recent contribution to this field, see Peter Burke, *Towards a Social History of Dutch* (Amsterdam: Amsterdam University Press, 2007).

6. On the Indian context, see Sudipta Kaviraj's seminal essay on the subject, "Writing, Speaking, Being: Language and the Historical Formation of Identities in India," in *Nationalstaat und Sprachkonflikte in Sud- und Sudostasien,* ed. Dagmar Hellman-Rajanayagam and Dietmar Rothermund (Stuttgart: Steiner, 1992), 25–65. Also see David Washbrook, "'To Each a Language of His Own': Language, Culture, and Society in Colonial India," in *Language, History, and Class,* ed. Penelope Corfield, 179–203.

7. Eric Hobsbawm provides the most succinct analysis of the importance of languages to modern European nationalisms in his *Nations and Nationalisms since 1780: Programme, Myth, Reality* (Cambridge: Cambridge University Press, 1990).

8. For a broad overview of linguistic reorganization, see Paul Brass, *The Politics of India since Independence* (Cambridge: Cambridge University Press, 1994), chap. 5; and Robert D. King, *Nehru and the Language Politics of India* (New Delhi: Oxford University Press, 1994).

9. Sumathi Ramaswamy makes this important point in *Passions of the Tongue: Language Devotion in Tamil India, 1891–1970* (Berkeley: University of California Press, 1997), 2–5.

10. Lisa Mitchell, *Language, Emotion, and Politics in South India: The Making of a Mother Tongue* (Bloomington: University of Indiana Press, 2009).

11. On the Marathi movement see: Y. D. Phadke, *Politics and Language* (Bombay: Himalaya Publishing House, 1979); on Assamese, Sanjib Baruah, *India against Itself: Assam and the Politics of Nationality* (Philadelphia: University of Pennsylvania Press, 1999); on Bengali and Sindhi, Tariq Rahman, *Language and Politics in Pakistan* (Karachi: Oxford University Press, 1996), chaps. 6 and 7, respectively.

12. Paul Brass, *Language, Religion, and Politics in North India* (Cambridge: Cambridge University Press, 1974), 277–400.

13. On the Unionists, see: Ian Talbot, *Khizr Tiwana, the Punjab Unionist Party, and the Partition of India* (Richmond, Surrey: Curzon Press, 1996); and David Gilmartin, *Empire and Islam: Punjab and the Making of Pakistan* (London: I. B. Tauris, 1988).

14. The Indian National Congress contested the Akali Dal's claim to represent Sikh interests, just as it contested the Muslim League claim to be the representative of Indian Muslims. Branding both the Akali Dal and the Muslim League "communalist," the Congress portrayed itself to be India's sole "nationalist" party. Both Akali Dal and Muslim League leaders contested that position, of course, as staunch nationalists in their own right.

15. On Akali Dal politics in the early twentieth century, see J. S. Grewal, *The Sikhs of the Punjab*, rev. ed. (Cambridge: Cambridge University Press, 1998 [1990]), 157–80.

16. This rendering of the Akali Dal's politics is based on Brass, *Language, Religion, and Politics in North India*, 318–27; and Baldev Raj Nayar, *Minority Politics in the Punjab* (Princeton, NJ: Princeton University Press, 1966).

17. Having adopted the principle that India's administrative units should dovetail with its linguistic map in 1920, the Indian National Congress could scarcely deem such a demand illegitimate once in power.

18. Brass, *Language, Religion, and Politics in North India*, 323.

19. Punjab was one of only two states that were not reorganized. The other was Bombay, which was left untouched so as not to alter the status of Bombay (city), which was claimed by both Gujarati-speakers and Marathi-speakers. Subsequently, in 1960, Maharashtra state was created, with Bombay as its capital.

20. Nayar, *Minority Politics in the Punjab*, 44–45.

21. Tariq Rahman provides an overview of the politics of national and regional languages in his *Language and Politics in Pakistan*.

22. See Alyssa Ayres, *Speaking Like a State: Language and Nationalism in Pakistan* (Cambridge: Cambridge University Press, 2009).

23. Rahman, *Language and Politics in Pakistan*, chap. 11.

24. Ibid., chap. 10.

25. Christopher Shackle, "Pakistan," in *Language and National Identity in Asia*, ed. Andrew Simpson (New York: Oxford University Press, 2007), 114. Also see his "Siraiki: A Language Movement in Pakistan," *Modern Asian Studies* 11, 3 (1977): 379–403.

26. Christopher Shackle provided one of the earliest assessments of the movement in his "Punjabi in Lahore," *Modern Asian Studies* 4, 3 (1970): 239–67.

27. Alyssa Ayres, "Language, the Nation, and Symbolic Capital: The Case of the Punjab," *Journal of Asian Studies* 67, 3 (2008): 917–46.

28. Ibid., 923.

29. Nadir Ali, "Celebrating a Rich Theatre Tradition," *The News* (Lahore, Pakistan) 20 December 1998.

30. For example, according to John McDonnell, Member of Parliament, Punjabi is the second most widely used language in Great Britain, with 1.3 million speakers. McDonnell cited these figures before Parliament on 7 March 2000. See www.publications.parliament.uk/pa/cm199900/cmhansrd/vo000307/halltext/00307h02.htm (accessed 1 June 2009).

BIBLIOGRAPHY

UNPUBLISHED SOURCES

Bhai Gurdas Library, Guru Nanak Dev University, Amritsar
Manuscripts and Rare Books Section.

Bhai Kahan Singh Nabha Library, Punjabi University, Patiala
Ganda Singh Punjabi Reference Library.
Theses Section.

Bhasha Vibhag (Languages Department), Patiala
Manuscripts Collection.

Musafir Memorial Central State Library, Patiala
Manuscripts Collection.

National Archives of India, New Delhi
Foreign Department Proceedings.
Home Department Proceedings.

Oriental and India Office Collections, British Library, London
Board of Control Records, 1784–1858 (F series).
East India Company: General Correspondence, 1602–1859 (E series).
European Manuscripts Division (MS EUR)
India Office Records Official Publications Series, c. 1760–1957 (V series).
Papers of George Abraham Grierson (E223).
Papers of John Laird Mair Lawrence (F90).

Papers of Charles James Napier (C123).
Papers of Herbert Hope Risley (E100).
Papers of Richard Carnac Temple (F98).
Records Division (IOR).

Panjab University Library, Chandigarh
Manuscripts and Rare Books Section.
Theses and Text Books Section.

Patiala State Archives, Patiala
Manuscripts Collection.

Punjab Provincial Archives, Chandigarh
Education, Science, and Art Department Proceedings.

OTHER SOURCES

Abbott, J. "On the Ballads and Legends of the Punjab." *Journal of the Asiatic Society of Bengal* 23, 1 (1854): 59–91, 123–63.

Ahmad, Fassi Niaz. *Hir Niaz Ranjha* (Niaz's *Hir-Ranjha*). Lahore: Munshi Aziz al-Din wa Najm al-Din, n.d. [c. 1914].

Ahmad, Imtiaz. "Caste and Kinship in a Muslim Village of Eastern Uttar Pradesh." In *Family, Kinship, and Marriage among Muslims in India,* ed. Imtiaz Ahmad, 319–46. New Delhi: Manohar, 1976.

———, ed. *Caste and Social Stratification among Muslims in India.* New Delhi: Manohar, 1978.

———, ed. *Family, Kinship, and Marriage among Muslims in India.* New Delhi: Manohar, 1976.

———. "Preface to the First Edition (1973)." Preface to *Caste and Social Stratification among Muslims in India,* ed. Imtiaz Ahmad, viii–x. New Delhi: Manohar, 1978.

Ahmad, Saghir. "Social Stratification in a Punjabi Village." *Contributions to Indian Sociology* 4, 1 (1970): 105–25.

Aiyar, Swarna. "'August Anarchy': The Partition Massacres in Punjab, 1947." *South Asia* 18, supplement 1 (1995): 13–36.

Akbar, Muhammad Sadiq Sahib. *Ranjhe di Faryad* (Ranjha's Plea). Lahore: Shaikh Zafar Muhammad, n.d.

Alam, Muzaffar. "The Pursuit of Persian Language in Mughal Politics." *Modern Asian Studies* 32, 2 (1998): 317–50.

Alavi, Hamza. "The Two Biraderis: Kinship in Rural West Pakistan." In *Muslim Communities of South Asia,* ed. T. N. Madan, 1–62. New Delhi: Manohar, 1995.

al-Baksh, Khaksar [Munir]. *Faryad Hir* (Hir's Plea). Lahore: Munshi Aziz al-Din Najm al-Din, n.d.

Ali, Hasan. "Elements of Caste among the Muslims in a District in Southern Bihar." In *Caste and Social Stratification among Muslims in India,* ed. Imtiaz Ahmad, 19–40. New Delhi: Manohar, 1978.

Ali, Imran. *The Punjab under Imperialism, 1885–1947.* Princeton, NJ: Princeton University Press, 1988.

Ali, Khawaish. *Hir-Ranjha.* Lahore: Pandit Labo Ram and Sons Tajran Kutab, n.d. [1933].

Ali, Mian Sher. *Chitthi Ranjhe di* (Ranjha's Letter). Amritsar: Vazir Hind Press, n.d. [c. 1915].

Ali, Muhammad Akbar. *Qissa Warburton.* Lahore: n.p., 1891.

Ali, Nadir. "Celebrating a Rich Theatre Tradition." *The News* (Lahore, Pakistan), 20 December 1998.

Allender, Tim. *Ruling through Education: The Politics of Schooling in the Colonial Punjab.* Elgin, IL: New Dawn Press, 2006.

American Baptist Magazine and Missionary Intelligencer 3, 11 (1822).

Amol, S. S., ed. *Sade Purane Kavi* (Our Historic Poets). Amritsar: Likhari Book Depot, 1941.

Anand, Tarlok Singh. "Sohni Jan Pecchan" (A Critical Introduction to *Sohni*). In *Sohni (Fazl Shah),* by Fazl Shah, ed. Tarlok Singh Anand, 1–41. Patiala: Punjabi University Publication Bureau, 1987.

Anderson, Benedict. *Imagined Communities: Reflections on the Origin and Spread of Nationalism.* Rev. ed. London: Verso, 1991 [1983].

Anderson, Flemming. "Technique, Text, and Context: Formulaic Mode and the Question of Genre." In *The Ballad and Oral Literature,* ed. Joseph Harris, 174–202. Cambridge, MA: Harvard University Press, 1991.

Anglo–Vernacular Pleasant Stories. Lahore: Shams-ul-Hind, 1897.

'Arif, Kishan Singh. *Qissa Hir te Ranjhe da* (The *Qissa* of Hir and Ranjha). Amritsar: Bhai Vasava Singh Juneja Pustak Wale, 1889.

Arora, Poonam. "Role of Singh Sabha Movement in the Promotion of Female Education in Punjab." In *Punjab History Conference, Twenty Sixth Session, March 18–20, 1994, Part I, Proceedings,* ed. Gursharan Singh, 209–14. Patiala: Department of Punjab Historical Studies, Punjabi University, 1994.

Arora, Seema. "J. D. Cunningham on Decline of the Lahore Kingdom." *Punjab History Conference, Twenty-Sixth Session, March 18–20, 1994, Part I, Proceedings,* ed. Gursharan Singh, 147–56. Patiala: Department of Punjab Historical Studies, Punjabi University, 1994.

Asad, Talal, ed. *Anthropology and the Colonial Encounter.* New York: Humanities Press, 1973.

Awan, Chiragh. *Qissa Hir-Ranjha.* Ed. Ain al-Haq Faridkoti. Lahore: Pakistan Punjabi Adabi Board, 1978.

Ayres, Alyssa. "Language, the Nation, and Symbolic Capital: The Case of the Punjab." *Journal of Asian Studies* 67, 3 (2008): 917–46.

———. *Speaking Like a State: Language and Nationalism in Pakistan.* Cambridge: Cambridge University Press, 2009.

Azim, Muhammad. *Hir Azim Ranjha* (Azim's *Hir-Ranjha*). Lahore: Munshi Aziz al-Din Najm al-Din, 1914.

———. *Hir Azim Ranjha* (Azim's *Hir-Ranjha*). Lahore: Munshi Aziz al-Din Najm al-Din, n.d. [c. 1922].

Bahawalpuri, Miran Shah. *Hir Miran Shah Mukamal* (The Complete Hir Miran Shah). Multan: Maulvi Khuda Yar wa Nur Ahmad wa Nur Muhammad wa Faiz Ahmad Tajar Kutab, 1316 h. [1898–99].

Bailey, T. Graham. *A Brief Grammar of Panjabi As Spoken in the Wazirabad District.* Lahore: Punjab Government Press, 1904.

Bailey, T. Graham, and Thomas F. Cummings. *Panjabi Manual and Grammar: A Guide to the Colloquial Panjabi of the Northern Panjab.* Sialkot: Sialkot Mission of the United Presbyterian Church of North America, 1912.

Banerjee, Sumanta. *The Parlour and the Streets: Elite and Popular Culture in Nineteenth Century Calcutta.* Calcutta: Seagull Books, 1998 [1989].

Banga, Indu. The *Agrarian System of the Sikhs: Late Eighteenth and Early Nineteenth Century.* Columbia, MO: South Asia Books, 1978.

———, ed. *Five Punjabi Centuries: Polity, Economy, Society and Culture, c. 1500–1990.* New Delhi: Manohar, 1997.

Barrier, N. G. *Banned: Controversial Literature and Political Control in British India, 1907–1947.* Columbia: University of Missouri Press, 1974.

———, ed. *The Census in British India: New Perspectives.* New Delhi: Manohar, 1981.

———. *The Punjab Alienation of Land Bill of 1900.* Durham, NC: Duke University Press, 1966.

———. *The Punjab in Nineteenth Century Tracts: An Introduction to the Pamphlet Collections in the British Museum and India Office.* East Lansing: Michigan State University Press, 1969.

———. *The Sikhs and Their Literature.* New Delhi: Manohar, 1970.

———. "Vernacular Publishing and Sikh Public Life in the Punjab, 1880–1910." In *Religious Controversy in British India: Dialogues in South Asian Languages,* ed. Kenneth W. Jones, 200–226. Albany: State University of New York Press, 1992.

Barrier, N. G., and Paul Wallace. *The Punjab Press, 1880–1905.* East Lansing: Michigan State University, 1970.

Barrow, Ian. *Making History, Drawing Territory: British Mapping in India, c. 1765–1905.* New Delhi: Oxford University Press, 2003.

Barstow, A. E. *The Sikhs: An Ethnology.* Delhi: Low Price Publications, 1994 [1928].

Baruah, Sanjib. *India against Itself: Assam and the Politics of Nationality.* Philadelphia: University of Pennsylvania Press, 1999.

Barz, Richard K., and Monika Thiel-Horstmann, eds. *Living Texts from India.* Wiesbaden: Otto Harrassowitz, 1989.

Basianwala, Gokalchand Sharma. *Qissa Hir Gokalchand.* Ludhiana: Allah Baksh Maula Baksh, n.d.

Bayly, C. A. *Empire and Information: Intelligence Gathering and Social Communication in India, 1780–1870.* Cambridge: Cambridge University Press, 1996.

Bayly, Susan. *Caste, Society, and Politics in India from the Eighteenth Century to the Modern Age.* Cambridge: Cambridge University Press, 1999.

———. "Islam in Southern India: Purist or Syncretic?" In *Two Colonial Empires,* ed. Christopher Bayly and D. H. A. Kolff, 35–73. Boston: Martinus Nijhoff, 1986.

Beames, John. *Memoirs of a Bengal Civilian.* London: Chatto and Windus, 1961.

———. *Outlines of Indian Philology and Other Philological Papers.* Calcutta: Indian Studies Past and Present, 1960 [1867].

Beck, Brenda E. F. *The Three Twins: The Telling of a South Indian Folk Epic.* Bloomington: Indiana University Press, 1982.

Bedi, Ganga Singh. "Bhumika." Introduction to *Hir Damodar,* by Damodar. Lahore: n.p., n.d. [1927].

Beissinger, Margaret, Jane Tylus, and Susanne Wofford, eds. *Epic Traditions in the Contemporary World: The Poetics of Community.* Berkeley: University of California Press, 1999.

Bhatia, H. S., and B. S. Ghumman, eds. *Punjabi Sahit di Itihaskari* (A History of Punjabi Literature). 2 vols. Amritsar: Guru Nanak Dev University, n.d.

Bhatia, Uttam Singh. *Qissa-Kav ate Hir Damodar* (*Qissa* Literature and Damodar's Hir). Patiala: Pavitar Pramanik, 1982.

Bhattacharya, Neeladri. "Remaking Custom: The Discourse and Practice of Colonial Codification." In *Tradition, Dissent, and Ideology,* ed. R. Champakalakshmi and S. Gopal, 20–51. New Delhi: Oxford University Press, 1996.

Bingley, A. H. *Sikhs.* New Delhi: Nirmal Publishers, 1986 [1899].

Blackburn, Stuart. "Patterns of Development for Indian Oral Epics." In *Oral Epics in India,* ed. Stuart Blackburn et al., 15–32. Berkeley: University of California Press, 1989.

———. *Print, Folklore, and Nationalism in Colonial South India.* Delhi: Permanent Black, 2003.

Blackburn, Stuart, and Vasudha Dalmia, eds. *India's Literary History: Essays on the Nineteenth Century.* Delhi: Permanent Black, 2004.

Blackburn, Stuart, and Joyce Flueckiger. Introduction to *Oral Epics in India,* ed. Stuart Blackburn et al., 1–14. Berkeley: University of California Press, 1989.

Blackburn, Stuart, and A. K. Ramanujan. Introduction to *Another Harmony: New Essays on the Folklore of India,* ed. Stuart Blackburn and A. K. Ramanujan, 1–40. Berkeley: University of California Press, 1986.

———, eds. *Another Harmony: New Essays on the Folklore of India.* Berkeley: University of California Press, 1986.

Blackburn, Stuart, et al., eds. *Oral Epics in India.* Berkeley: University of California Press, 1989.

Bose, Sugata, and Ayesha Jalal. *Modern South Asia: History, Culture, Political Economy.* New York: Routledge, 1998.

Boyarin, Jonathan, ed. *The Ethnography of Reading.* Berkeley: University of California Press, 1993.

Brass, Paul. *Language, Religion, and Politics in North India.* Cambridge: Cambridge University Press, 1974.

———. *The Politics of India since Independence.* Cambridge: Cambridge University Press, 1994.

Briggs, George Weston. *Gorakhnath and the Kanphata Yogis*. Delhi: Motilal Banarsidass, 1973 [1938].

Bruce, J. F. "A Brief History of the University of the Panjab." *Journal of the Panjab University Historical Society* 2, 4 (1933): 97–116.

Burke, Peter. *Towards a Social History of Dutch*. Amsterdam: Amsterdam University Press, 2007.

Burke, Peter, and Roy Porter, eds. *Language, Self, and Society: A Social History of Language*. Cambridge: Polity Press, 1991.

———, eds. *Languages and Jargons: Contributions to a Social History of Language*. Cambridge: Polity Press, 1995.

———, eds. *A Social History of Language*. Cambridge: Cambridge University Press, 1987.

Burton, Antoinette. *Dwelling in the Archive: Women Writing House, Home, and History in Late Colonial India*. New York: Oxford University Press, 2003.

Carey, Eustace. *Memoir of William Carey, D.D.* Hartford, CT: Canfield and Robins, 1837.

Carey, William. *A Grammar of the Punjaubee Language*. Serampore: Serampore Mission Press, 1812.

Carroll, Lucy. "The Temperance Movement in India: Politics and Social Reform." *Modern Asian Studies* 10, 3 (1976): 417–47.

Caton, Brian. "Social Categories and Colonisation in Panjab, 1849–1920." *Indian Economic and Social History Review* 41, 1 (2004): 33–50.

Chand, Bhagat Diwan. *Si Harfi Hir*. Gujranwala: Prem Bilas Press, 1916.

Chand, Kishore. *Navan Qissa Hir Kishore Chand* (Kishore Chand's New *Qissa* Hir). Amritsar: Bhai Harnam Singh Karam Singh, 1914.

———. *Navan Qissa Hir Kishore Chand* (Kishore Chand's New *Qissa* Hir). Amritsar: Bhai Harnam Singh Karam Singh, 1918.

Chapman, Graham, et al., eds. *The Asian City: Processes of Development, Characteristics, and Planning*. New York: Springer, 1994.

Chartier, Roger. *The Cultural Uses of Print in Early Modern France*. Trans. Lydia Cochrane. Princeton, NJ: Princeton University Press, 1987.

———. *Forms and Meanings: Texts, Performances, and Audiences from Codex to Computer*. Philadelphia: University of Pennsylvania Press, 1994.

Chatterjee, Partha. *The Nation and Its Fragments: Colonial and Postcolonial Histories*. Princeton, NJ: Princeton University Press, 1993.

Chaudhury, Muhammad Azam. *Justice and Practice: Legal Ethnography of a Pakistani Punjabi Village*. Oxford: Oxford University Press, 1999.

Chishti, Noor Ahmad. *Tahqiqaat-i Chishti: Tarikh-i Lahore Ka Encyclopedia* (Chishti's Inquiries: An Encyclopedia of Lahore's History). Lahore: al-Fasl Nashraan-o-Tajran Kitab, 1996 [1867].

———. *Yadgar-i Chishti* (Chishti's Memories). Lahore: Sang-e-Meel Publications, n.d. [1854].

Chowdhry, Prem. "Customs in a Peasant Economy: Women in Colonial Haryana." In *Recasting Women: Essays in Indian Colonial History*, ed. Kumkum Sangari and Sudesh Vaid, 302–36. Delhi: Kali for Women, 1989.

Churchill, Edward. "Muslim Societies of the Punjab, 1860–1890." *Panjab Past and Present* 8, 1 (1974): 69–91.

Cohn, Bernard. "The Census, Social Structure, and Objectification in South Asia." In *An Anthropologist among the Historians and Other Essays*, 224–54. New Delhi: Oxford University Press, 1987.

———. *Colonialism and Its Forms of Knowledge: The British in India*. Princeton, NJ: Princeton University Press, 1996.

———. "The Command of Language and the Language of Command." In *Colonialism and Its Forms of Knowledge: The British in India*, 16–56. Princeton, NJ: Princeton University Press, 1996.

Cole, Juan R. *Roots of North India Shi'ism in Iran and Iraq: Religion and State in Awadh, 1722–1859*. Berkeley: University of California Press, 1989.

Comaroff, Jean, and John Comaroff. *Of Revelation and Revolution*. Vol. 1. Chicago: University of Chicago Press, 1991.

Copley, Antony. *Religions in Conflict: Ideology, Cultural Contact, and Conversion in Late Colonial India*. New Delhi: Oxford University Press, 1997.

Corfield, Penelope. "Historians and Language." Introduction to *Language, History, and Class*, ed. Penelope Corfield, 1–29. Oxford: Basil Blackwell, 1991.

Cox, Jeffrey. *Imperial Fault Lines: Christianity and Colonial Power in India, 1818–1940*. Stanford, CA: Stanford University Press, 2002.

Crane, Ralph, and Anna Johnston. "Flora Annie Steel in the Punjab." In *Writing, Travel, and Empire*, ed. Peter Hulme and Russell McDougall, 71–96. London: I. B. Tauris, 2007.

Cunningham, Joseph Davey. *A History of the Sikhs from the Origin of the Nation to the Battles of the Sutlej*. Rev. ed. Ed. H. L. O. Garrett. New Delhi: Asian Educational Services, 1994 [1918].

Cust, Robert Needham. "Another Chapter in the History of the Conquest of the Panjab." *Calcutta Review* 108 (1899): 316–37.

———. "A Chapter in the History of the Conquest of the Panjab." *Calcutta Review* 102 (1898): 257–93.

———. *Linguistic and Oriental Essays: Written from the Years 1840 to 1903*. 7 vols. London: Trubner, 1880–1904.

———. *Memoirs of the Past Years of a Septuagenarian*. London: n.p., 1899.

———. *Self-Reflections of an Octogenarian*. London: n.p., n.d.

———. *A Sketch of the Modern Languages of the East Indies*. London: n.p., 1878.

Dalmia, Vasudha. *The Nationalization of Hindu Traditions: Bharatendu Harischandra and Nineteenth-Century Banaras*. New Delhi: Oxford University Press, 1997.

Damodar. *Hir Damodar*. Ed. Muhammad Asif Khan. Lahore: Pakistan Punjabi Adabi Board, 1986.

———. *Hir Damodar*. Ed. Jagtar Singh. Patiala: Punjabi University Publication Bureau, 1987.

Daniel, E. Valentine. *Fluid Signs: Being a Person the Tamil Way*. Berkeley: University of California Press, 1984.

Darnton, Robert. "Book Production in British India, 1850–1900." *Book History* 5 (2002): 239–62.

Das, Pandit Gopal. *Faryad Hir* (Hir's Plea). Lahore: Bhatia and Co. Tajran Kutab, n.d. [c. 1933].

Datta, Nonica. *Forming an Identity: A Social History of the Jats*. New Delhi: Oxford University Press, 1999.

Datta, Pradip Kumar. *Carving Blocs: Communal Ideology in Early Twentieth-Century Bengal*. New Delhi: Oxford University Press, 1999.

Davis, Emmett. *Press and Politics in British Western Punjab, 1836–1947*. Delhi: Academic Publications, 1983.

Davis, Natalie Zemon. *Fiction in the Archives: Pardon Tales and Their Tellers in Sixteenth-Century France*. Stanford, CA: Stanford University Press, 1987.

Davis, Richard. Introduction to *The Religions of India in Practice*, ed. Donald Lopez, Jr., 3–52. Princeton, NJ: Princeton University Press, 1995.

de Tassy, Garcin. *Muslim Festivals in India and Other Essays*. Ed. and trans. M. Waseem. New Delhi: Oxford University Press, 1995 [1831].

Denny, Frederick. *An Introduction to Islam*. 2nd ed. New York: Macmillan, 1986.

Deol, Jeevan. "Sex, Social Critique, and the Female Figure in Premodern Punjabi Poetry: Varis Shah's 'Hir.'" *Modern Asian Studies* 36, 1 (2002): 141–71.

Dimock, Edward. *The Place of the Hidden Moon: Erotic Mysticism in the Vaisnava-Sahajiya Cult of Bengal*. Chicago: University of Chicago Press, 1989 [1966].

Din, Hafiz Muhammad. *Ranjhan Par* (Ranjha, the Distant Shore). Amritsar: Munshi Muhammad Ismail Sahib Mushtaq, n.d. [c. 1920].

Dirks, Nicholas. *Castes of Mind: Colonialism and the Making of Modern India*. Princeton, NJ: Princeton University Press, 2001.

Duggal, Kartar Singh. *Sain Bulleh Shah: The Mystic Muse*. Delhi: Abhinav Publications, 1996.

During, Jean. "Hearing and Understanding in the Islamic Gnosis." *World of Music* 39, 2 (1997): 127–37.

———. "Revelation and Spiritual Audition in Islam." *World of Music* 24, 3 (1982): 68–81.

Eaton, Richard. "Approaches to the Study of Conversion to Islam in South Asia." In *Approaches to Islam in Religious Studies*, ed. Richard C. Martin, 106–23. Tucson: University of Arizona Press, 1985.

———. "The Political and Religious Authority of the Shrine of Baba Farid." In *Moral Conduct and Authority: The Place of Adab in South Asian Islam*, ed. Barbara Metcalf, 333–56. Berkeley: University of California Press, 1984.

———. *The Rise of Islam and the Bengal Frontier, 1204–1760*. Berkeley: University of California Press, 1993.

———. *A Social History of the Deccan, 1300–1761: Eight Indian Lives*. Cambridge: Cambridge University Press, 2005.

———. "Sufi Folk Literature and the Expansion of Indian Islam." *History of Religions* 14, 2 (1974): 117–27.

———. *Sufis of Bijapur, 1300–1700: Social Roles of Sufis in Medieval India*. Princeton, NJ: Princeton University Press, 1978.

———. "Women's Grinding and Spinning Songs of Devotion in the Late Medieval Deccan." In *Islam in South Asia in Practice*, ed. Barbara Metcalf, 87–92. Princeton, NJ: Princeton University Press, 2009.

Edney, Matthew. *Mapping an Empire: The Geographical Construction of British India, 1765–1843*. Chicago: University of Chicago Press, 1997.

Effendi, Sirdar Mohammad Abdul Kadir Khan. *Hir and Ranjha*. Lahore: Punjabi Adabi Laihr, 1982 [1917].

Eisenstein, Elizabeth. *Print Culture and Enlightenment Thought*. Chapel Hill: University of North Carolina Press, 1986.

———. *The Printing Press as an Agent of Change: Communication and Cultural Transformation in Early-Modern Europe*. 2 vols. Cambridge: Cambridge University Press, 1979.

———. *The Printing Revolution in Early Modern Europe*. Cambridge: Cambridge University Press, 1983.

Ewing, Katherine P. "The Politics of Sufism: Redefining the Saints of Pakistan." *Journal of Asian Studies* 42, 2 (1983): 251–68.

———, ed. *Shari'at and Ambiguity in South Asian Islam*. Berkeley: University of California Press, 1988.

Fabian, Johannes. *Language and Colonial Power: The Appropriation of Swahili in the Former Belgian Congo, 1880–1938*. Cambridge: Cambridge University Press, 1986.

Faqir, Faqir Muhammad. Introduction to *Hir Muqbal*, by Shah Jahan Muqbal, ed. Faqir Muhammad Faqir. N.p.: n.p., n.d. [1990].

Farshi, Munshi Muhammad Baksh Sahib. *Farshi di Hir (Hissa Chaharam)* (Farshi's Hir [the Fourth Part]). Lahore: Munshi Aziz al-Din Najm al-Din, 1929.

Faruqi, Shamsur Rahman. *Early Urdu Literary Culture and History*. New Delhi: Oxford University Press, 2001.

Fattehu'd-Din, Mian. "*Qissa Nahir Firozpur Panjab*." *Indian Antiquary* 11 (June 1882): 166–67.

Febvre, Lucien, and Henri-Jean Martin. *The Coming of the Book: The Impact of Printing, 1450–1800*. Trans. David Gerard. New York: Verso, 1976 [1958].

Finnegan, Ruth. *Literacy and Orality: Studies in the Technology of Communication*. Oxford: Basil Blackwell, 1988.

———. *Oral Poetry: Its Nature, Significance, and Social Context*. Cambridge: Cambridge University Press, 1977.

Flueckiger, Joyce Burkhalter. "Appropriating the Epic: Gender, Caste, and Regional Identity in Middle India." In *Epic Traditions in the Contemporary World*, ed. Margaret Beissinger et al., 131–52. Berkeley: University of California Press, 1999.

———. "Caste and Regional Variants in an Oral Epic Tradition." In *Oral Epics in India*, ed. Stuart Blackburn et al., 33–54. Berkeley: University of California Press, 1989.

———. *Gender and Genre in the Folklore of Middle India*. Ithaca, NY: Cornell University Press, 1996.

Fox, Richard. *Lions of the Punjab: Culture in the Making*. Berkeley: University of California Press, 1985.

Fraser, Nancy. "Rethinking the Public Sphere: A Contribution to the Critique of Actually Existing Democracy." In *Habermas and the Public Sphere,* ed. Craig Calhoun, 109–43. Cambridge, MA: MIT Press, 1992.

Freitag, Sandria. *Collective Action and Community: Public Arenas and the Emergence of Communalism in North India.* Berkeley: University of California Press, 1989.

Friedmann, Yohanan. *Prophecy Continuous: Aspects of Ahmadi Religious Thought and Its Medieval Background.* Berkeley: University of California Press, 1989.

Gaborieau, Marc. "The Cult of Saints among the Muslims of Nepal and Northern India." In *Saints and Their Cults: Studies in Religious Sociology, Folklore and History,* ed. Stephen Wilson, 291–308. Cambridge: Cambridge University Press, 1983.

Gardezi, Hasan. "Sufi Cosmology: An Indigenous Oral Tradition." In *East-West Dialogue in Knowledge and Higher Education,* ed. Ruth Hayhoe and Julia Pan, 195–205. Armonk: M. E. Sharpe, 1996.

Garrett, H. L. O., ed. *A History of Government College Lahore, 1864–1914.* Lahore: Government College, 1964 [1914].

Ghosh, Anindita, ed. *Behind the Veil: Resistance, Women, and the Everyday in Colonial South Asia.* Delhi: Permanent Black, 2007.

———. "Cheap Books, 'Bad' Books: Contesting Print Cultures in Colonial Bengal." *South Asia Research* 18, 2 (1998): 173–94.

———. *Power in Print: Popular Publishing and the Politics of Language and Culture in a Colonial Society, 1778–1905.* New Delhi: Oxford University Press, 2006.

———. "'An Uncertain Coming of the Book': Early Print Cultures in Colonial India." *Book History* 6 (2003): 23–55.

Gilmartin, David. "*Biraderi* and Bureaucracy: The Politics of Muslim Kinship Solidarity in Twentieth Century Punjab." *International Journal of Punjab Studies* 1, 1 (1994): 1–29.

———. "Customary Law and *Shari'at* in British Punjab." In *Shari'at and Ambiguity in South Asian Islam,* ed. Katherine P. Ewing, 43–62. Berkeley: University of California Press, 1988.

———. *Empire and Islam: Punjab and the Making of Pakistan.* London: I. B. Tauris, 1988.

———. "Religious Leadership and the Pakistan Movement in the Punjab." *Modern Asian Studies* 13, 3 (1979): 485–517.

———. "Shrines, Succession, and Sources of Moral Authority." In *Moral Conduct and Authority,* ed. Barbara Metcalf, 221–40. Berkeley: University of California Press, 1984.

Gilmartin, David, and Bruce B. Lawrence, eds. *Beyond Turk and Hindu: Rethinking Religious Identities in Islamicate South Asia.* Gainesville: University of Florida Press, 2000.

Gingley, A. H. *History, Caste, and Culture of Jats and Gujars.* New Delhi: Ess Ess Publications, 1978 [1899].

Glover, William J. *Making Lahore Modern: Constructing and Imagining a Colonial City.* Minneapolis: University of Minnesota Press, 2008.

Gordon, John J. H. *The Sikhs.* Patiala: Languages Department, 1970 [1904].

Goody, Jack. *The Domestication of the Savage Mind.* Cambridge: Cambridge University Press, 1977.

———. *The Interface between the Written and the Oral.* Cambridge: Cambridge University Press, 1987.

——. *Literacy in Traditional Societies.* Cambridge: Cambridge University Press, 1968.

——. *The Logic of Writing and the Organization of Society.* Cambridge: Cambridge University Press, 1986.

——. *The Power of the Written Tradition.* Washington, DC: Smithsonian Institution Press, 2000.

Goody, Jack, and Ian Watt. "The Consequences of Literacy." *Comparative Studies in History and Society* 5, 3 (April 1963): 304–335.

Goswami, Manu. "From Swadesh to Swaraj: Nation, Economy, Territory in Colonial South Asia, 1870 to 1907." *Comparative Studies in Society and History* 40, 4 (October 1998): 609–36.

——. *Producing India: From Colonial Economy to National Space.* Chicago: University of Chicago Press, 2004.

Goulding, H. R. *Old Lahore: Reminiscences of a Resident.* Lahore: Sang-e-Meel Publications, n.d. [1924].

Government of India. *The Census of India, 1901.* Vol. 1A, pt. 2. Calcutta: Superintendent of Government Printing, 1903.

——. *The Census of India, 1901.* Vol. 17, pt. 1. Simla: Government of India, 1902.

——. *The Imperial Gazetteer Atlas of India.* Delhi: Low Price Publications, n.d. [1931].

——. *Imperial Gazetteer of India: Provincial Series Punjab.* Vol. 2. Calcutta: Superintendent of Government Printing, 1908.

——. *Prices and Wages in India.* Calcutta: Office of the Superintendent of Government Printing, 1900.

——. *Report on Publications Issued and Registered in the Several Provinces of British India.* Calcutta: Office of the Superintendent of Government Printing, various dates.

——. *Selections from the Records of the Government of India. Various Numbers.* Calcutta: Office of the Superintendent of Government Printing, various dates.

Government of Punjab. *Bahawalpur State Gazetteer, 1904.* Lahore: Punjab Government, n.d. [1908].

——. *The Beginnings of Western Education in the Punjab: Mr. Arnold's Report on Public Instruction for the Year 1856–57.* Lahore: n.p., n.d.

——. *The Development of Urdu As Official Language in the Punjab, 1849–1974.* Comp. Nazir Ahmad Chaudhry. Lahore: Government of the Punjab, 1977.

——. *General Report of the Administration of the Punjab for the Years 1849–50 and 1850–51.* Lahore: Government of the Punjab, 1852.

——. *Punjab District Gazetteers, Jhelum District, 1904.* Lahore: Punjab Government, n.d. [1907].

——. *Punjab District Gazetteers, Lahore District, 1883–1884.* Lahore: Sang-e-Meel Publications, 1989 [1884].

——. *Report on the Administration of the Punjab and Its Dependencies, for 1887–88.* Lahore: Government of the Punjab, 1889.

——. *Report on Popular Education in the Punjab and Its Dependencies, for the Year 1860–61, by A. R. Fuller.* Lahore: Government of the Punjab, 1865.

——. *Report on Popular Education in the Punjab and Its Dependencies, for the Year 1874–75, by W. R. M. Holroyd.* Lahore, Government of the Punjab, 1876.

———. *Report on Popular Education in the Punjab and Its Dependencies, for the Year 1878–79, by W. R. M. Holroyd.* Lahore: Government of the Punjab, 1880.

———. *Report on Popular Education in the Punjab and Its Dependencies, for the Year 1884–85, by Denzil Ibbetson.* Lahore: Government of the Punjab, 1885.

Grewal, J.S. "The Emergence of Punjabi Drama: A Cultural Response to Colonial Rule." *Journal of Regional History* 5 (1984): 115–62.

———. "The Hir of Ahmad." In *Punjab History Conference, Twenty Sixth Session, March 18–20, 1994, Part–I, Proceedings,* ed. Gursharan Singh, 110–19. Patiala: Department of Punjab Historical Studies, Punjabi University, 1995.

———. *In the By-Lanes of History: Some Persian Documents from a Punjab Town.* Simla: Indian Institute of Advanced Study, 1975.

———. *The Sikhs of the Punjab.* Rev. ed. Cambridge: Cambridge University Press, 1998 [1990].

———. "The World of Waris." In *Social Transformations and Creative Imagination,* ed. Sudhir Chandra, 115–62. Delhi: Allied Publishers, 1984.

Grewal, J.S., and Indu Banga, trans. and eds. *Early Nineteenth Century Panjab: From Ganesh Das's "Char Bagh-i-Panjab."* Amritsar: Guru Nanak Dev University, 1975.

Grewal, J.S., and B.N. Goswamy. *The Mughals and the Jogis of Jakhbar: Some Madad-i-Ma'ash and Other Documents.* Simla: Indian Institute of Advanced Study, 1967.

Grierson, George. "A Bibliography of the Panjabi Language." *Indian Antiquary* 35 (1906): 65–72.

———. *Grierson on Panjabi* [reprint of Punjabi sections of *Linguistic Survey of India,* vol. 9]. Patiala: Languages Department, 1961 [1919].

———. "John Beames" [obituary]. *Journal of the Royal Asiatic Society* (1902): 722–25.

———. *Linguistic Survey of India.* 11 vols. Calcutta: Office of the Superintendent of Government Printing, 1903–1922.

———. *The Modern Vernacular Literature of Hindustan.* Calcutta: Asiatic Society, 1889.

Gujar, Ahmad. *Hir Ahmad.* Ed. Piara Singh Padam. Patiala: Punjabi University Publication Bureau, 1960.

Gupta, Charu. *Sexuality, Obscenity, Community: Women, Muslims, and the Hindu Public in Colonial India.* Delhi: Permanent Black, 2001.

Hadayatullah. *Baran Masa Hadayatullah* (Hadayatullah's *Baran Mah*). Amritsar: n.p., 1876.

Haider, Mian Ali. *Si Harfi Ali Haider.* Lahore: Chiragh al-Din Kutab Farosh, 1879.

———. *Si Harfian Ma'anah Hir* (*Si Harfis* on Hir). Lahore: Shaikh al-Baksh, 1885.

Hansen, Kathryn. *Grounds for Play: The Nautanki Theatre of North India.* Berkeley: University of California Press, 1992.

Harding, Christopher. *Religious Transformation in South Asia: The Meanings of Conversion in Colonial Punjab.* New York: Oxford University Press, 2008.

Hayes, Glen. "The Vaisnava Sahijya Traditions." In *The Religions of India in Practice,* ed. Donald Lopez, Jr., 333–51. Princeton, NJ: Princeton University Press, 1995.

Hindman, Sarah, ed. *Printing and the Written Word: The Social History of Books, circa 1450–1520.* Ithaca, NY: Cornell University Press, 1991.

Hirschkind, Charles. *The Ethical Soundscape: Cassette Sermons and Islamic Counterpublics.* New York: Columbia University Press, 2006.

Hobsbawm, Eric. *Nations and Nationalism since 1780: Programme, Myth, Reality.* Cambridge: Cambridge University Press, 1990.

Hodgson, Marshal. *Venture of Islam.* 3 vols. Chicago: University of Chicago Press, 1977.

Horovitz, J. "Dabistan al-Madhahib." *Encyclopaedia of Islam.* 2nd ed. Ed. P. Bearman et al. Leiden: E. J. Brill, 2009.

Husain. *Hir Husain.* Lahore: Gulab Singh and Sons, 1898.

———. *Hir Husain, Si Harfi Ashraf, Si Harfi Arora Rai, Si Harfi Ghulam.* Lahore: Chiragh al-Din Siraj al-Din, n.d. [c. 1888].

———. *Hir Husain, Si Harfi Ashraf, Si Harfi Arora Rai, Si Harfi Ghulam.* Lahore: Matbah Sultani, 1873.

———. *Hir Husain, Si Harfi Ashraf, Si Harfi Arora Rai, Si Harfi Ghulam.* Lahore: Munshi Aziz al-Din Najm al-Din, 1928.

———. *Hir Husain, Si Harfi Ashraf, Si Harfi Arora Rai, Si Harfi Ghulam.* Lahore: Munshi Gulab Singh, 1891.

———. *Hir Husain, Si Harfi Ashraf, Si Harfi Arora Rai, Si Harfi Ghulam.* Lahore: Shaikh Barkat Ali Mohsen Ali, n.d.

Husain, Munshi Ghulam. *Jhok Ranjhe di* (Ranjha's Abode). Lahore: Munshi Nawab Ali Brothers, 1322 h. [1904–5].

Hyder, Syed Akbar. *Reliving Karbala: Martyrdom in South Asian Memory.* New York: Oxford University Press, 2006.

Ibbetson, Denzil. *Panjab Castes.* Lahore: Sang-e-Meel Publications, 1994 [1883].

Irving, Miles. "The Shrine of Baba Farid Shakarganj at Pakpattan." *Journal of the Panjab University Historical Society* 1, 1 (1911–12): 70–76.

Ismail, Munshi Muhammad [Maskin]. *Maskin di Hir* (Maskin's Hir). Lahore: Munshi Aziz al-Din Najm al-Din Tajran Kutab, 1929.

Jaggi, Ratan Singh. "Bhumika." Introduction to *Sohni (Fazl Shah),* by Fazl Shah, ed. Tarlok Singh Anand, v–vi. Patiala: Punjabi University Publication Bureau, 1987.

Jalal, Ayesha. *Self and Sovereignty: Individual and Community in South Asian Islam since 1850.* New York: Routledge, 2000.

Janvier, Rev. L. *Idiomatic Sentences in English and Punjabi.* Lodiana: American Presbyterian Mission Press, 1846.

Johns, Adrian. *The Nature of the Book: Print and Knowledge in the Making.* Chicago: University of Chicago Press, 1998.

Jones, Kenneth W. *Arya Dharm: Hindu Consciousness in 19th-Century Punjab.* New Delhi: Manohar, 1989 [1976].

———. "Communalism in the Punjab: The Arya Samaj Contribution." *Journal of Asian Studies* 28, 1 (1968): 39–54.

———. "Ham Hindu Nahin: Arya-Sikh Relations, 1877–1905." *Journal of Asian Studies* 32, 3 (1973): 457–75.

———, ed. *Religious Controversy in British India: Dialogues in South Asian Languages.* Albany: State University of New York Press, 1992.

————. "Religious Identity and the Indian Census." In *The Census in British India: New Perspectives,* ed. N. G. Barrier, 73–101. New Delhi: Manohar, 1981.

————. *Socio-Religious Reform Movements in British India.* New Delhi: Foundation Books, 1994 [1989].

Jones, Kenneth W., and W. Eric Gustafson, comps. *Sources on Punjab History.* New Delhi: Manohar, 1975.

Joshi, Priya. *In Another Country: Colonialism, Culture, and the English Novel in India.* New York: Columbia University Press, 2002.

Joshi, Sanjay. *Fractured Modernity: Making of a Middle Class in Colonial North India.* New Delhi: Oxford University Press, 2001.

Kang, Kulbir Singh. *Hir Damodar: Itihasak te Sahitik Mulankan* (Hir Damodar: A Historical and Literary Assessment). Amritsar: Ruhi Prakashan, 1998.

Kanhayalal. *Tarikh-i Lahore* (History of Lahore). Lahore: Sang-e-Meel Publications, 1990 [1871].

————. *Tarikh-i Punjab* (History of Punjab). Lahore: Sang-e-Meel Publications, 1989 [1877].

Kapur, Prithipal Singh. Prologue to *The First Punjab War: Shah Mohammed's Jangnama,* by Shah Mohammed, ed. and trans. P. K. Nijhawan, 7–10. Amritsar: Singh Brothers, 2001.

Kaviraj, Sudipta. "The Imaginary Institution of India." In *Subaltern Studies: Writings on South Asian History and Society,* 12 vols., ed. Partha Chatterjee and Gyanendra Pandey, 7: 1–39. New Delhi: Oxford University Press, 1992.

————. "Writing, Speaking, Being: Language and the Historical Formation of Identities in India." In *Nationalstaat und Sprachkonflikte in Sud- und Sudostasien,* ed. Dagmar Hellman-Rajanayagam and Dietmar Rothermund, 25–65. Stuttgart: Steiner, 1992.

Kerr, Ian. "British Relations with the Golden Temple, 1849–90." *Indian Economic and Social History Review* 21, 2 (1984): 139–51.

Khadam, M. M. Y. *Mukamal Drama Hir-Ranjha* (The Complete Drama *Hir-Ranjha*). N.p.: N.D. Haskal and Sons, n.d. [c. 1923].

Khan, Muhammad Asif. Introduction to *Hir Damodar,* by Damodar, ed. Muhammad Asif Khan, 7–34. Lahore: Pakistan Punjabi Adabi Board, 1986.

Khan, Yasmin. *The Great Partition: The Making of India and Pakistan.* New Haven, CT: Yale University Press, 2007.

King, Christopher. "Images of Virtue and Vice: The Hindi-Urdu Controversy in Two Nineteenth-Century Hindi Plays." In *Religious Controversy in British India: Dialogues in South Asian Languages,* ed. Kenneth W. Jones, 123–48. Albany: State University of New York Press, 1992.

————. *One Language, Two Scripts: The Hindi Movement in Nineteenth Century North India.* New Delhi: Oxford University Press, 1994.

King, Robert D. *Nehru and the Language Politics of India.* New Delhi: Oxford University Press, 1994.

Kishwar, Madhu. "The Daughters of Aryavarta." In *Women and Social Reform in Modern India: A Reader,* 2 vols., ed. Sumit Sarkar and Tanika Sarkar, 1: 298–340. Delhi: Permanent Black, 2007.

Kohli, S. S. *History of Punjabi Literature.* Delhi: National Book Shop, 1993.

Kopf, David. *The Brahmo Samaj and the Shaping of the Indian Mind.* Princeton, NJ: Princeton University Press, 1979.

Kozlowski, Gregory. *Muslim Endowments and Society in British India.* New York: Cambridge University Press, 1985.

Krishna, Lajwanti Rama. *Panjabi Sufi Poets, A.D. 1460–1900.* New Delhi: Ashajanak Publications, 1973 [1938].

Krishna, Lajwanti Rama, and A.R. Luther. *Madho Lal Husain: Sufi Poet of the Punjab.* Lahore: Mubarak Ali, 1982.

Kurin, Richard. "The Culture of Ethnicity in Pakistan." In *Shari'at and Ambiguity in South Asian Islam,* ed. Katherine P. Ewing, 220–47. Berkeley: University of California Press, 1988.

Kurin, Richard, and Carol Morrow. "Patterns of Solidarity in a Punjabi Muslim Village." *Contributions to Indian Sociology* 19, 2 (1985): 235–49.

Kushta, Maula Baksh. *Punjab de Hire: Punjabi Shairan te Kavian da Itihas* (Gems of Punjab: A History of Punjabi Poets). Amritsar: Sudarshan Press, 1939.

———. *Punjabi Shairan da Tazkira* (A Dictionary of Punjabi Poets). Ed. Chaudhry Muhammad Afzal Khan. Lahore: Aziz Publishers, 1988 [1960].

Lafont, Jean Marie. *Fauj-i-Khas Maharaja Ranjit Singh and His French Officers.* Amritsar: Guru Nanak Dev University, 2002.

Lal, Harbans. "The Western Gateway to Sikhism: The Life and Works of Max Arthur Macauliffe." In *Sikh Art and Literature,* ed. Kerry Brown, 129–42. New York: Routledge, 1999.

Latif, Syad Muhammad. *History of the Panjab.* New Delhi: Kalyani Publishers, 1994 [1889].

———. *Lahore: Its History, Architectural Remains and Antiquities, with an Account of Its Modern Institutions, Inhabitants, Their Trade, Customs, &c.* Lahore: Sang-e-Meel Publications, 1994 [1892].

Lawrence, Bruce B. "The Early Chishti Approach to Sama'." In *Sacred Sound: Music in Religious Thought and Practice,* ed. Joyce Irwin, 93–110. Chico, CA: Scholars Press, 1983.

Leitner, G.W. *History of Indigenous Education in the Panjab since Annexation and in 1882.* Patiala: Languages Department, 1971 [1883].

Lelyveld, David. "*Zuban-e Urdu-e Mu'alla* and the Idol of Linguistic Origins." *Annual of Urdu Studies* 9 (1994): 57–67.

Lindholm, Charles. "Caste in Islam and the Problem of Deviant Systems: A Critique of Recent Theory." In *Muslim Communities of South Asia,* ed. T.N. Madan, 449–68. New Delhi: Manohar, 1995.

Lopez, Donald Jr., ed. *The Religions of India in Practice.* Princeton, NJ: Princeton University Press, 1995.

Lowrie, John. *Two Years in Upper India.* New York: R. Carter and Brothers, 1850.

Lutgendorf, Philip. *The Life of a Text: Performing the Ramcaritmanas of Tulsidas.* Berkeley: University of California Press, 1991.

Lyall, James. "Hindostani Literature." In *Encyclopedia Brittanica,* 11th ed., 29 vols., ed. Hugh Chisholm, 12: 483–91. New York: Encyclopedia Brittanica, 1910.

Macauliffe, Max Arthur. "The Fair at Sakhi Sarwar." *Calcutta Review* 60 (1875): 78–102.

———. *The Sikh Religion, Its Gurus, Sacred Writings and Authors.* 6 vols. New Delhi: S. Chand, 1985 [1909].

MacLean, Derryl. *Religion and Society in Arab Sind.* Leiden: E. J. Brill, 1989.

Madan, T. N., ed. *Muslim Communities of South Asia: Culture, Society, and Power.* New Delhi: Manohar, 1995.

Mahmood, Syed. *A History of English Education in India.* Aligarh: Muhammadan Anglo-Oriental College, 1895.

Major, Andrew J. *Return to Empire: Punjab under the Sikhs and British in the Mid-Nineteenth Century.* Karachi: Oxford University Press, 1996.

Malcolm, Lt. Col. John. *Sketch of the Sikhs.* New Delhi: Asian Educational Services, 1986 [1812].

Malhotra, Anshu. *Gender, Caste, and Religious Identities: Restructuring Class in Colonial Punjab.* New Delhi: Oxford University Press, 2002.

———. "The Quack of Patran and Other Stories." *Seminar* 569 (2007): 74–78.

Malik, Ikram Ali. *The History of the Punjab, 1799–1947.* Delhi: Low Price Publications, 1993 [1970].

———. "Muslim Anjumans and Communitarian Consciousness." In *Five Punjabi Centuries: Polity, Economy, Society and Culture, c. 1500–1990,* ed. Indu Banga, 112–25. New Delhi: Manohar, 1997.

———. "Muslim Anjumans in the Punjab." *Journal of Regional History* 5 (1984): 97–115.

Malik, Salim. *Qissa Hir-Ranjha wa Sehti-Murad (Qissa Hir-Ranjha and Sehti-Murad).* Lahore: Munshi Aziz al-Din, n.d.

Malik, Shahbaz. *Punjabi Kitabiyat* (A Bibliography of Punjabi Printed Books Written in Perso-Arabic Script). Islamabad: Akademi Adabiyat Pakistan, 1991.

Mann, Gurinder Singh. *Sikhism.* Upper Saddle River, NJ: Prentice Hall, 2004.

Martin, Henri-Jean. *The History and Power of Writing.* Trans. Lydia Cochrane. Chicago: University of Chicago Press, 1994 [1988].

Matringe, Denis. "'The Future Has Come Near, the Past Is Far Behind': A Study of Saix Farid's Verses and Their Sikh Commentaries in the Adi Granth." In *Islam and Indian Regions,* ed. Anna Libera Dallapiccola and Stephanie Zingel-Ave Lallemant, 417–43. Stuttgart: Franz Steiner Verlag, 1993.

———. "Hir Varis Shah: A Story Retold." In *Narrative Strategies: Essays on South Asian Film and Literature,* ed. Vasudha Dalmia and Theo Damsteegt, 19–30. New Delhi: Oxford University Press, 1999.

———. Introduction to *Hir Varis Sah,* by Varis Shah, 296–304. Pondicherry: Institut Francais, 1988.

———. "Krsnaite and Nath Elements in the Sufi Poetry of the Eighteenth-Century Panjabi Sufi Bullhe Sah." In *Devotional Literature in South Asia: Current Research, 1985–1988,* ed. R. S. McGregor, 190–206. Cambridge: Cambridge University Press, 1992.

Mazumder, Rajit. *The Indian Army and the Making of Punjab.* Delhi: Permanent Black, 2003.

McLeod, W. H. *The Early Sikh Tradition: A Study of the Janam-Sakhis.* Oxford: Clarendon Press, 1980.

Mehta, H. R. *A History of the Growth and Development of Western Education in the Punjab, 1846–84.* Delhi: Nirmal Publications, 1987 [1929].

Metcalf, Barbara. *Islamic Revival in British India: Deoband, 1860–1900*. Princeton, NJ: Princeton University Press, 1982.

———, ed. *Moral Conduct and Authority: The Place of Adab in South Asian Islam*. Berkeley: University of California Press, 1984.

———. *Perfecting Women: Maulana Ashraf Ali Thanawi's Bihishti Zewar: A Partial Translation with Commentary*. Berkeley: University of California Press, 1990.

Metcalf, Thomas. *Ideologies of the Raj*. Cambridge: Cambridge University Press, 1994.

M'gregor, William Lewis. *The History of the Sikhs*. Patiala: Languages Department, 1970 [1846].

Miller, Barbara Stoler. *Love Song of the Dark Lord: Jayadeva's Gitagovinda*. New York: Columbia University Press, 1977.

Minault, Gail. "Delhi College and Urdu." *Annual of Urdu Studies* 14 (1999): 119–34.

———. *Secluded Scholars: Women's Education and Muslim Social Reform in Colonial India*. New Delhi: Oxford University Press, 1998.

Mir, Farina. "Genre and Devotion in Punjabi Popular Narratives: Rethinking Cultural and Religious Syncretism." *Comparative Studies in Society and History* 48, 3 (July 2006): 727–58.

———. "Imperial Policy, Provincial Practices: Colonial Language Policy in Nineteenth-Century India." *Indian Economic and Social History Review* 43, 4 (2006): 395–427.

Mirza, Shafqat Tanveer. *Resistance Themes in Punjabi Literature*. Lahore: Sang-e-Meel Publications, 1992.

Mitchell, Lisa. *Language, Emotion, and Politics in South India: The Making of a Mother Tongue*. Bloomington: University of Indiana Press, 2009.

Mohammed, Shah. *The First Punjab War: Shah Mohammed's Jangnama*. Ed. and Trans. P. K. Nijhawan. Amritsar: Singh Brothers, 2001.

Muqbal, Shah Jahan. *Hir Muqbal*. Lahore: Chiragh al-Din, n.d. [c. 1873].

———. *Hir Muqbal*. Lahore: Chiragh al-Din Siraj al-Din, 1890.

———. *Hir Muqbal*. Lahore: Haji Chiragh al-Din Siraj al-Din, n.d.

———. *Hir Muqbal*. Lahore: Rai Sahib Munshi Gulab Singh and Sons, 1912.

———. *Hir Muqbal*. Lahore: n.p., 1875.

———. *Hir Muqbal Punjabi*. Lahore: Haji Chiragh al-Din Siraj al-Din, n.d.

———. *Hir Ranjha Muqbal*. Ed. Banarsi Das Jain. Lahore: Punjab University, 1921.

———. *Hir Muqbal*. Ed. Faqir Muhammad Faqir. N.p.: n.p., n.d. [1990].

Na'at, Abd al-Karim. *Na'at di Hir* (Na'at's Hir). Multan: Hafiz Muhammad al-Din Aziz al-Din Bashir al-Din Tajran Kutab, n.d. [c. 1880].

Naim, C. M. "Prize-Winning *Adab*: A Study of Five Urdu Books Written in Response to the Allahabad Government Gazette Notification." In *Moral Conduct and Authority: The Place of Adab in South Asian Islam*, ed. Barbara Metcalf, 290–314. Berkeley: University of California Press, 1984.

Naregal, Veena. *Language Politics, Elites, and the Public Sphere: Western India under Colonialism*. Delhi: Permanent Black, 2001.

Nath, Amar. *Hir-Ranjha Natak* (*Hir-Ranjha*, a Play). N.p.: Amar Press, 1900.

Nath, Lala Dina. "The Cult of Mian Bibi." *Indian Antiquary* 34 (June 1905): 125–31.

Nayar, Baldev Raj. *Minority Politics in the Punjab.* Princeton, NJ: Princeton University Press, 1966.

Nayyar, Adam. "Punjab." In *The Garland Encyclopedia of World Music,* ed. Alison Arnold, vol. 5, *South Asia: The Indian Subcontinent,* 762–72. New York: Garland Publishing, 2000.

Neuman, Daniel. *The Life of Music in North India: The Organization of an Artistic Tradition.* Detroit: Wayne State University Press, 1980.

Newton, Rev. E. P. *Panjabi Grammar: With Exercises and Vocabulary.* Ludhiana: Ludhiana Mission Press, 1898.

Newton, Rev. J. *A Grammar of the Panjabi Language, with Appendices.* Lodiana: American Presbyterian Mission Press, 1851.

Newton, Rev. J., and Rev. L. Janvier. *A Dictionary of the Panjabi Language, Prepared by a Committee of the Lodiana Mission.* Lodiana: American Presbyterian Mission Press, 1854.

Nijhawan, Michael. *Dhadi Darbar: Religion, Violence, and the Performance of Sikh History.* New Delhi: Oxford University Press, 2006.

Nijhawan, P. K. Introduction to *The First Punjab War: Shah Mohammed's Jangnama,* by Shah Mohammed, ed. and trans. P. K. Nijhawan, 19–52. Amritsar: Singh Brothers, 2001.

Oberoi, Harjot. *The Construction of Religious Boundaries: Culture, Identity, and Diversity in the Sikh Tradition.* Chicago: University of Chicago Press, 1994.

O'Brien, E. *Glossary of the Multani Language.* Lahore: Punjab Government Press, 1903.

O'Connell, Joseph, et al., eds. *Sikh History and Religion in the Twentieth Century.* Toronto: University of Toronto Press, 1988.

Oman, John Campbell. *Cults, Customs, and Superstitions of India* [originally published as *Indian Life, Religious and Social*]. Rev. ed. London: T. Fisher Unwin, 1908 [1889].

Ong, Walter. *Orality and Literacy: The Technologizing of the Word.* New York: Methuen, 1982.

Orsini, Francesca, "Detective Novels: A Commercial Genre in Nineteenth-Century North India." In *India's Literary History: Essays on the Nineteenth Century,* ed. Stuart Blackburn and Vasudha Dalmia, 435–82. Delhi: Permanent Black, 2004.

———. *The Hindi Public Sphere, 1920–1940: Language and Literature in the Age of Nationalism.* New York: Oxford University Press, 2002.

———. Introduction to *Love in South Asia: A Cultural History,* ed. Francesca Orsini, 1–42. Cambridge: Cambridge University Press, 2006.

———, ed. *Love in South Asia: A Cultural History.* Cambridge: Cambridge University Press, 2006.

Padam, Piara Singh. Introduction to *Hir Ahmad,* by Ahmad Gujar. Patiala: Punjabi University Publication Bureau, 1960.

———. *Kalam De Dhani* (The Wealth of Poets). Patiala: Piara Singh Padam, 1998.

———. *Sufi Kavidhara* (Sufi Poetry). Patiala: Piara Singh Padam, 1993.

Page, David. *Prelude to Partition: The Indian Muslims and the Imperial System of Control, 1920–1932.* New York: Oxford University Press, 1982.

Pandey, Gyanendra. *The Construction of Communalism in Colonial North India.* New Delhi: Oxford University Press, 1990.

———. *Remembering Partition: Violence, Nationalism, and History in India.* Cambridge: Cambridge University Press, 2001.

Peabody, Norbert. *Hindu Kingship and Polity in Precolonial India.* Cambridge: Cambridge University Press, 2003.

Perrill, Jeffrey Price. "Punjab Orientalism: The Anjuman-i-Punjab and Punjab University, 1865–1888." Ph.D. diss., University of Missouri, 1976.

Perry, Erskine. "On the Geographical Distribution of the Principal Languages of India, and the Feasibility of Introducing English as a Lingua Franca." *Journal of the Bombay Branch of the Royal Asiatic Society* 4 (1853): 289–317.

Pershad, Pandit Dabee. *Tarikh-i Punjab* (History of Punjab). Bareilly, n.p., 1850.

Petievich, Carla. *Assembly of Rivals: Delhi, Lucknow, and the Urdu Ghazal.* Lahore: Vanguard, 1992.

———. *When Men Speak as Women: Vocal Masquerade in Indo-Muslim Poetry.* New Delhi: Oxford University Press, 2007.

Phadke, Y. D. *Politics and Language.* Bombay: Himalaya Printing House, 1979.

Platts, John T. *A Dictionary of Urdu, Classical Hindi, and English.* Lahore: Sang-e-Meel Publications, 1994 [1911].

Pollock, Sheldon. "Cosmopolitan and Vernacular History." *Public Culture* 12, 3 (2000): 591–625.

———, Introduction to *Literary Cultures in History: Reconstructions from South Asia,* ed. Sheldon Pollock, 1–36. Berkeley: University of California Press, 2003.

———, ed. *Literary Cultures in History: Reconstructions from South Asia.* Berkeley: University of California Press, 2003.

Poovey, Mary. *Making a Social Body: British Cultural Formation, 1830–1864.* Chicago: University of Chicago Press, 1995.

Potts, E. Daniel. *British Baptist Missionaries in India, 1793–1837.* Cambridge: Cambridge University Press, 1967.

Prindle, Carol. "Occupation and Orthopraxy in Bengali Muslim Rank." In *Shari'at and Ambiguity in South Asian Islam,* ed. Katherine P. Ewing, 259–87. Berkeley: University of California Press, 1988.

Pritam, Amrita. *Alone in the Multitude.* Ed. and trans. Suresh Kohli. New Delhi: Indian Literary Review, 1979.

———. "I Call on Varis Shah!" Trans. Gib Schreffler. *Journal of Punjab Studies* 13, 1–2 (2006): 79.

Pritchett, Frances. *Marvelous Encounters: Folk Romances in Urdu and Hindi.* Riverdale, MD: Riverdale Company, 1985.

———. *Nets of Awareness.* Berkeley: University of California Press, 1994.

———. "Urdu Literary Culture, Part 2." In *Literary Cultures in History,* ed. Sheldon Pollock, 864–911. Berkeley: University of California Press, 2003.

Qureshi, Mian Muhammad Fazil. *Hir Viragan* (The Mendicant Hir). Jhelum: n.p., n.d. [c. 1923].

Qureshi, Regula. "His Master's Voice: Exploring Qawwali and 'Gramophone Culture' in South Asia." *Popular Music* 18, 1 (1999): 63–98.

———. "Sama' in the Royal Court of Saints: The Chishtiyya of South Asia." In *Manifestations of Sainthood in Islam*, ed. Grace Martin Smith and Carl Ernst, 111–28. Istanbul: Isis Press, 1987.

———. "Sufi Music and the Historicity of Oral Tradition." In *Ethnomusicology and Modern Music History*, ed. Stephen Blum, Philip Bohlman, and Daniel Neuman, 103–20. Chicago: University of Illinois Press, 1991.

———. *Sufi Music of India and Pakistan: Sound, Context, and Meaning in Qawwali*. Karachi: Oxford University Press, 2006 [1986].

Raheja, Gloria Goodwin. "The Illusion of Consent: Language, Caste, and Colonial Rule in India." In *Colonial Subjects: Essays on the Practical History of Anthropology*, ed. Peter Pels and Oscar Salemink, 117–52. Ann Arbor: University of Michigan Press, 1999.

Raheja, Gloria Goodwin, and Ann Gold. *Listen to the Heron's Words: Reimagining Gender and Kinship in North India*. Berkeley: University of California Press, 1994.

Rahman, Tariq. *Language and Politics in Pakistan*. Karachi: Oxford University Press, 1996.

Ram, Kirpa. *Qissa Hir-Ranjha*. Nawan Shahr (Jalandhar): Lala Nand Lal Basanta Mal Zaini, 1927.

Ram, Pandit Sardha. *Panjabi Bat Chit* (Conversational Punjabi). Lodiana: Panjab Text Book Committee, 1884.

Ramanujan, A. K. "Three Hundred *Ramayanas*: Five Examples and Three Thoughts on Translation." In *Many Ramayanas: The Diversity of a Narrative Tradition in South Asia*, ed. Paula Richman, 22–49. Berkeley: University of California Press, 1991.

Ramaswamy, Sumathi. *Passions of the Tongue: Language Devotion in Tamil India, 1891–1970*. Berkeley: University of California Press, 1997.

Ramdev, Joginder Singh. *Punjabi Likhari Kosh* (A Dictionary of Punjabi Writers). Jalandhar: New Book Company, 1964.

Rani, Aneeta. "Evolution of Press in the Punjab (1855–1910)." *Panjab Past and Present* 21, 1 (1987): 148–54.

Rao, Velcheru Narayana, David Shulman, and Sanjay Subrahmanyam. *Textures of Time: Writing History in South India, 1600–1800*. New York: Other Press, 2003.

Richman, Paula, ed. *Many Ramayanas: The Diversity of a Narrative Tradition in South Asia*. Berkeley: University of California Press, 1991.

Roberts, Peter A. *From Oral to Literate Culture: Colonial Experience in the English West Indies*. Kingston, Jamaica: University of the West Indies Press, 1997.

Robinson, Francis. "Technology and Religious Change: Islam and the Impact of Print." *Modern Asian Studies* 27, 1 (1993): 229–51.

Rocher, Ludo. *Orality and Textuality in the Indian Context*. Philadelphia: Department of Asian and Middle Eastern Studies, University of Pennsylvania, 1994.

Rose, H. A. "Hir and Ranjha." *Indian Antiquary* 52 (1923): 65–78.

———. "Mohiye Ki Har, or Bar." *Indian Antiquary* 37 (1908): 299–308.

———. "The Sequel to Hir and Ranjha Told by a Peasant Proprietor of Jhang." *Indian Antiquary* 60 (1926).

———. "A Version of Hir and Ranjha by Asa Singh of Maghiana, Jhang District." *Indian Antiquary* 54 (1925): 176–79, 210–19.

Roshan. *Hir Roshan*. Lahore: Mian Chiragh al-Din, n.d. [c. 1873].

——. *Hir Roshan.* N.p.: n.p., 1893.

——. *Hir Roshan.* Lahore: Hafiz Muhammad Din, 1895.

——. *Hir Roshan.* Lahore: n.p., 1895.

——. *Hir Roshan.* Lahore: Munshi Gulab Singh and Sons, 1896.

——. *Hir Roshan.* Lahore: Rai Sahib Munshi Gulab Singh and Sons, 1900.

Roy, Asim. *Islam in South Asia: A Regional Perspective.* New Delhi: South Asian Publishers, 1996.

——. *The Islamic Syncretistic Tradition in Bengal.* Princeton, NJ: Princeton University Press, 1983.

Rypka, Jan. *History of Iranian Literature.* Dordrecht: Reidel, 1968.

Saberwal, Satish. *Spirals of Contention: Why India Was Partitioned.* New Delhi: Routledge, 2007.

Sabir, Muhammad Sharif. "Ta'aruf." Introduction to *Hir Waris Shah,* by Waris Shah, ed. Muhammad Sharif Sabir. Lahore: Waris Shah Memorial Committee, 1985.

Saini, Pritam. "Kavi Kishan Singh 'Arif: Ik Alochnatmik Adhiain" (Poet Kishan Singh 'Arif: A Critical Study). Ph.D. diss., Punjabi University, n.d.

Sakin, Muhammad Shah. *Qissa Hir wa Ranjha.* Amritsar: Prem Singh Sachdio and Sons, n.d.

——. *Qissa Hir wa Ranjha.* Lahore: Malik Din Muhammad and Sons, n.d.

——. *Qissa Hir wa Ranjha.* Lahore: Malik Din Muhammad Tajar Kutab, n.d.

——. *Qissa Hir wa Ranjha.* Lahore: Malik Din Muhammad Tajran Kutab, 1924.

——. *Qissa Hir wa Ranjha.* Lahore: Munshi Aziz al-Din, n.d. [c. 1929].

Saksena, Ram Babu. *A History of Urdu Literature.* Lahore: Sang-e-Meel Publications, 1996 [1927].

Sanyal, Usha. *Devotional Islam and Politics in British India: Ahmad Riza Khan Barelwi and His Movement, 1870–1920.* New Delhi: Oxford University Press, 1996.

Sarwar, Mufti Ghulam. *Tarikh-i Makhzan-i Punjab* (History and Record of Punjab). Lahore: Dost Associates, 1996 [1884].

Schimmel, Annemarie. *Islamic Literatures of India.* Wiesbaden: Otto Harrassowitz, 1973.

——. *Mystical Dimensions of Islam.* Chapel Hill: University of North Carolina Press, 1975.

Schmidt, Ruth. "Urdu." In *The Indo-Aryan Languages,* ed. Dhanesh Jain and George Cardona, 286–350. New York: Routledge, 2003.

Sekhon, S. S. *A History of Panjabi Literature.* 2 vols. Patiala: Punjabi University Publication Bureau, 1993, 1996.

Sekhon, S. S., and K. S. Duggal. *A History of Punjabi Literature.* New Delhi: Sahitya Akademi, 1992.

Shackle, Christopher. "Between Scripture and Romance: The Yusuf-Zulaikha Story in Panjabi." *South Asia Research* 15, 2 (1995): 153–88.

——. "Beyond Turk and Hindu: Crossing the Boundaries in Indo-Muslim Romance." In *Beyond Turk and Hindu: Rethinking Religious Identities in Islamicate South Asia,* ed. David Gilmartin and Bruce B. Lawrence, 55–73. Gainesville: University of Florida Press, 2000.

——. "Early Vernacular Poetry in the Indus Valley: Its Context and Its Character." In *Islam and Indian Regions*, ed. Anna Libera Dallapiccola and Stephanie Zingel-Ave Lallemant, 259–89. Stuttgart: Franz Steiner Verlag, 1993.

——. Introduction to *Sassi Punnun*, by Hasham Shah, trans. Christopher Shackle, 1–48. Lahore: Vanguard Books, 1985.

——. "Making Punjabi Literary History." In *Sikh Religion, Culture, and Ethnicity*, ed. Christopher Shackle et al., 97–117. Richmond, Surrey: Curzon Press, 2001.

——. "The Multani 'Marsiya.'" *Islam* 55 (1978): 281–311.

——. "Pakistan." In *Language and National Identity in Asia*, ed. Andrew Simpson, 100–115. New York: Oxford University Press, 2007.

——. "Panjabi." In *The Indo-Aryan Languages*, ed. Dhanesh Jain and George Cardona, 581–621. New York: Routledge, 2003.

——. "Punjabi in Lahore." *Modern Asian Studies* 4, 3 (1970): 239–67.

——. "Rival Linguistic Identities in Pakistan Punjab." In *Rule, Protest, Identity: Aspects of Modern South Asia*, ed. Peter Robb and David Taylor, 213–34. London: School of Oriental and African Studies, 1979.

——. "The Shifting Sands of Love." In *Love in South Asia: A Cultural History*, ed. Francesca Orsini, 87–108. Cambridge: Cambridge University Press, 2006.

——. "Siraiki: A Language Movement in Pakistan." *Modern Asian Studies* 11, 3 (1977): 379–403.

——. "Some Observations of the Evolution of Modern Standard Punjabi." In *Sikh History and Religion in the Twentieth Century*, ed. Joseph O'Connell et al., 101–9. Toronto: University of Toronto Press, 1988.

——. "Transition and Transformation in Varis Shah's *Hir*." In *The Indian Narrative: Perspectives and Patterns*, ed. Christopher Shackle and Rupert Snell, 241–64. Wiesbaden: Otto Harrassowitz, 1992.

Shah, Fazl. *Majmu'a Si Harfian Fazl Shah* (A Collection of Fazl Shah's *Si Harfi*s). Lahore: Mir Amir Baksh and Sons, n.d.

——. *Qissa Hir wa Ranjha Punjabi*. Lahore: Munshi Muhammad Abdul Aziz, n.d. [c. 1911].

——. *Si Harfi Hir, Si Harfi Sassi, Si Harfi Sohni*. Lahore: Chiragh al-Din Kutab Farosh, n.d. [c. 1886].

——. *Si Harfi Hir, Si Harfi Zulaikha, Si Harfi Sohni, Si Harfi Laila, Si Harfi Sassi*. Lahore: Shaikh Muhammad Ashraf, n.d.

——. *Sohni (Fazl Shah)*. Ed. Tarlok Singh Anand. Patiala: Punjabi University Publication Bureau, 1987.

Shah, Hamid. *Hir Hamid Shah*. Lahore: n.p., 1908.

Shah, Maula. *Hir wa Ranjha*. Amritsar: Imam al-Din Miraj al-Din, 1330 h. [1911–12].

Shah, Muhammad. *Qissa Hir wa Ranjha*. Lahore: n.p., n.d.

——. *Qissa Hir wa Ranjha*. Rawalpindi: Lala Butamal Sahib, n.d. [c. 1908].

Shah, Waris. *The Adventures of Hir and Ranjha*. Trans. Charles Frederick Usborne. London: Peter Owen, 1966.

——. *Hir*. Ed. Muhammad Baqir. Lahore: Pakistan Punjabi Adabi Board, 1993 [1988].

——. *Hir Waris*. Ed. Jit Singh Sital. Patiala: Muni Lal Gupta and Sons, n.d.

———. *Hir Waris Shah.* Ed. Muhammad Sharif Sabir. Lahore: Waris Shah Memorial Committee, 1985.

———. *Hir Waris Shah.* Lahore: Sang-e-Meel Publications, 1997.

———. *Hir Waris Shah.* Ed. Piara Singh Padam. New Delhi: Navyug Publishers, 1998 [1977].

———. *The Love of Hir and Ranjha.* Trans. Sant Singh Sekhon. Ludhiana: Punjab Agricultural University, 1978.

Shahrd, Babu Firoz Din. *Hir Sial.* Lahore: Punjabi Pustak Bhandar, 1933.

Shapiro, Michael. "Hindi." In *The Indo-Aryan Languages,* ed. Dhanesh Jain and George Cardona, 250–85. New York: Routledge, 2003.

Sharma, Sunil. *Amir Khusraw: The Poet of Sufis and Sultans.* Oxford: Oneworld Publications, 2005.

———. *Persian Poetry at the Indian Frontier: Mas'ud Sa'd Salman of Lahore.* Delhi: Permanent Black, 2000.

Sharma, Ursula. *Caste.* Philadelphia: Open University Press, 1999.

Shaw, Graham W. "The First Printing Press in the Panjab." *Library Chronicle* 43, 2 (1979): 159–79.

———. "The Parameters of Publishing in Nineteenth-Century North India: A Study Based Loosely on Delhi." New Literary Histories for the Nineteenth Century Workshop, University of California, Berkeley, 17 September 1999.

Siddiqi, Akhtar Husain. "Small Town Growth and Development Policy in Pakistan." In *The Asian City: Processes of Development, Characteristics, and Planning,* ed. Graham Chapman et al., 181–204. New York: Springer, 1994.

Singh, Ajmer. *Maharaja Ranjit Singh ate Punjabi Sahit* (Maharaja Ranjit Singh and Punjabi Literature). Patiala: Punjabi University Publication Bureau , 1982.

Singh, Bhagat. *A History of Sikh Misals.* Patiala: Punjabi University Publication Bureau, 1993.

Singh, Bhagwan. *Bhagwan Singh Rachnavli* (Bhagwan Singh's Compositions). Ed. S.S. Padam. Barnala: Punjabi Sahit Sabha, n.d.

———. *Hir Bhagwan Singh.* Amritsar: Bhai Chattar Singh Jivan Singh, n.d.

———. *Hir Bhagwan Singh.* Amritsar: Lala Dhani Ram Sahib, n.d.

———. *Hir Bhagwan Singh.* Amritsar: Lala Ram Nath Tajar Kutab, 1892.

———. *Hir Bhagwan Singh.* Lahore: Rai Sahib Munshi Gulab Singh and Sons, 1924.

Singh, Bhai Lakma. *Qissa Hir wa Mian Ranjha.* Peshawar: Bhai Lakma Singh, n.d. [c.1876].

Singh, Bhai Rann. *Navan Qissa Hir* (A New *Qissa* Hir). Amritsar: Gurmat Press, 1913.

Singh, Bhai Sant Bajara. *Qissa Hir te Ranjhe da* (The *Qissa* of Hir and Ranjha). Amritsar: Bhai Hari Singh, 1951 b. [1894].

Singh, Chetan. *Region and Empire: Panjab in the Seventeenth Century.* New Delhi: Oxford University Press, 1991.

Singh, Gurbaksh. *Baran Mah Gurbaksh Singh.* N.p.: n.p., n.d.

Singh, Jog. *Hir Jog Singh.* Lahore: Chiragh al-Din Siraj al-Din Tajran Kutab, n.d.

———. *Hir Jog Singh.* Lahore: Mian Chiragh al-Din Siraj al-Din Tajran Kutab, n.d.

———. *Hir Jog Singh.* Lahore: Hafiz Muhammad Din wa Ahmad Din Tajran Kutab, 1887.

———. *Hir Jog Singh.* Lahore: Munshi Gobind Singh, n.d. [c. 1888].

——. *Qissa Hir Jog Singh*. Lahore: Chiragh al-Din Kutab Farosh, 1877.

——. *Qissa Hir Jog Singh*. Lahore: Chiragh al-Din Tajar Kutab, 1880.

——. *Qissa Hir Jog Singh*. Lahore: Malik Hira Tajar Kutab, 1882.

Singh, Khushwant. *A History of the Sikhs*. Vol. 2, 1839–1964. Princeton, NJ: Princeton University Press, 1966.

——. *Ranjit Singh: Maharajah of the Punjab, 1780–1839*. Bombay: George Allen and Unwin, 1962.

——. *The Sikhs*. London: G. Allen and Unwin, 1953.

Singh, Lahora. *Hir Lahori* (Lahora's Hir). Lahore: Gurdial Singh and Sons, 1931.

Singh, Nazar. "Newspapers, Politics, and Literature in the Nineteenth Century Delhi and Punjab." *Panjab Past and Present* 24, 2 (1990): 392–407.

——. "Notes on the Anjuman-i-Punjab, Aligarh Movement, Brahmo Samaj, Indian Association, Arya Samaj and Singh Sabha in the Context of Colonial Education in the Punjab, 1865–1885." *Panjab Past and Present* 26, 1 (1992): 35–69.

Singh, Pankaj K. "Reconstruction of Legend in Contemporary Panjabi Drama in India." *Modern Drama* 38, 1 (1995): 109–22.

——. *Re-Presenting Woman: Tradition, Legend, and Panjabi Drama*. Simla: Indian Institute of Advanced Study, 2000.

Singh, Pritam. *Bhai Gurdas*. New Delhi: Sahitya Akademi, 1992.

Singh, Radha. "Some Aspects of the Demography of the Punjab in the Mid-Nineteenth Century." *Panjab Past and Present* 24 (1990): 384–91.

Singha, Radika. *A Despotism of Law: Crime and Justice in Early Colonial India*. New Delhi: Oxford University Press, 1998.

Sinha, Mrinalini. "The Lineage of the 'Indian' Modern: Rhetoric, Agency and the Sarda Act in Late Colonial India." In *Gender, Sexuality, and Colonial Modernities,* ed. Antoinette Burton, 207–20. New York: Routledge, 1999.

——. *Specters of Mother India: The Global Restructuring of an Empire*. Durham, NC: Duke University Press, 2006.

Sirani, Malik Ahmad Baksh Toba [Ghafil], *Qissa Hir wa Ranjha*. Lahore: Matba' Kadimi, n.d.

Sital, Jit Singh. "Hir Waris." In *Hir Waris,* by Waris Shah, ed. Jit Singh Sital, 10–21. Delhi: Aarsi Publishers, 2004.

Sood, Jyotika, and Anuradha Shukla. "Udham Singh's 'Heer' in for a Makeover." *The Tribune* (Chandigarh), 26 July 2007.

Stark, Ulrike. *An Empire of Books: The Naval Kishore Press and the Diffusion of the Printed Word in Colonial India*. Delhi: Permanent Black, 2007.

Steel, Flora Annie. *The Garden of Fidelity: Being the Autobiography of Flora Annie Steel*. London: Macmillan, 1930.

——. *Tales of the Punjab Told by the People*. London: Macmillan, 1894.

Steel, Flora Annie, and R. C. Temple. "Folklore in the Panjab." *Indian Antiquary* 11 (1882): 32–43, 73–76.

Steinbach, Henry. *The Punjaub*. Patiala: Languages Department, 1970 [1846].

Stewart, Charles. "Syncretism and Its Synonyms: Reflections on Cultural Mixture." *Diacritics* 29, 3 (1999): 40–62.

Stock, Brian. *Listening for the Text: On the Uses of the Past.* Philadelphia: University of Pennsylvania Press, 1990.

Stocking, George. *Victorian Anthropology.* New York: Free Press, 1987.

Sweeney, Amin. *A Full Hearing: Orality and Literacy in the Malay World.* Berkeley: University of California Press, 1987.

Swynnerton, Charles. *Romantic Tales from the Panjab.* London: Archibald Constable, 1903.

Syed, Najm Hossain. *Recurrent Patterns in Punjabi Poetry.* 2nd ed. Lahore: Punjab Adbi Markaz, 1978.

Talbot, Ian. *Khizr Tiwana, the Punjab Unionist Party, and the Partition of India.* Richmond, Surrey: Curzon Press, 1996.

Tandon, Prakash. *Punjabi Century, 1857–1947.* Berkeley: University of California Press, 1961.

Taunsvi, Tahir. *Siraiki Kitabiyat: Aghaz ta 1993* (A Bibliography of Siraiki Books: Up to 1993). Islamabad: Akademi Adabiyat Pakistan, 1994.

Taylor, Charles. *Modern Social Imaginaries.* Durham, NC: Duke University Press, 2004.

Temple, R. C. "The Administrative Value of Anthropology." *Indian Antiquary* 42 (1913): 289–300.

———. "Analysis of the Tales on the Plan Adopted by the Folklore Society of England." In *Tales of the Punjab Told by the People,* by F. A. Steel, 327–55. London: Macmillan, 1894.

———. *Legends of the Panjab.* 3 vols. Lahore: Sang-e-Meel Publications, n.d. [1884–1900].

———. "A Song about Sakhi Sarwar." *Calcutta Review* 73 (1881): 253–74.

———. "The Story of the Ferozpur Canal." *Indian Antiquary* 11 (June 1882): 167–69.

———. "A Survey of the Incidents in Modern Indian Folk-Tales." In *Tales of the Punjab Told by the People,* by F. A. Steel, 356–95. London: Macmillan, 1894.

Thapar, Romila. *Somanatha: The Many Voices of a History.* New York: Verso, 2005 [2004].

Trautmann, Thomas. *Aryans and British India.* Berkeley: University of California Press, 1997.

———. *Languages and Nations: Conversations in Colonial South India.* Berkeley: University of California Press, 2006.

Trevaskis, Hugh Kennedy. *The Punjab of To-Day: An Economic Survey of the Punjab in Recent Years (1890–1925).* Vol. 2. Lahore: Civil and Military Gazette, 1932.

Ubaidurrahman, Muhammad. *Siraiki Kitabiyat* (A Bibliography of Siraiki Books). Bahawalpur: Siraiki Adabi Majlis, 1980.

Uberoi, Mohan Singh. *A History of Panjabi Literature, 1100–1932.* Jalandhar: Bharat Prakashan, 1971 [1933].

———. *Punjabi Sahit di Itihas Rekha* (A Timeline of Punjabi Literature). Chandigarh: Panjabi University, 1962 [1958].

Usborne, C. F. "Appendix: Hir and Ranjha of Waris Shah, 1776 A.D. (A Critical Analysis) by Multani." *Indian Antiquary* 51 (1922): 58–64.

———. "Hir and Ranjha." *Indian Antiquary* 51 (1922): 33–40, 42–58.

———. "The Story of Hir and Ranjha." *Indian Antiquary* 52 (1923).

van den Dungen, P. H. M. "Changes in Status and Occupation in Nineteenth-Century Punjab." In *Soundings in Modern South Asian History,* ed. D. A. Low, 59–94. Berkeley: University of California Press, 1968.

van der Linden, Bob. *Moral Languages from Colonial Punjab: The Singh Sabha, Arya Samaj, and Ahmadiyahs*. New Delhi: Manohar, 2008.

van der Veer, Peter. *Imperial Encounters: Religion and Modernity in India and Britain*. Princeton, NJ: Princeton University Press, 2001.

Viswanathan, Gauri. *Masks of Conquest: Literary Study and British Rule in India*. New York: Columbia University Press, 1989.

Warner, Michael. *Publics and Counterpublics*. Cambridge: Zone Books, 2002.

———. "Publics and Counterpublics." *Public Culture* 14, 1 (2002): 49–90.

Waseem, M., trans. and ed. *On Becoming an Indian Muslim: French Essays on Aspects of Syncretism*. New Delhi: Oxford University Press, 2003.

Washbrook, David. "'To Each a Language of His Own': Language, Culture, and Society in Colonial India." In *Language, History, and Class*, ed. Penelope Corfield, 179–203. Oxford: Basil Blackwell, 1991.

Wasti, Razi. "Anjuman Himayat-i-Islam, Lahore: A Brief History." In *The Political Triangle in India*, ed. Razi Wasti, 25–36. Lahore: People's Publishing House, 1976.

White, David Gordon. *The Alchemical Body: Siddha Traditions in Medieval India*. Chicago: University of Chicago Press, 1996.

———. "The Wonders of Mastnath." In *Religions of India in Practice*, ed. Donald Lopez, Jr., 399–411. Princeton, NJ: Princeton University Press, 1995.

Wikeley, J. M. *Punjabi Musalmans*. New Delhi: Manohar, 1991 [1915].

Yar, Maulvi Ahmad. *Hir wa Ranjha*. Lahore: Matba' Mufid-i Am, 1928.

Yar, Qadir. *Qissa Sohni Mahival M'a Tasvir* (The *Qissa* Sohni-Mahival with Illustrations). Lahore: Chiragh al-Din Tajar Kutab, 1877.

Yong, Tan Tai. *The Garrison State: The Military, Government and Society in Colonial Punjab, 1849–1947*. Thousand Oaks, CA: Sage Publications, 2005.

Zamindar, Vazira. *The Long Partition and the Making of Modern South Asia*. New York: Columbia University Press, 2007.

Zastoupil, Lynn, and Martin Moir, eds. *The Great Indian Education Debate: Documents Relating to the Orientalist-Anglicist Controversy, 1781–1843*. London: Curzon Press, 1999.

INDEX

Pothohari, 5, 210n7
Prahlad, 116, 122
Pritam, Amrita, 3, 4, 25, 183
Pritchett, Frances, 39, 57
Puadhi, 5, 210n7
public sphere, 6, 19, 31, 58, 59
Punjab Alienation of Land Act of 1900, 132
Punjab Department of Public Instruction, 55, 56, 60
Punjab Unionist Party, 186
Punjab University College Senate, 62, 221n1
Punjabi: association with Sikhs, 22, 43, 44–46, 46, 49, 52, 60, 187; colloquial use of, 4, 6, 31, 35, 47–49, 193, 218n65, 218n66; colonial conceptions of, 64; continuing vitality of, 193–94, 243n30; definition of, 210n7 ; distribution of printed books in, 81, 82; manuscripts in, 7, 8, 9, 15, 16, 37, 63, 71, 91–93, 121, 211n19; marginalization of, 4; newspapers in, 14, 75–78; in Pakistan, 191–93; in postcolonial India, 186–91; printed books in, 14, 15, 62, 63, 71, 77–85, 120; at Punjab University, 62–63; relative independence from colonial intervention, 64, 87; resilience of, 32; Singh Sabha promotion of, 23; tract publishing in, 21; type fonts for, 14
Punjabi literary formation: definition of, 6, 17–18, 19, 24, 97–100; coherence of, 107; diversity of, 107–10, 115, 120–21; *qissa* as foundation of, 90; tenacity of, 191, 193–94; vitality of, 32, 103, 194
Punjabi literature: history of, 36–38; indigenous patronage for, 17, 105, 117, 185; marginalization of, 4; performance of, 103–22, 193; pleasure in, 99–100, 117; print market 13, 15, 16, 24, 63, 79, 80–81; relative independence from colonial intervention, 64, 69; as resistance to colonialism, 4
Punjabi Suba movement, 184, 186–91
Puran-Bhagat, 7

qawwali, 104–7, 122, 229n41
qisse: episodic texts of, 15–16, 89, 140–41, 143, 150–51, 153, 163, 168, 178, 238n7; historical imagination and, 4; historical significance of, 16, 98; history of, 3–4, 15–16; history of Punjabi composition of, 7–12, 15–16, 85–90, 151–52; invocations in, 16, 152–55; moral sensibility of, 6; performance of, 16–17, 114, 117–20; pleasure in, 17, 149; popularity of, 15;

Punjabi literary formation and, 6; regional history and, 2; as social commentary, 90, 98, 132, 141, 149, 151
Qissa Hir te Ranjhe da (by Kishan Singh 'Arif), 12, 196; fakir(s) in, 174, 175; genealogy of poets in, 11, 16, 89; gender in, 145–47; invocation in, 154, 155; Krishnaite imagery in, 162–63; saint veneration in 180–81; *zat* in, 127–29
Qureshi, Mian Muhammad Fazil, 199
Qureshi, Regula, 104–5

Raheja, Gloria Goodwin, 130, 147
Rahman, Tariq, 192
Rai, Arora, 207
Rai, Hursookh, 33
Rai, Khush-Waqt, 36, 216n37
Ram, Kirpa, 199
Ramanujan, A. K., 97, 181
Ramaswamy, Sumathi, 185
Rao, Ram Sukh, 215n23
rebellion of 1857–58, 36, 39
Reed, William, 44
Risley, H. H., 101
Rose, H. A., 101
Roshan, 12, 16, 89; *Hir Roshan*, 89, 178–79, 199–200

Sabir, Muhammad Sharif, 78
Safdar, Huma, 193
Sakin, Muhammad Shah, 16, 144–45, 152–53, 163, 200
saint veneration (Sufi), 175–82. *See also* Sufism
Salman, Mas'ud Sa'd, 36
Sama', 99, 103, 106–7, 112
Sanskrit, 16, 22, 42; colonial officials' abilities in, 30; printed books in, 34, 63, 67; sacrality of, 36
Sarwar, Mufti Ghulam, 39, 100, 108, 118
Sarwar, Sakhi, 102, 120; shrine of, 108, 110, 112
Sassi-Punnun, 7, 38, 86, 100
Saxena, Ram Babu, 39
Schimmel, Annemarie, 155–56
scribe(s): 92; in lithography, 71, 72, 93; in pre-print book production, 92, 227n8
script(s). *See* Gurmukhi script; Indo-Persian script; Devnagari script
Sekhon, Sant Singh, 156
Serampore Mission, 42; language map by, 44, 45, 46, 47, 49; publishing activity of, 42–44

TEXT
10/12.5 Minion Pro

DISPLAY
Minion Pro

COMPOSITOR
BookComp, Inc.

PRINTER AND BINDER
IBT Global